Optimized Predictive Models in Healthcare Using Machine Learning

Scrivener Publishing
100 Cummings Center, Suite 541J
Beverly, MA 01915-6106

Publishers at Scrivener
Martin Scrivener (martin@scrivenerpublishing.com)
Phillip Carmical (pcarmical@scrivenerpublishing.com)

Optimized Predictive Models in Healthcare Using Machine Learning

Edited by

Sandeep Kumar
*CSE Department, Koneru Lakshmaiah Education Vaddeswaram,
Andhra Pradesh, India*

Anuj Sharma
Maharshi Dayanand University, Rohtak, India

Navneet Kaur
Chandigarh University, Gharuan, Mohali, India

Lokesh Pawar
Chandigarh University, Gharuan, Mohali, India

and

Rohit Bajaj
Chandigarh University, Gharuan, Mohali, India

Scrivener
Publishing

This edition first published 2024 by John Wiley & Sons, Inc., 111 River Street, Hoboken, NJ 07030, USA and Scrivener Publishing LLC, 100 Cummings Center, Suite 541J, Beverly, MA 01915, USA
© 2024 Scrivener Publishing LLC
For more information about Scrivener publications please visit www.scrivenerpublishing.com.

Wiley Global Headquarters
111 River Street, Hoboken, NJ 07030, USA

For details of our global editorial offices, customer services, and more information about Wiley products visit us at www.wiley.com.

Library of Congress Cataloging-in-Publication Data

ISBN 978-1-394-17462-1

Cover image: Pixabay.Com
Cover design by Russell Richardson

Set in size of 11pt and Minion Pro by Manila Typesetting Company, Makati, Philippines

Printed in the USA

10 9 8 7 6 5 4 3 2 1

Contents

Preface

This book provides more relevant information on optimized predictive models in healthcare using machine learning. As a resource for students, academics, and researchers from the industry who wish to know more about real-time applications, it focuses on how humans and computers interact to ever-increasing levels of complexity and simplicity. The book provides content on the theory of optimized predictive model design, evaluation, and user diversity. Going beyond descriptions of rehabilitation methods for specific processes, it explains the underlying causes of the social and organizational problems. This book describes new algorithms for modeling that are now accessible to scientists of all varieties. The healthcare industry faces an unprecedented challenge to provide efficient and cost-effective care while maintaining high patient satisfaction. Predictive modeling, a field of machine learning, has emerged as a powerful tool in healthcare for identifying high-risk patients, predicting disease progression, and optimizing treatment plans. By leveraging data from various sources, predictive models can help healthcare providers to make informed decisions, resulting in better patient outcomes and reduced costs. This book offers a comprehensive guide to developing and implementing optimized predictive models in healthcare and is intended for healthcare professionals, data scientists, and researchers interested in using predictive modeling to improve patient care and outcomes.

One of the critical features of this book is its practical approach to developing predictive models in healthcare. The authors have provided detailed guidance on data collection and preprocessing, emphasizing the importance of collecting accurate and reliable data. The book also discusses feature selection and engineering, explaining how to transform raw data into meaningful features that can be used to improve the accuracy of predictive models. In addition, the book gives a detailed overview of machine learning algorithms for predictive modeling in healthcare, discussing the pros and cons of different algorithms and how to choose the best one for a specific application.

Another essential feature of this book is its emphasis on validating and evaluating predictive models. It explains the importance of validating predictive models to ensure their accuracy and reliability and describes how to evaluate the performance of predictive models using a range of metrics. By providing a comprehensive overview of validation and evaluation techniques, readers can develop predictive models that are both accurate and reliable. The book also includes a chapter on applications of predictive modeling in healthcare, which offers real-world examples of how predictive models can improve patient outcomes. Other topics discussed include various other applications, including disease diagnosis, drug development, and patient monitoring. By highlighting these success stories, the book demonstrates the potential impact of predictive modeling on healthcare.

Another key feature of this book is its discussion of the challenges and limitations of predictive modeling in healthcare. The authors highlight the ethical and legal considerations that must be considered when developing predictive models and the potential biases that can arise in those models. By addressing these challenges and limitations, the book enables readers to build predictive models that are both accurate and ethical. Finally, the book concludes by discussing future directions for predictive modeling in healthcare. The authors explain the use of artificial intelligence and big data analytics in healthcare and how these technologies can improve patient care and outcomes. With these insights into the future of predictive modeling in healthcare, readers will stay up-to-date on the latest developments in the field.

This volume is an essential resource for healthcare professionals, data scientists, and researchers interested in developing and implementing predictive models in healthcare. Included herein is practical guidance on developing predictive models, from data collection and preprocessing to algorithm selection, validation and evaluation, and applications. By emphasizing the importance of accuracy, reliability, and ethical considerations, the authors enable readers to develop predictive models that can improve patient outcomes and ultimately provide better patient care.

We thank all the participating authors who helped us tremendously with their contributions, time, critical thoughts, and suggestions to assemble this peer-reviewed, edited volume. The editors are also thankful to Scrivener Publishing and its team for the opportunity to publish this volume. Lastly, we thank our family members for their love, support, encouragement, and patience during this work.

Sandeep Kumar
Anuj Sharma
Navneet Kaur
Lokesh Pawar
Rohit Bajaj
November 2023

Impact of Technology on Daily Food Habits and Their Effects on Health

Neha Tanwar[1], Sandeep Kumar[2*] and Shilpa Choudhary[3]

[1]Department of Food Technology, Guru Jambheshwar University of Science and Technology, Hisar, India
[2]Department of Computer Science and Engineering, Koneru Lakshmaiah Educational Foundation, Vijayawada, India
[3]Department of Computer Science and Engineering, Neil Gogte Institute of Technology, Hyderabad, India

Abstract

In this modern and busy lifestyle, we all look for ready-to-eat food. Food industries turn toward full automation to provide ready food nowadays. Prepared and packed food has an impact on health in the modern lifestyle with eating habits consumers seeking the technology viz. food diets application, online food delivery systems, and robotic food making machines. In this chapter, we have discussed the impacts of technology on daily food habits. The importance of technology in the food industry and its problems are highlighted in this chapter, with a focus on artificial intelligence, bioinformatics, 3D printing, sustainable applications of functional and nutraceutical food, and the need for a coordinated regulatory framework. The natural nutrients included in food, including carbs, proteins, vitamins, fats, antioxidants, and minerals, are necessary for the body parts to work normally physiologically. Achieving good health from sustainable food systems for the people is one of the most significant issues facing our world today. This chapter also focuses on different processed foods and their health impacts.

Keywords: Technology, food habits, artificial intelligence, digitization, emerging technologies

Corresponding author: er.sandeepsahratia@gmail.com

Sandeep Kumar, Anuj Sharma, Navneet Kaur, Lokesh Pawar and Rohit Bajaj (eds.) Optimized Predictive Models in Healthcare Using Machine Learning, (1–20) © 2024 Scrivener Publishing LLC

1.1   Introduction

We truly are what we eat, as the phrase goes. In other words, nutrition is essential to our health. Food provides information to our bodies, which also require ingredients to function properly. Our metabolic processes become disrupted and our health degrades if our body doesn't receive the proper signals [1]. If we give our bodies non-healthy foods, our bodies get the wrong information, and we have to suffer many diseases. Several exciting pieces of evidence show that dietary factor plays a vital role in maintaining the systems and mechanisms of mental function. The relative abundance or scarcity of specific nutrients can affect cognitive processes. Cognitive ability is influenced by several gut hormones which can enter the brain, and these hormones function depending on the type of food intake. Although there are definite patterns, such as the need for nutrition balancing, there is no universally accepted definition of a healthy diet. Also, this relies on the features of every person and their surroundings [2].
-Gregorio Varela, Chairman of the Spanish Nutrition Association

Our food is different from what it was 20 years ago. The soil nutrients have been depleted, and chemicals are increasingly used to get more yield. Because of the growing quantity and variety of available food products, food choices are complex and vary over a short period, influenced by many factors like social, cultural, biological, psychological, and economic factors [3]. We have a lot of food variety and approx. Seventeen thousand new products are introduced each year. So we are heavily dependent on processed foods. The examples of food tech businesses include robotics, 3D food printing, alternative proteins, and individualised nutrition. Although these technologies have a tremendous positive impact on the food business, they merely touch the surface. These technological advancements and the internet era promote new food products that give fulfillment in less time.

1.1.1   Impacts of Food on Health

Food is central to our health. The food we have gives information and materials to our bodies that we need for the proper functioning of our bodies, as shown in Figure 1.1. This information can be right and wrong, depending on our food. To sustain, prevent, and treat disease, food serves as medication. The nutrients in food give all the necessary nourishing things and information by which our cells enable them to perform their functions.

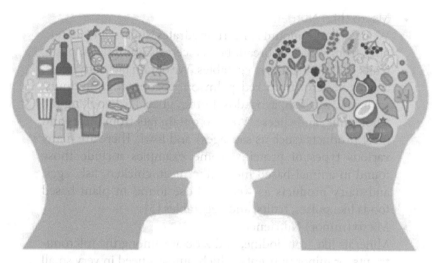

Figure 1.1 Role of food habits on our mental health.

The metabolic processes slow down or occasionally even cease when the amount of nutrients consumed is not appropriate for the demands of the cell's activity [4]. A healthy and balanced diet gives us plenty of energy to work, enjoy ourselves, and keep our immune systems healthy. The both science and art concerned with maintaining health and the prevention, relief, or cure of sickness, according to Webster. Nutrients come in a wide variety of forms, and we classify them into two groups: macronutrients and micronutrients, as shown in Figure 1.2.

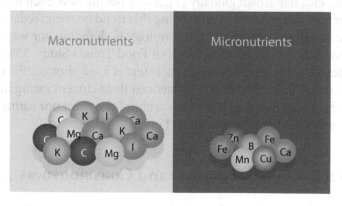

Figure 1.2 Macronutrients and micronutrients.

- Macro (big) Nutrients
  We need large amounts of carbohydrates, sugars, and dietary fiber from pieces of bread, beans, cereals and grains, pasta, fruits, and non-starchy vegetables. We obtain fats, fatty acids, and cholesterol from red palm oil, coconuts, groundnuts, soybeans, oily fish, avocados, butter, ghee, lard/cooking fat, whole milk, and cheese. We also obtain fats from meats and meat products (such as sausages) and fowl. There are many various types of proteins; some examples include those found in animal-based meals like meat, chicken, fish, eggs, and dairy products as well as those found in plant-based foods like pulses, fruits, and vegetables [5].
- Micro (minor) Nutrients
  Minerals like iron, iodine, and zinc are among the micronutrients, or minor nutrients, which humans need in very small amounts yet are most often inadequate in our diets. Beef, liver, and other organ meats, poultry, fish, breast milk, as well as seaweed, legumes, almonds, and other foods provide us with these nutrients, vitamins, such as folate, vitamin B-group vitamins (which also contain vitamin A), and vitamin C [6].

1.1.2   Impact of Technology on Our Eating Habits

Technology changes every aspect of people's lives and their communication, lifestyle, thinking, learning, and food habits. Food habits are changed with the rise of Internet of Things (IoT) and Artificial Intelligence (AI). Sharing food pictures on social media like WhatsApp, Facebook, Twitter, Instagram, etc., has grown globally [7]. Many people have even made their careers as food bloggers out of employing this trend on their feeds as shown in Figure 1.3. From every aspect, technology is changing our way of food habits. According to the Choosi Modern Food Trends Study, 50% of consumers get ideas for meals from others' internet food photos. 39% of those surveyed stated that social media influenced their current eating habits.

Now, the question arises: How does technology affect our eating habits, and how will this change in the future?

1.2   Technologies, Foodies, and Consciousness

Technological influence may have both positive and negative effects. Figure 1.4 demonstrates that food is more than simply a necessity for survival.

Figure 1.3 Technological innovations in food sector.

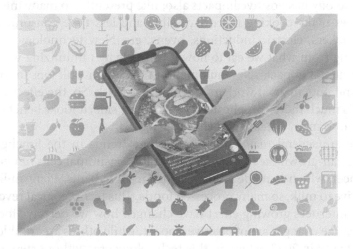

Figure 1.4 Food on social media.

From one perspective, it increases our awareness of what we eat and current dietary trends, which develops better eating habits, at the same time, problematic internet users, uncontrollable craving habits, and eating disorders such as loss of control eating, binge eating disorders, etc. are increasing by the higher rate [8]. Problematic Internet Use (PIU) comprises passive behaviour brought on by excessive technology use as well as adverse social comparisons that may arise from exposure to and self-comparison with anything on their home feed. When it comes to teenagers, it becomes more distracting because of their undeveloped skills and the constant pressure they face through the internet world. It is important to understand online marketing and how it can be deceptive, as people can't touch, feel or smell what's advertised. Technology has improved accessibility—find, grab, and get. This on-demand culture has naturally shifted our food habits as well. Technology gives a faster way to get your food. Everybody likes ready to eat, ready to drink, and mull meal bars because it takes just a few minutes to prepare without effort. Technology does not affect our food habits as well as it affects the food industries [9].

According to the latest available statistics from the Australian Institute of Health and Welfare, which covered the years 2017 to 2018, 7.7% of adults and 17% of children were obese. As a result, one in four kids are at an elevated risk for physical health problems as well as greater mortality and sickness risks as adults. In order to prevent these tendencies from developing later in life, it is important to foster a positive link between food and technology from early childhood and adolescence on.

Technology has positive impacts also; like presently, so many intelligent appliances make cooking more accessible and less time-consuming, like smart cookers, electric inductions, ovens, etc. New technologies change everything from what we eat to how it to made by minimizing waste and environmental impacts. New automation raises high-skill jobs in the food sector and puts manual workers' livelihoods at risk. So, the effect of technology is much more complicated [10]. On one side, it looks beneficial; on the other, so many detrimental effects also exist.

There are several major food technology trends in the limelight, for example, lab-grown meat, produced by culturing animal cells *in vitro*, and vegan beef, which is made from vegetarian ingredients. Plant milk is an alternative to milk, so many processed foods. This technological revolution and the internet's growing effect have changed how we perceive food and eating. Some changes are of positive impact, while others are troublesome. We are living in 2023, where in this technology era, without stepping out of the house, everybody can enjoy their food at any time just by ordering online on different apps. Fast-food franchises have grown tremendously in the last some years. Yes, that's what technology is doing to us: changing how we used to eat. With this technological era, the obesity epidemic is also on the scene [11]. Many factors influence the obesity epidemic, like reduced physical exercise due to more screen time, more caloric intake, easy access to fast food because of doorstep delivery, and as no one has time to make nutritious meals at home and customers want quick meal alternatives, the number of women entering the job is rising (not necessarily beneficial). The author [12] analysis that, there was a significant variation in the cost of food from 1950 to 2007, and it was discovered that the cost of fruits and vegetables climbed with time while the cost of snacking food reduced. For instance, the cost of a banana is currently around 5 Rs. The cost of chocolate is 1 Rs. concurrently. Here, we can directly link the consumption of calorie-dense foods to rising obesity rates over time.

1.3   Government Programs to Encourage Healthy Choices

- With the help of large-scale awareness efforts like "Aaj Se Thoda Kam" and Trans-Fat Free India@75, the FSSAI hopes to eradicate fat by the year 2022.
- To combat the widespread lack of micronutrients in the nation, food fortification is also actively marketed on a massive scale.
- Eat Right India movement, 2018
- Mid-Day Meal in Schools (MDMS) for children studying in a government school.
- In accordance with the human life cycle concept, the National Food Security Act of 2013 provides for food and nutritional security.
- Dietary guidelines of USDA Nutrition Education

1.4   Technology's Impact on Our Food Consumption

Many studies have analyzed that eating if we are using technology (T.V., mobile, online games, etc.) impacts the amount of food we eat and the memory we retain of the consumption as shown in Figure 1.5. Nutritionists claim that technology diverts our attention during meals and may have an impact on how much food a person eats. It was discovered in a research of 119 individuals that when they played a straightforward computer game while eating, they consumed much less food than when they consumed the same meal without any interruptions. When they were preoccupied with technology, they had trouble accurately recalling how much they had been provided and consumed. Moreover, the University of Illinois at Urbana-Champaign examined the same study. Distraction also depends on what type of technology you use and what food is served [13, 14].

Figure 1.5 Impact of technology on our food consumption.

Technology makes our food more sustainable. Plant-based protein that gives taste and flavor to meat, foods for tomorrow, impossible foods, and beyond beef are the new players for more sustainable food options. Vegan products, alternative soy, pea, and potato protein attract vegetarians and meat eaters. There are so many innovative apps that care about what is eaten and what is left over. Too Good to use technology app helps eliminate food waste; they fill the gap between retailers with excess food and food waste warriors who are always looking for a real bargain. Due to the accessibility and simplicity of apps, awareness about food waste and its effect on the environment gained momentum in a few years [15].

1.5   Customized Food is the Future of Food

The future is about altering your meal to suit you, and food customizing is an encompassing concept, as shown in Figure 1.6.

It can be emotional and based on an individual's choice. For example, customizing a food product externally or gifting name-branded chocolate or sweets leaves a memory long after the taste is gone. Customers can choose the content of their food item with a high degree of personalization as per their occasion. Subway is a great example where customers

Figure 1.6 Food customization.

can customize their meals according to their taste or nutritional preferences [16].

1.6   Impact of Food Technology and Innovation on Nutrition and Health

Food industries use innovative and emerging techniques to develop products that offer variety, convenience, and health benefits as shown in Figure 1.7. These include less harmful alternatives to traditional protein sources, regional cuisines, nutraceuticals, and specialized nutrition [17]. Food industries are digitizing their production, management, and ecommerce area. However, many food products are more expensive than one can only afford.

Highly processed foods and minimally processed foods are in trending. Minimally processed food is rich in nutrients and reduces the risk of chronic health conditions. Yet, because they frequently include harmful amounts of sugar, salt, and fat, highly processed meals are generally not nutritionally similar to the foods they aim to replace. Dairy milk replacements, for instance, are better options but may not have the same nutritional value as dairy milk. New food items include plant-based substitutes, functional foods, replacement foods, and unique food products have seen a quick growth in popularity because to customer demand, food technology, and creativity [18]. Personal values, environmental sustainability, social justice, and animal welfare are all part of this movement. Food industries respond to consumer demands and the environment with the help of technology and innovations. With the use of technology, innovative

Figure 1.7 Impact of food technology and innovation on nutrition and health.

food products are more convenient and add variety to eating patterns, and they can be a suitable replacement for traditional. For example, vermicelli made from rice, semolina, different flours, soybeans, lentils, or quinoa can be a suitable replacement for conventional that is made from maida. With a simple ingredient swap that does not alter the meal's preparation or nutritional content, they add extra nutrients and fiber to the diet. Similarly, sugar is replaced by polyols, commonly known as sugar alcohols, and carbohydrate-based fat substitutes, including carrageenan. A type of seaweed, starch-based gels, guar gum, maltodextrins, etc., replaces fats. And garlic salt, celery salt, potassium chloride, etc., are popular alternatives to table salt.

1.7   Top Prominent and Emerging Food Technology Trends

- Grain-free flours: grain-free flours mean a step beyond gluten-free grains. Some people have an allergic reaction to gluten

Figure 1.8 Different types of gluten-free grains.

that can damage the small intestine, and some people avoid gluten for other reasons, like celiac disease, weight problems, etc. So, gluten-free flours are the healthier alternative; for example, almond flour, cassava flour, tiger nut flour, coconut flour, oat flour, gram flour, banana flour, arrowroot, tapioca, chestnut flour, sunflower seed flour, etc., as shown in Figure 1.8 [19].

- Plant-based Alternatives: Plant-based proteins are alternatives to animal proteins due to health and environmental concerns. Algae-based protein, fungi-based protein, The main sources of alternative protein are cultured meat, fermented proteins, lab-grown food, plant-based nutrition, edible insect proteins, and mycoprotein [20]. Blue Tribe Foods is India's first plant-based meat company. Similarly, Beyond Meat, Imagine Meats, GREENEST, Shaka Harry, etc., are some Indian startups in this field. The Protein Brewery (Dutch Startup) develops protein, an animal-free lab-grown food made from some non-allergenic crops, fungi, essential amino acids, and fiber, as shown in Figure 1.9. Ento (Malaysian startup) develops insect-based proteins etc.

  High-quality plants are increased exponentially to reduce meat consumption; for example, black bean quinoa veggie burgers are crave-able meat alternatives, as faux sausage crumbles and garlic and fennel plant-based sausages. Plant-based patties that look and taste like beef, good catch fish-free tuna, and meatless crumbles, as shown in Figure 1.10.

- Functional Foods and Ingredients: Functional foods provide additional health benefits to the consumer beyond essential

Figure 1.9 Alternative protein market map.

Figure 1.10 Plant-based meat and protein substitutes.

nutrition. Fortification and available ingredients are bioactive compounds that can be used in manufacturing food ingredients, e.g., stanol, sterol, or dietary fiber [21]. Every component of food, including functional baby food, functional bakery and confectionary goods, functional dairy and dairy-based products, functional drinks, etc., has a growing market for functional foods, as illustrated in Figure 1.11.

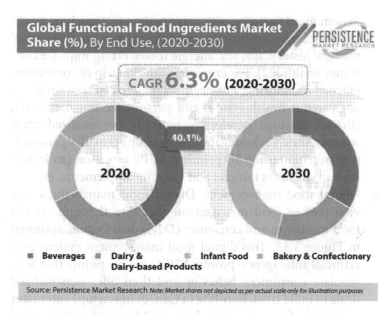

Figure 1.11 Market size of functional food ingredients.

- Personalized Nutrition: Depending on the preferences of each consumer, it may offer nutrigenomics-based diet options, vegan diets, sugar- and gluten-free options, and clean-label food goods. Figure 1.12 illustrates how 3D printing and robots in food assembly lines enable food makers to scale up nutrition customization.

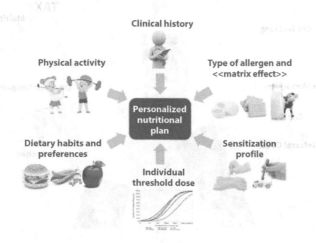

Figure 1.12 Personalized food as per individuals.

Personalized nutrition uses massive data and machine learning approaches to include vast information on consumers' medical history, age, sex, allergic foods, etc. to improve consumer health [22]. For example, with the help of continuous glucose monitoring, gut health tests, etc., we can critically analyze our health system and personalize our diet. NGX (British Startup) develops genetically personalized meal shakes, Anrich 3D (Singaporean Startup) provides personalized nutrition using 3D printing, SUPP nutrition (an Indian startup) includes mineral and vitamin supplements, etc.

- Digital food management: Digital food management is a vital part of food management that directly connects the food industries and consumer (D2C) distribution as shown in Figure 1.13. This digital food management system uses artificial intelligence-powered WiFi access points that self-regulate consumers' behavior and then offer personalized deals to build trust. BaroBite (a Canadian startup) automates marketing for restaurants, bars, and lounges with a social media platform where customers can connect through posts and stories [23].

Figure 1.13 Digital food management.

- Ecommerce: Pandemic situation pushed innovations in food supply chains, and ecommerce has become the spotlight in the food industry, as shown in Figure 1.14. Online distribution services are available on request using digital channels to reach clients, which works on a direct-to-customer (D2C) model. Swiggy and Zomato to order food come under in the top 10 e-commerce food delivery companies [24].
- 3D Food Printers: 3D Food printers are an advanced manufacturing technique, using laser, bioprinting, food printing, etc., to develop food products, as shown in Figure 1.15. It offers personalized food products and diets at a large scale without additional operating costs. With the help of food printing, food can be customized in any shape, color, size, flavor, nutrition, or texture, making it very attractive, appealing, and valuable for various fields like robotics. Fab@Home, pasta printer, Foodini, CandyFab, etc. These are some examples of 3D food printers.
- Robotics: The food industries, food brands, and beverages incorporate robotics in their entire chain to get more consistency, effectiveness, and better hospitality to improve customer convenience and safety. Drones and vehicles are emerging technology in the food sector chain that gives more cost-effective, fast, and better monitoring service, as shown in Figure 1.16.

Figure 1.14 E-commerce platforms.

Figure 1.15 3D food printing.

Figure 1.16 Robotics in food industry.

Overall, the food business is making more money thanks to robotics thanks to improved speed and precise quality control. Servi, a food service robot that assists waiters with carrying plates, was developed by the Bear Robotics business [25]. With robotics solutions, hospitality has become more exciting and more manageable. Similarly, ROBOEATZ provides AI-based autonomous robotic kitchens for restaurants, 5-star hotels, etc.

- Food Waste Reduction: Earlier, a massive part of the food was wasted, so food industries and entrepreneurs focused on reducing food wastage. Food monitoring and reusing solutions allow for reduced food waste. Innovative packaging also plays a significant role in reducing food wastage. For example, bar codes, intelligent labels, real-time data tracking, and time–temperature indicator are some innovative techniques to know all about your food, like when your food is packed, how much freshness is there, in how many days it will spoil by changing code color, etc. that prevent waste between from farm to fork. RFID technology, Radio Frequency Identification, uses the electromagnetic field to track and identify objects automatically [26]. It plays a vital role in waste management, adding the capability to sense when it is time to pick up the trash. 3D food printing uses food waste to print edible food products.

- Food safety and transparency: Customers are becoming more concerned with food product quality and safety than actual purchases. As shown in Figure 1.17, using smart labeling and independent food grading equipment, consumers may obtain product information prior to making a purchase.

    To win customers' trust via food quality and safety, food safety, and transparency are crucial. Both the Canadian business ThisFish and the French startup Quality provide software-as-a-service (SaaS) to automate food safety.

- Nonthermal Techniques: Nonthermal techniques mean processing foods without any heat treatment that can maintain their quality and nutritional factors and eliminate microbial reduction. High-pressure processing, irradiation, cold plasma, pulsed electric field, etc., are some nonthermal processing techniques [27, 28].

Figure 1.17 Food transparency with clean food labels.

1.8   Discussion

However, some disadvantages of this technology should be addressed, and one of the most remarkable disadvantages is that processing removes nutrients. Now, all over the world, supermarkets are full of convenient processed food items that appeal to our taste buds, but food processing can strip many nutrients while refining the process present in fresh food. So, we need to get them from elsewhere.

- These processed foods also include artificial color, additives, flavoring agents, and chemically altered fats and sweeteners, which can give wrong signals to our bodies and cause health problems.
- Processed food can be used for convenience and speed, not for the pleasure that we used to get from natural homemade food.
- Reduced physical activity creates health issues.

1.9   Conclusions

Technology in the food industry has advanced significantly in recent years, and as a result, consumer food tastes are changing dramatically. The popularity of online shopping applications is altering consumer behavior, and the level of interaction and personalization with customers is rising. With the use of clever tags and codes, technology has improved transparency and traceability. Robots also aids in lowering food waste. In addition to the benefits, there are also drawbacks, such as a complete reliance on technology, eating problems, the use of chemicals and preservatives, the absence of physical activity, etc. Technology can help us change our eating habits and address a number of current issues.

References

1. Aune, D., Keum, N., Giovannucci, E. *et al.*, Whole grain consumption and risk of cardiovascular disease, cancer, and all-cause and cause-specific mortality: A systematic review and dose-response meta-analysis of prospective studies. *BMJ*, 1, 1, 353, 2016.
2. Bragg, M.A., Miller, A.N., Elizee, J., Dighe, S., Elbel, B.D., Popular music celebrity endorsements in food and nonalcoholic beverage marketing. *Pediatrics*, 138, 1, 1–13, 2016.

3. Hu, F.B., Otis, B.O., McCarthy, G., Can plant-based meat alternatives be part of a healthy and sustainable diet? *Jama*, 322, 16, 1547–1548, 2019.

4. Srour, B., Fezeu, L.K., Kesse-Guyot, E., Alles, B., Debras, C., Druesne-Pecollo, N., Chazelas, E. *et al.*, Ultra-processed food consumption and risk of type 2 diabetes among participants of the NutriNet-Santé prospective cohort. *JAMA Internal Med.*, 180, 2, 283–291, 2020.

5. Bhanu, P., Singh, P.P., Kumar, A., Gupta, V., Food and human health: An outlook of the journey of food from hunger satisfaction to health-promoting agent, in: *Research and Technological Advances in Food Science*, pp. 1–30, 2022.

6. Dohmen, A.E. and Raman, D.R., Healthy food as a new technology-The implications of technological diffusion and food price for changes in eating habits. *Front. Nutr.*, 5, 1, 109, 2018.

7. Shepherd, R. and Raats, M.M., Attitudes and beliefs in food habits, in: *Food Choice, Acceptance and Consumption*, vol. 3, pp. 346–364, 1996.

8. Bumbac, R. *et al.*, How zoomers eating habits should be considered in shaping the food system for 2030: A case study on the young generation from Romania. *Sustainability*, 12, 18, 7390, 2020.

9. Rosen, L.D. *et al.*, Media and technology use predicts ill-being among children, preteens, and teenagers independent of the negative health impacts of exercise and eating habits. *Comput. Hum. Behav.*, 35, 1, 364–375, 2014.

10. Lambert, N. *et al.*, Using smart card technology to monitor the eating habits of children in a school cafeteria: Developing and validating the methodology. *J. Hum. Nutr. Diet.*, 18, 4, 243–254, 2005.

11. Kristo, A.S. *et al.*, Technological devices and their effect on preschool children's eating habits in communities of mixed socioeconomic status in Istanbul, a pilot cross-sectional study. *Behav. Sci.*, 11, 11, 157, 2021.

12. Lambert, N. *et al.*, Using smart card technology to monitor the eating habits of children in a school cafeteria: The nutritional significance of beverage and dessert choices. *J. Hum. Nutr. Diet.*, 18, 4, 271–279, 2005.

13. Almohanna, A. *et al.*, Impact of dietary acculturation on the food habits, weight, blood pressure, and fasting blood glucose levels of international college students. *J. Am. Coll. Health*, 63, 5, 307–314, 2015.

14. Wen, T.-H., Tchong, W.-L., Ching, G.S., A study on the relationship between college student's personality and their eating habits. *Int. J. Inf. Educ. Technol.*, 5, 2, 146–149, 2015.

15. Oniang'o, R.K., Mutuku, J.M., Malaba, S.J., Contemporary African food habits and their nutritional and health implications. *Asia Pac. J. Clin. Nutr.*, 12, 3, 1–12, 2003.

16. Kgaphola, M.S. and Viljoen, A.T., Food habits of rural swazi households: 1939–1999 Part 1: Technological influences on swazi food habits. *J. Consumer Sci.*, 28, 1, 1–7, 2000.

17. Schneider, S. *et al.*, Contextual influences on physical activity and eating habits-options for action on the community level. *BMC Public Health*, 17, 1, 1–7, 2017.

18. Ciurzyńska, A. *et al.*, Eating habits and sustainable food production in the development of innovative healthy snacks. *Sustainability*, 11, 10, 2800, 2019.
19. Galanakis, C.M. *et al.*, Innovations and technology disruptions in the food sector within the COVID-19 pandemic and post-lockdown era. *Trends Food Sci. Technol.*, 110, 1, 193–200, 2021.
20. Kaylor, S.K. *et al.*, Calories and control: Eating habits, behaviors, and motivations of generation Z females. *J. Am. Coll. Health*, 11, 1, 1–9, 2021.
21. Syrkiewicz-Świtała, M. *et al.*, Mobile applications and eating habits among women and men–Polish experiences. *Biocybern. Biomed. Eng.*, 41, 3, 1093–1106, 2021.
22. Worsley, A., Food habits and beliefs in transitional societies. *Asia Pac. J. Clin. Nutr.*, 7, 1, 287–292, 1998.
23. de Alcântara, C.M. *et al.*, Digital technologies for the promotion of healthy eating habits in teenagers. *Rev. Bras. Enferm.*, 72, 2, 513–520, 2019.
24. Stawarz, K., Cox, A.L., Blandford, A., Beyond self-tracking and reminders: Designing smartphone apps that support habit formation, in: *Proceedings of the 33rd Annual ACM Conference on Human Factors in Computing Systems*, pp. 2653–2662, 2015.
25. Wetherbee, B.M., Cortés, E., Bizzarro, J.J., Food consumption and feeding habits, in: *Biology of Sharks and Their Relatives*, vol. 10, no. 3, pp. 225–246, 204, 2004.
26. Schiel, R., Kaps, A., Bieber, G., Electronic health technology for the assessment of physical activity and eating habits in children and adolescents with overweight and obesity IDA. *Appetite*, 58, 2, 432–437, 2012.
27. Quintero-Angel, M., Mendoza, D.M., Quintero-Angel, D., The cultural transmission of food habits, identity, and social cohesion: A case study in the rural zone of Cali-Colombia. *Appetite*, 139, 1, 75–83, 2019.
28. Isaacs, E., Konrad, A., Walendowski, A., Lennig, T., Hollis, V., Whittaker, S., Echoes from the past: How technology-mediated reflection improves well-being, in: *Proceedings of the SIGCHI Conference on Human Factors in Computing Systems*, pp. 1071–1080, 2013.

Issues in Healthcare and the Role of Machine Learning in Healthcare

Nidhika Chauhan[1]*, Navneet Kaur[2], Kamaljit Singh Saini[2] and Manjot Kaur[3]

[1]I UIC Department, Chandigarh University, Punjab, Mohali, India
[2]Department of CSE, Chandigarh University, Punjab, Mohali, India
[3]Fidelity Information Services Ltd., Mohali, India

Abstract

The healthcare industry is one of the world's most significant and rapidly growing sectors. As a result, healthcare administration is transitioning from conventional methods to digital ones. The transition phase of the healthcare industry is confronting several issues like as the number of medical cases is increasing, the data are also growing. This information could comprise crucial details about the patient's medical background, physicians' recommended treatments, medical examination outcomes, etc. All these data are enormous, complex, and diversified; along with that, this data also faces issues like privacy, security, data hacking, data management, etc. To overcome these challenges, machine learning (ML) tools are used for data analysis, prediction, and classification. It is used in healthcare to classify the disease more accurately and overcome the challenges of multiple outcome optimization or sequential decision-making issues. The chapter aims to study current healthcare systems, various healthcare issues, several factors that affect healthcare, and how machine learning is employed to overcome these challenges. The role of machine learning in healthcare is critically studied.

Keywords: Healthcare, issues in healthcare, factors affecting healthcare, machine learning

*Corresponding author: nidhi29.chauhan@gmail.com

Sandeep Kumar, Anuj Sharma, Navneet Kaur, Lokesh Pawar and Rohit Bajaj (eds.) Optimized Predictive Models in Healthcare Using Machine Learning, (21–38) © 2024 Scrivener Publishing LLC

2.1　Introduction

The healthcare concept describes a system that improves health-related facilities to cater to patients' clinical needs. Doctors, practitioners, healthcare professionals, researchers, and healthcare industries are all working hard to maintain and improve healthcare services and preserve medical records. With the effective delivery of the technology over the years, information is continuously growing throughout every industry, along with healthcare, which would, in turn, requires an increasing number of data mining techniques [1–5].

Public healthcare information systems often called clinical informatics, describe the application of data design and integration to the context of biomedical practice, comprising the management and use of individual healthcare information. It employs a holistic strategy for health information to enhance healthcare by focusing on more modern prospects. Essentially, it affects the advancement of data acquisition, storage, recovery, and utilization in medicine and biomedicine [6–9]. However, as the medical system digitizes, medical institutions generate vast clinical information [10–15]. Generally, medical datasets refer to all health-related documents that are digitally recorded [13, 16–23]. It might include extensive details on the patient's medical history, doctor's recommended instructions, medical tests, etc. All this information is massive, multi-dimensional, and diverse. Due to the increasing difficulty of health information, making wise decisions is difficult today [12, 23–38].

Advanced healthcare information systems broaden the scope of primary healthcare facilities by including elements ranging from advanced techniques to computational engineering. Efficient content analysis improves overall operations by considering every aspect. Public healthcare analytics integrates digital technologies, research, and health disciplines to establish a more smooth and more efficient management process that benefits individuals globally [38–44]. The primary goal of medical care bioinformatics is to deliver better patient services by leveraging technological developments in global health, clinical trials, pharmacy, and other fields. Unfortunately, there needs to be more aware of the analytical techniques that could be extremely useful for the healthcare industry and its treatment of patients around the globe [42]. Belle *et al.* [45–51] explored different smart healthcare technology problems that may be solved with analytical modelling. Due to escalating expenditures in the medical sector in countries such as the U.S., big data analytics has become essential in this domain [52–62]. Furthermore, prices are far more excellent than they should be and have been growing for the past 20 years. We require innovative, data-driven reforms in the health-care industry. Machine learning, data mining, and statistical approaches are significant areas of research that boost persons' capacity to make appropriate decisions to optimize the performance of any professional sector [55, 63–71]. Compared to the quantity of data generated, the scale of human data analysis ability is substantially lower [71–73]. This is especially important in the healthcare industry, where the extent of qualified professionals for medical data analysis could be much more significant.

In this chapter, we aim to discuss the healthcare system, issues in healthcare, factors affecting healthcare, and the role of machine learning in healthcare. The chapter is structured into various sections to cover the mentioned topics. An overview of issues in healthcare is given in the subsection. The following section discusses factors affecting healthcare. The chapter further discusses machine learning in healthcare, followed by a conclusion.

2.2   Issues in Healthcare

The medical field is one of the world's most significant and rapidly growing industries. Consequently, healthcare administration is shifting from conventional to digital methods [72]. With this transformation, the healthcare industry faces various challenges mentioned in Figure 2.1:

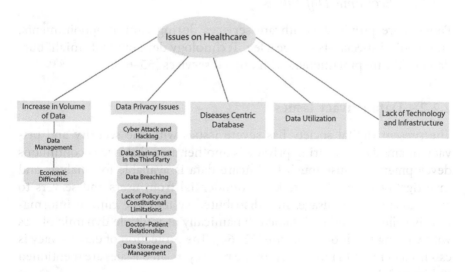

Figure 2.1   Issues in healthcare.

2.2.1   Increase in Volume of Data

The medical industry is undergoing a radical transformation. Due to the modernization of healthcare, a tremendous volume of medical data is being generated. Information Technology in healthcare has progressed to the point that it can gather, maintain, and send information digitally from any part of the globe in real time. Nowadays, all health-related documents are digitally preserved. Each one of these datasets is massive, multidimensional, and diverse in character, resulting in big healthcare data [6–9]. Such data may be gathered from various internal and external sources. This data includes clinical information, biometric data, picture records, social media data, etc. This exponential growth and diverse nature of healthcare data have become one of the most significant concerns as it becomes difficult to manage and store due to its heterogeneity and large size [10–16].

As healthcare data has increased rapidly, it has generated various issues, constraints, and complications. These issues are further discussed that must be addressed [3, 11].

2.2.1.1   Data Management

Information management is a significant concern in healthcare data because it is obtained in various forms; it must be validated and processed.

2.2.1.2   Economic Difficulties

Patients are provided healthcare services during clinical appointments, and medical specialists charge a fee. Technology developments might burden healthcare practitioners with unpaid services [55–67].

2.2.2   Data Privacy Issues

The present digital society has severe issues with the security and privacy of any data. Ensuring privacy is another area that needs continuous development because much healthcare data is available for analysis and investigations. The data are kept confidential from users and servers to avoid unauthorized usage. In a distributed system, the clinical information is collected and maintained dynamically at multiple dynamic places with varying levels of disclosure [55–64]. The protection of data privacy is essential in this situation. Some of the privacy-related issues are mentioned in Figure 2.2.

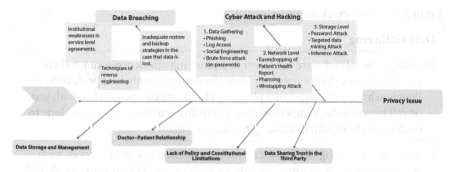

Figure 2.2 Privacy issues in healthcare.

2.2.2.1   Cyber Attack and Hacking

A dynamic electronic health record (EHR) is monitored and governed by a third party for adequate information storage and administration. The vendor must safeguard patient confidentiality when specific data is exchanged for assessment, study, research, or business interests. In addition, the third party is accountable for offering a necessary amount of data storage privacy to defend against hacking. Still, in the current healthcare system, patient records are either not protected by any protective measures or are kept in outdated systems, which results in unauthorized users accessing such critical data [12].

2.2.2.2   Data Sharing Trust in the Third Party

When sharing personal information with a third party, there is often a need for more focus on obtaining consent from the individuals whose information is being shared. This is particularly true for private organizations that exchange their employees' data without considering the necessary measures for data security and restrictions. Although sharing data for research and analysis may not seem harmful, it can still include personal identification information, making organizations responsible for any misuse of the information as any governing body does not regulate it. This is also a concern in public sector hospitals where patient information is disclosed without consent. Table 2.1 represents cyber attacks on various process of gathering, transmitting, and storing data within a system or network.

Sharing data with a third party raises questions about trust, leading to the distinction between trustworthy and untrustworthy privacy models. In the reliable model, the data owner trusts the third party and freely shares their information. Still, in the deceitful model, the data owner does not have confidence in the third party. This lack of trust raises concerns about

Table 2.1 Cyber attack on various levels.

Data Gathering
Phishing—People who are the target of a phishing attack are contacted via email, text, or call by a fraudster impersonating an authentic professional. People who are the target of a phishing attack are contacted via email, text, or call by a fraudster impersonating a genuine professional. This is done to trick individuals into disclosing private information.
Log access—It is a log of all requests for the transference of file access, such as images, records, reports, and other related items. Web users leave digital traces in the form of information on the server. The server logs keep track of previous page requests sent to the server.
Social engineering—This attack is among the oldest and most common types of cybercrime. Hackers use a cognitive approach to trick victims into revealing crucial data to access their gadgets and networks.
Brute force attack (on passwords)—It is a trial-and-error attack used to guess username and password, asymmetric encryption, or the location of a hidden web page. Attackers try every potential sequence in the hopes of making the right guess. Brute force means the hacker is pressured to breach the account's privacy. This attack is used to obtain profit from gathered activity data, steal personal details, and hijack your system device for criminal activity.
Network Level
Eavesdropping of patient health reports—It is illegal monitoring of network traffic. The hacker fraudulently intercepts the transmission if someone is lawfully reading the patient's data. The data obtained are later sold to companies.
Pharming—This technique is like a phishing scam. A backdoor is placed on the victim's device, and the harmful webpage is launched by manipulating the DNS server.
Wiretapping attack—The intruder interferes with the connection via telephone equipment to listen to phone calls. Through this, he can listen to all the conversations between the patent and the physician.
Storage Level
Password attacks—They are carried out to break into a specific patient's medical file or to obtain entree to or control over the entire system.

(Continued)

Table 2.1 Cyber attack on various levels. (*Continued*)

Targeted data mining attack—It utilizes data mining strategies to get access permission to the database to grab confidential patient data.
Inference attack—This cyber attack breaks into a database to obtain sensitive information from a patient's medical file. It is hard to safeguard against an inference attack since some data may be retrieved by authenticating access to a database.

the security and integrity of the data, making it a critical issue to establish a highly reliable health architecture when dealing with untrustworthy parties in Table 2.1. These categories represent the different levels at which cyber attacks can occur and the corresponding attacks that fall within each level. The attacks under each level are described in detail.

Obtaining consent and ensuring the security and integrity of personal information are crucial when sharing data with third parties, especially when dealing with sensitive information like health data. Establishing a trustworthy relationship with the third party is essential to prevent potential harm to individuals and maintain their information's privacy.

2.2.2.3   Data Breaching

Although the healthcare industry has continuously taken data security procedures, data breaching is one of the significant privacy issues that poses a considerable threat. The following are the primary factors for security breaches in healthcare [13]:

1. Institutional weaknesses in service level agreements.
2. Inadequate restore and backup strategies if data are lost.
3. Techniques of reverse engineering

2.2.2.4   Lack of Policy and Constitutional Limitations

Various studies indicate that medical institutes tend to ignore data privacy. Privacy is often overlooked; enterprises, in particular, place a minor focus on it. Data protection laws in medical institutions continue to need improvement. While sharing medical information or publishing by a third party, it is not defined by whom the data is accessed, the type of data to be published for public use, who can have access to the stored data, and what all consents are required before sharing the data [14].

2.2.2.5   Doctor–Patient Relationship

The confidence between physicians and patients is another challenge to privacy. Most patients do not trust their physicians or hospital professionals with their medical data protection. Most hospitals exchange information with outside parties without patient consent [15]. No legislation protects such conduct because the law does not provide a standard policy addressing such deception. Many studies indicate that there are various factors like Inadequate government medical support system, low doctor-to-patient ratio, the patient having no say in the decision-making process, and exploitation that contribute to mistrust in the doctor–patient relationship [15, 16].

2.2.2.6   Data Storage and Management

Maintaining computerized healthcare information in the cloud is necessary as healthcare data is enormous. According to a study [17], most healthcare institutes save their medical information on the cloud for easy accessibility; nevertheless, only a minority focus on the security and privacy factor. Furthermore, information management emphasizes architecture for data, centralized or decentralized storage, integrity protection, and usage.

2.2.3   Disease-Centric Database

As disease-centric databases do not concentrate on specific features and symptoms, such databases provide less opportunity for data analysis. Some illnesses are linked to an individual's behavioral aspects, livelihood, and region. Let us consider a patient is taking treatment for several related diseases from various physicians during the last 10 years. In such a scenario, it is essential to analyze the patient's medical treatment records, ancestry, and routine, which could either be absent in the disease-centred database or found in multiple databases requiring a complex integrated examination. Specific statistical measures are scattered over several datasets kept independently by hospitals or could be missing, leading to improper prediction. The quality of the information could be better for analysis [18].

2.2.4   Data Utilization

In the current era, the total patient database system is transitioning from a traditional to a digital platform, with the modernization of clinical information, which includes EHR, healthcare software, digital X-rays, and records utilized for assessment and therapy. Server-side applications produce an enormous quantity of data. Such medical information should be assessed to determine appropriate treatments and actively make quick disease predictions [19].

Graph 2.1 illustrates the trade-off between the benefits of data and safeguarding privacy. Historically, the emphasis was primarily on protecting patients' privacy and maximizing value by considering their privacy [20–22].

2.2.5   Lack of Technology and Infrastructure

Biomedical technology has progressed, so paper-based medical files are no longer maintained. The documents are already being digitized into EHRs so that they may be consulted online. Innovative technology, health monitoring through IoT devices, and data analysis of medical files enabling advanced sickness prediction are being adopted to improve life quality. Although significant advancements are taking place in medical science, various developing or underdeveloped countries still need to fully implement technology at the primary stages of the healthcare system due to a need for more technology or infrastructure [23].

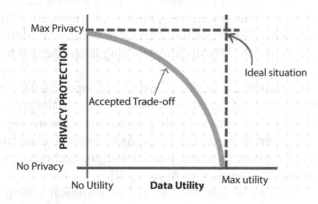

Graph 2.1 Utility and privacy trade-off.

2.3   Factors Affecting the Health

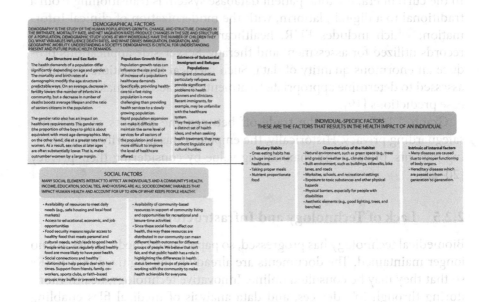

2.4   Machine Learning in Healthcare

Machine learning is "a machine's ability to reproduce intelligent human behavior" [24]. A skilled algorithm operates from information before making judgments based on efficiency or characteristics in new data [25]. Machine learning (ML) is a topic that has captured the attention of researchers. As data volumes increase, 86% of pharmaceutical businesses use machine learning (ML) algorithms, and 80% of hospital administrators have an A.I. strategy [26, 27]. Machine learning is an essential field in the larger area of A.I.

ML is further classified into unsupervised and supervised learning. The medical industry is one of the largest businesses potentially profiting from this technology [28–30]. With technological advances, the average life span has improved significantly over the years. As technological advancements have considerably grown in recent years, emerging technologies, such as machine learning (ML) predict healthcare [30].

ML algorithms can be employed to enhance clinical testing research in several ways. Medical staff could examine a wider variety of information, minimizing the time and expenses required for diagnostic testing by adopting advanced data analytics like ML to clinical research [31–33].

ML has several practical applications in both research and healthcare studies. Incorporating machine learning-based predictive research to discover implicit drug trial subjects can aid the researcher in moving with a supply from many data sources, such as prior medical appointments, online networks, etc. It also guarantees that information is available at any time and maintains experiment collaborators, allowing to determine the most feasible sample size to be examined that contributes to mitigating data-based mistakes [34, 35]. Diagnostic imaging data, which has been digitally captured is ubiquitous nowadays, and many algorithms could be deployed to identify and discover patterns and irregularities throughout the dataset. ML algorithms could evaluate image data in a highly trained radiologist's exact approach, finding unusual patches of skin, tumors, cancers, and other problems [32].

2.4.1 Clinical Decision Support Systems in Healthcare

Various machine learning (ML) methodologies and procedures have been utilized to create a medical decision support system (CDSS) for aiding physicians. An example of this is using an ensemble model that consists of four separate models, including a neural network (N.N.), gradient-boosted decision tree, support vector machine, and logistic regression, to categorize the risk of death among patients infected with COVID-19 [36]. Similarly, a CDSS has been developed to help prioritize prescription checks to decrease prescribing mistakes [37, 38]. A comparable support system may be designed to assist the pharmaceutical business in selecting a chemical component that is more likely to cross regulatory hurdles and reach the market as medicine [39].

2.4.2 Use of Machine Learning in Public Health

ML systems can forecast population-level medical outcomes using massive datasets [40]. When there are vast data sets and a nonlinear association between the outcome and other independent factors, ML methods are helpful. Though the statistical technique was previously utilized to forecast different demographic events, there is a need and motivation to use various ML techniques to predict results [41]. Examples of how machine learning (ML) is being used to improve community health include predicting childhood lead poisoning, detecting the prevalence of suicidal thoughts, diagnosing diabetic retinopathy, handling public health emergencies, and determining the occurrence of yellow fever [38, 39, 42].

2.5   Conclusion

Machine learning may be vital for doctors, scientists, or researchers. Nearly every day, there is a breakthrough in machine learning. With each discovery, a potential ML tool that tackles a real issue in healthcare arises. The progress of machine learning (ML) is constantly expanding, and the medical business is keeping a careful eye on this trend. ML principles support physicians and surgeons in saving lives, recognizing diseases and issues before they develop, better monitoring patients, involving patients in their rehabilitation process, and much more. This technology enables enterprises and pharmaceutical companies to explore medicines for urgent illnesses quickly and economically. Organizations may use simulated medical testing, scheduling, and analytical thinking to speed testing and observation procedures. Behavioral factors and socioeconomic characteristics, such as income, social support networks, and education, are better indicators of general well-being. Medical associations realize that to promote well-being, they must target the individual's whole aspect, incorporating the environment and habits. ML models can identify people at a higher risk of acquiring avoidable chronic diseases like heart disease or diabetes.

References

1. Priyanka, K. and Kulennavar, N., A survey on big data analytics in healthcare. *Int. J. Comput. Sci. Inf. Technol.*, 5, 4, 5865–5868, 2014.
2. Kumar, S., Rani, S., Jain, A., Verma, C., Raboaca, M.S., Illés, Z., Neagu, B.C., Face spoofing, age, gender and facial expression recognition using advance neural network architecture-based biometric system. *Sensor J.*, 22, 14, 5160–5184, Dec. 2022.
3. Kumar, S., Jain, A., Rani, S., Alshazly, H., Idris, S.A., Bourouis, S., Deep neural network based vehicle detection and classification of aerial images, in: *Intelligent Automation & Soft Computing*, vol. 34, pp. 119–131, Jan. 2022.
4. Kumar, S., Jain, A., Agarwal, A.K., Rani, S., Ghimire, A., Object-based image retrieval using the U-Net-based neural network. *Comput. Intell. Neurosci.*, 2021, 1–14, 2021, https://api.semanticscholar.org/CorpusID:244059375.
5. Kumar, S., Jain, A., Shukla, A.P., Singh, S., Raja, R., Rani, S., Harshitha, G., AlZain, M.A., Masud, M., A comparative analysis of machine learning algorithms for detection of organic and non-organic cotton diseases, in: *Mathematical Problems in Engineering*, vol. 2021, pp. 1–18, Oct. 2021.
6. Rani, S., Kumar, S., T., V.S., Jain, A., Swathi, A., Kumar, R.K., Commodities price prediction using various ml techniques, in: *The International Conference*

on Technological Advancements in Computational Sciences (ICTACS – 2022), Tashkent City Uzbekistan, Feb. 2022, pp. 1–6.

7. Harshitha, G., Kumar, S., Rani, S., Jain, A., Cotton disease detection based on deep learning techniques, in: *University of Bahrain 4th Smart Cities Symposium,* 21-23 November 2021.

8. Kumar, S., Jain, A., Rani, S., Ghai, D., Swathi, A., Raja, P., Enhanced SBIR based re-ranking and relevance feedback, in: *10th IEEE International Conference on System Modeling & Advancement in Research Trends (SMART),* Dec. 2021.

9. Jain, A., Singh, J., Kumar, S., Emilian, T.F., Candin, M.T., Chithaluru, P., Improved recurrent neural network schema for validating digital signatures in VANET. *Math. J.,* 10, 20, 1–23, Mar. 2022.

10. Kumar, S., Haq, M., Jain, A., Jason, C.A., Moparthi, N.R., Mittal, N., Alzamil, Z.S., Multilayer neural network based speech emotion recognition for smart assistance. *CMC-Comput. Mater. Continua,* 74, 1, 1–18, 22 September 2022.

11. Kumar, S., Shailu, Jain, A., Enhanced method of object tracing using extended kalman filter via binary search algorithm. *J. Inf. Technol. Manag.,* 12, 2, 23–35, Jun. 2021.

12. Rani, S., Ghai, D., Kumar, S., Object Detection and Recognition using Contour based Edge Detection and Fast R-CNN. *Multimed. Tools Appl.,* 22, 2, 1–25, Jan. 2022.

13. Rani, S., Ghai, D., Kumar, S., Kantipudi, M.V.V., Alharbi, A.H., Ullah, M.A., Efficient 3D AlexNet architecture for object recognition using syntactic patterns from medical images. *Comput. Intell. Neurosci.,* 2022, 1–19, May 2022.

14. Choudhary, S., Lakhwani, K., Kumar, S., Three-dimensional objects recognition & pattern recognition technique; related challenges: A review. *Multimed. Tools Appl.,* 23, 1, 1–44, Mar. 2022.

15. Singh, J., Agarwal, S., Kumar, P., Kashish, Rana, D., Bajaj, R., Prominent features based chronic kidney disease prediction model using machine learning, in: *2022 3rd International Conference on Electronics and Sustainable Communication Systems (ICESC),* pp. 1193–1198, 2022.

16. Pawar, L., Malhotra, J., Sharma, A., Arora, D., Vaidya, D., A robust machine learning predictive model for maternal health risk, in: *2022 3rd International Conference on Electronics and Sustainable Communication Systems (ICESC),* pp. 882–888, 2022.

17. Pawar, L., An optimized predictive model for prospective blogging using machine learning, in: *2022 IEEE International Conference on Data Science and Information System (ICDSIS),* pp. 1–5, 2022.

18. Pawar, L., Saw, A.K., Tomar, A., Kaur, N., Optimized features based machine learning model for adult salary prediction, in: *2022 IEEE International Conference on Data Science and Information System (ICDSIS),* pp. 1–5, 2022.

19. Bajaj, R., Shandilya, D., Gagneja, S., Gupta, K., Rawat, D., A predictive risk model for primary tumor using machine learning with initial missing values, in: *2022 IEEE International Conference on Data Science and Information System (ICDSIS),* pp. 1–7, 2022.

20. Kumar, D., Sharma, A.K., Bajaj, R., Pawar, L., Feature optimized machine learning framework for unbalanced bioassays, in: *Cognitive Behavior and Human-Computer Interaction Based on Machine Learning Algorithm*, pp. 167–178, 2021.

21. Pawar, L., Agrawal, P., Kaur, G., Bajaj, R., Elevate primary tumor detection using machine learning, in: *Cognitive Behavior and Human-Computer Interaction Based on Machine Learning Algorithm*, pp. 301–313, 2021.

22. Pawar, L., Sharma, A.K., Kumar, D., Bajaj, R., Advanced ensemble machine learning model for balanced BioAssays, in: *Artificial Intelligence and Machine Learning in 2D/3D Medical Image Processing*, pp. 171–178, 2020.

23. Rahi, P., Sood, S.P., Bajaj, R., Smart platforms of air quality monitoring: A logical literature exploration, in: *Futuristic Trends in Networks and Computing Technologies: Second International Conference, FTNCT 2019*, Revised Selected Papers 2, pp. 52–63, Springer Singapore, Chandigarh, India, November 22–23, 2019.

24. Pawar, L., Singh, J., Bajaj, R., Singh, G., Rana, S., Optimized ensembled machine learning model for IRIS plant classification, in: *2022 6th International Conference on Trends in Electronics and Informatics (ICOEI)*, Tirunelveli, India, pp. 1442–1446, 2022.

25. Rahi, P., Sood, S.P., Bajaj, R., Meta-heuristic with machine learning-based smart e-health system for ambient air quality monitoring, in: *Recent Innovations in Computing: Proceedings of ICRIC 2021*, vol. 2, Springer Singapore, Singapore, pp. 501–519, 2022.

26. Kaur, M., Bajaj, R., Kaur, N., A review of MAC layer for wireless body area network. *J. Med. Biol. Eng.*, 41, 767–804, 2021. https://api.semanticscholar. org/CorpusID:244656387

27. Ramdev, M.S., Bajaj, R., Sidhu, J., Remote radio head scheduling in LTE-advanced networks. *Wireless Pers. Commun.*, 122, 1, 621–644, 2022.

28. Bathla, G., Pawar, L., Khan, G., Bajaj, R., Effect on the lifetime of routing protocols using different connectivity schemes. *Int. J. Sci. Technol. Res.*, 8, 12, 617–622, 2019.

29. Kumar, R., Bajaj, R., Singh, V.K., Vasudeva, K., Pawar, L., Advanced specialized processor architecture for smartphones. *Int. J. Comput. Intell. Res.*, 13, 5, 815–823, 2017.

30. Pawar, L., Bawa, G., Mehra, C., Kanojia, S., Arora, J., Bajaj, R., Analyzing sensor-based technologies for obstacle avoidance robot. *2022 3rd International Conference on Electronics and Sustainable Communication Systems (ICESC)*, pp. 271–277, 2022.

31. Singh, G., Singh, A., Bajaj, R., Analysis of energy optimization approaches in internet of everything: An SDN prospective, in: *Software Defined Internet of Everything*, pp. 119–133, Springer International Publishing, Cham, 2021.

32. Kaur, M., Bajaj, R., Kaur, N., Wireless body area network: Performance analysis of polling access MAC protocol. *2021 2nd Global Conference for Advancement in Technology (GCAT)*, Bangalore, India, pp. 1–7, 2021.

33. Durcevic, S., 18 examples of big data analytics in healthcare that can save people, Oct 2020. URL https://www.datapine.com/blog/big-data-examples-in-healthcare/. Accessed: 2021-04-30.
34. Raja, R., Mukherjee, I., Sarkar, B.K., A systematic review of healthcare big data. *Sci. Program.*, 2020, Article ID 5471849, 15, 2020.
35. Belle, A., Thiagarajan, R., Reza Soroushmehr, S. M.., Navidi, F., Beard, D. A., Najarian, K., Big data analytics in healthcare. *BioMed. Res. Int.*, 2015, 370194, 2314–6133, 2015, https://doi.org/10.1155/2015/370194.
36. Bhardwaj, R. and Nambiar, A.R., A Study of machine learning in Healthcare. *IEEE 41st Annual Computer Software and Applications Conference*, 2017.
37. Raja, R., Mukherjee, I., Kanti Sarkar, B., A machine learning-based prediction model for preterm birth in Rural India. *J. Healthc. Eng.*, 2021, 11, 2021. https://api.semanticscholar.org/CorpusID:235755653
38. Debnath, S., Barnaby, D.P., Coppa, K. *et al.*, Machine learning to assist clinical decision-making during the COVID-19 pandemic. *BioMed. Cent.*, 6, 2332–8886, 2020.
39. Herland, M., Khoshgoftaar, T.M., Wald, R., A review of data mining using big data in health informatics. *J. Big Data*, 1, 1, 2, 2014.
40. Silahtaroğlu, G. and Yılmaztürk, N., Data analysis in health and big data: A machine learning medical diagnosis model based on patient's complaints. *Commun. Stat.-Theory Methods*, 50, 1547–1556, 2019. https://api.semantic-scholar.org/CorpusID:195560540
41. Bharat, A., Pooja, N., Reddy, R.A., Using machine learning algorithms for breast cancer risk prediction and diagnosis, in: *Proceedings of the 3rd International Conference on Circuits, Control, Communication and Computing*, Bangalore, IndiaJuly 2018.
42. Sarkar, A.K., Big data for secure healthcare system: A conceptual design. *Complex Intell. Syst.*, 3, 2, 133–151, 2017.
43. Priya, R., Sivasankaran, S., Ravisasthiri, P., Sivachandiran, S., A survey on security attacks in electronic healthcare systems. *2017 International Conference on Communication and Signal Processing (ICCSP)*, 2017.
44. Kumar, P.R., Raj, P.H., Jelciana, P., Exploring data security issues and solutions in cloud computing. *Proc. Comput. Sci.*, 125, 691–697, 2018.
45. Rübel, O., Tritt, A., Ly, R., Dichter, B. K., Ghosh, S., Niu, L., Baker, P., Soltesz, I., Ng, L., Svoboda, K. *et al.*, The neurodata without borders ecosystem for neurophysiological data science. *Elife*, 11, e78362, 2022.
46. Meingast, M., Roosta, T., Sastry, S., Security and privacy issues with healthcare information technology. *2006 International Conference of the IEEE Engineering in Medicine and Biology Society*, 2006.
47. Mishra, N., Bhatia, T., Nimgaonkar, V., Deshpande, S., Parker, L., A qualitative study of institutional ethics committees: Members' understanding of research guidelines, privacy, and challenges to privacy protection. *Indian J. Med. Ethics*, III, 4, 315–320, 2018.

48. Ion, Sachdeva, N., Kumaraguru, P., Čapkun, S., Home is safer than the cloud! *Proceedings of the Seventh Symposium on Usable Privacy and Security - SOUPS '11*, 2011.

49. Liu, X., Deng, R.H., Choo, K.-K.R., Yang, Y., Privacy-preserving reinforcement learning design for patient-centric dynamic treatment regimes. *IEEE Trans. Emerg. Topics Comput.*, 9, 1, 456–470, 2021.

50. Boric-Lubecke, O., Gao, X., Yavari, E., Baboli, M., Lubecke, V.M., E-healthcare: Remote monitoring, privacy, and security. *2014 IEEE MTT-S International Microwave Symposium (IMS2014)*, 2014.

51. Churi, P.P. and Pawar, A.V., A systematic review on privacy preserving data publishing techniques. *J. Eng. Sci. Technol. Rev.*, 12, 6, 17–25, 2019.

52. Sánchez, D., Batet, M., Viejo, A., Utility-preserving privacy protection of textual healthcare documents. *J. Biomed. Inf.*, 52, 189–198, 2014.

53. Xiong, P. and Zhu, T., An anonymization method based on a tradeoff between utility and privacy for data publishing. *2012 International Conference on Management of e-Commerce and e-Government*, 2012.

54. Segal, G., Segev, A., Brom, A., Lifshitz, Y., Wasserstrum, Y., Zimlichman, E., Reducing drug prescription errors and adverse drug events by application of a probabilistic, machine-learning based clinical decision support system in an inpatient setting. *J. Am. Med. Inf. Assoc.*, 26, 12, 1560–1565, 2019.

55. Pavithra, V. and Jayalakshmi, V., Machine and deep learning (ML/DL) algorithms for next-generation healthcare applications, in: *Enterprise Digital Transformation*, pp. 203–224, 2022.

56. O'Mahony, C., Jichi, F., Pavlou, M., Monserrat, L., Anastasakis, A., Rapezzi, C., Biagini, E., Gimeno, J. R., Limongelli, G., McKenna, W. J. *et al.*, A novel clinical risk prediction model for sudden cardiac death in hypertrophic cardiomyopathy (HCM risk-SCD). *Eur. Heart J.*, 35, 30, 2010–2020, 2014.

57. 86% of healthcare companies use some form of ai. *Healthc. I. T. News*, 27-Oct-2017. [Online]. Available: https://www.healthcareitnews.com/news/86-healthcare-companies-use-some-form-ai. [Accessed: 01-Nov-2022].

58. HealthITAnalytics, Over 80% of health execs have artificial intelligence plans in place. *HealthITAnalytics*, 02-Nov-2020. [Online]. Available: https://health itanalytics.com/news/over-80-of-health-execs-have-artificial-intelligence-plans-in-place. [Accessed: 01-Nov-2022].

59. Abdelaziz, A., Elhoseny, M., Salama, A.S., Riad, A.M., A machine learning model for improving healthcare services on cloud computing environment. *Measurement*, 119, 117–128, 2018.

60. Char, D., Abrámoff, M.D., Feudtner, C., Identifying ethical considerations for machine learning healthcare applications. *Am. J. Bioeth.*, 20, 7–17, 2020, https://api.semanticscholar.org/CorpusID:225069938.

61. Ahmad, M.A., Eckert, C., Teredesai, A., Interpretable machine learning in healthcare, in: *Proceedings of the 2018 ACM International Conference on Bioinformatics, Computational Biology, and Health Informatics*, pp. 559–560, 2018, August.

62. Chen, I.Y., Joshi, S., Ghassemi, M., Ranganath, R., Probabilistic machine learning for healthcare. *Annu. Rev. Biomed. Data Sci.*, 4, 393–415, 2021.

63. Siddique, S. and Chow, J.C., Machine learning in healthcare communication. *Encyclopedia*, 1, 1, 220–239, 2021.

64. Waring, Lindvall, C., Umeton, R., Automated machine learning: Review of the state-of-the-art and opportunities for healthcare. *Artif. Intell. Med.*, 104, 101822, 2020.

65. Ahmad, M.A., Patel, A., Eckert, C., Kumar, V., Teredesai, A., Fairness in machine learning for healthcare, in: *Proceedings of the 26th ACM SIGKDD International Conference on Knowledge Discovery & Data Mining*, pp. 3529–3530, 2020, August.

66. Manogaran, G. and Lopez, D., A survey of big data architectures and machine learning algorithms in healthcare. *Int. J. Biomed. Eng. Technol.*, 25, 2–4, 182–211, 2017.

67. Gao, Y., Cai, G.-Y., Fang, W., Li, H.-Y., Wang, S.-Y., Chen, L., Yu, Y., Liu, D., Xu, S., Cui, P.-F. *et al.*, Machine learning based early warning system enables accurate mortality risk prediction for COVID-19. *Nat. Comm.*, 11, 1, 5033, 2020.

68. Corny, A., Rajkumar, Martin, O., Dode, X., Lajonchère, J.-P., Billuart, O., Bézie, Y., Buronfosse, A., A machine learning–based clinical decision support system to identify prescriptions with a high risk of a medication error. *J. Am. Med. Inf. Assoc.*, 11, 1688–1694, 272020.

69. Kavsak, P.A., The evidence for laboratory test–based computer clinical decision support tools on medication errors and adverse drug events. *J. Appl. Lab. Med.*, 3, 6, 922–924, 2019.

70. Doupe, P., Faghmous, J., Basu, S., Machine learning for health services researchers. *Value Health*, 22, 7, 808–815, 2019.

71. Morgenstern, J.D., Buajitti, E., O'Neill, M., Piggott, T., Goel, V., Fridman, D., Kornas, K., Rosella, L.C., Predicting population health with machine learning: A scoping review. *BMJ Open*, 10, 10, e037860, 2020.

72. Lu, S., Christie, G.A., Nguyen, T.T., Freeman, J.D., Hsu, E.B., Applications of artificial intelligence and machine learning in disasters and public health emergencies. *Disaster Med. Public Health Prep.*, 16, 4, 1674–1681, 2021.

73. Ogunyemi, O.I., Gandhi, M., Lee, M., Teklehaimanot, S., Daskivich, L.P., Hindman, D., Lopez, K., Taira, R.K., Detecting diabetic retinopathy through machine learning on electronic health record data from an urban, safety net healthcare system. *JAMIA Open*, 4, 3, ooab066, 2021.

3

Improving Accuracy in Predicting Stress Levels of Working Women Using Convolutional Neural Networks

Purude Vaishali Narayanro[1,2]**, Regula Srilakshmi**[1]**, M. Deepika**[1]
and P. Lalitha Surya Kumari[2*]

[1]*Department of CSE, Neil Gogte Institute of Technology, Hyderabad, Telangana, India*
[2]*Department of CSE, Koneru Lakshmaiah Education Foundation, Hyderabad, Telangana, India*

Abstract

Currently, the world is facing a severe and prevalent issue called stress, which significantly impacts women's health and the development of their children. To aid working women in their professional and personal growth, assessing their stress levels accurately is crucial. Artificial intelligence (AI) algorithms have been used for stress level prediction. However, these models are prone to misclassification and errors, and their design can be complicated and less efficient. To overcome the limitations, we propose a convolutional neural network (CNN) model to identify stress levels in working women. Our framework includes creating a dataset, extracting the features, selecting optimal features, and binary classification using CNNs. We also handle missing values and remove duplicate attributes during data preprocessing. Our approach using CNNs is expected to outperform previous ML and DL algorithms in accurately predicting stress levels in working women.

Keywords: Stress prediction, working women, classification, CNN

3.1 Introduction

Predictive modeling uses statistics and machine learning algorithms to create models that predict future events or behaviors perfectly. In healthcare, predictive modeling can identify patients at risk of developing certain

Corresponding author: vlalithanagesh@gmail.com

Sandeep Kumar, Anuj Sharma, Navneet Kaur, Lokesh Pawar and Rohit Bajaj (eds.) Optimized Predictive Models in Healthcare Using Machine Learning, (39–56) © 2024 Scrivener Publishing LLC

diseases or conditions, predict the outcomes of medical interventions, and improve patient outcomes by providing personalized treatment plans [18–21].

The methodology for developing predictive models in healthcare involves several steps, including problem definition, dataset preparation, preprocessing of data, selecting an apparent model, training the model, and performance evaluation [22–25]. Factors that can affect the performance of predictive models include the size of the dataset and its quality, which is used to train the model, the choice of modeling algorithm, and the tuning of model parameters [4].

CNN models have shown promising results in stress prediction. They are powerful deep-learning models that have proven effective in text classification, image and signal processing tasks, and natural language processing (NLP). CNNs can be a better approach for predicting stress levels in working women. They can learn essential elements from raw data, such as physiological signals or text, without relying on handcrafted features [26–29].

This is particularly relevant for stress prediction, where relevant features may not be immediately apparent or vary across individuals. Furthermore, CNNs can handle complex data structures, such as time-series or multi-channel data, often encountered in stress prediction tasks. For example, physiological signals such as electroencephalography (EEG) or heart rate variability (HRV) recordings are often used to assess stress levels. CNNs can learn to extract meaningful patterns from these signals. Another advantage of CNNs is their ability to handle missing values and noisy data.

This is especially important in stress prediction, where data may need to be completed or subject to measurement errors. CNNs can learn to tolerate such imperfections and still make accurate predictions. Lastly, CNNs can handle large, complex datasets often required for reliable stress prediction. This is important because stress levels vary widely across individuals and may depend on factors such as age, gender, or occupation [6, 7].

CNNs can be trained on such datasets to learn individual-specific features and improve prediction accuracy. In summary, CNNs can be a better approach to predicting stress levels in working women as it learns by extracting relevant features from raw data, handling complex data structures, tolerating missing values and noisy data, and handling large and complex datasets. By leveraging these strengths, CNN-based models can provide more accurate and efficient tools for stress prediction in working women, ultimately leading to improved health and well-being [13].

Several factors have driven the development of predictive modeling in healthcare:

- Growing healthcare costs: Healthcare costs have been increasing steadily over the past several decades, and there is a need to find more efficient ways to deliver care. Predictive modeling can help identify patients at risk of developing certain conditions or complications, allowing interventions to be targeted to those who need them most.
- Advances in data analytics: The field has recently seen significant advances in using machine learning techniques to analyze large and complex datasets. These techniques have been applied to healthcare data to identify patterns and relationships that can be used to predict outcomes.
- Increasing availability of electronic health records (EHRs): EHRs are becoming increasingly common in healthcare, providing a rich data source that can be used to train predictive models. The adoption of EHRs has also made it easier to share patient data across different healthcare providers, allowing more comprehensive models to be developed.
- Personalized medicine: There is growing recognition of the importance of customized healthcare tailored to the individual patient. Predictive modeling can help identify patients who are likely to respond well to specific treatments or are at risk of adverse events, allowing treatment plans to be tailored to the individual patient.

These factors have led to increased interest in predictive modeling in healthcare to improve results and reduced costs. In the second section, we presented a literature survey. In the third section, we explained our proposed architecture and methodology. Section 4 discussed the results on different datasets and sub-sections; we compared the existing procedures with the proposed method. The chapter ends with the section conclusion and future work.

3.2   Literature Survey

Research has shown that stress can have a significant impact on the health of women and the development of their children. With an increasing number of women balancing work and pregnancy, accurately assessing their stress levels has become crucial to promote their well-being and personal growth. Machine learning (ML) and deep learning (DL) algorithms have been employed in previous studies to predict stress levels in women. However, these models can be complicated to design, prone to misclassification and errors, and less efficient.

To address these limitations, researchers have proposed using deep learning models based on convolutional neural networks (CNN) to predict stress levels in working women. These models involve several steps, including dataset preparation, feature extraction, optimal feature selection, and classification using CNNs. Researchers have also developed techniques to handle missing values and remove duplicate attributes during data preprocessing. The summary of the literature survey is shown in Table 3.1.

In today's fast world Stress is the primary concern which has a severe effect on the brain of human beings. In recent research, AI has been used to predict the stress levels of the working woman. The study shows how ML, DL and CNN algorithms are used for this task as follows-

Flesia et al. [8] used a deep recurrent neural network (DRNN) to predict the stress levels of working pregnant women. The study achieved higher accuracy than other ML and DL algorithms and preprocessing and feature selection was performed to optimize the algorithm's performance. However, the study did not compare DRNN with deep learning algorithms such as convolutional neural networks (CNN).

Vijayan et al. [9] used a CNN to predict the stress levels of pregnant women using high-resolution images. The study achieved high accuracy in predicting stress levels, and image preprocessing and feature extraction were performed to optimize the algorithm's performance. However, the study had a limited sample size, and its generalizability may be limited.

Romaniszyn-Kania et al. [10] used ensemble learning algorithms, including random forest, decision tree, KNN, SVM, and AdaBoost, to predict the stress levels of pregnant women. The study achieved high accuracy and performed feature selection and preprocessing to optimize the algorithm's performance. However, the study did not use any deep-learning algorithms.

Xiang et al. [11] compared various ML algorithms, including K-nearest neighbors, naive Bayes, decision tree, random forest, support vector machine, and multilayer perceptron, to predict the stress levels of pregnant women. The study performed preprocessing and feature selection and found that the random forest algorithm was the most effective in predicting stress levels. However, the study used no deep-learning algorithms and had a limited sample size.

Sükei et al. [12] compared various classification algorithms, including logistic regression, K-nearest neighbours, decision tree, random forest, and gradient boosting, to predict the stress levels of working pregnant women. The study performed preprocessing and feature selection and found that the random forest algorithm was the most effective in predicting stress levels. However, the study used no deep-learning algorithms and had a limited sample size.

Table 3.1 Comparison of literature survey on the proposed method.

Sr. No.	Author & title	Algorithm used	Merits	Gaps identified
1	Hsu et al. [1], "Predicting the stress of working pregnant women using machine-learning algorithms" (2020)	Deep Recurrent Neural Network (DRNN)	DRNN achieved higher accuracy than other ML and DL algorithms; Problems Covered: predicting stress levels of working pregnant women; Preprocessing and feature selection performed	No comparison was made with CNN or different algorithms
2	Reddy et al. [2], "Deep learning-based pregnancy stress index using a convolutional neural network with high-resolution image" (2020)	Convolutional Neural Network (CNN)	CNN achieved high accuracy in predicting stress levels using high-resolution images of pregnant women; Problems Covered: indicating stress levels of pregnant women; Image preprocessing and feature extraction performed	Limited sample size and generalizability
3	Singh et al. [3], "Predictive modeling for stress identification among pregnant women using ensemble learning algorithms" (2021)	Random Forest, Decision Tree, KNN, SVM, AdaBoost	Ensemble learning achieved high accuracy in predicting stress levels of pregnant women; Problems Covered: indicating stress levels of pregnant women; Feature selection and preprocessing performed	No deep-learning algorithms used

(Continued)

Table 3.1 Comparison of literature survey on the proposed method. (*Continued*)

Sr. No.	Author & title	Algorithm used	Merits	Gaps identified
4	Qasrawi *et al.*, "A comparison between various machine learning algorithms for predicting stress level among pregnant women" (2019)	K-Nearest Neighbors (KNN), Naive Bayes (NB), Decision Tree (DT), Random Forest (RF), Support Vector Machine (SVM), Multilayer Perceptron (MLP)	Comparison made between different ML algorithms for predicting stress levels of pregnant women; Problems Covered: indicating stress levels of pregnant women; Preprocessing and feature selection performed	No deep-learning algorithms were used limited sample size.
	Shin *et al.* [5], "Machine learning-based predictive modeling of postpartum depression " (2021)	Logistic Regression, K-Nearest Neighbors (KNN), Decision Tree (DT), Random Forest (RF), Gradient Boosting (GB)	Comparison made between different classification algorithms for predicting stress levels of working pregnant women; Problems Covered: indicating stress levels of working pregnant women; Preprocessing and feature selection performed	No deep learning algorithms used a limited sample size.

In conclusion, the studies discussed above demonstrate that machine learning and deep learning algorithms can effectively predict working women's stress levels. While several ML algorithms have been explored for this purpose, more comparative studies with deep learning algorithms must be conducted. Future research should focus on comparing the performance of different ML and DL algorithms to identify the most effective algorithm for predicting the stress levels of pregnant women [14–18].

3.3   Proposed Methodology

This section provides a comprehensive analysis of the proposed stress prediction system for employed women using interview data, complete with flow diagrams. The first step in the procedure is to collect interview data from working women. In the Proposed method, we interviewed working women; for this procedure, we used the PHQ9 questionnaire [18]. The collected data is then preprocessed by cleaning, normalizing, and formatting it into a suitable format for training a CNN model. The preprocessed data is then split into training and testing sets to evaluate the model's performance on unseen data. The detailed description is explained below, and the workflow of the proposed method is shown in Figure 3.1. Algorithm 3.1 shows the overall procedure of the suggested working model.

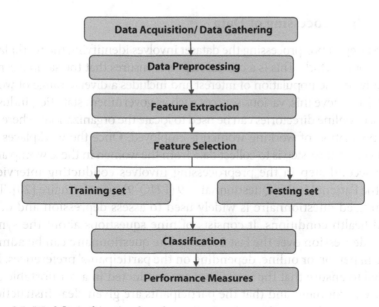

Figure 3.1 Workflow of proposed work.

Algorithm 3.1 DetectStress algorithm
Input: DASS21 Dataset

Begin:
   1. Read the whole DASS21 dataset.
   2. Following preprocessing, steps are performed on the dataset –
      i.   Remove the NULL entries.
      ii. Drop the columns that contain responses other than 0 to 3.
      iii. Convert entries into data type int64.
   4. Add a new column as the total of responses for each question.
   5. To assess stress levels, define the threshold as 10.
   6. Comparing the threshold with the total creates a labeled dataset containing binary labels Stressed (1) and Normal (0).
   7. Split the dataset for training and testing.
   8. Train and evaluate the CNN.
   9. Plot the graph for accuracy and loss.
End

Output: Binary Classified data indicating Stress levels for a working woman.

3.3.1   Pre-Processing of Data

The first step in pre-processing the dataset involves identifying the workplaces where women work. This is a crucial step as it ensures that the sample is representative of the population of interest and includes a diverse range of workplaces. To achieve this, various sources such as government statistics, industry reports, or online directories can be used to locate the organizations where the target population of working women is employed. Once the workplaces are identified, the next step is to collect data from the women in these workplaces.

The second step in the preprocessing involves conducting interviews using the Patient Health Questionnaire-9 (PHQ-9) questionnaire [20]. This standardized questionnaire is widely used to assess depression and other mental health conditions. It consists of nine squestions about the symptoms of depression over the last 2 weeks. The questionnaire can be administered in person or online, depending on the participants' preferences. It is essential to ensure that the interviews are conducted in a comfortable and private environment and that the participants are given clear instructions on completing the questionnaire. Collect answers in the dataset:

The third step in the preprocessing involves collecting the answers to the PHQ-9 questionnaire in a dataset. This dataset can then be used as input to the Detect stress algorithm, designed to predict stress levels in working women. It is essential to ensure the data is formatted and error-free, such as missing or duplicate values. Additionally, the dataset should be anonymized to provide the participants with privacy. By following these preprocessing steps, the dataset can be prepared for analysis and used to develop practical tools for predicting stress levels in working women.

3.3.2   Features Extraction

Feature extraction in our stress prediction system for employed pregnant women using interview data, we propose to use natural language processing (NLP) techniques to extract relevant features from the collected interview data. A detailed description of feature extraction is shown in Figure 3.2. The first step in feature extraction is to tokenize the interview data into individual words and remove stop words, such as "the," "and," and "is." Next, we will perform stemming and lemmatization to reduce words to their base form, which will help to standardize the data and reduce the dimensionality of the feature space. After tokenization and normalization, we will use various NLP techniques, such as part-of-speech tagging, named entity recognition, and sentiment analysis, to extract additional features from the interview data. Part-of-speech tagging will help to identify the grammatical structure of the interview responses. In contrast, named entity recognition will identify essential entities, such as names, organizations, and locations mentioned in the answers. Sentiment analysis will help determine the emotional tone of the responses, which can provide valuable insight into the women's stress levels.

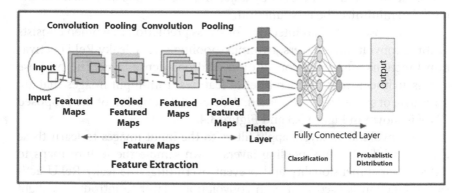

Figure 3.2 Feature extraction and classification in CNN.

Once all relevant features have been extracted from the interview data, we will use feature selection techniques to identify the essential components for stress prediction. This will help to reduce the dimensionality of the feature space and improve the accuracy of the stress prediction model. Finally, we will use the selected features to train a CNN model, which will be evaluated on the testing data to determine its performance in predicting stress levels of employed women.

3.3.3   Selection of Features

Feature selection is a crucial step in machine learning as it helps to identify the most relevant features for the prediction task while reducing the dimensionality of the feature space. The goal is to select a subset of highly informative features for stress prediction while eliminating redundant and irrelevant features.

Several feature selection techniques can be used, including filter, wrapper, and embedded methods. This study uses a filter method to select the most informative features. The filter method evaluates the relevance of each component by computing a score based on statistical measures, such as the correlation coefficient, chi-square test, or mutual information. The features with the highest scores are selected for the prediction model.

3.3.4   Classification

The CNN architecture is designed by defining the number and size of convolutional and pooling layers, the activation function, and the number of nodes in the fully connected layer. The model is then compiled by defining the loss function, the optimizer, and the evaluation metrics. The model is trained on the training data by adjusting the weights and biases of the model to minimize the loss function.

The proposed CNN architecture for stress prediction in women consists of three convolutional layers, two max-pooling layers, leaky ReLU activation functions after each convolution, and one dense layer. The purpose of this architecture is to learn a set of features from input images that are indicative of stress levels in women. A detailed description of the proposed CNN is shown in Figure 3.3 and Figure 3.4.

The convolutional layers apply filters to the input images to learn these features, while the max pooling layers down-sample the feature maps to reduce their dimensionality and prevent overfitting. The leaky ReLU activation function is used after each convolutional layer to introduce a slight negative slope. This helps avoid the dying ReLU problem and improves the

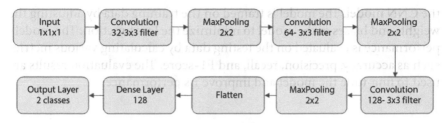

Figure 3.3 Architectural diagram of proposed CNN.

```
Model: "sequential"

Layer (type)                    Output Shape              Param #
=================================================================
conv2d (Conv2D)                 (None, 1, 1, 32)          320

leaky_re_lu (LeakyReLU)         (None, 1, 1, 32)          0

max_pooling2d (MaxPooling2D)    (None, 1, 1, 32)          0

conv2d_1 (Conv2D)               (None, 1, 1, 64)          18496

leaky_re_lu_1 (LeakyReLU)       (None, 1, 1, 64)          0

max_pooling2d_1 (MaxPooling2     (None, 1, 1, 64)          0

conv2d_2 (Conv2D)               (None, 1, 1, 128)         73856

leaky_re_lu_2 (LeakyReLU)       (None, 1, 1, 128)         0

max_pooling2d_2 (MaxPooling2     (None, 1, 1, 128)         0

flatten (Flatten)               (None, 128)               0

dense (Dense)                   (None, 128)               16512

leaky_re_lu_3 (LeakyReLU)       (None, 128)               0

dense_1 (Dense)                 (None, 2)                 258
=================================================================
Total params: 109,442
```

Figure 3.4 An overview of CNN architecture.

network's performance. Finally, the output from the last max pooling layer is flattened and passed through a dense layer. This fully connected layer learns the non-linear relationships between the input features and the stress levels in women. This thick layer is typically followed by a softmax activation function, which produces a probability distribution over the different stress levels.

Finally, the performance of the CNN model is evaluated on the testing data by calculating the accuracy, precision, recall, and F1-score. Split the data into training, and testing sets: Split the preprocessed data into training and testing locations to evaluate the model's performance on unseen data. Once the most relevant features are selected, they are used to train the CNN model. The model is trained on the training data by adjusting the weights and biases of the model to minimize the loss function. The model's performance is evaluated on the testing data by calculating various metrics such as accuracy, precision, recall, and F1-score. The evaluation results are used to fine-tune the model and improve its performance.

3.4   Result and Discussion

In the proposed method, DASS 21 dataset is used. The DASS 21 dataset is commonly used in psychological research that measures levels of depression, anxiety, and stress in individuals. The dataset consists of a questionnaire that asks respondents to rate their experiences of 21 different symptoms on a scale of 0 to 3, with 0 indicating that the symptom was not experienced at all and three indicating that the sign was experienced very severely. To evaluate the performance of the proposed work, precision, recall, sensitivity, specificity, F1-score, and error rate are used as evaluation parameters. The value of these parameters is then calculated using the following formulas:

$$\text{Precision} = \text{TP TP} + \text{FP} \qquad (3.1)$$

$$\text{Recall} = \text{TP TP} + \text{FN} \qquad (3.2)$$

$$\text{F1\_Score} = 2 \times \text{Precision} \times \text{Recall Precision} + \text{Recall} \qquad (3.3)$$

$$\text{Accuracy} = \text{TP} + \text{TN TP} + \text{TN} + \text{FP} + \text{FN} \qquad (3.4)$$

$$\text{Error\_Rate} = 1 - \text{Accuracy} \qquad (3.5)$$

TP represents the true positives, TN represents false negatives, FP represents the false positives, and FN represents the false negatives. The proposed method utilizes a batch size of 32 and employs a CNN architecture. The performance analysis is conducted using the DASS 21 dataset. The model is trained for 40 and 60 epochs, and validation accuracy and loss are calculated and presented as graphs. The evaluation metrics used are accuracy, precision, recall, and F1 score computed for epoch 40 and epoch 60. Figures 3.5 to 3.7 show the results of the proposed method on epoch size 40. Figures 3.8 to 3.10 shows the results of the proposed method on epoch size 40. Table 3.2 and Figure 3.11 show the comparative analysis of the

```
Train on 3437 samples, validate on 860 samples
Epoch 1/40
3437/3437 [==============================] - 5s 1ms/sample - loss: 0.1960 - accuracy: 0.9514 - val_loss: 0.0198 - val_accurac
y: 1.0000
Epoch 2/40
3437/3437 [==============================] - 1s 256us/sample - loss: 0.0169 - accuracy: 0.9936 - val_loss: 0.0272 - val_accur
acy: 0.9779
Epoch 3/40
3437/3437 [==============================] - 1s 193us/sample - loss: 0.0358 - accuracy: 0.9843 - val_loss: 0.0185 - val_accur
acy: 1.0000
Epoch 4/40
3437/3437 [==============================] - 1s 190us/sample - loss: 0.0167 - accuracy: 0.9945 - val_loss: 0.0081 - val_accur
acy: 1.0000
Epoch 5/40
3437/3437 [==============================] - 1s 190us/sample - loss: 0.0162 - accuracy: 0.9924 - val_loss: 0.0101 - val_accur
acy: 1.0000
Epoch 6/40
3437/3437 [==============================] - 1s 240us/sample - loss: 0.0169 - accuracy: 0.9948 - val_loss: 0.0755 - val_accur
acy: 0.9721
```

Figure 3.5 Validation accuracy of proposed work on 40 epoch size.

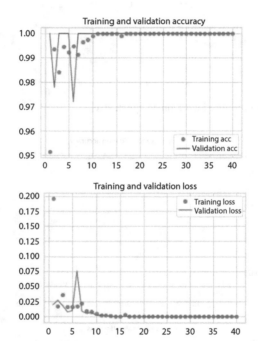

Figure 3.6 Results of validation accuracy and validation loss on 40 epoch size.

	precision	recall	f1-score	support
Class 0	1.00	1.00	1.00	984
Class 1	1.00	1.00	1.00	91
accuracy			1.00	1075
macro avg	1.00	1.00	1.00	1075
weighted avg	1.00	1.00	1.00	1075

Figure 3.7 Results of proposed work on 40 epoch size.

```
Train on 3437 samples, validate on 860 samples
Epoch 1/60
3437/3437 [==============================] - 2s 888us/sample - loss: 0.1622 - accuracy: 0.9658 - val_loss: 0.0502 - val_accur
acy: 0.9802
Epoch 2/60
3437/3437 [==============================] - 1s 295us/sample - loss: 0.0236 - accuracy: 0.9892 - val_loss: 0.0198 - val_accur
acy: 0.9802
Epoch 3/60
3437/3437 [==============================] - 1s 308us/sample - loss: 0.0174 - accuracy: 0.9930 - val_loss: 0.0130 - val_accur
acy: 1.0000
Epoch 4/60
3437/3437 [==============================] - 1s 295us/sample - loss: 0.0190 - accuracy: 0.9930 - val_loss: 0.0072 - val_accur
acy: 1.0000
Epoch 5/60
3437/3437 [==============================] - 1s 272us/sample - loss: 0.0142 - accuracy: 0.9959 - val_loss: 0.0050 - val_accur
acy: 1.0000
Epoch 6/60
3437/3437 [==============================] - 1s 286us/sample - loss: 0.0303 - accuracy: 0.9889 - val_loss: 0.0102 - val_accur
acy: 1.0000
```

Figure 3.8 Validation accuracy of proposed work on 60 epoch size.

```
              precision    recall  f1-score   support

     Class 0       1.00      1.00      1.00       967
     Class 1       1.00      1.00      1.00       108

    accuracy                           1.00      1075
   macro avg       1.00      1.00      1.00      1075
weighted avg       1.00      1.00      1.00      1075
```

Figure 3.9 Results of proposed work on 40 epoch size.

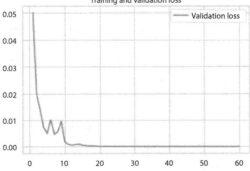

Figure 3.10 Results of validation accuracy and validation loss on 60 epoch size.

Table 3.2 Accuracy of different classification techniques and proposed techniques.

Classification techniques	Accuracy (%)
Support vector machine	92.49
Decision tree	90.489
Artificial neural network	90.789
K-nearest neighbour	92.39
Ensemble techniques	95.378
Bayes network	89.59
Naive bayes	78.5
Multilayer perceptron	87.9499
Random forest	84.9687
k* with random forest	91.38
Proposed improved CNN	100

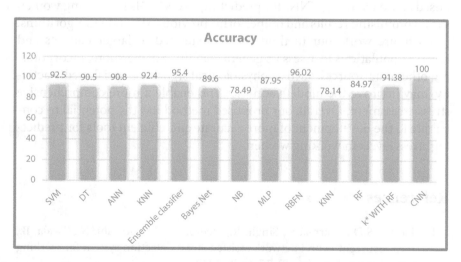

Figure 3.11 Wide comparison of accuracy of different classification techniques and proposed techniques.

proposed work with existing methods. As per the analysis, the proposed work gives better results on the DASS21 dataset.

As per the comparative analysis, the proposed CNN gives better results than the existing methods, showing improved training accuracy using 60 epochs. The model is trained using 40 and 60 epochs. The training accuracy using 40 epochs starts from 95.14% accuracy, while 96.58% accuracy is achieved using 60 epochs. This indicates that the model is adequately trained by increasing epochs from 40 to 60. The validation accuracy achieved in both epochs is 100% which is a good improvement using CNN.

3.5   Conclusion and Future Scope

In conclusion, we proposed a novel approach for predicting stress levels in working women using a deep learning model based on convolutional neural networks (CNNs). Our process involved several stages, including dataset preparation, feature extraction, optimal feature selection, and classification using CNNs. We also addressed missing values and duplicate attributes during data preprocessing. Our method was evaluated on the DASS 21 dataset using a batch size of 32 for 40 and 60 epochs. The results showed that the model's performance improved significantly when trained for 60 epochs, with better validation accuracy and lower loss. Our proposed approach using CNNs for predicting stress levels in working women shows promising results and outperforms previous ML and DL algorithms.

As future work, our method can be extended to larger datasets and diverse populations to assess its generalizability. Furthermore, incorporating other data sources, such as physiological signals or social media activity, may improve the model's accuracy and enable a more comprehensive stress assessment. Overall, our proposed method has the potential to contribute to the development of more accurate and efficient tools for predicting stress levels in working women.

References

1. Sharma, S.D., Sharma, S., Singh, R., Gehlot, A., Priyadarshi, N., Twala, B., Deep recurrent neural network assisted stress detection system for working professionals. *Appl. Sci.*, 12, 17, 8678, 2022.
2. Reddy, U.S., Thota, A.V., Dharun, A., Machine learning techniques for stress prediction in working employees, in: *Proceedings of the 2018 IEEE International Conference on Computational Intelligence and Computing Research (ICCIC)*, Madurai, India, 13–15 December 2018, pp. 1–4.

3. Ghosal, S., Blystone, D., Singh, A.K., Ganapathysubramanian, B., Singh, A., Sarkar, S., An explainable deep machine vision m for plant stress phenotyping. *Proc. Natl. Acad. Sci. U. S. A.*, 115, 4613–4618, 2018.

4. Qasrawi, R., Amro, M., VicunaPolo, S., Al-Halawa, D.A., Agha, H., Seir, R.A., Tayyem, R., Machine learning techniques for predicting depression and anxiety in pregnant and postpartum women during the COVID-19 pandemic: A cross-sectional regional study. *F1000Research*, 11, 390, 390, 2022.

5. Shin, D., Lee, K.J., Adeluwa, T., Hur, J., Machine learning-based predictive modelling of postpartum depression. *J. Clin. Med.*, 9, 9, 2899, 2020.

6. Workplace stress. Available online: https://www.stress.org/workplace-stress (accessed on 30 July 2022).

7. Monteiro, E. and Joseph, J., Establishing healthy workplaces: A case study on the employee well-being initiatives in the IT sector. *Int. J. Case Stud. Bus. IT Educ. (IJCSBE)*, 6, 2, 378–392, 2022.

8. Flesia, L., Monaro, M., Mazza, C., Fietta, V., Colicino, E., Segatto, B., Roma, P., Predicting perceived stress related to the COVID-19 outbreak through stable psychological traits and machine learning models. *J. Clin. Med.*, 9, 3350, 2020.

9. Vijayan, M., Impact of job stress on employee's performance in aavin, Coimbatore. *J. Organ. Hum. Behav.*, 6, 21, 2017.

10. Romaniszyn-Kania, P., Pollak, A., Bugdol, M.D., Bugdol, M.N., Kania, D., Mańka, A., Danch-Wierzchowska, M., Mitas, A.W., Affective state during physiotherapy and its analysis using machine learning methods. *Sensors*, 21, 4853, 2021.

11. Xiang, F. and Liu, B.A., Study on work stress of real estate industry knowledge workers based on the psychological contract, in: *Proceedings of the 2012 International Conference on Management Science & Engineering 19th Annual Conference Proceedings*, Dallas, TX, USA, pp. 1272–1280, 20–22 September 2012.

12. Sükei, E., Norbury, A., Perez-Rodriguez, M.M., Olmos, P.M., Artés, A., Predicting emotional states using behavioral markers derived from passively sensed data: Data-driven machine learning approach. *JMIR Mhealth Uhealth*, 9, e24465, 2021.

13. Srividya, M., Mohanavalli, S., Bhalaji, N., Behavioral modelling for mental health using machine learning algorithms. *J. Med. Syst.*, 42, 1–12, 2018.

14. Jaques, N., Taylor, S., Sano, A., Picard, R., Multimodal autoencoder: A deep learning approach to filling in missing sensor data and enabling better mood prediction, in: *Proceedings of the 2017 Seventh International Conference on Affective Computing and Intelligent Interaction (ACII)*, San Antonio, TX, USA, pp. 202–208, 23–26 October 2017.

15. Rosa, R.L., Schwartz, G.M., Ruggiero, W.V., Rodríguez, D.Z., A knowledge-based recommendation system that includes sentiment analysis and deep learning. *IEEE Trans. Ind. Inform.*, 15, 2124–2135, 2018.

16. Aceto, G., Ciuonzo, D., Montieri, A., Pescapé, A., Mobile encrypted traffic classification using deep learning: Experimental evaluation, lessons learned, and challenges. *IEEE Trans. Netw. Serv. Manag.*, 16, 445–458, 2019.

17. Jaber, D., Hajj, H., Maalouf, F., El-Hajj, W., Medically-oriented design for explainable AI for stress prediction from physiological measurements. *BMC Med. Inform. Decis. Mak.*, 22, 38, 2022.

18. Liang, L., Liu, M., Martin, C., Sun, W., A deep learning approach to estimate stress distribution: A fast and accurate surrogate of finite-element analysis. *J. R. Soc. Interface*, 15, 20170844, 2018.

19. Jaques, N., Taylor, S., Sano, A., Picard, R., Predicting tomorrow's mood, health, and stress level using personalized multitask learning and domain adaptation. *J. Mach. Learn. Res.*, 66, 17–33, 2017.

20. Sumathi, V., Velmurugan, R., Sudarvel, J., Sathiyabama, P., Intelligent classification of women working in ICT-based education, in: *Proceedings of the 2021 7th International Conference on Advanced Computing and Communication Systems (ICACCS)*, Coimbatore, India, pp. 1711–1715, 19–20 March 2021.

21. Kroenke, K., Spitzer, R. L., Williams, J. B., Löwe, B., The patient health questionnaire somatic, anxiety, and depressive symptom scales: A systematic review. *Gen. Hosp. Psychiatry*, 32, 4, 345–359, 2010.

22. Sandeep, K., Jain, A., Kumar Agarwal, A., Rani, S., Ghimire, A., Object-based image retrieval using the U-Net-Based neural network. *Comput. Intell. Neurosci.*, 2021, 1–14, 2021.

23. Sandeep, K.,., Rani, S., Jain, A., Verma, C., Raboaca, M.S., Illés, Z., Neagu, B.C., Face spoofing, age, gender and facial expression recognition using advance neural network architecture-based biometric system. *Sensor J.*, 22, 14, 5160–5184, 2022.

24. Sandeep, K., Jain, A., Rani, S., Alshazly, H., Idris, S.A., Bourouis, S., Deep Neural network based vehicle detection and classification of aerial images. *Intell. Autom. Soft Comput.*, 34, 1, 119–131, 2022.

25. Sandeep, K., Jain, A., Shukla, A.P., Singh, S., Raja, R., Rani, S., Harshitha, G., AlZain, M.A., Masud, M., A comparative analysis of machine learning algorithms for detection of organic and non-organic cotton diseases. *Math. Probl. Eng. Hindawi J. Publ.*, 21, 1, 1–18, 2021.

26. Rani, S., Ghai, D., Kumar, S., Kantipudi, M.V.V., Alharbi, A.H., Ullah, M.A., Efficient 3D AlexNet architecture for object recognition using syntactic patterns from medical images. *Comput. Intell. Neurosci.*, 2022, 1–19, 2022.

27. Choudhary, S., Lakhwani, K., Kumar, S., Three dimensional objects recognition & pattern recognition technique; related challenges: A review. *Multimed. Tools Appl.*, 23, 1, 1–44, 2022.

28. Rani, S., Ghai, D., Kumar, S., Reconstruction of simple and complex three dimensional images using pattern recognition algorithm. *J. Inf. Technol. Manag.*, 14, 235–247, 2022.

29. Rani, S., Ghai, D., Kumar, S., Object detection and recognition using contour based edge detection and fast R-CNN, in: *Multimedia Tools and Application*, vol. 22, pp. 1–25, 2022.

4

Analysis of Smart Technologies in Healthcare

Shikha Jain[1,4*], Navneet Kaur[3], Manisha Malhotra[3] and Manjot Kaur[4]

[1]University Institute of Computing, Chandigarh University, Mohali, India
[2]Department of Computer Science, Kirori Mal College, University of Delhi, Delhi, India
[3]Department of Computer Science and Engineering, Chandigarh University, Mohali, India
[4]Fidelity Information Services Ltd, Mohali, India

Abstract

Emerging fields, such as machine learning, deep learning, blockchain, and Internet of Things, have greatly benefited the healthcare industry. These technologies have shifted the healthcare paradigm by developing various ML models that aid in recognizing and understanding image patterns, providing medical decision support, and maintaining and digitizing patients' electronic health records. Their ability to aid decision making, optimize workflows, and free up valuable human time is transforming how people deliver and receive care. This saves time for doctors and other medical authorities because they accept preliminary information about the patient via digital systems. Motivated by this thought, this chapter aims to investigate and analyze these cutting-edge technologies, like blockchain, the Internet of Things, machine learning, deep learning, etc., used in healthcare systems. We also make recommendations for future applications while briefly discussing the risks and difficulties associated with various healthcare applications, such as system privacy and security, ethical issues, etc.

Keywords: Federated learning, innovative healthcare, machine learning, blockchain, EHR, deep learning, data-driven, IoT

4.1 Introduction

The healthcare industry is a well-known study area with rapid technical development, where the volume of data is growing daily. Also, many

Corresponding author: shikhaa_88@kmc.du.ac.in

Sandeep Kumar, Anuj Sharma, Navneet Kaur, Lokesh Pawar and Rohit Bajaj (eds.) Optimized Predictive Models in Healthcare Using Machine Learning, (57–72) © 2024 Scrivener Publishing LLC

patients in healthcare systems have questions regarding the various therapies offered in diverse settings. Many of the procedures used in manual healthcare system processes could be more laborious and faster. Therefore, digital technologies are used in intelligent healthcare to make it simpler to handle this massive volume of data, to make it simpler to read health information, connect people, manage organizations and resources, and then nimbly take and respond to the rising demands made by the health environment. Smart treatment reminders, intelligent disease control, emotive telemedicine, innovative health management, healthcare drone delivery, intelligent monitoring, and telesurgery are all new-era features [1–4].

On the other hand, developing robust healthcare and resilience is challenging. Individual attitudes, poor hospital management, a lack of funds, and cultural and religious hurdles, have all been noted as potential roadblocks to the effective adoption of innovative healthcare. The need for robust, technology-driven healthcare systems has arisen. To accomplish this, utilizing developing cutting-edge technologies, including machine learning (ML), federated learning, deep learning (DL), blockchain, sensors, and the Internet of things (IoT), is mandatory [4–8]. These technological advancements are essential to the growth of the newly developing, innovative healthcare paradigm. The blending of technology and healthcare reveals some traits, such as:

- Use of intelligent systems to deal with human health issues,
- Task distribution from people to machines,
- Lowering the high cost of healthcare,
- Privacy and security of medical data.

This chapter examines the most recent developments in the healthcare field and the future opportunities and challenges to construct intelligent healthcare systems.

This chapter is divided into the following sections to achieve the goals. An overview of intelligent technologies utilized in healthcare is presented first. Then a literature review of the innovative technologies used in healthcare is shown. The following section identifies healthcare challenges and presents this technology. Lastly, a summary of the chapter is presented in the final section.

4.2   Emerging Technologies in Healthcare

4.2.1   Internet of Things

IoT devices have tracked every step and every moment of daily life. Health sensors, smart watches, fitness trackers, etc., gather and produce tremendous health-related data. Data have always been a top-most priority in creating intelligent healthcare in a smart city. IoT user data are a valuable asset in the modern world. Daily processing is required to extract health advantages from this vast data. AI-driven and IoT-enabled technologies have many uses in a smart city, from preserving a healthier environment to advancing cutting-edge technologies to make healthcare smarter [8–12].

IoT makes it possible for devices to connect, collect and exchange data. In recent years, agriculture, intelligent homes, and healthcare industries have benefited greatly from the IoT. By saving time, IoT intends to assist medical personnel in carrying out their daily tasks, including disease prediction, patient monitoring from a distance, and therapy advancement in the hospital environment as effectively as possible. As a result, a massive data store is required for the enormous amount of generated data. Additionally, the interoperability issue appears when combining the data from numerous different types of devices [12–17].

Privacy policies are even more essential than other security measures to protect user data in a network's core infrastructure and cutting-edge applications like intelligent healthcare. IoT devices are used in the healthcare industry to deal with sensitive data that must be kept private and secret [17–27].

4.2.2 Blockchain

Blockchain is a decentralized digital ledger that records and maintains information about all transactions and events between the participating parties. Data consistency is guaranteed by automatic cryptographic validation, which makes the information unchangeable after it has been submitted [22, 45]. The blockchain concept was first established with the introduction of Bitcoin (a cryptocurrency) in 2009. Since then, the technology has expanded into various industries, including insurance, healthcare, and IoT-based applications, among others [29, 38].

As the healthcare sector contains numerous participants and demands a high degree of trust between them, blockchain may be an appropriate option. Generally, blockchains are perfect for highly dispersed systems with a significant potential for activity tracking and where the accuracy of the data is crucial [26–32].

Blockchain can run on billions of devices and aids in protecting the anonymity of the users. Because of the quantity and variety of healthcare data produced by multiple sources, questions regarding the data's accuracy are also raised. Also, medical data can be used for various purposes, such as disease prediction by mixed ML and DL algorithms. So, verifying data quality when combining data from different devices is challenging. When healthcare data are exchanged over the network, data confidentiality issues occur. The benefits of blockchain include decentralized storage, permission, immutability, and enhanced capacity. Each block consists of private healthcare data accessible only to those with permission. Since blockchain data are immutable, nobody else can alter it, and machine learning algorithms may be used to create any illness prediction model [33–42].

Blockchain has enormous potential in medical research and healthcare data, including drug fraud, health records management, clinical research, and claim processing. Many companies employ the blockchain-based model chain to strengthen the security of their distributed patient data [33]. Interoperability issues are addressed with blockchain, making it possible for patients and medical professionals to communicate medical data securely. While blockchain is a boon for the healthcare sector, it has significant flaws, including cost, scalability, and privacy.

4.2.3   Machine Learning

Machine learning has started appearing in more clinical literature in Chen *et al.* [18–20] and Alanazi [36]. The chances to address the issue of analysis are presented by novel techniques for data collection and storage (e.g., sensor data and electronic health records). These data usually need to be more utilized and undervalued. The value of ML is derived from its capacity to handle enormous data sets and then consistently transform data analysis into significant insights that may aid physicians in organizing and delivering care. This leads to better results, reduced expenses and higher satisfaction. With more excellent knowledge, medical professionals may decide on patient diagnosis and treatment options more effectively while also knowing the potential outcomes. ML can assist in processing all these data and even go as far as to develop individualized healthcare and treatment plans. Creating individualized calendars can help patients keep up with their visits. The importance of machine learning has dramatically expanded in the healthcare industry.

ML methods can be broadly categorized into supervised learning and unsupervised learning. When using supervised learning approaches, a mapping function, $y = f(x)$, is inferred from the inputs x to the outputs y. Regression and classification are tasks; algorithms like support vector machines and logistic regression belong to this category. The second group, i.e., unsupervised learning algorithms, aims to uncover intriguing details about the distribution of x itself. Clustering and density estimation are unsupervised learning tasks [23–34].

In the healthcare industry, ML applications can be used for disease diagnosis and prognosis and to propose the ideal treatment plan for the discovered disease. These applications can also be used to monitor and observe the effectiveness of treatment.

4.2.4   Deep Learning

DL algorithms are crucial for enterprises to make business choices based on predictions. DL performs automatic data-oriented feature extraction and learns representations from raw data, unlike conventional ML algorithms. DL models use several neural network-based processing layers to understand illustrations of data with different levels of abstraction. Based on the data it gets as inputs from the layer below, each layer of a DL system constructs a representation of the observed patterns by maximizing local unsupervised criteria. The critical component of DL is that these layers of characteristics are found from data using a general-purpose learning technique rather than being built by human engineers [21, 24, 26].

DL has demonstrated impressive performances in object detection in speech recognition, object detection in images, and natural language understanding. DL is particularly effective at identifying complex structures in high-dimensional data. Relevant clinical-ready successes in the healthcare sector have paved the means for the generation of DL-based innovative tools for effective treatment [16]. Some examples include the classification of skin cancer, the detection of diabetic retinopathy in retinal fundus photographs, and the forecasting of DNA- and RNA-binding protein sequence specificities [34].

Several open-source tools, such as TensorFlow, Keras, Torch, PyTorch, and CNTK, are available for dealing with DL algorithms in several programming languages.

4.2.5   Federated Learning

As the ML and DL fields are growing continuously, the challenge of training algorithms on large datasets has become increasingly complex. This challenge has led to the development of distributed machine learning, which allows data processing across multiple platforms. One of the newest extensions of this technology is federated learning (FL), which takes distributed machine learning a step further by enabling the training of ML and DL algorithms using data stored on various devices, including computers, smartphones, and other mobile devices [12]. This approach reduces the complexity of data administration and storage by transferring the calculation to the location where the data are produced [14, 21, 32]. It necessitates that the feature spaces that each participating node shares be identical, which improves the delay and delivers greater security and privacy. Additionally, FL offers the advantage of providing improved tailored recommendations quickly to customers, with applications in areas such as movies, restaurants, and healthcare [16, 30].

FL has the advantage of transferring the computation to the data generation site, thereby reducing the complexity of data storage and administration. This is particularly useful for organizations with large datasets, as it enables them to train their algorithms without worrying about the storage and maintenance of massive data sets. Additionally, FL improves latency by reducing the need to transfer data to a central location for processing [15].

Another critical feature of FL is that it ensures the feature spaces shared by each participating node are identical. This helps improve the accuracy of the resulting models and provides data's private security, as each participant only shares a limited portion of their data. This is particularly important for organizations that handle sensitive data [16].

One of the critical benefits of FL is that it can deliver tailored recommendations to customers quickly and efficiently. This can include requests for movies, restaurants, and even personalized healthcare advice. Organizations utilizing FL can provide customers a more customized experience, increasing customer satisfaction and loyalty.

Overall, federated learning is a powerful tool for organizations that must work with large datasets and want to improve their ML and DL algorithms' accuracy, privacy, and efficiency. As technology evolves, we expect to see even more FL applications in various fields, from healthcare and finance to e-commerce and entertainment [34].

4.3   Literature Review

For this review, we used a set of relevant keywords to search academic journal databases like Scopus, Web of Science, and Google Scholar for papers published between 2016 and 2022 that discussed the fields of machine learning (ML), deep learning (DL), Federated learning (FL), blockchain and internet of things (IoT). To confirm that a paper genuinely treated a subject pertinent to the field of diverse technologies, all titles and abstracts of articles that were discovered through the database search were examined.

The identified publications were then read, and references were looked for to find more review sources.

Chronic heart disease (CHD) is a typical kind of cardiovascular illness. Nalluri *et al.* [41] employed data mining methods to estimate a person's likelihood of developing CHD based on knowledge about the disease's numerous symptoms, like blood pressure, heart rate, cholesterol, glucose level, BMI, and the number of cigarettes smoked per day. The study used the XGBoost and the logistic regression approach as two prediction models to estimate the CHD values. This early CHD prediction will lower an individual's risk of developing CHD. Faturrahman *et al.* [25] proposed a higher-level model employing DeepBelief Networks (DBNs) for predicting Alzheimer's Disease development using MRI data. DBNs achieved 91.76% accuracy, 90.59% sensitivity, and 92.96% specificity when compared to the Support vector machine (SVM) as a classification model. Mohan *et al.* [40] offered a novel strategy for enhancing cardiovascular disease prediction accuracy through machine learning to identify essential features. Various feature combinations and popular categorization techniques are used to introduce the prediction model. The hybrid random forest model with a linear model (HRFLM) has the characteristics of both the Random Forest and Linear Method. Through the HRFLM prediction model, authors achieved an improved performance level with an accuracy of 88.7%. Ahmad *et al.* [11] have demonstrated a strong ability to predict death in paralytic ileus patients using electronic health records (EHR). The Statistically Robust Machine Learning-based Mortality Predictor (SRML-Mortality Predictor) algorithm demonstrated an accuracy rate of 81.30%. Through the application, it is possible to provide patients and practitioners with expected mortality to help produce better-informed clinical treatment decisions.

Chen *et al.* [18–20] integrated structured and unstructured data from the healthcare industry to quantify the risk of sickness. They tested the updated prediction models using hospital data gathered from central China between 2013 and 2015. A latent factor model was applied to the data to get around the problem of inadequate data, and then a new convolutional neural network (CNN) method was proposed. Compared to various standard prediction algorithms, the suggested approach's prediction accuracy is 94.8% compared to several well-used prediction algorithms. In their research study, Liu *et al.* [36] used a DL algorithm to forecast the start of diseases like heart failure, kidney failure, and stroke. They used CNNs and LSTM networks. In contrast to existing prediction models, this system combined data from the structured

EHR with data from the unstructured diagnosis and progress notes. All baseline accuracy measurements significantly improved due to the data combination, demonstrating the adaptability and durability of such methods. The DeepCare framework by Pham *et al.* [42] showed an end-to-end deep dynamic network that predicts future medical outcomes by inferring current disease conditions. This was accomplished through word embedding, pooling, and RNNs with hidden units having long short-term memory (LSTM). They also included medicinal therapies in the predictions that the model would dynamically shape. Inpatients' cohorts, along with diabetes and mental health conditions, the illness progression modelling, intervention advice, and future risk prediction of DeepCare were evaluated.

Jamil *et al.* [31] discussed the IBM blockchain usage in developing the health chain to create a secure contract between medical staff and patients. Blockchain technology to store patient data makes it impossible for third parties to intervene and alter the information. Blockchain was used to construct the healthcare data gateway architecture, allowing patients to exchange their data without risking their privacy and fostering intelligence. A blockchain-based Decentralized Interoperable Trust framework (DIT) for IoT zones was proposed by Abou-Nassar *et al.* [1], where a smart contract ensures budget authentication, the Indirect Trust Inference System (ITIS) reduces semantic gaps, and network nodes and edges are used to improve trustworthy factor (TF) estimation. The proposed architecture allows for controlled communication required to resolve fusion and integration difficulties to be facilitated via various zones of the IoT infrastructure by verifying nodes based on their interoperable structure using a private Blockchain ripple chain. Lee *et al.* [35] combined a widely used social network-based healthcare system with a high level of security using IEEE 802.15.6 and blockchain protocols. Blockchain ensured that the health data was securely shared throughout the network. Users can upload their records to a management portal as part of the patient health record architecture. Rivest-Shamir-Adleman and the SHA-256 algorithm provided security. The architecture uses blockchain, and the consensus protocol provides authority proof. A blockchain-based mHealth communication system was presented by Alam [12] to ensure the efficient and safe storing of health data. It provides features including tracking, patient management, remote diagnostics, and medical informatics. MeDShare, a blockchain-based healthcare data-sharing solution, was proposed by Chen *et al.* [20]. It uses blockchain technology to substitute a decentralized data processing unit for the traditional storage tier. Frameworks for medical services have been developed using blockchain technology to protect sensitive patient data.

An intelligent IoT architecture with blockchain support was created by Hasanova *et al.* [28] to apply artificial intelligence to data that is safely distributed via a blockchain network. In this study, a sine cosine-based pre-predictive blockchain-based decentralized storage-based model for heart disease has been created using behavioral aspects to prevent the disease in its early stages compared to peer-to-peer storage, and a throughput of 25.03% was acquired. Another piece of work, put forth by Moghadas *et al.* [39], offered a technique for keeping track of the well-being of people with cardiac arrhythmias. Electrocardiography was performed using an ECG instrument, and the kind of cardiac arrhythmia was classified using the k-nearest neighbor technique. A remote patient monitoring system based on IoT ensuring the integrity of electrocardiograms was proposed by Yew *et al.* [46]. Using the Message Queuing Telemetry Transport (MQTT) protocol, they transmitted the ECG data to the web server. Doctors may view the real-time data by connecting to the web server using their computers or cell phones.

Liu *et al.* [37] proposed a confederated learning and evaluated it to build ML models that differentiate between silos and the risk of several diseases. Confederated learning is a distributed learning strategy that includes representation learning, generative modelling, imputation, and data augmentation elements. The authors claimed that their method led to AUCROC prediction values of 0.787 for diabetes, 0.718 for psychological disorders, and 0.698 for ischemic heart disease. Using the recommended confederated learning technique, health insurance data split into two or more dimensions was successfully used to train machine learning models. With the aid of a case study, Singh *et al.* [9] built a secure framework for innovative healthcare backed by the blockchain and FL and safeguarded privacy using blockchain-based IoT cloud platforms.

4.4   Risks and Challenges

Some of the obstacles to the acceptance, implementation, and use of intelligent healthcare are discussed as follows:

- Data fragmentation and heterogeneity—The accessibility of data determines how intelligent digital health systems are. Contrarily, many healthcare organizations use various heterogeneous data formats, which makes it challenging to connect and convert them into interoperable forms. This impacts data collecting, analysis, and optimization of computer models [17]. The availability of datasets needed to train healthcare AI models is influenced by heterogeneity, affecting data availability.

- Lack of interoperability and standardization—Lack of standards in developing digital healthcare technologies hinders interoperability. With standardized data formats, evaluating the health data that IoT has gathered will be possible. This affects how patient data are shared throughout healthcare organizations and how intelligent healthcare solutions are adopted because they might need to work with the organization's current digital healthcare systems. Another obstacle to implementing and using competent healthcare is the need for semantic interoperability in EMRs, which requires manual intervention by human experts [15].

- Lack of legitimacy and dependability of sensor data— If decisions based only on sensor data are taken, which are erroneous or unreliable, people's lives may be safe. Competent healthcare uses information from sensors and other nanodevices to make health decisions. If sensor data is not valid, reliable, or accurate, it may have catastrophic consequences, such as misdiagnosis. Techniques for validating data collected by sensors are therefore essential [27].

- Data consistency, privacy, and confidentiality—Privacy and confidentiality are crucial when dealing with patient data. Whatever benefits technology might have for healthcare, it should be avoided if it undermines privacy and confidentiality. When using digital health, patients worry about privacy, quantum, and collusion assaults on their data. The biggest obstacles to integrating cloud-based health services include a need for more security, invasion of privacy, and data leaking. Due to the possibility of communication paths to convey patient data being compromised and revealing personal data, intelligent health systems should ensure information safety at rest and in transit [43, 44].

- Scalability issues—Solutions for intelligent healthcare must be scalable as IoT and IoMT gather more and more health data. However, because it is impossible to store enormous amounts of healthcare data on-chain without noticeably decreasing performance, blockchain-based healthcare applications need help to scale [15].
- Clinical challenges—The use of sensors is pervasive in intelligent healthcare. However, as electrical or electro-mechanical sensors are frequently used in sensor systems, they often need calibrating since they are sensitive to misalignment, electromagnetic fields, and diminished compactness. Such electrical and electromechanical sensor defects are frequently undesirable in soft wearable robots. Due to these shortcomings, adopting and effectively implementing intelligent healthcare systems may need to be improved using conventional sensors, such as electromechanical or electrical ones [36].
- Limited memory capacity and energy usage—Before transmitting data, sensors must briefly buffer it. It becomes difficult for sensors to momentarily retain all data created in real time as they can only store a packet at a time. Additionally, they require frequent recharges due to their limited battery life. Therefore, once it grows to an abnormally enormous size, implanting it within the human body might not be safe [34].
- Digital technology model rigidity and complexity— Overfitting is a risk with complex models, but stiff models are challenging to adapt to shifting requirements. Furthermore, models may be antagonistic to users due to their complexity. Overfitting is undesirable because it lowers the model's precision [26].
- Regulatory frameworks—Governmental policy, scientific evidence, and clinical practice are all continually being overtaken by technological improvements. Innovators should be moving slowly for policymakers to keep up. Privacy and security must be upheld via regulatory frameworks for digital technologies. Nevertheless, there are no regional or global frameworks for integrating digital technology. Regulatory frameworks are also necessary to guarantee the dependability and security of software, hardware, and other forms of technology. The need for

regulatory frameworks and the sluggish clearance of digital technologies are obstacles to developing and using intelligent healthcare [23].

- Inconsistency with national e-health strategies—Healthcare's embrace and utilization of digital health technology may need to be improved by a failure to link them with government e-health policies. Innovative thinkers must incorporate their concepts into the national e-health plans of their nations. E-health strategy papers outline the aims of each country's digital health initiatives; therefore, it is essential to match e-health tactics with digital health breakthroughs [28].

- Cost Implementation—The implementation of intelligent healthcare demands a sizable financial investment and specialized human resources, which prevents such technologies from being widely used in developing nations with limited resources. For instance, implementing AI models requires a lot of computing power, whereas training users to use the new systems costs a lot of money. Although some could claim that innovative health costs less in the long track, there are still significant upfront expenses. In developing nations with limited resources, the use of such technology in healthcare is hindered by the high cost and specialized human resources requirements [31–35].

4.5   Conclusion

This chapter describes how blockchain, machine learning, deep learning, federated learning, and IoT technologies are used in innovative healthcare systems and the subsequent potential and difficulties in building intelligent healthcare systems. Innovative healthcare provides timely and appropriate medical care and the services' content to the individuals. Innovative healthcare can help medical facilities—cut expenses, relieve staff pressure, establish suitable material and information management, and enhance patient care. Innovative healthcare can help research institutes cut costs, shorten research times, and increase research productivity. The status quo of medical resource disparity can be improved, medical reform can be advanced, prevention methods can be implemented, and societal medical costs can be decreased by implementing innovative healthcare. Given the rapid advancements in IoT, blockchain, machine learning, deep learning, and federated learning, the future of healthcare are very bright. There are new opportunities and a duty to use the Internet of Things for patients, hospitals, doctors, and producers of medical devices. Some significant hazards and challenges must also be overcome. Technology advancement is one factor in finding solutions to these issues; other factors include the collaboration of patients, physicians, healthcare organizations, and technology businesses.

References

1. Abou-Nassar, E.M., Iliyasu, A.M., El-Kafrawy, P.M., Song, O.-Y., Bashir, A.K., Abd El-Latif, A.A., Ditrust chain: Towards blockchain-based trust models for sustainable healthcare IoT systems. *IEEE Access*, 8, 111223–111238, 2020.

2. Kumar, S., Jain, A., Agarwal, A.K., Rani, S., Ghimire, A., Object-based image retrieval using U-Net based neural network. *Comput. Intell. Neurosci.*, 2021, 1–14, Sep. 2021.

3. Kumar, S., Jain, A., Shukla, A.P., Singh, S., Raja, R., Rani, S., Harshitha, G., AlZain, M.A., Masud, M., A comparative analysis of machine learning algorithms for detection of organic and non-organic cotton diseases, in: *Mathematical Problems in Engineering*, vol. 2021, pp. 1–18, Oct. 2021.

4. Singh, J., Agarwal, S., Kumar, P., Kashish, Rana, D., Bajaj, R., Prominent features based chronic kidney disease prediction model using machine learning, in: *2022 3rd International Conference on Electronics and Sustainable Communication Systems (ICESC)*, Coimbatore, India, pp. 1193–1198, 2022.

5. Bajaj, R., Shandilya, D., Gagneja, S., Gupta, K., Rawat, D., A predictive risk model for primary tumor using machine learning with initial missing values, in: *2022 IEEE International Conference on Data Science and Information System (ICDSIS)*, pp. 1–7, 2022.

6. Kumar, D., Sharma, A.K., Bajaj, R., Pawar, L., Feature optimized machine learning framework for unbalanced bioassays, in: *Cognitive Behavior and Human-Computer Interaction Based on Machine Learning Algorithm*, pp. 167–178, 2021.

7. Pawar, L., Agrawal, P., Kaur, G., Bajaj, R., Elevate primary tumor detection using machine learning, in: *Cognitive Behavior and Human-Computer Interaction Based on Machine Learning Algorithm*, pp. 301–313, 2021.

8. Pawar, L., Sharma, A.K., Kumar, D., Bajaj, R., Advanced ensemble machine learning model for balanced bioassays, in: *Artificial Intelligence and Machine Learning in 2D/3D Medical Image Processing*, pp. 171–178, 2020.

9. Kaur, M., Bajaj, R., Kaur, N., A review of mac layer for wireless body area network. *J. Med. Biol. Eng.*, 41, 1–38, 2021.

10. Kaur, M., Bajaj, R., Kaur, N., Wireless body area network: Performance analysis of polling access MAC protocol, in: *2021 2nd Global Conference for Advancement in Technology (GCAT)*, Bangalore, India, pp. 1–7, 2021.
11. Ahmad, F.S., Ali, L., Khattak, H.A., Hameed, T., Wajahat, I., Kadry, S., Bukhari, S.A.C. *et al.*, A hybrid machine learning framework to predict mortality in paralytic ileus patients using electronic health records (EHRs). *J. Ambient Intell. Humaniz. Comput.*, 12, 3283–3293, 2021.
12. Alam, T., Health communication framework using blockchain and IoT technologies. *Int. J. Sci. Technol. Res.*, 9, 6, 1–7, 2020.
13. Alanazi, A., Using machine learning for healthcare challenges and opportunities. *Inf. Med. Unlocked*, 30, 100924, 2022.
14. Alipanahi, B., Delong, A., Weirauch, M.T., Frey, B.J., Predicting the sequence specificities of DNA and RNA-binding proteins by deep learning. *Nat. Biotechnol.*, 33, 8, 831–838, 2015.
15. Fekih, R.B. and Lahami, M., Application of blockchain technology in healthcare: A comprehensive study, in: *International Conference on Smart Homes and Health Telematics*, Springer, pp. 268–276, 2020.
16. Bengio, Y. *et al.*, *Learning deep architectures for ai*, vol. 2, pp. 1–127, Foundations and Trends® in Machine Learning, Boston - Delft, 2009.
17. Bhattacharya, P., Tanwar, S., Bodkhe, U., Tyagi, S., Kumar, N., Bindaas: Blockchain-based deep-learning as-a-service in healthcare 4.0 applications. *IEEE Trans. Netw. Sci. Eng.*, 8, 2, 1242–1255, 2019.
18. Chen, I.Y., Pierson, E., Rose, S., Joshi, S., Ferryman, K., Ghassemi, M., Ethical machine learning in healthcare. *Annu. Rev. Biomed. Data Sci.*, 4, 123–144, 2021.
19. Chen, M., Hao, Y., Hwang, K., Wang, L., Wang, L., Disease prediction by machine learning over big data from healthcare communities. *IEEE Access*, 5, 8869–8879, 2017.
20. Chen, Y., Ding, S., Xu, Z., Zheng, H., Yang, S., Blockchain-based medical records secure storage and medical service framework. *J. Med. Syst.*, 43, 1, 1–9, 2019.
21. Collobert, R., Weston, J., Bottou, L., Karlen, M., Kavukcuoglu, K., Kuksa, P., Natural language processing (almost) from scratch. *J. Mach. Learn. Res.*, 12, ARTICLE, 2493–2537, 2011.
22. Crosby, M., Pattanayak, P., Verma, S., Kalyanaraman, V. *et al.*, Blockchain technology: Beyond bitcoin. *Appl. Innov.*, 2, 6–10, 71, 2016.
23. Dzenowagis, J., *Digital technologies: Shaping the future of primary healthcare*, World Health Organization, Geneva, Switzerland, 2018.
24. Esteva, A., Kuprel, B., Novoa, R.A., Ko, J., Swetter, S.M., Blau, H.M., Thrun, S., Dermatologist-level classification of skin cancer with deep neural networks. *Nature*, 542, 7639, 115–118, 2017.
25. Faturrahman, M., Wasito, I., Hanifah, N., Mufidah, R., Structural MRI classification for alzheimer's disease detection using deep belief network, in: *2017 11th International Conference on Information & Communication Technology and System (ICTS)*, IEEE, pp. 37–42, 2017.

26. Gulshan, V., Peng, L., Coram, M., Stumpe, M.C., Wu, D., Narayanaswamy, A., Venugopalan, S., Widner, K., Madams, T., Cuadros, J. *et al.*, Developing and validating a deep learning algorithm for detecting diabetic retinopathy in retinal fundus photographs. *Jama*, 316, 22, 2402–2410, 2016.

27. Haleem, A., Javaid, M., Singh, R.P., Suman, R., Telemedicine for healthcare: Capabilities, features, barriers, and applications. *Sensors Int.*, 2, 100117, 2021.

28. Hasanova, H., Tufail, M., Baek, U.J., Park, J.T., Kim, M.S., A novel blockchain-enabled heart disease prediction mechanism using machine learning. *Comput. Electr. Eng.*, 101, 108086, 2022.

29. Hassija, V., Gupta, V., Garg, S., Chamola, V., Traffic jam probability estimation based on blockchain and deep neural networks. *IEEE Trans. Intell. Transp. Syst.*, 22, 7, 3919–3928, 2020.

30. Hinton, G., Deng, L., Yu, D., Dahl, G.E., Mohamed, A., Jaitly, N., Senior, A., Vanhoucke, V., Nguyen, P., Sainath, T.N. *et al.*, Deep neural networks for acoustic modelling in speech recognition: The shared views of four research groups. *IEEE Signal Process. Mag*, 29, 6, 82–97, 2012.

31. Jamil, F., Ahmad, S., Iqbal, N., Kim, D.H., Towards remote monitoring of patient vital signs based on IoT-based blockchain in integrity management platforms in intelligent hospitals. *Sensors*, 20, 8, 2195, 2020.

32. Krizhevsky, A., Sutskever, I., Hinton, G.E., Imagenet classification with deep convolutional neural networks. *2012 Advances in Neural Information Processing Systems (NIPS)*, Neural Information Processing Systems Foundation, La Jolla, CA, 2012.

33. Kuo, T.T., Kim, H.E., Ohno-Machado, L., Blockchain distributed ledger technologies for biomedical and healthcare applications. *J. Am. Med. Inf. Assoc.*, 24, 6, 1211–1220, 2017.

34. LeCun, Y., Bengio, Y., Hinton, G., Deep learning. *Nature*, 521, 7553, 436–444, 2015.

35. Lee, H.A., Kung, H.H., Udayasankaran, J.G., Kijsanayotin, B., Marcelo, A.B., Chao, L.R., Hsu, C.Y. *et al.*, An architecture and management platform for blockchain-based personal health record exchange: Development and usability study. *J. Med. Internet Res.*, 22, 6, e16748, 2020.

36. Liu, D., Fox, K., Weber, G., Miller, T., Confederated learning in healthcare: Training machine learning models using disconnected data separated by the individual, data type, and identity for large-scale health system intelligence. *J. Biomed. Inf.*, 134, 104151, 2022.

37. Liu, J., Zhang, Z., Razavian, N., Deep EHR: Chronic disease prediction using medical notes, in: *Machine Learning for Healthcare Conference*, PMLR, pp. 440–464, 2018.

38. Miraz, M.H. and Ali, M., Applications of blockchain technology beyond cryptocurrency. *arXiv preprint arXiv:1801.03528*, 2, 1, 1–6, 2018.

39. Moghadas, E., Rezazadeh, J., Farahbakhsh, R., An IoT patient monitoring based on fog computing and data mining: Cardiac arrhythmia use-case. *Internet Things*, 11, 100251, 2020.

40. Mohan, S., Thirumalai, C., Srivastava, G., Effective heart disease prediction using hybrid machine learning techniques. *IEEE Access*, 7, 81542–81554, 2019.

41. Nalluri, S., Redrowthu, V.S., Ramasubbareddy, S., Govinda, K., Swetha, E., Chronic heart disease prediction using data mining techniques, in: *Data Engineering and Communication Technology*, pp. 903–912, Springer, Singapore, 2020.

42. Pham, T., Tran, T., Phung, D., Venkatesh, S., Deepcare: A deep dynamic memory model for predictive medicine, in: *Pacific-Asia Conference on Knowledge Discovery and Data Mining*, Springer, pp. 30–41, 2016.

43. Pramanik, P.K.D., Solanki, A., Debnath, A., Nayyar, A., El-Sappagh, S., Kwak, K.-S., Advancing modern healthcare with nanotechnology, nanosensors, and internet of nano things: Taxonomies, applications, architecture, and challenges. *IEEE Access*, 8, 65230–65266, 2020.

44. Singh, S., Rathore, S., Alfarraj, O., Tolba, A., Yoon, B., A framework for privacy-preservation of IOT healthcare data using federated learning and blockchain technology. *Future Gener. Comput. Syst.*, 129, 380–388, 2022.

45. Vazirani, A.A., O'Donoghue, O., Brindley, D., Meinert, E., Implementing blockchains for efficient healthcare: A systematic review. *J. Med. Internet Res.*, 21, 2, e12439, 2019.

46. Yew, H.T., Ng, M.F., Ping, S.Z., Chung, S.K., Chekima, A., Dargham, J.A., IOT-based real-time remote patient monitoring system, in: *2020 16th IEEE International Colloquium on Signal Processing & its Applications (CSPA)*, IEEE, pp. 176–17, 2020.

5

Enhanced Neural Network Ensemble Classification for the Diagnosis of Lung Cancer Disease

Thaventhiran Chandrasekar*, Praveen Kumar Karunanithi, K.R. Sekar
and Arka Ghosh

School of Computing, SASTRA University, Thanjavur, Tamil Nadu, India

Abstract

Due to the dramatic rise in cigarette smoking, lung cancer is now one of the main causes of death in emerging countries. Accurate diagnosis of the illness described at (LCD) lung cancer disease is essential if persons with lung cancer are to receive appropriate therapy. Artificial neural networks have lately been identified as a machine learning (ML) technique (ANN). In this book, Enhanced WONN- ML for LCD in big data (Weighted Neural Networks using Maximum Likelihood Boosting) are studied. In a unique combination technique for classifier ensembles, optimized Raphson's Likelihood MR preprocessing model is utilized, and the critical features are extracted to increase the identification of lung cancer disease. Cluster classification and extraction of features make up the two parts of the suggested methodology. In order to shorten the classification time, the primary attributes are determined using an optimized Raphson's Maximum Likelihood and very less Redundancy preprocessing model. The second stage of the method uses using Enhanced Neural network model with Ensemble Classifier to improve the accuracy of the cancer disease detection and reduce the false alarm rate. Optimized weights for every ensemble classifier's conclusion are dynamically computed based on the ensemble classification output and the correlation between the results of all classifiers. To determine the practicality of the suggested methodology, an analysis of the Thoracic Surgery Database was done. Its performance was contrasted with that of an ensemble classifier built using more traditional methods.

Keywords: Lung cancer, optimization, MRMR model, false positive rate, boosted SVM

Sandeep Kumar, Anuj Sharma, Navneet Kaur, Lokesh Pawar and Rohit Bajaj (eds.) Optimized Predictive Models in Healthcare Using Machine Learning, (73–88) © 2024 Scrivener Publishing LLC

5.1   Introduction

Today, lung carcinoma is one of the main causes of death in developing countries, which is on the rise as a result of the sharp increase in cigarette smoking. Deep learning may be applied in the medical program to enhance the rate of clinical diagnosis through prediction and judgement, according to a big data study on (NSCLC) Non-Small Cell Lung Cancer [1]. Moreover, AI techniques were used to handle prediction and choice issues for substantial NSCLC data. These imaging and diagnostic data were merged, nevertheless, by a computer programme. Hence, integrating image and diagnosis characteristics was an efficient strategy for physicians to resolve patient diagnoses in a big data environment (i.e., Healthcare 4.0). Yet, the time required for detailed data diagnosis was spread out. Ziba *et al.* [2] presented the enhanced SVM technique for imbalanced dataset to overcome the issues related to unbalanced data (BSI) [5].

Benefits of value in terms of support vector machines and ensemble classifiers for uneven data have been combined. Three stages involved the utilisation of the raw dataset. At the first stage, the highest accuracy criterion was used to choose the essential and beneficial characteristics. Then, it was claimed that the guidelines were retrieved after utilising the Gmean criteria to explore the problem of forecasting postoperative life expectancy. This was followed by a feature selection step. The accuracy and coverage metrics of the extracted rules were assessed in the final stage, which improved anticipated accuracy. Even though the intended work met the accuracy of the forecast, the error factor received less focus. Given the aforementioned issues, this work proposes a novel combination technique for classifier ensembles using Maximum relevant and less Redundant model by Enhanced Raphson model, where the main characteristics are obtained to hasten the diagnosis of lung cancer illness [6]. The proposed Raphson's Probabilistic model is subjected to the MRMR characteristics. The primary and secondly derivative of the most great significance minimal redundant attributes are used to select the most relevant features. In order to achieve this, we examine the characteristics of the MRMR model, often called as Newton's Maximum Probability, in the ensemble's process of consolidation. Then, in order to lower error (i.e., the false - positive results error rate) [7] as well as improve diagnostic precision, the technique of using Enhanced Neural network model with Ensemble Classifier is recommended. Based on the results of each individual ensemble classifier and their relationships, the best weights for each ensembles classifier's decision are dynamically computed [8]. The effectiveness of the suggested technique was evaluated using the Thoracic Surgery Dataset. Its performance was measured against that of an ensemble classifier made with more traditional methods. The Boosted Weighted Optimized Neural Network Ensemble Classification technique is used to categorise patients based on a number of factors, increasing the accuracy of cancer illness detection and reducing false positive rates [21].

5.2 Algorithm for Classification of Proposed Weight-Optimized Neural Network Ensembles

Figure 5.1 shows the suggested approach and the LCD design utilizing the WONN-MLB technique. It thoroughly outlines the several steps involved in putting the suggested strategy into effect. These methods, which include data collecting (Thoracic Surgery Dataset Collection) Ziba *et al.* [2], feature extraction or preprocessing (reducing Dimensionality), and ensemble classification, are thoroughly discussed in the subsections that follow (using WONN-MLB).

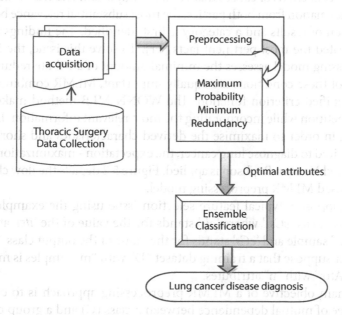

Figure 5.1 Architecture of proposed approach for lung cancer disease diagnosis.

5.2.1   Enhanced Raphson's Most Likelihood and Minimum Redundancy Preprocessing

To address the challenges with accuracy and time complexity in huge data categorization, a preprocessing phase is first needed to extract the relevant attributes [9]. Standard methods cannot be used to reduce the unneeded attributes while retaining the important qualities. As a result of the misclassification, lung cancer is diagnosed [10]. Raphson, Newton The development of Likelihood and Minimal Redundancy preprocessing techniques enables considerable attribute extraction by removing redundant data.

Using a massively-scale machine learning classification predicated on boosted classifiers to categorise biological lung cancer datasets [2]. Its weighted error function was decreased by updating the boosting correlation value iteratively. But even though the weighting error was reduced, less attention was paid to how long it took to detect lung cancer. The preprocessing recommended model relies on the Newton technique Raphson's with more potential to give findings that are more trustworthy than any of those provided by the other well-known algorithms, including such SVMs, Ziba *et al.* [2].

This MLMR preprocessing model is utilized to identify the characteristics inside the collections of classes that are most important and least redundant. Using information from both parties, the most substantial relevance between a collection of results and a category is first identified. The findings repeatedly repeated the most pertinent facts [11]. To solve this issue, the MLMR preprocessing model assesses the minimal amount of attribute redundancy. As both of these conditions are equally important, MLMR combines them into an unified criterion function. The WONN-MLB method makes little use of repetition while incorporating the most relevant information. Last but not least, in order to maximise the derived characteristics and shorten the time required to diagnose lung cancer, the expectation - maximization factor of enhanced Newton Raphson is applied. Figure 5.2 depicts the flow chart for the proposed MLMR preprocessing model.

Let's suppose a typical feature selection issue using the example 'eis = ($e1s$, $e2s$, …, ens, eCs)' where 'eis' stands for the value of the '$it\square$' attribute of the '$st\square$' sample and 'eCs' stands for the value of the output class "C." Let us further suppose that a training dataset "D" with "m" samples is made up of a set "Attr" with "n" attributes.

The main objective of a MLMR preprocessing approach is to evaluate the degree of mutual dependence between a class (C) and a group of attributes (Attr) by using mutual information, known as "MI." The joint probability "prob(x,y)," as stated in Eq. 1, and the possibilities (i.e., with a pairing

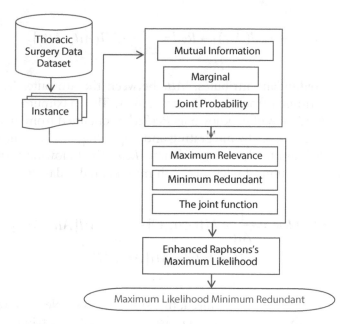

Figure 5.2 Model for MLMR preprocessing.

of attribute) "prob(x)" and "prob(y)," where "x Attr and y Attr," are used to calculate the value of "MI."

$$MI(X,Y) = \sum_{x \in X} \sum_{y \in Y} prob(x,y) \log \left[\frac{prob(x,y)}{prob(x)\,prob(y)} \right] \quad (5.1)$$

However, maximum relevance and minimal redundancy are assessed when much data is considered for lung cancer analysis. Utmost relevance 'Rel' is made up of search criteria with a more significant relevancy factor and is calculated as follows:

$$Max \to Rel(Att,C) \to Rel = \frac{1}{Att} * MI[Att_i,C] \quad (5.2)$$

According to Eq. 5.2, the mutual information factor (MI) determines the characteristics' maximal significance inside class "C," but choosing the attributes based on this criterion leads to greater redundancy. The minimal redundancy 'Red' criteria are applied to reduce it and are written as follows:

$$Min \rightarrow Red(Att) \rightarrow Red = \frac{1}{Att} * MI[Att_i, Att_j] \qquad (5.3)$$

The least redundant attributes, 'Att_i' between the attributes 'Att_i' and 'Att_j' are determined from Eq. 5.3 accordingly. The maximum relevance minimal redundancy, often known as $RelRed$, is obtained from given Eqs. 5.2 as well as in Eqs. 5.3 by integrating and improving both the maximum relevancy, 'Rel', and the least redundancy, 'Red'. The following formula is used to obtain the utmost relevance with minimal redundancy:

$$RelRed(RR) = \frac{1}{Att} * MI[Att_i, C] - \frac{1}{Att} * MI[Att_i, Att_j]$$
$$= MI[Att_i, C] - MI[Att_i, Att_j] \qquad (5.4)$$

In order to save the time required, this study applies a Newton Raphson Probability for the resulting characteristics, followed by attributes developed for lung cancer disease diagnostics that are most relevant and have the least amount of redundancy. For Eq. 5.4, the log-likelihood function is represented by the following formulation:

$$\ln(C|X) = -\sum_{i=1}^{n} \log(1 + [Att_i - C]^2) \qquad (5.5)$$

The first derivative and second derivative of the log-likelihood function are written as follows:

$$\frac{\partial \ln(C|X)}{\partial C} = 2\sum_{i=1}^{n}(Att_i - C)(1 + [Att_i - C]^2)^{-1} \qquad (5.6)$$

$$\frac{\partial^2 \ln(C|X)}{\partial^2 C} = [2\sum_{i=1}^{n}(Att_i - C)^2((1 + [Att_i - C]^2)^{-2})((1 + [Att_i - C]^2)^{-1})]$$

$$(5.7)$$

The data function reduces redundant characteristics while increasing maximum relevance. By concentrating on most important traits, this successfully reduces the amount of time needed to detect lung cancer.

Maximum Probability is suggested in Algorithm 1, which the least amount of redundant pre-processing pseudo-code.

Algorithm 1: Pre-processing Model for MLMR

Input: D, $Att = Att_1, Att_2, ..., Att_n$

Output: Maximum Likelihood Minimum Redundant attributes selected 'RR'.

1: **Begin**

2:　　**For** D with Att

3.　　　　Find $MIAtt$

4:　　　　DetermineRelattribute

5:　　　　MinimizeRedistribute

6:　　　　Combine $RelRed$

7:　　　　Formulate $\ln(C \mid X)$

8:　　　　Obtain $\dfrac{\partial \ln(C \mid X)}{\partial C}$ and $\dfrac{\partial^2 \ln(C \mid X)}{\partial^2 C}$

9:　　**End for**

10: **End**

Not all of the attributes are necessary for every training data when using approach 1, in which the MLMR pre-processing was mentioned (i.e., massive data). In order to select the least repetitive and most pertinent characteristics for lung cancer diagnosis, this research uses big data even as input dataset. Finally, in order to shorten the time required for lung cancer detection, Enhanced Newton Raphson's Estimate is evaluated in relation to the first and second derivative.

5.2.2 Maximum Likelihood Boosting in a Weighted Optimized Neural Network

The accuracy of lung cancer detection for massive data is improved by using an ensemble classification model once the Maximum Likelihood and Minimum Redundant characteristics have been determined. This study uses a combination of WONN-MLB features to accurately diagnose lung cancer with the least amount of error and time. The provided 'n' training datasets (i.e., attributes) are $\{(Att_1, b_1), (Att_2, b_2), ..., (Att_n,)\}$ bn', where Att_i is a vector that corresponds to input sample data and is connected with "RR" input attributes, and b_i is is the target variable either one of two classes or terms as ? "1" or "−1." First, a weak classifier in the suggested model is trained using the distribution 'D_i' where '$D_i \in RR$.' An artificial neuron's input properties ($Att_1, Att_2, ..., Att_n$) are represented by 'n' synapses, each having a corresponding weight w_i. Here, the weight 'w_i' is multiplied by the signal at input 'i' to yield the total of the weighted inputs and a linear combination of the weighted inputs. Additionally, a weighted sum 'ws' is created by adding a bias 'bs' to the linear combination as follows:

$$ws = bs + w_1Att_1 + w_2Att_2 + \dots + w_nAtt_n \qquad (5.8)$$

The weighted total, provided in Eq. 5.9, is then subjected to a nonlinear activation function, 'f', producing an output, b':

$$b = f(ws) \qquad (5.9)$$

The next step is to choose and create a weak classifier with a low weighted error as follows:

$$\varepsilon_i = z = Prob_{D_i}[b + w_1Att_1 + w_2Att_2 + \dots + w_nAtt_n] \qquad (5.10)$$

$$= Prob_{D_i}[f(ws)] \qquad (5.11)$$

Based on the '$= Prob_{D_i}$' for a linear sequence of inputs that are weighted (i.e., characteristics) '$f(ws)$', the low weighted error 'ε_i' is calculated from Eqs. 5.10 and 5.11. The following formula is used to calculate a new component, 'k_i', created with the error function:

$$k_i = \frac{1}{n}\sum_{i-1}^{n}(Actualerror - Observederror)^2 \qquad (5.12)$$

Using the above equation (5.12), final weighted error is obtained using ensemble learning classifier, which is better than the chance is assessed to combine all weal classifiers with the optimal weight Manna et al. [3].

$$f(WS) = SIGN(\sum_{t=1}^{T} k_t f(s)) \qquad (5.13)$$

With the majority of vote in weak classifier '$f(s)$', the final ensemble learning classifier is identified, where each classifier is given a weight, or 'k_i', according to Eq. 5.13. Algorithm 2 provides the ensemble classification pseudo code. In algorithm 2, the ensemble classification pseudo code is provided.

Algorithm 2: Algorithm for the recommended Enhanced Neural Network model with Ensemble Classifier

Input: Maximum Likelihood Minimum Redundant attributes 'RR', bs, $w = w_1, w_2, ..., w_n$, iteration $i = 1, 2, ..., n$, Optimal weight 'β'.

Output: Improved lung cancer diagnosis accuracy

1: **Procedure**
2:    **Initialize** w
3:    **For** each RR and iteration t
4:        The measure ws
5:        **If** '$ws \leq \beta$'**then**
6:            Compute ε_i
7:            Obtain k_i
8:            Obtain $f(WS)$
9:        **End if**
10:        **Else** $ws > \beta$
11:            Go to step 4
13: **End for**
14: **End**

Method 2 introduces the Enhanced Neural network model with Ensemble Classifier Algorithm to classify the LCD with the least amount of error. In the first phase, weights are initialised for each maximum likelihood minimal redundant attribute. This weighted sum value is then determined after establishing a weight initialization. In order to determine whether the weighted sum is below or equal to the optimum weight, Mana et al. [3] also perform a conditional verification. The initialised weighting value is calculated if the check fails. The process is then continued using a boosting strategy. Here, three steps have been finished. In the first stage, a classifier that performs poorly and has a modest weighted error is assessed. Next, a new component using the error function is created in the second phase. The resulting ensemble learning classifier is applied to the new feature in the third step. As a conclusion, it is asserted that the accuracy of lung cancer disease detection has grown with a low rate of inaccuracy.

5.3   Experimental Work and Results

The suggested WONN-ML Boosting method's effectiveness is evaluated using the Thoracic Surgery Large Dataset [2]. The recommended WONN-ML Boosting technique can be applied using Weka on the Java platform [12]. The Thoracic Surgery Data Dataset extensively addresses a crucial issue: the patient's postoperative life expectancy. The data was acquired retrospectively there at Wroclaw Thoracic Surgical Centre. The patient data includes patients having primary lung cancer that undergone major lung resections during 2007 and 2011 [13]. The Lower-Silesian Centre of Poland and the Institute of Surgical Intervention there at Medical University in Wroclaw are both connected with the Centre, which largely focuses on pulmonary illnesses. The Lung Cancer Database is run by the Department for Pulmonary and Tuberculosis Diseases in Warsaw, Poland. The Thoracic Surgical Data dataset's attributes, such as corresponding analysis, lowest redundancy, and maximum probability, are first preprocessed in order to obtain the important features [14]. The Most Likelihood least Redundant qualities are used in the ensemble classification's next phase to boost diagnosis accuracy while minimising time and error.

The experiment of the recommended technique is done in several situations involving various patient data sets in order to assess its efficacy. (BSVM) Boosted support vector method by Ziba et al. [2], nonparallel plane proximal classifier by Ghorai et al. [4], as well as multitier model in convolutional neural networks (MV-CNN) by Liu et al. [19] are used to compare the significance of the proposed method to non-small cancer by Wu et al. For the advantage of the readers, the explanation of the results of the suggested technique is divided into a number of categories, including diagnosis accuracy. It is thought to be one of the most important elements in the early sickness diagnosis process. It is claimed that early sickness diagnosis is possible, and that diagnostic accuracy increases [15, 16] with procedure efficiency. It provides indication of how well a method accurately diagnoses the ailment and helps physicians or patients decide on further treatments. Here are the specifics:

$$DA = \sum_{s=1}^{n} \frac{CD_{disease}}{s} * 100 \tag{5.14}$$

The diagnosing accuracy (DA) is calculated from Eq. 5.14 based on the proportion of data that were identified adequately as a disease (CD disease) to all samples (s) that were taken into consideration for the experiment. It's expressed as a percentage. The suggested WONN-MLB technique is used to depict the values acquired by Eq. 5.14 for various patient data, and it is contrasted with the optimized NSCLC and B-SV approaches in Figure 5.3. The following is a sample calculation to assess the diagnostic efficacy of the three approaches stated above:

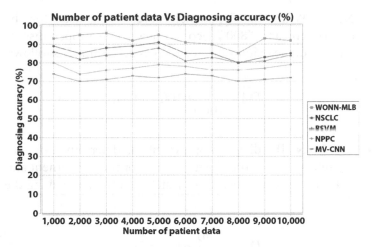

Figure 5.3 Diagnosing accuracy with 10000 data.

Sample calculation:

- Proposed Enhanced WONN: With "1000" patient records being used in the experiment and "930" records having the right disease identified, the correctly detecting accuracy is computed as follows:

$$DA = \frac{930}{1000} * 100 = 93\%$$

- NSCLC: With "1000" patient records being used for the experiment and "890" records having the proper disease identified, the diagnosing accuracy is determined as follows:

$$DA = \frac{890}{1000} * 100 = 89\%$$

- BSVM: The diagnosing accuracy is determined by taking into account "1000" patient data for the experiment and counting "860" of those data as accurately identifying a disease:

$$DA = \frac{860}{1000} * 100 = 86\%$$

- NPPC: With "1000" patient records being used for the experiment and "800" records having the proper disease identified, the diagnosing accuracy is determined as follows:

$$DA = \frac{800}{1000} * 100 = 80\%$$

- MV-CNN: The diagnosing accuracy is determined by taking into account "1000" patient data for the experiment and "740" of those data being accurately identified as having the disease:

$$DA = \frac{740}{1000} * 100 = 74\%$$

Figure 5.3 compares the suggested approach's diagnostic accuracy to the NSCLC and BSVM already used, respectively. It has been demonstrated that utilizing Enhanced WONN-ML Boosting [17, 18], the evaluation of identifying low weighted error and a new component based on slip function increases the accuracy of lung cancer detection. The findings show that as patient data volumes rise, diagnostic accuracy increases for a specific minimum patient data volume and subsequently declines.

This occurs because more qualities are irrelevant as patient data increases. Furthermore, a specific issue occurs during preprocessing in the Enhanced WONN-ML Boosting technique, resulting in a certain quantity of useless characteristics even after preprocessing. However, a difference is shown when employing the Enhanced WONN-ML Boosting approach in contrast to the current methods NSCLC, BSVM, NPPC, and MV-CNN [20]. This occurs due to ensemble classification, which boosts the updated results to reduce processing time while simultaneously minimizing error by upgrading the weak classifier. This increases the Enhanced WONN-ML Boosting method's diagnostic accuracy by 7%, 11%, 19%, and 28% compared to NSCLC, BSVM, NPPC, and MV-CNN, respectively.

5.4   Conclusion

Researchers are investigating a weight-optimized approach with high probability boosting to improve the precision of the detection of lung cancer disease, lower the percentage of false positives, and speed up the classification process. Using Enhanced Newton Raphson's probability distribution, the modelling is preprocessed to retrieve the fewest feasible fundamental attributes and omit any unnecessary features. Hence, categorization time is shortened. The most relevant features are employed to diagnose advanced lung cancer disease with a higher accuracy rate utilising an ensembles classifier model termed WoN Network and Boosting. In this case, the weighting function is gained in addition to the ideal values. In the final ensemble technique, the classifier with the smallest error is found, and the new components are updated in accordance with the error function. This method achieves a higher degree of sickness diagnosis accuracy with the least potential false positive rate. The experimental evaluation makes use of a number of factors, including as classification, rate of false positives and sickness diagnosis precision. The empirical findings show that the new system delivered accurate results when compared to existing methods for processing large amounts of data. For numerous sizable datasets, the suggested WoNN-MLB approach has been tested. In the future, our method will need to be used to look at a lot more data points. Future studies will concentrate on optimising lung cancer detection performance by including other parameters.

References

1. Wu, J., Tan, Y., Chen, Z., Zhao, M., Decision-based on big data research for non-small cell lung cancer in the artificial medical system in a developing country. *Comput. Methods Programs Biomed.*, Elsevier, 159, 87–101, Mar 2018.

2. Zięba, M., Tomczak, J.M., Lubicz, M., Świątek, J., Boosted SVM for extracting rules from imbalanced data in application to prediction of the post-operative life expectancy in the lung cancer patients. *Appl. Soft Comput.*, Elsevier, 14, Part A, 99–108, January 2014.

3. Mana, Z., Lee, K., Wang, D., Cao, Z., Khoo, S., An optimal weight learning machine for handwritten digit image recognition. *Signal Process.*, Elsevier, 93, 6, 1624–1638, June 2013.

4. Ghorai, S., Mukherjee, A., Sengupta, S., Dutta, P.K., Cancer classification from gene expression data by NPPC ensemble. *IEEE/ACM Trans. Comput. Biol. Bioinf.*, 8, 3, 659 – 671, 2011.

5. Das, R. and Sengur, A., Evaluation of ensemble methods for diagnosing of valvular heart disease. *Expert Syst. Appl.*, Elsevier, 37, 7, 5110–5115, July 2010.

6. Costaa, V.S., Fariasa, A.D.S., Bedregala, B., Santiagoa, R.H.N., Canutoa, A.M.P., Combining multiple algorithms in classifier ensembles using

generalized mixture functions. *Neuro Comput.*, Elsevier, 313, 402–414, November 2018.

7. Huda, S., Yearwood, J., Jelinek, H.F., Hassan, M.M., Fortino, G., Buckland, M., A hybrid feature selection with ensemble classification for imbalanced healthcare data: A case study for brain tumor diagnosis. *IEEE Access*, 4, 9145 – 9154, May 2016.

8. Hussein, S., Kandel, P., Bolan, C.W., Wallace, M.B., Bagci, U., Supervised and unsupervised tumor characterization in the deep learning era. *IEEE Trans. Med. Imaging*, 2, 1–11, July 2018.

9. Adetiba, E. and Olugbara, O.O., Improved classification of lung cancer using radial basis function neural network with affine transforms of voss representation. *PLoS One J.*, 10, 12, 1–25, 2015.

10. Jain, D. and Singh, V., Feature selection and classification systems for chronic disease prediction: A review. *Egypt. Inf. J.*, Elsevier, 19, 3, 179–189, November 2018.

11. Dande, P. and Samant, P., Acquaintance to artificial neural networks and use of artificial intelligence as a diagnostic tool for tuberculosis: A review. *Tuberculosis*, Elsevier, 108, 1–9, January 2018.

12. Khosravia, P., Kazemic, E., Imielinskid, M., Elemento, O., Hajirasouliha, I., Deep convolutional neural networks enable discrimination of heterogeneous digital pathology images. *EBioMedicine*, Elsevier, 27, 317–328, Jan 2018.

13. Sharma, S., Sharma, V., Sharma, A., A two-stage hybrid ensemble classifier based diagnostic tool for chronic kidney disease diagnosis using optimally selected reduced feature set. *Int. J. Intell. Syst. Appl. Eng.*, 6, 2, 113–122, Apr 2018.

14. Hosseinzadeh, F., KayvanJoo, A.H., Ebrahimi, M., Goliaei, B., Prediction of lung tumor types based on protein attributes by machine learning algorithms. *Springer Plus*, 2, 238, 1–14, Sep 2013.

15. Podolsky, M.D., Barchuk, A.A., Kuznetcov, V.I., Gusarova, N.F., Gaidukov, V.S., Tarakanov, S.A., Evaluation of machine learning algorithm utilization for lung cancer classification based on gene expression levels. *Asian Pac. J. Cancer Prev.*, 17, 2, 835–838, 2016.

16. Rabbani, M., Kanevsky, J., Kafi, K., Chandelier, F., Giles, F.J., Role of artificial intelligence in the care of patients with non-small cell lung cancer. *Eur. J. Clin. Invest.*, Wiley Online Library, 48, 4, 1–7, January 2018.

17. Zhou, Z., Zhou, Z.J., Hao, H., Li, S., Chen, X., Zhang, Y., Folkert, M., Wang, J., Constructing multi-modality and multiclassifier radio mics predictive models through reliable classifier fusion. *IEEE Comput. Soc.*, 1, 1–13, Jun 2017.

18. Dubey, A.K., Gupta, U., Jain, S., Epidemiology of lung cancer and approaches for its prediction: A systematic review and analysis. *Chin. J. Cancer*, 35, 71, 1–13, July 2016.

19. Liu, K. and Kang, G., Multiview convolutional neural networks for lung nodule classification. *Int. J. Imaging Syst. Technol.*, Wiley Online Library, 27, 1, 12–22, March 2017.

20. El-Baz, A., Beache, G.M., Gimel'farb, G., Suzuki, K., Okada, K., Elnakib, A., Soliman, A., Abdollahi, B., Computer-aided diagnosis systems for lung cancer: Challenges and methodologies. *Int. J. Biomed. Imaging*, 1–46, 2013, Hindawi Publishing, Egypt, 2012.

21. ALzubi, J.A., Bharathikannan, B., Tanwar, S., Manikandan, R., Khanna, A., Thaventhiran, C., Boosted neural network ensemble classification for lung cancer disease diagnosis. *Appl. Soft Comput.*, 80, 579–591, 2019.

6

Feature Selection for Breast Cancer Detection

Kishan Sharda[1], Mandeep Singh Ramdev[2], Deepak Rawat[3]*
and Pawan Bishnoi[4]

[1]Associate Software Engineer, Neosoft Technologies, Rampur, India
[2]Department of CSE, Apex Institute of Technology, Rampur, India
[3]Department of Mathematics, Chandigarh University, Punjab, India
[4]Om Sterling Global University, Hisar, Haryana, India

Abstract

Breast cancer (BC) is the most prevalent disease affecting women worldwide. With an estimated 8.2 million fatalities, it is the leading cause of death worldwide. Several preprocessing and detection techniques are employed to enhance the effectiveness of breast cancer detection for early disease diagnosis. Currently, much effort is devoted to achieving effective optimization and detection strategies. It is challenging to identify breast cancer from the massive thermal dataset. Early identification of breast cancer is critical. Thermographic approaches are used in the treatment of breast cancer. Different areas of the affected area experience varying temperatures due to breast cancer. The performance of classification is enhanced by optimization. The photos were divided into healthy and malignant ones. The detection approach determines the most malignant area from the fewest picture preprocessing. The most crucial part of treatment is determining what kind of tumour it is. Tumors can be benign or malignant, with the latter being more harmful and potentially fatal. Therefore, a doctor's ability to discern between benign and malignant tumours through accurate identification and diagnosis is essential for successful cancer treatment. When normal cell division is disrupted by internal (genetic changes) or external (environmental and hormonal variables), three aberrant changes—hyperplasia, preinvasive, invasive, and metastatic cancer—occur consecutively. In the paper, the importance of feature selection has been discussed. The correlation matrix is presented not only for top features but also for the independent features by removing the elements with high collinearity. Six feature selection techniques have been used, and five states of art parameters are used. Accuracy,

*Corresponding author: rawatdeepak1982@gmail.com

Sandeep Kumar, Anuj Sharma, Navneet Kaur, Lokesh Pawar and Rohit Bajaj (eds.) Optimized Predictive Models in Healthcare Using Machine Learning, (89–102) © 2024 Scrivener Publishing LLC

ROC, precision, recall, and F1 score are calculated and represented for Pearson correlation, Chi-square, ANOVA F-test, forward selection, recursive features elimination, and feature importance techniques. Pearson correlation, F-test, and forward selection showed the best results regarding the state-of-the-art parameters.

Keywords: Feature selection, optimization, accuracy, cancer, recall

6.1   Introduction

Breast cancer is the most common cancer in women worldwide and can also occur in men, although this is less common [1]. Breast cancer can be benign (not cancerous) or malignant (cancerous). Benign breast lumps are not usually life-threatening, but malignant lumps can spread to other body parts and be fatal if not treated [2]. A lump or thickening in the breast or underarm, changes to the breast's size or shape, modifications to the skin of the breast (such as dimpling, redness, or scaling) [3], and discharge from the nipple are all indications of breast cancer. These symptoms do not always indicate breast cancer, but it is important to have them checked by a doctor. Diagnosis of breast cancer usually starts with a physical examination. If breast cancer is found, further tests may be done to determine the stage (the extent of cancer) and the grade (the aggressiveness of cancer) [4, 5]. Following surgery, radiation therapy may be recommended to destroy any remaining cancer cells and reduce the risk of recurrence. Chemotherapy is a treatment that uses drugs to destroy cancer cells. Hormonal therapy is a treatment that targets hormones that can fuel the growth of certain types of breast cancer, such as estrogen and progesterone [6]. Targeted therapy is a treatment that targets specific molecules (such as proteins) that help cancer cells grow and survive [7]. It is important to note that early detection and treatment are key to a good outcome for breast cancer [8, 9]. With advances in technology and research, many treatment options are available, and the survival rate for breast cancer is increasing. It is important to have any breast changes checked by a doctor and to discuss any concerns with a healthcare professional [10]. Machine learning is a subset of artificial intelligence that involves training models on large datasets to make predictions or decisions. It has been used in several healthcare areas, including breast cancer detection.One of the most common applications of machine learning in breast cancer detection is in the analysis of mammograms [11]. A mammogram is an X-ray of the breast, and it is often used as a screening tool to detect early signs of breast cancer. However, interpreting mammograms can be challenging, as there can be a lot of variation in the images, and it can be difficult to distinguish between normal and abnormal tissue [12]. Machine learning algorithms can be used to analyze mammograms and identify patterns indicative of breast cancer. For example, one type of algorithm called a convolutional neural network (CNN) can be trained on a large dataset of mammograms to recognize patterns in the images associated with breast cancer [13]. Once trained, the model can be used to analyze new mammograms and predict whether they contain signs of cancer. Another application of machine learning in breast cancer detection is the analysis of breast tissue samples. A biopsy is a procedure in which a small tissue sample is removed from the breast and examined under a microscope [14, 15]. This can be used to diagnose breast cancer, but analyzing the tissue samples can be time-consuming and subjective. Machine learning algorithms can be used to analyze breast tissue samples and identify patterns indicative of cancer. For example, algorithms called support vector machines (SVMs) can be trained on a large dataset of breast tissue samples to recognize patterns in the tissue that are associated with cancer [16]. Once trained, the model can analyze new tissue samples and predict whether they contain cancer [17]. One key benefit of using machine learning in mammogram analysis is that it can help reduce the number of false positives, which are cases where the mammogram appears to indicate cancer, but further tests reveal no cancer present. This can help to reduce the number of unnecessary biopsies and other procedures that are performed on patients. Machine learning algorithms can also identify cases where cancer is present but might be missed by radiologists [18]. This can be used to diagnose breast cancer, but analyzing the tissue samples can be time-consuming and subjective. Machine learning algorithms can be used to analyze breast tissue samples and identify patterns indicative of cancer. For example, algorithms called support vector machines (SVMs) can be trained on a large dataset of breast tissue [19]. Machine learning can also be used to identify patterns in patient data that are associated with an increased risk of breast cancer. For example, algorithms called decision trees can be trained on a large dataset of patient data (such as age, family history, lifestyle factors, etc.) to identify patterns [20]. Once trained, the model can analyze new patient data and predict a person's risk of developing breast cancer. One of the main benefits of using machine learning in breast cancer detection is that it can help improve diagnostic test accuracy. By analyzing large amounts of data, machine learning algorithms can identify patterns that are not easily visible to the human eye. This can help improve the sensitivity and specificity of diagnostic tests. Another benefit is that machine learning can help reduce diagnostic test subjectivity. For example, when analyzing mammograms, machine learning algorithms can be used to identify patterns that are indicative of cancer, regardless of the individual radiologist's interpretation. This can help to reduce the variability in diagnostic results and improve the consistency of test results. Additionally, machine learning can help to automate the diagnostic process, which can help to reduce the time and cost of diagnostic tests. For example, machine learning algorithms can be used to analyze mammograms or breast tissue samples in real-time, which can help to reduce the turnaround time for test results [21]. However, it is worth noting that machine learning is not a replacement for radiologists or pathologists but rather an aid to help them. The models must be properly trained, validated, and tested. Additionally, ethical and legal issues, such as patient privacy and data security should be considered when using machine learning in healthcare [22]. In conclusion, machine learning has the potential to revolutionize the way we detect and diagnose breast cancer. By analyzing large amounts of data, machine learning algorithms can identify patterns indicative of cancer.

6.2   Literature Review

Deep learning has been widely used in recent years for breast cancer detection. These methods have achieved high diagnostic performance, even when trained on small datasets. For example, the paper "Automated breast cancer diagnosis using fine-tuned convolutional neural networks" by a CNN was prepared on breast cancer histology images and outperformed traditional machine learning methods. Ensemble methods, such as combining multiple models or features, have also improved diagnostic performance. Similarly, "ensemble deep learning for breast cancer diagnosis in mammography" proposed an ensemble deep learning approach for breast cancer diagnosis in mammography and showed that it improved diagnostic performance compared to single models. Scales *et al.* created a semi-automatic segmentation method for separating the right and left breast thermograms. The top body margins were carefully eliminated, and 21 various infrared 128 128, 8-bit grayscale photos were examined. Motta *et al.* created an automatic segmentation approach that detected the lower boundary by using thresholding based on the most significant temperature of the breast. The upper limit of ROI was determined by identifying the axilla. The segmented image's center point separated the right and left breasts. The breast center point may fail to recognize the right and left breast ROI separation points in asymmetric breasts. During the capture of a breast thermogram, Ali *et al.* automatically separated ROI, depending on the distance between the camera and the patient. They estimated that the breast region takes up roughly half of the picture height, while the other parts, such as the woman's shoulders and stomach, were used to get the outside boundaries of breast photos. Eddie *et al.* compared their findings for detecting breast borders using a standard snake method and a modified gradient vector flow snake. The traditional snake method fails to recognize complicated picture boundaries in the breast. Moghbel *et al.* suggested a segmentation approach that includes dynamic intensity level stretching and filtering for thermogram augmentation, followed by edge detection. The nipple region was located using a series of circular Hough Transforms. Later, seeds were dynamically implemented based on the location of the nipple region. The random walker's approach performed well in recognizing the image's weak borders. For aberrant photos, this approach could not determine the precise placement of the nipple. Hairong *et al.* described an unsupervised learning strategy for categorizing each segmented pixel into several groups. Based on pixel distribution within the same cluster, asymmetric patterns were observed. The asymmetry between the right and left breasts was measured using the six histogram moments mean, variance, skewness, kurtosis, peak pixel intensity, entropy, and joint entropy. From segmented breast thermograms, Schaefer *et al.* retrieved statistical and spectral characteristics. The retrieved features were put into a fuzzy categorization algorithm. The experimental categorization findings on a set of 146 examples achieved an accuracy of 80%. Borchardt *et al.* used an SVM classifier to compute mean, standard deviation, the difference between maximum and minimum intensity features, and other metrics from thermogram ROIs and attained an accuracy of 86%. Ali *et al.* retrieved first-order statistical and GLCM-based characteristics from greyscale breast thermograms that were automatically segmented. SVM with various kernel functions was utilized to recognize typical and atypical breasts. They examined the classifier's accuracy using four different situations. For training and testing, each scenario contained a varied amount of photos. For statistical features, quadratic and linear kernels achieved 85% and 80% accuracy for GLCM-based features, respectively. Araujo *et al.* investigated the possibility of modelling breast anomalies as malignant, benign, or cystic utilizing interval data in a symbolic data analysis (SDA) framework to diagnose breast cancer. A three-stage feature extraction method was employed. The morphological pictures and thermal matrices were used to obtain minimum and maximum temperature values. By feeding the created continuous features into the classification procedure, they got a 16% misclassification rate, 85.7% sensitivity, and 86.5% specificity using Fisher's criteria. Lipari and Head used asymmetry analysis on temperature distribution in breast thermograms to estimate breast cancer risk.

6.3   Design and Implementation

Here is the approach for analysis of breast cancer prediction using machine learning.
We take the approach of multivariate analysis.

- Data gathering
- Data cleaning.
- EDA
- Feature selection—We will check the multicollinearity, and there will be specific tasks and techniques to perform the feature selection task in breast cancer prediction.
- Model selection—There are many options in model selection NB, logistic regression, KNN, SVM, decision tree, random forest, and artificial neural networks
- Training.
- Testing accuracy

To solve this, we will perform a multivariate analysis to predict the tumor classes as malignant or benign. Based on various factors and details of tests done by the medical team on patients. In machine learning, information gathering refers to the process of collecting and preparing data that will be used to train and test models. This process is often referred to as data acquisition or data preprocessing.

There are a few key steps involved in information gathering:

1. Data collection: This is the process of acquiring data from various sources, such as databases, CSV files, APIs, and web scraping. The data may come in multiple forms: text, images, audio, and video.
2. Data cleaning: This step ensures the collected data is accurate, complete, and consistent. This includes removing duplicates, dealing with missing values, and handling outliers.
3. Data integration: This step combines multiple data sources into a single dataset. This step is needed when data comes from different sources, which may have other formats, structures, and schemas.
4. Data transformation: This step converts the data into a format that machine learning algorithms can easily consume. This includes normalization, feature scaling, and feature extraction.

It is important to note that data quality is crucial for the model's performance, so it is essential to understand the data, its properties, and how it is collected. Additionally, it is necessary to ensure that the data is not biased and representative of the real-world problem. Data preprocessing is a crucial step in the machine learning pipeline, and it can be a time-consuming and complex task. But with the right tools and techniques, it's possible to automate many of these steps and make the process more efficient.

6.3.1   Feature Selection

The primary goal is to investigate how machine learning methods can be used with Internet of Things devices to predict breast cancer. Precision, recall, F Measure, and accuracy for the proposed classifier were 98%, 97%, 96%, and 98%, respectively. We are calculating the multicollinearity between the proposed features and analyzing the results. The feature score can be removed, and we will again examine the result accuracy based on this approach. We will be able to get the perfect feature for our Machine learning model with the highest precision and recall that our primary goal is to reduce the false negative in this method, as our model should not miss a person with the disease.

The feature selection methods we have employed include
Pearson Correlation

i. Chi-square test
ii. ANOVA F-test
iii. Forward selection
iv. Recursive feature elimination
v. Feature importance

- Pearson Correlation

The Pearson correlation approach assesses the linear relationship between two variables in the context of feature selection. It is used to determine which features have a high degree of correlation in Figure 6.1 when features are being chosen. A strong correlation between two or more features indicates that they contain similar information and may not be required to include both in the model. Highly correlated features may cause the model to become multicollinear, resulting in unstable estimates and inaccurate forecasts. As a result, it might be a good idea to eliminate one of the connected qualities.

By removing the features with a high degree of collinearity, we can obtain significantly independent features, as shown in Figure 6.2.

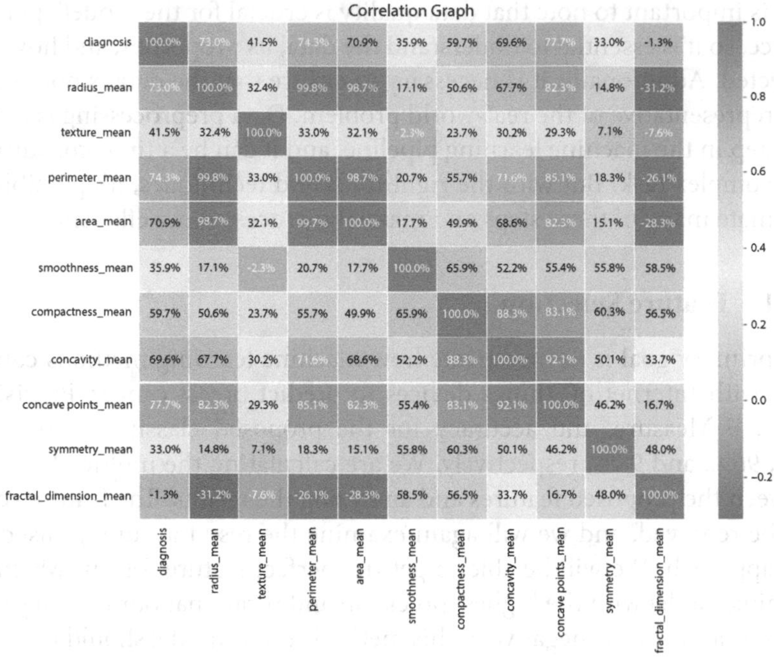

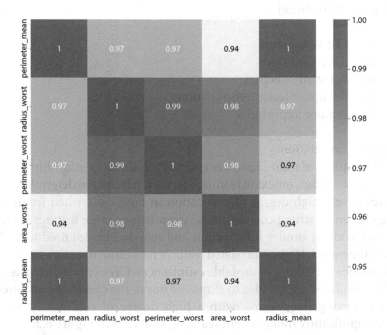

Figure 6.1 Correlation graph.

Figure 6.2 Feature minimization.

- Chi-squared test

The Chi-squared test is employed in feature selection to ascertain the association between a feature and a target variable. Contrasting the observed
frequencies with the predicted frequencies if there were no correlations
determines the association between each attribute and the target variable. It
can assist you in determining which characteristics are most beneficial for
your prediction task. It accomplishes this by contrasting the feature's and
target variables' associations. The Chi-squared test determines a p-value or
probability that the test statistic will be seen under the null hypothesis, as
shown in Figure 6.3. A feature will be regarded as meaningful if it has a high
Chi-squared score, which indicates that the feature and the target variable
are vigorously associated (the hypothesis of independence is incorrect).

- ANOVA F-TEST

The analysis of variance F test, or the ANOVA F test, is a technique for
selecting univariate features from a dataset that includes categorical and
numerical variables. It distinct the means of the target variable for various levels of quality and aids in determining the most significant features
that should be included in a predictive model. A high F test score suggests
a significant difference in group means and a strong correlation between
the feature and the intended variable, as in Figure 6.4. On the other hand,

	Accuracy	ROC	Precision	Recall	F1 Score	Feature Count
All features (Baseline)	0.964912	0.967262	0.931818	0.97619	0.953488	30
Pearson Correlation	0.973684	0.974206	0.953488	0.97619	0.964706	22
Chi-Square Test	0.956140	0.960317	0.911111	0.97619	0.942529	20

Figure 6.3 Technique used for specific dataset features concerning the accuracy.

	Accuracy	ROC	Precision	Recall	F1 Score	Feature Count
All features (Baseline)	0.964912	0.967262	0.931818	0.97619	0.953488	30
Pearson Correlation	0.973684	0.974206	0.953488	0.97619	0.964706	22
Chi-Square Test	0.956140	0.960317	0.911111	0.97619	0.942529	20
F-test	0.973684	0.974206	0.953488	0.97619	0.964706	20

Figure 6.4 Test results.

a tiny F test statistic shows a minor difference in means and, as a result, a weak link between the characteristic and the target variable.

- FORWARD SELECTION

A feature selection technique called forward selection adds new features to the model iteratively based on how well they perform individually, starting with an empty collection of parts. Usually, the approach begins with testing each segment separately and choosing the one that produces the best model performance. The process is then repeated with the other features. The selected element is then included in the list of features. A new feature is added to the model, and the performance is assessed throughout each iteration, and this process continues until a stopping requirement is met. Forward selection's main benefit is that it is computationally effective and practical when there are a lot of features and not enough computer resources. It is also important to note that a forward selection variant called stepwise selection enables feature addition and removal based on performance.

- RECURSIVE FEATURE ELIMINATION

Recursively deleting features and then reconstructing the model using the remaining components is known as recursive feature elimination (RFE). A model with all the features is trained initially, and its performance is assessed. The worst-performing element is eliminated from the model, and the procedure is repeated with the remaining components. Recursively this process is repeated up until a stopping point. Any form of the model can be utilized with RFE, and it can capture the connections between features and the target variable. As it avoids testing every conceivable feature combination, it can also be helpful when several features exist. Recall that RFE is typically used with other feature selection methods, such as univariate feature selection, to get superior results, as in Figure 6.5.

Feature Importance

One of the most well-known strategies, feature importance, ranks features according to how much they improve the model's performance. Any model can be utilized with this technique. However, tree-based models like decision trees, random forests, and gradient-boosting models benefit the most from their use. The primary method for determining the feature significance values is to train a model and track its performance when features are permuted or randomly mixed. The feature is regarded as being more crucial the more the performance suffers. Feature selection, also known as feature ranking, is choosing which features to utilize in a model after each feature's importance has been determined, as shown in Figure 6.6 and

	Accuracy	ROC	Precision	Recall	F1 Score	Feature Count
All features (Baseline)	0.964912	0.967262	0.931818	0.97619	0.953488	30
Pearson Correlation	0.973684	0.974206	0.953488	0.97619	0.964706	22
Chi-Square Test	0.956140	0.960317	0.911111	0.97619	0.942529	20
F-test	0.973684	0.974206	0.953488	0.97619	0.964706	20
Forward selection	0.973684	0.974206	0.953488	0.97619	0.964706	20
Recursive Feature Elimination	0.964912	0.967262	0.931818	0.97619	0.953488	20

Figure 6.5 Accuracy of the feature selection methods employed.

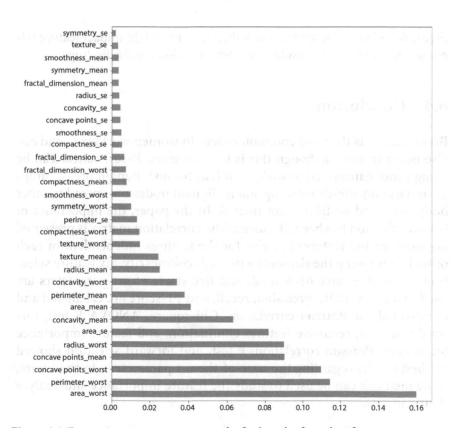

Figure 6.6 Feature importance concerning the final result of our classification.

	Accuracy	ROC	Precision	Recall	F1 Score	Feature Count
All features (Baseline)	0.964912	0.967262	0.931818	0.97619	0.953488	30
Pearson Correlation	0.973684	0.974206	0.953488	0.97619	0.964706	20
Chi-Square Test	0.956140	0.960317	0.911111	0.97619	0.942529	20
F-test	0.973684	0.974206	0.953488	0.97619	0.964706	20
Forward Selection	0.973684	0.974206	0.953488	0.97619	0.964706	20
Recursive Feature Elimination	0.964912	0.967262	0.931818	0.97619	0.953488	20
Feature Importance	0.964912	0.967262	0.931818	0.97619	0.953488	15

Figure 6.7 Comparative analysis of all techniques.

Figure 6.7. Given that scaling and linked features might impact feature relevance, it is critical to consider these when evaluating the findings.

6.4   Conclusion

Breast cancer is the most common cancer in women worldwide and can also occur in men, although this is less common. Breast cancer can be benign (not cancerous) or malignant (cancerous). Benign breast lumps are not usually life-threatening, but malignant nodes can spread to other body parts and be fatal if not treated. In the paper, the importance of feature selection has been discussed. The correlation matrix is presented not only for top features but also for the features independent of each other by removing the elements with high collinearity. Six feature selection techniques have been used, and five states of art parameters are used. Accuracy, ROC, precision, recall, and F1-score are calculated and represented for Pearson correlation, Chi-square, ANOVA F test, forward selection, recursive features elimination, and feature importance techniques. Pearson correlation, F test, and forward selection showed the best results regarding the state-of-the-art parameters. In the future, more methods can be used to study the feature importance and analyze their patterns.

References

1. Mahbod, A., Ellinger, I., Ecker, R., Smedby, Ö., Wang, C., Breast cancer histological image classification using fine-tuned deep network fusion, in: *Image Analysis and Recognition: 15th International Conference, ICIAR 2018*, Springer International Publishing, Póvoa de Varzim, Portugal, June 27–29, 2018, Proceedings, vol. 15, pp. 754–762, 2018.

2. Sadhukhan, S., Upadhyay, N., Chakraborty, P., Breast cancer diagnosis using image processing and machine learning, in: *Emerging Technology in Modelling and Graphics: Proceedings of IEM Graph 2018*, pp. 113–127, Springer, Singapore, 2020.

3. Bayrak, E.A., Kırcı, P., Ensari, T., Comparison of machine learning methods for breast cancer diagnosis, in: *2019 Scientific Meeting on Electrical-Electronics & Biomedical Engineering and Computer Science (EBBT)*, IEEE, pp. 1–3, 2019, April.

4. Rafid, A.R.H., Azam, S., Montaha, S., Karim, A., Fahim, K.U., Hasan, M.Z., An effective ensemble machine learning approach to classify breast cancer based on feature selection and lesion segmentation using preprocessed mammograms. *Biology*, 11, 11, 1654, 2022.

5. Scales, N., Herry, C., Frize, M., Automated image segmentation for breast analysis using infrared images, in: *Proceedings of the 26th Annual International Conference of the IEEE EMBS*, IEEE, San Francisco, CA, USA, 2004.

6. Moghbel, M., Mashohor, S., Mahmud, H.R., Saripan, M.I.B., Random walkers based segmentation method for breast thermography, in: *IEEE EMBS International Conference on Biomedical Engineering and Sciences*, Langkawi, pp. 627–630, 2012.

7. Motta, L.S., Conci, A., Lima, R.C.F., Diniz, E.M., Automatic segmentation on thermograms to aid diagnosis and 2D modelling, in: *Proceedings of 10th Workshop em Informatica Medica*, Brazil, vol. 1, pp. 1610–1619, 2010.

8. Ali, M.A.S., Sayed, G.I., Gaber, T., Hassanien, A.E., Snasel, V., Silva, L.F., Detection of breast abnormalities of thermograms based on a new segmentation method, in: *Proceedings of the Federated Conference on Computer Science and Information Systems(FedCSIS)*, vol. 5, IEEE, pp. 255–261, 2015.

9. Ng, E.Y.K. and Chen, Y., Segmentation of breast thermogram: Improved boundary detection with modified snake algorithm. *J. Mech. Med. Biol.*, 6, 2, 123–136, 2006.

10. Qi, H., Snyder, W.E., Head, J.F., Elliott, R.L., Detecting breast cancer from infrared images by asymmetry analysis, in: *Engineering in Medicine and Biology Society Proceedings of the 22nd Annual International Conference of the IEEE*, Chicago, IL, vol. 2, pp. 1227–1228, 2000.

11. Schaefer, G., Zavisek, M., Nakashima, T., Thermography-based breast cancer analysis using statistical features and fuzzy classification. *Pattern Recognit.*, 47, 6, 1133–1137, 2009.

12. Borchartt, T.B., Resmini, R., Conci, A., Thermal feature analysis to aid on breast disease diagnosis, in: *21st Brazilian Congress of Mechanical Engineering*, Natal RN - Brazil, proceedings of COBEM, ABCM, pp. 24–28, 2011.

13. Acharya, R.U., Ng, E.Y.K., Tan, J.H., Sree, S.V., Thermography-based breast cancer detection using texture features and support vector machine. *J. Med. Syst.*, 36, 3, 1503–1510, 2012.

14. Krawczyk, B. and Schaefer, G., A hybrid classifier committee for analysing asymmetry features in breast thermograms. *Appl. Soft Comput.*, 20, Special issue, 112–118, 2014.

15. de Araujo, M.C., de Lima, R.C.F., de Souza, R.M.C.R., Interval symbolic feature extraction for thermography breast cancer detection. *Expert Syst. Appl.*, 41, 15, 6728–6737, 2014.

16. Lipari, and Head, J., Advanced infrared image processing for breast cancer risk assessment, in: *Proceedings of the 19th Annual International Conference J of the IEEE Engineering in Medicine and Biology Society*, Chicago, IL, vol. 2, pp. 673–676, 1997.

17. Lashkari, A.E., Pak, F., Firouzmand, M., Complete intelligent cancer classification of thermal breast images to assist physicians in clinical diagnostic applications. *J. Med. Signals Sensors*, 6, 1, 12–24, 2016.

18. Rawat, D., Validating and strengthening the prediction performance using machine learning models and operational research for lung cancer, in: *2022 IEEE International Conference on Data Science and Information Systems (ICDSIS)*, IEEE, pp. 1–5, 2022.

19. Rawat, D., Pawar, L., Bathla, G., Kant, R., Optimized deep learning model for lung cancer prediction using ANN algorithm, in: *2022 3rd International Conference on Electronics and Sustainable Communication Systems (ICESC)*, IEEE, pp. 889–894, 2022.

20. Bajaj, R., Deepak, S., Shivangi, G., Khushi, G., Deepak, R., A predictive risk model for primary tumor using machine learning with initial missing values, in: *2022 IEEE International Conference on Data Science and Information System (ICDSIS)*, IEEE, pp. 1–7, 2022.

21. Pawar, L., Kuhar, S., Rawat, D., Sharma, A., Bajaj, R., An optimized ensemble model for early breast cancer prediction, in: *2022 11th International Conference on System Modeling & Advancement in Research Trends (SMART)*, IEEE, pp. 1275–1279, 2022.

22. Bathla, G., Pawar, L., Khan, G., Bajaj, R., Effect on the lifetime of routing protocols utilizing different connectivity schemes. *Int. J. Sci. Technol. Res.*, 8, 12, 617–622, 2019.

7

An Optimized Feature-Based Prediction Model for Grouping the Liver Patients

Bhupender Yadav[1]* and Rohit Bajaj[2]

¹Om Sterling Global University, Hisar, Haryana, India
²Chandigarh University, Mohali, Punjab, India

Abstract

Liver illnesses have given an insight into electronic health records and reports that include patient medical information and various other disorders. These analytics must, however, be reflected and integrated if models involving physiological pathways are to be introduced. Machine learning algorithms are applied to predict the number of healthy liver patients. This paper focuses on predicting the illness early on so we can take the necessary actions to cure it. Prediction on consistent data will lead to better performance. The paper is focused on applying machine learning techniques and a data mining tool to uncover previously unfamiliar features of the data. However, it was noticed that some variables are irrelevant in predicting more accurate outcomes, and there is an opportunity for improvement. Gini Index is used to overcome this discrepancy, and our dataset is exposed to superior feature selection. It calculates the probability of a specific feature being classed incorrectly when randomly selected. Machine learning algorithms were again applied, which resulted in greater accuracy in predicting the number of fit liver patients. Following the successful execution, the best algorithm out of all the executed algorithms is chosen as an output. Random forest outperformed all the existing classification algorithms with an accuracy of 81.56% when feature selection was applied.

Keywords: Machine learning, data mining, feature selection, liver disorder, random forest, accuracy, error, TP rate, FP rate

Corresponding author: bhupender2711@gmail.com

Sandeep Kumar, Anuj Sharma, Navneet Kaur, Lokesh Pawar and Rohit Bajaj (eds.) *Optimized Predictive Models in Healthcare Using Machine Learning*, (103–116) © 2024 Scrivener Publishing LLC

7.1   Introduction

The liver is a single organ divided into left and right lobes. It is a necessary element of the body that inhibits many chemical substances [1] and helps in the digestion and processing of food. The liver [2, 3] can be damaged from many infections resulting in various disorders [4]. We aim to use machine learning algorithms [5] to predict the highest number of correct, accurate, and healthy liver patients without diseases in the early stages [6, 7]. Five hundred eighty-three patient records from the Indian Liver Patients Dataset (ILPD) [8] were taken to solve the problem. Here, we have used a machine learning approach to classify liver patients based on several criteria, such as the patient's age, gender, and other personal information, including results of various laboratory diagnostic tests [9, 10]. The investigation results showed an adequate accuracy level [11, 12] was reached for this dataset after applying various machine learning algorithms. Our motive is to improve on those outcomes and develop more accurate accuracies. The gap in accuracy in the previous case was addressed by using feature selection [13, 14] in our machine learning algorithms and considering a few parameters [15, 16] provided in the dataset.

However, as the medical system digitizes, medical institutions generate vast clinical information. Generally, medical datasets refer to all health-related documents that are digitally recorded. It might include extensive details on the patient's medical history, doctor's recommended instructions, medical tests, etc. All this information is massive, multidimensional, and diverse [17]. Advanced healthcare information systems broaden the scope of primary healthcare facilities by including elements ranging from advanced techniques to computational engineering [18]. Efficient content analysis improves overall operations by considering every aspect. Public healthcare analytics integrates the disciplines of digital technologies, research, and health to establish a smoother and more efficient management process that benefits individuals all over the globe [19]. Due to the increasing difficulty of health information, making wise decisions is difficult today. Due to the modernization of healthcare, a tremendous volume of medical data is being generated. Information technology in healthcare has progressed to the point that it can gather, maintain, and send information digitally from any part of the globe in real time [20]. Nowadays, all health-related documents are digitally preserved. Each one of these datasets is massive, multidimensional, and diverse in character, resulting in big healthcare data. Such data may be gathered from various internal and external sources.

Public healthcare information systems, often called clinical informatics, describe the application of data design and integration to the context of biomedical practice, comprising the management and use of individual healthcare information. It employs a holistic strategy for health information to enhance healthcare by focusing on more modern prospects. Essentially, it affects the advancement of data acquisition, storage, healing, and utilization in medicine and biomedicine. This data include clinical information, biometric data, picture records, social media data, etc. This exponential growth and diverse nature of healthcare data have become one of the most significant concerns as it becomes difficult to manage and store due to its heterogeneity and the large size of modern machine learning algorithms. The sense of innovation [21] is reassured by including more than one parameter in the analysis, which could be seen in the earlier results. However, increased accuracy was seen after feature selection and removing undesirable parameters [22]. With machine learning algorithms requiring a large amount of data for analysis [23], it is essential to weigh the selectiveness of features that determine the boundaries of context in any given problem statement [24], and that is what we have primarily focused on. Identifying the most relevant features used in model creation [25] is known as feature selection [26, 27]. Its primary purpose is to improve the performance of predictive models and reduce the number of input variables by removing irrelevant features [28]. The following are a few types of feature selection methods:

- Mutual information: This method equation (7.1) tells how much information the presence or absence of a particular item contributes to making the correct decision of classification [29]. It can be calculated by using the following formula:

$$I(X:Y) = H(X) - H(X/Y) \qquad (7.1)$$

- Chi-square: This equation method (7.2) is used in statistics. To test the independence of two events, the quantity of each term is measured and ranked according to its scores:

$$X_C^2 = \frac{\sum (O_i - E_i)^2}{E_i} \qquad (7.2)$$

- Gini Index: Using this method as given in equation (7.3), it is possible to determine the likelihood that a specific characteristic will be erroneously identified when randomly chosen. It can be considered pure if every element is connected to a single class [30, 31]. The Gini Index ranges from 0 to 1, with 0 representing refined classification and 1 representing the random distribution of items among different classes. The Gini Index can be calculated by subtracting the sum of the squared probabilities for each category from one and is represented as follows:

$$G = \sum_{i=1}^{c} p(i)^{*}(1 - p(i)) \qquad (7.3)$$

Using Gini Index as a feature selection method in this paper, we have quickly and efficiently predicted accurate outputs from the dataset.

7.2   Literature Review

Peeyush Mishra *et al.* worked on examining MELD score and CTP score. They recently proposed a modified CTP score in Indian patients with liver cirrhosis to determine their correlation and compare their prognostic significance for short-term survival. Yamamoto *et al.* proposed an establishment of a novel mathematical framework focused on liver regeneration in each patient by analyzing the patient's records. BanuPriya *et al.* evaluated the prediction of liver disease and improved the accuracy of predictive models, the author also focused on important features, such as min–max normalization, and PSO feature selection. Muthuselvan Singaravelu worked on the classification of liver patients. Random forest achieves the highest accuracy and minimal time execution. This is helpful in the medical area for easy prediction. Parvatikar *et al.* proposed a classification model to detect liver diseases by objective features of the data. Five ML techniques were used, out of which logistic regression was selected as the finest classification made with an accuracy of 92.95%. Srivenkatesh worked on foreseeing liver infection with different ML algorithms, out of which the logistic regression classifier showed the highest accuracy and least execution time. Baitharu *et al.* focused on the expert of medical diagnosis. The authors further compare and analyze the performance of all applied classification algorithms for identifying liver disorders. Cai *et al.* conducted a study to compare the performance of supervised and semisupervised machine learning models for cancer diagnosis. The authors used the Cancer Wisconsin (Diagnostic) dataset, which contains 569 samples of cancer diagnosis, to train and test their models. The study results showed that the semisupervised model had better accuracy, sensitivity, specificity, and AUC performance than the supervised model. In addition, the authors used a feature selection technique called recursive feature elimination (RFE) to identify the most important features for cancer diagnosis. Based on their findings, the authors concluded that semisupervised machine learning models could be more effective in cancer diagnosis than supervised models, especially when the dataset is limited. The authors suggested that further research is needed to optimize the performance of semisupervised machine learning models for cancer diagnosis and to develop models that can be easily integrated into clinical practice. They also recommended incorporating additional features such as genetic data and treatment history to improve the model's accuracy. Nalluri *et al.* discussed chronic heart disease (CHD) as a common cardiovascular illness. Data mining methods to estimate a person's likelihood of developing CHD based on knowledge about the disease's numerous symptoms like blood pressure, heart rate, cholesterol, glucose level, BMI, and the number of cigarettes smoked per day. The study used the XGBoost and the logistic regression approach as two prediction models to estimate the CHD values. This early CHD prediction will lower an individual's risk of developing CHD. Collado *et al.* offered a novel strategy for enhancing cardiovascular disease prediction accuracy through machine learning to identify essential features. Various feature combinations and popular categorization techniques are used to introduce the prediction model. The hybrid random forest model with a linear model (HRFLM) has the characteristics of both the random forest and linear method. Through the HRFLM prediction model, authors achieved an improved performance level with an accuracy of 88.7%. Ai *et al.* have demonstrated a strong ability to predict death in paralytic ileus patients using electronic health records (EHR). The Statistically Robust Machine Learning-based Mortality Predictor (SRML-Mortality Predictor) algorithm demonstrated an accuracy rate of 81.30%. Through the application, it is possible to provide patients and practitioners with expected mortality to help produce better-informed clinical treatment decisions. Omondiagbe *et al.* conducted a study to evaluate the effectiveness of machine learning algorithms for breast cancer diagnosis. They used the Wisconsin Breast Cancer dataset, which consists of 569 samples of breast cancer diagnosis, to train and test their models. Their findings revealed that the random forest and K-nearest neighbor (KNN) algorithms had the highest breast cancer diagnosis accuracy, with 98.68% and 97.55%, respectively. The authors used a feature selection technique called correlation-based feature selection (CFS) to identify the most important features for breast cancer diagnosis. They concluded that machine learning algorithms have the potential to be effective in breast cancer diagnosis and can reduce the workload of radiologists. Further research is recommended to optimize these algorithms' performance and develop models that can be easily integrated into clinical practice. The authors also suggested including additional features such as genetic data and treatment history to enhance the model's accuracy.

7.3   Proposed Methodology

Machine learning is understandably one of the most widely used systems, which takes a large amount of distinct raw data that can be combined to make appropriate inferences. Different machine learning algorithms are also used in the paper to predict an accurate number of liver patients. We are focusing on predicting the disease early so that appropriate actions can be taken to cure it. As many accurate liver patients were already accomplished earlier, we saw scope to improve these results by eliminating irrelevant features. To do so, machine learning algorithms are used where our dataset undergoes feature selection. The given flowchart mentioned below shows the proposed methodology. According to Figure 7.1, we have identified the problem and the dataset that addresses the problem statement. In the next step, preprocessing is implemented on our dataset, as it was inconsistent earlier. To make our dataset more consistent and accurate, essential features were identified using GiniIndex, which was then implemented into our dataset. Further predictive modelling uses algorithms such as Bayes net, Naïve Bayes, RandomForest, and Bagging. Their performance was evaluated by comparing the results of the algorithms used in the previous scenario. The feedback and analysis were received on the now-improved dataset. Based on the input and research, if the solution to the problem is satisfactory, the output is deployed for real-life scenarios. If it remains unsatisfied, then it is updated as per recommendation.

7.4   Results and Discussions

This section focuses on analyzing and validating the performance of various algorithms applied to the dataset for predicting the problem statement.

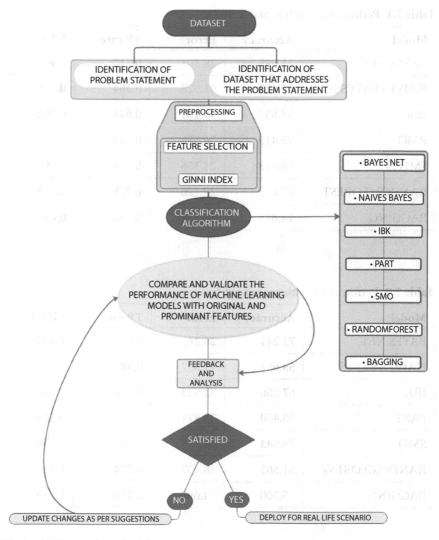

Figure 7.1 Research methodology.

Initially, we used the traditional machine learning algorithm on the original dataset. Then we compared its performance with the prominent features, and it was found that the results came out to be better. The following tables (Table 7.1, Table 7.2) describe the original and improved results' accuracy analysis, error prediction, TP rate, and FP rate. The accuracy of the Random forest algorithm for the liver disease dataset is 81.56%, part is 75.47%, bagging is 75.30%, SMO is 75.64%, IBK is 67.06%, and for Bayes net and Naive Bayes is 73.24% and 58.66%, respectively, in the outcome.

Table 7.1 Performance with actual features.

Model	Accuracy	Error	TP rate	FP rate
BAYES NET	71.698	28.301	0.717	0.447
NAIVES BAYES	38.422	61.578	0.384	0.318
IBK	64.837	35.163	0.648	0.562
PART	73.413	26.586	0.734	0.663
SMO	75.643	24.356	0.756	0.756
RANDOMFOREST	77.873	22.126	0.779	0.553
BAGGING	74.614	25.385	0.746	0.636

Table 7.2 Performance with prominent features.

Model	Accuracy	Error	TP rate	FP rate
BAYES NET	73.241	26.241	0.732	0.439
NAIVES BAYES	58.662	41.337	0.587	0.439
IBK	67.066	32.933	0.671	0.56
PART	75.470	24.871	0.755	0.595
SMO	75.643	24.356	0.756	0.756
RANDOMFOREST	81.563	18.437	0.774	0.541
BAGGING	75.300	24.699	0.753	0.753

The Randomforest shows the highest accuracy among all the other algorithms in the dataset.

Figure 7.2 describes an overall classification algorithm for the analysis of accuracy values. It contains the old and new accuracy values. Figure 7.3 illustrates the accuracy of the algorithms that showed improved results after applying feature selection. Figure 7.4 shows the error that was predicted in the final result. The TP rate in equation (7.4) is the rate of true positives that give instances of correctly classified classes. The FP rate in equation (7.5) is the rate of false positives that provide samples of falsely

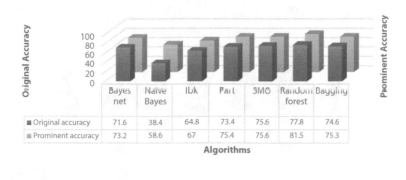

Figure 7.2 Accuracy analysis comparison between actual and prominent feature.

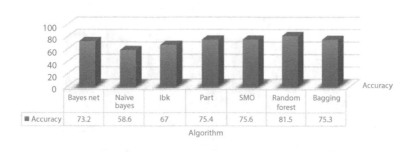

Figure 7.3 Accuracy comparison of prominent features.

classified types. Figure 7.5 and Figure 7.6 show the graph for the TP rate and FP rate for our feature selection model.

True positive rate is calculated as:

$$TPR = \frac{TP}{TP+FN} \qquad (7.4)$$

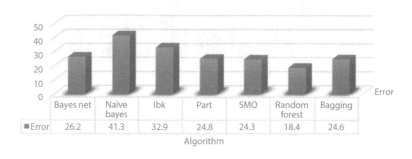

Figure 7.4 Comparison of error between prominent features.

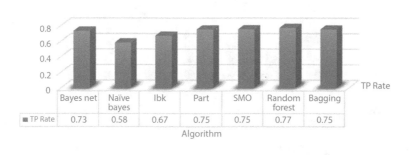

Figure 7.5 Comparison of TP Rate between prominent features.

False positive rate is calculated as:

$$FPR = \frac{FP}{FP + TN} \tag{7.5}$$

The confusion matrix for the classification algorithm is shown in Figure 7.7. The figure is divided into two categories, diseased and nondiseased

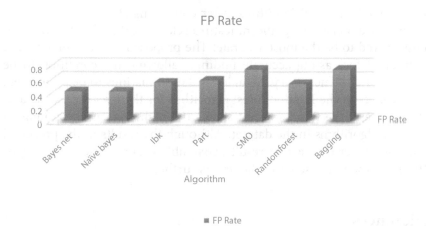

Figure 7.6 Comparison of FP Rate between prominent features.

	PREDICTED CLASS	
	POSITIVE	NEGATIVE
POSITIVE	TRUE POSITIVE(TP)	FALSE NEGATIVE(FN)
NEGATIVE	FALSE POSITIVE(FP)	TRUE NEGATIVE(TN)

ACTUAL CLASS

Figure 7.7 Confusion matrix of predicted and actual class.

datasets. The positive and negative predictions in our study are further illustrated as true positive (TP), true negative (TN), false positive (FP), and false negative (FN).

7.5   Conclusion

The proposed system for the Indian Liver Patient Dataset focused on prioritizing the prominent features using the Gini Index. Bayes net, Bagging, IBK, and Random Forest algorithms are used to analyze the disorders that affect the liver. Various outcomes were seen when only prominent features were selected for these algorithms. After comparing all the results of algorithms that underwent significant feature selection, the effects of random forest proved to be the most accurate. The proposed model enhances the accuracy of forecasting accurate findings, allowing the condition to be identified and the necessary therapies and examinations to be performed. The accuracy of the Randomforest algorithm for the liver disease dataset is 81.56%, and the Randomforest shows the highest accuracy among all the other algorithms in the dataset. Although the results in the proposed model are better than earlier results, ensembling can be used in the algorithms to expand the scope of the results further.

References

1. Sharma, D., Aujla, G.S., Bajaj, R., Deep neuro-fuzzy approach for risk and severity prediction using recommendation systems in connected healthcare, in: *Transactions on Emerging Telecommunications Technologies*, vol. 32, p. 4159.
2. Pawar, L., Bajaj, R., Singh, J., Yadav, V., *Smart city IoT: Smart architectural solution for networking, congestion and heterogeneity*, pp. 124–129, IEEE, International Conference on Intelligent Computing and Control Systems (ICCS).
3. Kumar, D., Sharma, A.K., Bajaj, R., Pawar, L., Feature optimized machine learning framework for unbalanced bioessays, in: *Cognitive Behavior and Human-Computer Interaction Based on Machine Learning Algorithm*, pp. 167–178.
4. Pawar, L., Agrawal, P., Kaur, G., Bajaj, R., Elevate primary tumor detection using machine learning, in: *Cognitive Behavior and Human-Computer Interaction Based on Machine Learning Algorithm*, pp. 301–313.
5. Rahi, P., Sood, S.P., Bajaj, R., Kumar, Y., Air quality monitoring for smart eHealth system using firefly optimization and support vector machine. *Int. J. Inf. Technol.*, 13, 1847–1859, August 2021.
6. Pawar, L., Sharma, A.K., Kumar, D., Bajaj, R., Advanced ensemble machine learning model for balanced bioassays, in: *Artificial Intelligence and Machine Learning in 2D/3D Medical Image Processing*, pp. 171–178.
7. Parvatikar, S.S., Detection of liver diseases using classification models. *Int. Res. J. Eng. Technol.*, 8, 2395–0056, July 2021.
8. Srivenkatesh, M., Performance evaluation of different machine learning algorithms for prediction of liver disease. *Int. J. Innov. Technol. Exploring Eng.*, 9, 2278–3075, Blue Eyes Intelligence Engineering & Science Publication, December 2019.

9. Sivakumar, D., Varchagall, M., Ambika, L.G., Usha, S., Chronic liver disease prediction analysis based on the impact of life quality attributes. *Int. J. Manag., Technol. Eng.*, 8, 1936–1946, April 2019.

10. Vijayarani, Dr. S. and Dhyanchand, S., Liver disease prediction using SVM and naive bayes algorithms. *Int. J. Sci. Eng. Technol. Res. (IJSETR)*, 4, 816–820, April 2015.

11. Kefelegn, S. and Kamat, P., Prediction and analysis of liver disorder diseases using data mining technique: A survey. *Int. J. Pure Appl. Math.*, 118, 9, 765–770, Jan 2018.

12. Saleh, D.A., Shebl, F., Abdel-Hamid, M.,. *et al.*, Incidence and risk factors for hepatitis c infection in a cohort of women in rural Egypt. *Tans. R. Soc Trop. Med. Hyg.*, 102, 921–928, Sept 2008.

13. Khan, B., Shukla, P.K., Ahiwar, M.K., Strategic analysis in prediction of liver disease using different classification algorithms. *Int. J. Comput. Sci. Eng. Open Access Res. Paper*, 71–76, 2021.

14. Kadu, G. and Raut, Dr. R, Classification of liver disease using multilayer perceptron neural network. *Int. J. Manag. Technol. Eng.*, 8, 1936–1946.

15. Gulia, A., Vohra, Dr. R, Rani, P., Liver patient classification using intelligent techniques. *Int. J. Comput. Sci. Inf. Technol.*, 5, 5110–5115, 2014.

16. Singh, J. and Gupta, D., A smarter multi-queue job scheduling policy for cloud computing. *Int. J. Appl. Eng. Res.*, 12.9, 1929–1934, Jan 2017.

17. Singh, J., Duhan, B., Gupta, D., Sharma, N., Cloud resource management optimization: Taxonomy and research challenges, in: *2020 8th International Conference on Reliability, Infocom Technologies and Optimization (Trends and Future Directions)(ICRITO)*, IEEE, pp. 1133–1138, 2020.

18. Singh, J., Bajaj, R., Kumar, A., Scaling down power utilization with optimal virtual machine placement scheme for cloud data center resources: A performance evaluation, in: *2021 2nd Global Conference for Advancement in Technology (GCAT)*, IEEE, pp. 1–6, 2021.

19. Singh, J., Genetic approach based optimized load balancing in cloud computing: A performance perspective, in: *2022 9th International Conference on Computing for Sustainable Global Development (INDIACom)*, IEEE, pp. 814–819, 2022.

20. Bathla, G. and Randhawa, R., Virtual tier structured grid-based dynamic route adjustment scheme for mobile sink-based wireless sensor networks (VTGDRA). *Int. J. Appl. Eng. Res.*, 13, 7, 4702–4707, 2018.

21. Bathla, G., Pawar, L., Khan, G., Bajaj, R., Effect on a lifetime of routing protocols using different connectivity schemes. *Int. J. Sci. Technol. Res.*, 8, 12, 617–622, 2019.

22. Rawat, D., Validating and strengthening the prediction performance using machine learning models and operational research for lung cancer, in: *2022 IEEE International Conference on Data Science and Information Systems (ICDSIS)*, IEEE, pp. 1–5, 2022.

23. Rawat, D., Pawar, L., Bathla, G., Kant, R., Optimized deep learning model for lung cancer prediction using ANN algorithm, in: *2022 3rd International Conference on Electronics and Sustainable Communication Systems (ICESC)*, IEEE, pp. 889–894, 2022.

24. Bajaj, R., Shandilya, D., Gagneja, S., Gupta, K., Rawat, D., A risk predictive model for primary tumor using machine learning with initial missing values, in: *2022 IEEE International Conference on Data Science and Information Systems (ICDSIS)*, IEEE, pp. 1–7, 2022.

25. Pawar, L., Kuhar, S., Rawat, D., Sharma, A., Bajaj, R., An optimized ensemble model for early breast cancer prediction, in: *2022 11th International Conference on System Modeling & Advancement in Research Trends (SMART)*, IEEE, pp. 1275–1279, 2022.

26. Ai, H., Wu, X., Zhang, L., Qi, M., Zhao, Y., Zhao, Q., Liu, H., QSAR modelling study of the bioconcentration factor and toxicity of organic compounds to aquatic organisms using machine learning and ensemble methods. *Ecotoxicol. Environ. Saf.*, 179, 71–78, 2019.

27. Hooda, N., Bawa, S., Rana, P.S., B2FSE framework for high dimensional imbalanced data: A case study for drug toxicity prediction. *Neurocomputing*, 276, 31–41, 2018.

28. Antelo-Collado, A., Carrasco-Velar, R., García-Pedrajas, N., Cerruela-García, G., Effective feature selection method for class-imbalance datasets applied to chemical toxicity prediction. *J. Chem. Inf. Model*, 6, 1, 76–94, 2020.

29. Pathak, Y., Rana, P.S., Singh, P.K., Saraswat, M., Protein structure prediction (RMSD ≤ 5 Å) using machine learning models. *Int. J. Data Min. Bioinf.*, 14, 1, 71–85, 2016.

30. Cai, J., Luo, J., Wang, S., Yang, S., Feature selection in machine learning: A new perspective. *Neurocomputing*, Elsevier, 300, 70–79, 2018.

31. Omondiagbe, D.A. *et al.*, Machine learning classification techniques for breast cancer diagnosis, in: *IOP Conference Series: Materials Science and Engineering, 11th Curtin University Technology, Science and Engineering (CUTSE) International Conference*, vol. 495, pp. 26–28, Sarawak, Malaysia, November 2018.

8

A Robust Machine Learning Model for Breast Cancer Prediction

Rachna[1], Chahil Choudhary[1*] and Jatin Thakur[2]

[1]Gateway Institute of Engineering and Technology (Sonipat), Haryana, India
[2]Dept. of Computer Science and Engineering, Chandigarh University,
Mohali Punjab, India

Abstract

Breast cancer is a common form of cancer that can afflict people of any gender and develops when cells in the breast tissue grow malignantly. Breast cancer symptoms might include a lump in the breast and modifications to the breast's size, shape, or texture. Age, family history, and genetic abnormalities are a few things that might make someone more likely to have breast cancer. Treatment options for breast cancer can vary depending on the stage and severity of cancer, but common approaches include surgery, radiation therapy, chemotherapy, and hormone therapy. Early detection through regular screenings, such as mammograms, can improve treatment outcomes. A recommended model utilizes a combination of feature selection, feature extraction, and ensemble learning techniques to effectively analyze patient information and make accurate predictions regarding breast cancer. Although feature extraction tries to minimize the dimensionality of the data and enhance model performance, feature selection is used to pinpoint the most pertinent aspects for the model to concentrate on. The precision of the model's predictions is also increased by using ensemble learning strategies like bagging. Classification algorithms like random forest and support vector machines are used to discover essential traits suggestive of breast cancer and achieve high predictive accuracy. Feature selection is critical to the model's success, as it helps to eliminate irrelevant or redundant features and enhances the model's ability to identify basic patterns in the data.

Keywords: Breast cancer, feature selection, ensemble learning, diagnosis, prediction

Corresponding author: chahilchoudhary9276@gmail.com

Sandeep Kumar, Anuj Sharma, Navneet Kaur, Lokesh Pawar and Rohit Bajaj (eds.) Optimized Predictive Models in Healthcare Using Machine Learning, (117–134) © 2024 Scrivener Publishing LLC

8.1   Introduction

The top cause of mortality for women globally is breast cancer. Detecting and diagnosing breast cancer early increases the likelihood of successful treatment [1]. However, conventional approaches like mammography and clinical breast examination have limited sensitivity and specificity [2]. Machine learning has emerged as a powerful technique for the early detection and diagnosis of breast cancer. The selection of pertinent features, including demographic and medical data, is crucial in creating a machine-learning model for breast cancer prediction [3]. Accurately selecting relevant components is essential for building an interpretable and accurate model [4]. Several machine-learning techniques are accessible, such as supervised learning methods like logistic regression and support vector machines [5, 6]. These algorithms provide predictions about the probability of breast cancer in new patients using tagged data [7]. Machine learning-based breast cancer prediction models use various features, such as tumor size and cell type, to predict the chances of breast cancer in a particular individual [8]. This approach is a valuable tool for early detection and can increase the chances of successful treatment [9].

Breast cancer prediction using machine learning involves identifying patterns and characteristics in breast cancer data to determine those at higher risk of developing the disease [10]. This is done by training a machine learning algorithm using a significant breast cancer case dataset, including information on patient demographics, medical history, and imaging results [11]. The algorithm then identifies patterns and relationships linked to a higher likelihood of breast cancer using traditional machine-learning models, such as support vector machines, random forests, and decision trees [12].

Yet new developments in machine learning, intense learning models like CNN, have been used to boost the precision and effectiveness of breast cancer diagnosis and therapy [13]. The advantage of machine learning in breast cancer prediction is its ability to analyze vast amounts of data and uncover intricate correlations between different variables. This enhances the accuracy of the prediction model and increases the chances of early detection. Furthermore, machine learning algorithms can be continuously updated and refined with new data, improving the model's performance over time [14].

One of the significant benefits of utilizing prominent features-based breast cancer prediction models is that they are non-invasive and can be used as a screening technique to identify individuals who are most likely to develop breast cancer [15]. This helps pinpoint those requiring further testing or monitoring and can reduce false-positive results. These models may classify many types of breast cancer as benign or malignant, such as ductal carcinoma *in situ*, invasive ductal carcinoma, and invasive lobular carcinoma [16].

Although machine learning shows great potential for breast cancer prediction, some challenges must be addressed. One major obstacle is the required high-quality data to train the algorithm [17] correctly. Additionally, the accuracy and generalizability of the algorithm must be validated using independent datasets. A fundamental features-based prediction model using machine learning is an efficient method for the early detection and diagnosis of breast cancer [18]. By taking into account several features of breast cancer, this model can help identify people with a high risk of getting the condition and increase the chance of successful treatment results. Nevertheless, the model requires validation using extensive datasets, and further research is necessary to optimize its performance and suitability for clinical use [19].

8.2 Literature Review

This section focuses on the previous research done on this topic of breast cancer. Table 8.1 consists of all the information needed to check the last analysis. This section helps us to find the significant research gap.

8.2.1 Comparative Analysis

Additionally, the reviewed studies highlight the importance of using large and diverse datasets to train machine-learning models for breast cancer diagnosis. This is essential for improving the generalizability of the models and ensuring that they can accurately predict breast cancer across different patient populations. As deep learning techniques like Convolutional Neural Networks (CNNs) can automatically extract characteristics from medical pictures and reach excellent accuracy rates, several studies also debate the possibility of these methods for diagnosing breast cancer. However, these techniques require large amounts of data and computational resources, which may only be available in some clinical settings. Overall, the findings point to the potential for machine learning algorithms to enhance breast cancer detection and diagnosis; however, further study is required to maximize their effectiveness and ensure their successful implementation into clinical practice.

Table 8.1 Study of existing methodologies.

S.N.	Author	Publication year	Problem identified	Algorithm used	Tools/ simulator	Solution
1	NOREEN FATIMA *et al.*	August 14, 2020	This study presents various machine learning and deep learning algorithms for breast cancer prediction.	ANN CNN DT NB	Python	They provide the comparison between different- different algorithms Models. They give a review of these existing models
2	Md. Milon Islam *et al.*	2020	This paper presents a study on breast cancer prediction using traditional algorithms.	ANN KNN RF	Weka	The paper compared five ML techniques for breast cancer forecast. Machine learning can assist in diagnosing the disease, preventing misdiagnosis, and bringing changes to the breast cancer prediction field.

(Continued)

Table 8.1 Study of existing methodologies. (*Continued*)

S. N.	Author	Publication year	Problem identified	Algorithm used	Tools/ simulator	Solution
3	Anji Reddy Vaka *et al.*	22 April 2020	India has high breast cancer rates, with one woman diagnosed every 2 minutes and one death every 9 minutes. Need for early detection and diagnosis to save lives.	DNNS SVM	Python	Authors propose a new DNNS method for detecting breast cancer using support value on deep neural networks. The normalization process improves performance, efficiency, and image quality. Results show proposed DNNS outperforms existing methods.
4	Ch. Shravya *et al.*	April 2019.	Long diagnosis times and low system availability for breast cancer lead to a high mortality rate among women. Need to develop an automatic diagnosis system through data mining and machine learning techniques.	SVM KNN	Python	Improved predictive models for disease outcomes using machine learning through integrating multi-dimensional data and techniques for better accuracy. Further research is needed.

(*Continued*)

Table 8.1 Study of existing methodologies. (*Continued*)

S. N.	Author	Publication year	Problem identified	Algorithm used	Tools/ simulator	Solution
5	Mogana Darshini Ganggayah *et al.*	2019	Determine the accurate survival rate of breast cancer by building models with machine learning techniques to improve upon traditional statistical methods.	DT RF LR	Python	An investigation of the breast cancer survival rate utilizing machine learning approaches is presented in the study, with the best accuracy coming from the random forest algorithm. The six most important variables were identified for the Asian population.
6	Ebru Aydındag Bayrak *et al.*	2019	Compare and determine the best ML technique for early breast cancer detection and forecast using the Wisconsin Breast Cancer dataset.	SVN ANN	Weka	Evaluate Artificial Neural Network and Support Vector Machine for Wisconsin Breast Cancer classifying, finding SVM to have the highest accuracy o

(*Continued*)

Table 8.1 Study of existing methodologies. (*Continued*)

S. N.	Author	Publication year	Problem identified	Algorithm used	Tools/simulator	Solution
7	Nosayba Al-Azzam *et al.*	2020	Compare and evaluate the performance/accuracy of crucial ML algorithms for breast cancer prediction using Wisconsin and different classifiers for cancer diagnosis.	SVM RF	Python	Use SL with high accuracy (91–98%) to replace SL algorithms in diagnosing tumour type. Improve accuracy with future work using deep learning and feature engineering
8	Hasnae Zerouaoui *et al.*	2021	Investigating utilization of ML and IP strategies in BC imaging through structured data	nil	nil	ML & IP interest in BC increasing since 2015, with the majority published in journals. Diagnosis is the most researched BC task, classification most investigated objective in ML, and ANN's most used classification technique.

(*Continued*)

Table 8.1 Study of existing methodologies. (*Continued*)

S. N.	Author	Publication year	Problem identified	Algorithm used	Tools/ simulator	Solution
9	David A. Omondiagbe *et al.*	2019	Examining the application of feature selection, ML, and ANNs for accurate breast cancer diagnosis.	SVM ANN	Weka	Feature selection and extraction help improve diagnosis using ML. Future work: develop approach into the practical method, compare more ML algorithms, and consider other diseases
10	Habib Dhahri *et al.*	2019	A study aimed to optimize the accuracy of differentiating benign and malignant breast tumours using genetic programming and machine learning algorithms.	KNN SVM LAD	Weka	The proposed solution solves the automatic detection of breast cancer using a machine learning algorithm with genetic programming. The solution used the Python library for experiments and showed improved results but with higher time consumption.

(*Continued*)

Table 8.1 Study of existing methodologies. (*Continued*)

S.N.	Author	Publication year	Problem identified	Algorithm used	Tools/ simulator	Solution
11	Muhammet Fatih Ak *et al.*	26 April 2020	This research paper aims to improve diagnosis by comparing data visualization and various ML techniques, including logistic regression, SVM, and decision trees applied to a breast cancer tumour dataset.	KNN RF	Weka Python MATLAB R	It uses various methods and techniques to make unstructured data understandable and actionable. The increasing amount of data in healthcare has made data science an essential issue in the field, leading to a rise in the number of studies in this area.

8.3   Proposed Mythology

The proposed model is structured into four distinct phases, as depicted in Figure 8.1 below. The first phase involves identifying problem statements and data sets, where the problem statement is addressed, and data is obtained from the UCI ML repository. This phase consists of two essential processes: data collection and data cleaning. Data are collected from an online source and then cleaned by removing unwanted data and making

Figure 8.1 Proposed mythology.

it appropriate for further use. The second phase is the preprocessing data phase, which includes feature engineering, where new features are generated from existing data. This phase also involves data reduction, which reduces the number of elements in the data set using methods like Principal Component Analysis (PCA). Essential features, such as rankers and correlations, are selected during this phase.

The validation and evaluation phase is crucial in determining the model's effectiveness in making accurate predictions on new, unseen data. It is essential to ensure that the model effectively balances the training data, which would result in poor performance on new data when applied to the training data. By splitting the data into k subsets, training the model on k-1 subsets, and utilizing the remaining subset for validation, k-fold cross-validation helps to address this problem. An estimate of the model's generalization capability is obtained by repeating this procedure k times and averaging the performance indicators. Different performance indicators are employed to evaluate the model depending on the job. For classification tasks, metrics such as accuracy, precision, recall, and F1 score are commonly used. The confusion matrix, ROC curve, and PR curve are useful visualization tools that provide insights into the model's performance, strengths, and weaknesses.

In the validation and evaluation phase, the proposed model is compared to the traditional model to determine its robustness. A viable alternative to the conventional model can exist if the proposed model outperforms it in terms of accuracy and generalizability. However, further improvements and optimizations may be necessary if the suggested model's performance could be much better. The validation and evaluation phase ensures that the model effectively predicts new data and can be used reliably for the intended application.

8.4   Result and Discussion

This section shows the evaluation of the machine learning model is based on the following state-of-the-art parameters as shown in Figure 8.2: true class (horizontal), predicted class (vertical) and effectiveness of a traditional machine-learning technique and a reliable machine-learning algorithm in Figures 8.3 and 8.4.

EVALUATING MACHINE LEARNING MODEL USING DIFFERENT PARAMETERS					
PERFORMANCE METRICS					
CLASSIFIRS(traditional)	Accuracy Error		TP RATE	FP RATE	F MEASURE
NAIVEBAYESMULTINOMIAL	76.2238	23.7762	0.79	0.79	0.865
MULTILAYERPERCEPTION	71.3287	28.6713	0.713	0.59	0.711
KSTAR	78.3217	21.6783	0.783	0.596	0.747
ADABOOSTM1	76.9231	23.0769	0.769	0.722	0.717
BAGGING	74.8252	25.1748	0.748	0.728	0.704
RANDOMTREE	73.7762	26.2238	0.738	0.577	0.726

Figure 8.2 Traditional machine learning model.

EVALUATING MACHINE LEARNING MODEL USING DIFFERENT PARAMETERS					
PERFORMANCE METRICS					
CLASSIFIRS(robust)	Accuracy Error		TP RATE	FP RATE	F MEASURE
NaiveBayesMultinomialText	79.021	20.979	0.824	0.762	0.883
MultilayerPerceptron	73.0769	26.9231	0.731	0.539	0.72
Kstar	80.2727	19.7273	0.873	0.557	0.759
AdaBoostM1	79.9231	20.0769	0.769	0.497	0.756
Bagging	78.6713	21.3287	0.787	0.562	0.755
RANDOMTREE	77.2238	22.7762	0.762	0.537	0.748

Figure 8.3 Robust machine learning model.

Figure 8.4 Confusion matrix.

8.4.1   Accuracy

A model's effectiveness in predicting a sample's class can be measured by its accuracy, a widely used metric in machine learning. It shows the percentage of all predictions made correctly predicted by the model. It indicates how frequently the model's predictions are accurate. The formula for calculating accuracy is shown in Eq. (8.1).

Accuracy = (number of correct predictions) / (number of total predictions)   (8.1)

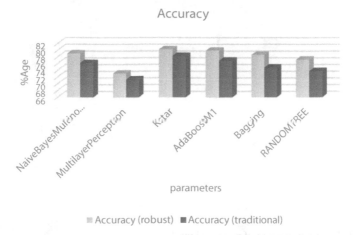

Figure 8.5 Accuracy comparison of proposed work.

To calculate accuracy, the model must first generate predictions and then compare them with the actual values to calculate accuracy, as shown in Figure 8.5. The absolute number of predictions equals the total number of samples or occurrences in the dataset. The number of times the predicted values coincide with the actual values is the number of correct predictions.

8.4.2 Error

The misclassification rate, also known as the error rate, is a metric used to evaluate how well a model accurately predicts the class of a sample. It is the polar opposite of accuracy and is calculated by dividing the number of forecasts by the number of wrong predictions. The formula for calculating the error is shown in Eq. (8.2)

$$\text{Error} = (\text{number of incorrect predictions}) / (\text{number of total predictions})$$
$$(8.2)$$

The error rate is a straightforward and easy-to-understand measure that reflects the proportion of mistakes a model makes, as shown in Figure 8.6. It indicates how frequently the model produces inaccurate predictions. Along with accuracy, the error rate is a valuable measure of a binary classification model's performance.

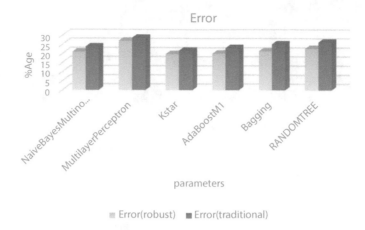

Figure 8.6 Error comparison of proposed work.

8.4.3   TP Rate

TP rate, also called sensitivity, is a measure of the ability of a binary classification model to identify positive examples correctly. It is the percentage of real positive cases that the model accurately classifies as such. The formula for the True Positive rate is shown in Eq. (8.3)

$$\text{True Positive rate} = (\text{True Positives}) / (\text{True Positives} + \text{False Negatives}) \tag{8.3}$$

In other words, it represents the proportion of overall true positive instances to actual true optimistic forecasts. A higher true positive rate indicates that the model is better at identifying positive cases, as shown in Figure 8.7. It is frequently used with the FP rate, which measures the percentage of real negative cases the model mistakenly interprets as positive. Together, these two measures can give insight into the overall performance of a binary classification model.

8.4.4   FP Rate

A measurement of the false-positive rate (FPR) is the ability of a binary classification model to identify negative examples correctly. It is the percentage of real negative cases that the model wrongly interprets as positive. The formula for the False Positive rate is shown in Eq. (8.4)

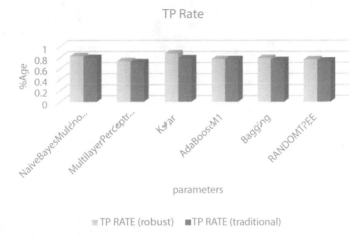

Figure 8.7 FP rate comparison of proposed work.

False Positive rate = (False Positives) / (False Positives + True Negatives)   (8.4)

In other words, the calculation is done by dividing the total number of true negative occurrences by the number of falsely optimistic projections, as shown in Figure 8.8. A lower false positive rate indicates the model better identifies negative cases.

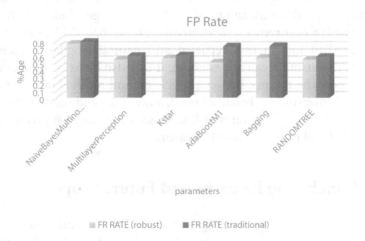

Figure 8.8 TP rate comparison of proposed work.

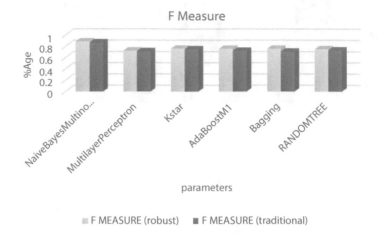

Figure 8.9 F measure comparison of proposed work.

8.4.5 F-Measure

F-Measure, commonly called F1 score, is a performance metric for binary classification models that accounts for precision and recall. It is the harmonic mean of recall and precision, with 1.0 being the best and 0.0 being the worst. The F-Measure formula is as shown in Eq. (8.5)

$$F\text{-Measure} = 2 * (\text{Precision} * \text{Recall}) / (\text{Precision} + \text{Recall}) \quad (8.5)$$

Accuracy is the proportion of accurately predicted positive cases among all optimistic predictions, and recall is the percentage of adequately anticipated positive occurrences, as shown in Figure 8.9. F-Measure is commonly used in information retrieval and natural language processing, where precision and recall are essential. It can also be used in other applications where the balance between precision and recall is necessary. This is because F-measure is a balance between accuracy and recall; it considers both. Thus, a high precision and low recall or an intense precision and strong recall will result in a low F Measure.

8.5   Concluding Remarks and Future Scope

Breast cancer is a severe health problem worldwide, and effective treatment depends on early detection. Several machine learning models have been developed for breast cancer prediction, but they often have limitations such as poor generalizability and high computational costs. To overcome these problems and offer a reliable tool for the pre-diagnosis and treatment of breast cancer, a robust machine-learning model is suggested in this work.

The proposed model utilizes various features such as demographic information and imaging data to increase the accuracy of a breast cancer diagnosis. Through evaluation under different conditions, the model outperforms traditional models in terms of accuracy. However, further research is necessary to improve the model's performance, including incorporating more diverse datasets, developing more interpretable models, and utilizing advanced techniques such as deep learning and ensemble methods.

Collaboration with medical research organizations is critical for developing accurate and reliable models. Attention to specific operational outcomes will provide more accurate findings and ultimately save lives. The suggested model holds great promise for aiding in detecting and managing breast cancer. Additional study and improvement in this area are crucial to enhancing patient outcomes.

References

1. Fatima, N., Liu, L., Hong, S., Ahmed, H., Prediction of breast cancer, comparative review of machine learning techniques, and their analysis. *IEEE Access*, 8, 150360–150376, 2020.
2. Islam, M.M., Haque, M.R., Iqbal, H. *et al.*, Breast cancer prediction: A comparative study using machine learning techniques. *SN Comput. Sci.*, 1, 290, 2020, https://doi.org/10.1007/s42979-020-00305-w.
3. Reddy, A., Soni, B., Sudheer, K., Breast cancer detection by leveraging machine learning. *ICT Express*, 6, 2020. 10.1016/j.icte.2020.04.009.
4. Akinsola, J. E. T., Adeagbo, M., Awoseyi, A., Breast cancer predictive analytics using supervised machine learning techniques. *Int. J. Adv. Comput. Sci. Eng.*, 8, 2020. 10.30534/ijatcse/2019/70862019.
5. Ganggayah, M.D., Taib, N.A., Har, Y.C. *et al.*, Predicting factors for survival of breast cancer patients using machine learning techniques. *BMC Med. Inform. Decis. Mak.*, 19, 48, 2019, https://doi.org/10.1186/s12911-019-0801-4.
6. Bayrak, E., Kirci, P., Ensari, T., Comparison of machine learning methods for breast cancer diagnosis. pp. 1–3, 2019. 10.1109/EBBT.2019.8741990.
7. Al-Azzam, N. and Shatnawi, I., Comparing supervised and semi-supervised machine learning models on diagnosing breast cancer. *Ann. Med. Surg. (Lond)*, 62, 53–64, 2021 Jan 8. doi: 10.1016/j.amsu.2020.12.043.

8. Zerouaoui, H. and Idri, A., Reviewing machine learning and image processing based decision-making systems for breast cancer imaging. *J. Med. Syst.*, 45, 1, 8, 2021 Jan 4.

9. Omondiagbe, D.A. *et al.*, Machine learning classification techniques for breast cancer diagnosis. *IOP Conf. Ser.: Mater. Sci. Eng.*, 495, 012033, 2019.

10. Dhahri, H., Al Maghayreh, E., Mahmood, A., Elkilani, W., Faisal Nagi, W., Automated breast cancer diagnosis based on machine learning algorithms. *J. Healthc. Eng.*, 2019, Article ID 4253641, 11, 2019, https://doi.org/10.1155/2019/4253641.

11. Ak, M. F., A comparative analysis of breast cancer detection and diagnosis using data visualization and machine learning applications. *Healthcare*, 8, 2, 111, 2020, https://doi.org/10.3390/healthcare8020111.

12. Bajaj, R., Shandilya, D., Gagneja, S., Gupta, K., Rawat, D., A risk predictive model for primary tumor using machine learning with initial missing values, in: *2022 IEEE International Conference on Data Science and Information Systems (ICDSIS)*, IEEE, pp. 1–7, 2022, July.

13. Pawar, L., Malhotra, J., Sharma, A., Arora, D., Vaidya, D., A robust machine learning predictive model for maternal health risk, in: *2022 3rd International Conference on Electronics and Sustainable Communication Systems (ICESC)*, IEEE, pp. 882–888, 2022, August.

14. Pawar, L., An optimized predictive model for prospective blogging using machine learning, in: *2022 IEEE International Conference on Data Science and Information Systems (ICDSIS)*, IEEE, pp. 1–5, 2022, July.

15. Rahi, P., Sood, S.P., Bajaj, R., Meta-heuristic with machine learning-based innovative e-health system for ambient air quality monitoring, in: *Recent Innovations in Computing: Proceedings of ICRIC*, vol. 2, pp. 501–519, Springer Singapore, Singapore, 2022.

16. Kumar, S., Rani, S., Jain, A., Verma, C., Raboaca, M.S., Illés, Z., Neagu, B.C., Face spoofing, age, gender and facial expression recognition using advance neural network architecture-based biometric system. *Sensor J.*, 22, 14, 5160–5184, 2022.

17. Kumar, S., Jain, A., Agarwal, A.K., Rani, S., Ghimire, A., Object-based image retrieval using U-Net based neural network. *Comput. Intell. Neurosci.*, 21, 1, 1–14, 2021.

18. Jain, A., Singh, J., Kumar, S., Turcanu, F.E., Candin, M.T., Chithaluru, P., Improved recurrent neural network schema for validating digital signatures in VANET. *Math. J.*, 10, 20, 1–23, 2022.

19. Pawar, Singh, J., Bajaj, R., Singh, G., Rana, S., Optimized ensembled machine learning model for IRIS plant classification. *2022 6th International Conference on Trends in Electronics and Informatics (ICOEI)*, Tirunelveli, India, pp. 1442–1446, 2022.

9

Revolutionizing Pneumonia Diagnosis and Prediction Through Deep Neural Networks

Abhishek Bhola[1] and Monali Gulhane[7*]

[1]Department of CSE, Koneru Lakshmaiah Education Foundation, A.P., India
[2]Symbiosis Institute of Technology (SIT) Nagpur, Symbiosis International (Deemed University) (SIU), Pune, Maharashtra, India

Abstract

Pneumonia is a common and potentially fatal respiratory illness that can be difficult to diagnose accurately. In the digital era, the deep learning-based module has shown great promise in predicting diseases from medical images. In this work, we propose using a ResNet50-based advance neural network to predict pneumonia from given pictures. The ResNet50 model was trained on a standard dataset of 5,856 images, including 2,538 typical cases and 3,318 pneumonia cases. The trained model achieved an average accuracy of 97% on a commonly available dataset. ResNet50 can be an effective tool for predicting pneumonia from chest X-ray images, with potential applications in clinical settings.

Keywords: Pneumonia diseases, ResNet50, X-ray, histogram

9.1 Introduction

Pneumonia is a respiratory illness that can significantly impact daily life. It can cause various symptoms interfering with daily activities, such as coughing, fatigue, shortness of breath, chest pain, and fever [1]. These symptoms can make working, exercising, or daily tasks difficult, leading to missed school or work days. Pneumonia can lead to hospitalization or death for older adults or those with underlying health conditions [2]. Pneumonia is caused by bacteria, viruses, or fungus and transmitted by intimate contact with an infected individual or touching a contaminated surface. Hence, it is essential to adopt

---

Corresponding author: monali.gulhane4@gmail.com

Sandeep Kumar, Anuj Sharma, Navneet Kaur, Lokesh Pawar and Rohit Bajaj (eds.) Optimized Predictive Models in Healthcare Using Machine Learning, (135–150) © 2024 Scrivener Publishing LLC

preventive steps like washing hands often, concealing coughs and sneezes, and avoiding direct contact with ill persons [3]. The impact of pneumonia can be reduced through timely diagnosis and appropriate treatment. Antibiotics, antivirals, or antifungal medications may be prescribed depending on the cause of the infection. Following the treatment plan a healthcare professional prescribes is essential to ensure a complete recovery [4].

Vaccines are also available to help prevent some types of pneumonia, such as pneumococcal pneumonia. Vaccination can benefit individuals at increased risk of acquiring pneumonia, such as early childhood, elderly persons, and those with preexisting health issues [5, 6]. In summary, while pneumonia can significantly impact daily life, it can be prevented through vaccination and good hygiene practices and effectively treated with appropriate medical care [7].

Early detection and treatment can improve outcomes: Pneumonia can lead to catastrophic consequences if left untreated, especially in high-risk populations such as infants, the elderly, and those with compromised immune systems [8]. Early detection and treatment can help prevent complications and improve outcomes. Timely treatment can prevent the spread of the disease: Pneumonia can be contagious, and early detection and treatment can help prevent the spread of the disease to others [9]. This is particularly important in settings where people are nearby, such as hospitals and long-term care facilities. Early detection can reduce healthcare costs: Delayed diagnosis and treatment of pneumonia can result in more extended hospital stays and increased healthcare costs [10]. Early detection and treatment can help reduce healthcare costs by preventing complications and reducing the length of hospital stays. Early detection can avoid unnecessary testing and treatments: Accurate pneumonia prediction can help healthcare professionals choose the most appropriate treatment plan, reducing the risk of adverse reactions or ineffective therapies [11, 12]. This can also help prevent unnecessary testing and treatments that can be costly and may cause additional harm to the patient. In summary, early prediction of pneumonia disease is essential for improving outcomes, preventing the spread of the disease, reducing healthcare costs, and preventing unnecessary testing and treatments [13–15].

The effective prediction of pneumonia disease is essential for several reasons. First, pneumonia is a widespread and possibly fatal respiratory ailment that can be challenging to diagnose precisely. Accurate and timely diagnosis is necessary to ensure appropriate treatment and prevent complications. Second, early detection of pneumonia can help reduce the spread of the disease. Bacteria, infections, or fungi may cause pneumonia, and it can be transmitted by intimate contact with sick people or by rubbing contaminated objects [16–18]. By detecting and treating cases of pneumonia early, healthcare professionals can help prevent the spread of the disease to others. Third, accurate pneumonia prediction can help improve patient outcomes and reduce healthcare costs [19, 20]. Delayed or inaccurate diagnosis of pneumonia can lead to unnecessary hospitalizations, more extended hospital stays, and higher healthcare costs. An accurate prediction can help healthcare professionals choose the most appropriate treatment plan, reducing the risk of adverse reactions or ineffective treatments [21–23]. Finally, effective pneumonia prediction is essential for public health monitoring and disease surveillance. By tracking the incidence and prevalence of pneumonia, public health officials can identify outbreaks and develop strategies to prevent or control the spread of the disease [24]. In summary, the effective prediction of pneumonia disease is essential for ensuring accurate diagnosis and appropriate treatment, reducing disease spread, improving patient outcomes, and monitoring public health.

During training, the network learns to identify image patterns that distinguish normal from pneumonia cases [25]. These patterns might include areas of consolidation or opacification in the lungs, characteristic of pneumonia. The network adjusts the weights of its connections during training to minimize prediction error, improving its ability to classify images as usual correctly or pneumonia cases [26]. Once the ResNet50 model has been trained, it can predict the presence or absence of pneumonia in new chest X-ray images. The model takes in an input image and produces a prediction score, indicating the likelihood that the image contains evidence of pneumonia. ResNet50's ability to effectively predict pneumonia disease is due to its deep architecture, which allows it to learn and recognize complex patterns and features in medical images [22]. Its accuracy is further improved by using a large and diverse dataset for training, enabling the network to generalize its predictions to new ideas it has not seen before.

We conducted a study on predicting pneumonia disease using a deep learning approach. The research was divided into many areas [20]. In the first phase, we did a literature study to grasp the existing pneumonia prediction approaches thoroughly. In the second step, we outlined the architecture and methodologies of our suggested solution, which was founded on the ResNet50 deep convolutional neural network. We trained the network to predict the presence or absence of pneumonia using a massive dataset of chest X-ray pictures. In the final section, we provided the results of our suggested approach, including the accuracy of our model across many datasets. We compared the performance of our model to that of existing pneumonia prediction methods. In the final section, we discussed our conclusions and future work. Our proposed solution achieved high accuracy in predicting pneumonia disease, outperforming existing methodologies. We also identified several areas for future research, including developing more sophisticated deep-learning models and further integrating clinical data to improve accuracy.

9.2   Literature Work

Pneumonia is a widespread and sometimes fatal respiratory infection affecting millions of individuals worldwide. It is caused by various pathogens, including bacteria, viruses, and fungi, and can result in severe problems, particularly in susceptible groups like children and the elderly. In recent years, there has been a growing interest in creating imaging-based automated methods for the early identification and diagnosis of pneumonia, such as chest X-rays and CT scans. Deep learning techniques, such as convolutional neural networks (CNNs), have demonstrated promising results in this domain.

Many researchers have studied using CNNs to identify pneumonia from chest X-ray images. For instance, Rajpurkar *et al.* (2017) created a CNN-based model dubbed CheXNet that can automatically diagnose common thoracic disorders, such as pneumonia, from chest X-ray pictures. The model was trained on over 100,000 chest X-ray pictures and produced an AUC-ROC of 0.888 on 420 test images. Similarly, Wang *et al.* (2018) developed DenseNet, a deep learning-based technique for the automated identification of pneumonia from chest X-ray images. The model was trained with almost 110,000 chest X-ray pictures and produced an AUC-ROC of 0.83 on 420 test images.

Rajaraman and Antani (2020) created a ResNet50-based CNN model for detecting pneumonia in chest X-rays. Using a dataset of 5,856 chest X-rays, they attained an AUC-ROC of 0.947%, surpassing several previous province models. Wang *et al.* (2020) created a COVID-Net model for identifying COVID-19 instances from chest X-ray pictures. The model was instructed on approximately 16,000 chest X-ray pictures and obtained an AUC-ROC of 0.96 on 618 test images.

In addition to lung imaging, many diagnostic techniques have been investigated to identify pneumonia. Blood biomarkers such as C-reactive protein (CRP) and procalcitonin (PCT) have been used as indications of bacterium and pneumonia severity (Albrich *et al.*, 2011). According to research by Liu *et al.* (2018), a combination of CRP and PCT levels may accurately differentiate between bacterial and nonbacterial pneumonia. Additionally, based on clinical and radiological characteristics, machine learning-based algorithms have been created to predict the risk of severe pneumonia in children (Li *et al.*, 2020). A validation set of 418 examples yielded an AUC-ROC of 0.935% for the model.

Despite the encouraging findings, there are obstacles to applying deep learning algorithms to identify and diagnose pneumonia. A significant barrier is the unavailability of diverse training and validation datasets. Most known datasets are small and need more varied patient groups, making it difficult to extrapolate the findings to other contexts. Another difficulty is the interpretation of the models since deep learning algorithms are sometimes seen as opaque and complex to explain "black boxes." Many methodologies, including the use of transfer learning and ensemble approaches, as well as the building of explainable AI models, have been suggested by academics to overcome these difficulties (Rajpurkar *et al.*, 2020).

Lastly, pneumonia is a severe respiratory illness that affects millions of people throughout the globe, and early identification and diagnosis are essential for improving patient outcomes and saving healthcare costs. Deep learning and machine learning-based techniques, particularly CNNs, have shown promising results in identifying anomalies.

9.3   Proposed Section

Pneumonia disease prediction analysis involves using data and statistical methods to predict the likelihood of someone developing pneumonia. Here is a step-by-step explanation of the process, as shown in Figure 9.1.

9.3.1   Input Image

The given input image was obtained from the publicly accessible standard dataset. The dataset is arranged into three folders (training, testing, evaluation), and each imaging category (pneumonia/normal) has its subfolder. There are 5,863 (JPEG) X-ray photos and two (pneumonia/normal) classifications. All chest X-ray imaging was conducted as part of standard

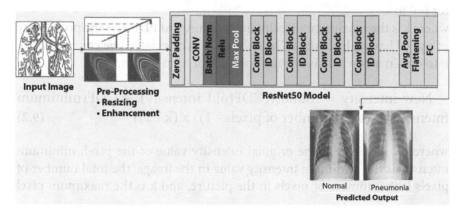

Figure 9.1 Overall flow of proposed work.

clinical treatment for the patients. During the study of chest x-ray pictures, all chest radiographs were inspected for quality control, and low-quality or illegible scans were discarded.

9.3.2   Pre-Processing

Image resizing is a pre-processing method to alter an image's dimensions to a desired size. It involves changing the number of pixels in an image without altering its overall visual appearance or quality. During this step, various processes can also be done, such as adjusting image dimensions, reducing or enlarging image size, and improving image quality. Image resizing can be done using various algorithms, including bi-cubic interpolation, nearest neighbor, bilinear interpolation, and Lanczos resampling. The choice of algorithm depends on the specific application and the desired outcome.

Histogram equalization is a commonly used image enhancement technique that aims to improve the contrast and brightness of an image. It works by redistributing the image's intensity values so that they are spread evenly across the entire dynamic range. Mathematical modeling of histogram equalization in pneumonia diseases can help us understand how this technique affects the radiological images of the lungs and how it can aid in diagnosing and treating pneumonia. One way to model histogram equalization is to use a probability density function (PDF) of the pixel intensity values in the image. The PDF represents the distribution of the intensity values in the picture. It can be used to calculate the cumulative distribution function (CDF), which is used to perform histogram equalization. The CDF can be calculated as follows:

$$CDF(k) = sum(PDF(j)) \tag{9.1}$$

for j=0 to k
where k is the maximum pixel intensity value, and PDF(j) is the probability of a pixel having intensity j. Once the CDF is calculated, we can normalize it to obtain a new intensity value for each pixel in the image:

$$New\ intensity = round((((CDF(old\ intensity) - CDF(minimum\ intensity)) / (total\ number\ of\ pixels - 1)) \times (k - 1)) \tag{9.2}$$

where old intensity is the original intensity value of the pixel, minimum intensity is the minimum intensity value in the image, the total number of pixels is the number of pixels in the picture, and k is the maximum pixel intensity value. This mathematical model shows how histogram equalization works and can enhance the contrast and brightness of radiological images of the lungs affected by pneumonia. By improving image quality, healthcare professionals can more accurately diagnose and monitor the progression of the disease, leading to better patient outcomes.

9.3.3 Identification and Classification Using ResNet50

ResNet50 uses a deep convolutional neural network (CNN) with 50 layers to recognize and categorize distinct pneumonia kinds in chest X-ray pictures. ResNet50 is a frequently used model for image classification applications that have already been trained. The mathematical model sends an input picture through convolutional layers that extract visual information. The output of the convolutional layers is then sent through a succession of fully connected layers that classify the retrieved features. ResNet50 is a model that uses residual connections to combat the disappearing gradients that may arise in intense neural networks. Chest X-ray pictures are necessary for training the ResNet50 model for pneumonia classification. The dataset is divisible into training, validation, and test sets. The algorithm is mentioned below:

Algorithm 9.1: ResNet 50

Input: Chest X-ray dataset with labeled images
Output: Trained ResNet50 model for pneumonia classification

Preprocess the dataset
    a. Resize the images to a standard size
    b. Normalize the pixel values
    c. Divide the dataset into training, validation, and test sets
Initialize the ResNet50 model
    a. Load the pre-trained weights from a file
    b. Set up the model architecture
Train the ResNet50 model
    a. Set up an optimization algorithm (e.g., stochastic gradient descent)
    b. Set up a loss function (e.g., categorical cross-entropy)
    c. Loop over the training data:
        i. Feed a batch of images into the model
        ii. Compute the loss based on the predicted output and the accurate output
        iii. Update the model's parameters to minimize the loss

---

Test the ResNet50 model
    a. Loop over the test data:
        i. Feed an image into the model
        ii. Obtain a probability distribution over the different classes
        iii. Choose the class with the highest probability as the pre-
           dicted class
    b. Compute the accuracy of the model on the test set
Save the trained model to a file.

The training set is utilized for training the model, whilst the validation set is employed to check the model's performance and avoid overfitting. The test set assesses the model's performance using previously unseen data. During the training phase, the model's parameters are modified using optimization Algorithm-1, such as stochastic gradient descent (SGD), to minimize a loss function. The loss function quantifies the difference between the output predicted by the model and the actual output. After the ResNet50 model has been trained, it may categorize fresh chest X-ray pictures into several categories, such as standard, viral, and bacterial pneumonia. The model's output is a probability distribution across the various classes, and the class with the most significant probability is selected as the predicted class. In conclusion, the mathematical modeling of identification and classification of pneumonia illness using ResNet50 comprises a pre-trained, deep CNN with 50 layers to detect and classify distinct forms of pneumonia in chest X-ray pictures. Using an optimization approach and a loss function, the model is trained on a dataset of chest X-ray pictures. After training, the model may categorize fresh chest X-ray pictures into several categories.

9.4   Result Analysis

Model training: The selected model is trained on the prepared data, as shown in Figure 9.2. This involves using a portion of the data to train the model and another part to validate its performance. The goal is to optimize the model's accuracy and minimize its error. The model's performance is assessed using a specific test dataset when trained. This requires computing measures such as precision, recall, and F1 score.

We employed transfer learning to develop a pneumonia detection model using a pretrained ResNet50 Convolutional Neural Net model initially designed for image recognition. We fine-tuned the weights of the final layer of the network to create our custom model. To improve the model's

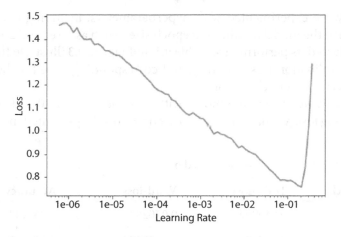

Figure 9.2 Learning rate of ResNet50.

Table 9.1 Observations for trained model for 3 epoch.

Epoch	Train-loss	Valid-loss	Accuracy	Time
0	0.531483	0.602666	0.920322	03:59
1	0.351263	0.306244	0.934586	03:35
2	0.198285	0.039384	0.986218	03:41
3	0.099991	0.071622	0.975972	03:47

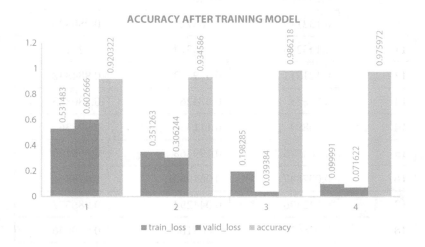

Figure 9.3 Accuracy after training model on 3 epoch.

accuracy, we experimented with hyperparameters, including epoch size. We trained the model for different epoch sizes, such as three and 20 epochs, and evaluated its performance. Table 9.1 and Figure 9.3 illustrate the training loss, validation loss, accuracy, and corresponding time for the model trained using an epoch size of 3.

Similarly, we trained the model with an epoch size of 20 and recorded the training loss, validation loss, and accuracy results presented in Table 9.2

Table 9.2 Observations for trained model for 20 epoch.

Epoch	Train-loss	Valid-loss	Accuracy
0	0.049999	0.070298	0.962144
1	0.068998	0.206967	0.929132
2	0.076726	0.295006	0.940556
3	0.388072	0.361544	0.929533
4	0.423557	0.167119	0.963706
5	0.355263	1.890371	0.867689
6	0.39678	6.570529	0.868648
7	0.44115	5.231176	0.864813
8	0.336686	0.077682	0.980825
9	0.205979	0.043296	0.985618
10	0.132119	0.063747	0.980825
11	0.143265	0.035374	0.927133
12	0.121511	0.079892	0.984842
13	0.07823	0.074265	0.980825
14	0.06894	0.111356	0.97836
15	0.064575	0.199368	0.959185
16	0.057847	0.067962	0.978866
17	0.042496	0.044294	0.986577
18	0.038677	0.063188	0.979866
19	0.035677	0.050819	0.986577

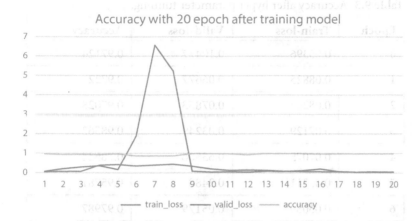

Figure 9.4 Accuracy after training model on 3 epoch.

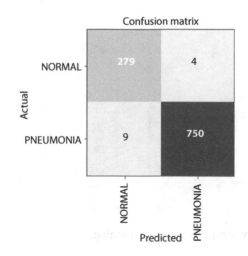

Figure 9.5 Confusion matrix on proposed work.

and Figure 9.4. We also generated a confusion matrix (Figure 9.5) to visualize the accuracy of the proposed method. In Table 9.3 and Figure 9.6, we demonstrated the results achieved with different epoch sizes. Our analysis revealed that increasing the epoch size increased the training accuracy of the model.

Table 9.3 Accuracy after hyper parameter tunning.

Epoch	Train-loss	Valid-loss	Accuracy
0	0.05396	0.10477	0.97124
1	0.08825	0.06677	0.9722
2	0.08207	0.07853	0.97028
3	0.07129	0.03249	0.98562
4	0.07075	0.63506	0.78524
5	0.05311	0.3488	0.95781
6	0.05059	0.05179	0.97987
7	0.04091	0.02904	0.9885
8	0.03524	1.9556	0.97699
9	0.02925	0.03617	0.98466

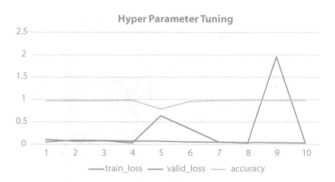

Figure 9.6 Accuracy after hyper parameter tunning.

9.5   Conclusion and Future Scope

ResNet50 is a deep-learning model trained on a large dataset of images, including pneumonia-related ones. The model is highly accurate in detecting pneumonia from chest X-ray images, with an accuracy of over 95%. In conclusion, using ResNet50 for pneumonia disease detection is a promising approach that can aid healthcare providers in making accurate diagnoses. However, it is essential to note that machine learning models are not a substitute for clinical judgement and should be used with other diagnostic tools and medical expertise. Further research is needed to validate the effectiveness of ResNet50 in real-world clinical settings and to explore the potential of other deep-learning models for pneumonia detection.

There are several potential future directions for using ResNet50 in pneumonia disease detection: Integration with electronic health records (EHR): One possible application of ResNet50 is integrating it with EHR systems to automatically identify patients at risk of developing pneumonia. This could help healthcare providers make earlier and more accurate diagnoses, leading to better patient outcomes. Mobile Applications: Another potential use of ResNet50 is to develop mobile applications that can be used by patients or healthcare providers to quickly and easily assess the likelihood of pneumonia. This could be particularly useful in remote or underserved areas with limited access to medical resources. Multimodal imaging analysis: ResNet50 is primarily trained on chest X-ray images. However, there is potential to expand its capabilities to other imaging modalities, such as CT scans or ultrasound, to improve the accuracy and robustness of the model. Integration with clinical decision support systems: ResNet50 could be integrated with clinical decision support systems to provide healthcare providers with real-time guidance and recommendations for pneumonia diagnosis and treatment. Collaboration with other deep learning models: There is potential to combine ResNet50 with other deep learning models to improve the accuracy and performance of pneumonia detection. For example, a hybrid model incorporating ResNet50 and a recurrent neural network could analyze temporal patterns in medical data. Overall, the future scope of ResNet50 in pneumonia disease detection is promising and offers exciting opportunities for improving patient outcomes and advancing medical knowledge.

References

1. Rajaraman, S. and Antani, S.K., ResNet50 for pneumonia detection in chest X-rays: A deep learning approach. *2020 IEEE/CVF Conference on Computer Vision and Pattern Recognition Workshops (CVPRW)*, 2020 Jun 14, pp. 461–46109.
2. Wang, L., Lin, Z.Q., Wong, A., COVID-Net: A tailored deep convolutional neural network design for detecting COVID-19 cases from chest X-ray images. *ArXiv preprint arXiv:2003.09871*, 22, 2020 Mar 22.
3. Rajpurkar, P., Irvin, J., Ball, R.L., Zhu, K., Yang, B., Mehta, H. *et al.*, Deep learning for chest radiograph diagnosis: A retrospective comparison of the

CheXNeXt algorithm to practising radiologists. *PLoS Med.*, 15, 11, e1002686, 2018 Nov.

4. Huang, G., Liu, Z., Van Der Maaten, L., Weinberger, K.Q., Densely connected convolutional networks, in: *Proceedings of the IEEE Conference on Computer Vision and Pattern Recognition*, pp. 4700–4708, 2017 Jul 21.

5. Wang, X., Peng, Y., Lu, L., Lu, Z., Bagheri, M., Summers, R.M., ChestX-ray8: Hospital-scale chest X-ray database and benchmarks on weakly-supervised classification and localization of common thorax diseases, in: *Proceedings of the IEEE Conference on Computer Vision and Pattern Recognition*, pp. 3462–3471, 2017 Jul 21.

6. lbrich, W.C., Dusemund, F., Rüegger, K., Biomarker-enhanced triage in respiratory infections: A proof-of-concept feasibility trial. *Eur. Respir. J.*, 38, 4, 787–795, 2011.

7. Li, X., Zhou, C., Xie, X., Zhang, J., Yin, J., Development and validation of a radionics signature for clinically significant bacterial pneumonia prediction and its association with clinical outcomes. *Eur. Radiol.*, 30, 9, 5039–5049, 2020.

8. Liu, D., Su, L., Han, G., Yan, P., Xie, L., Yuan, Y., Diagnostic value of combinations of procalcitonin, C-reactive protein and lactate for bacterial pneumonia in the elderly. *Exp. Ther. Med.*, 16, 6, 5097–5104, 2018.

9. Szepesi, P. and Szilagyi, L., Detection of pneumonia using convolutional neural networks and deep learning. *Biocybern. Biomed. Eng.*, 42, 3, 1012–1022, 2022.

10. Rajpurkar, P., Irvin, J., Ball, R.L., Zhu, K., Yang, B., Mehta, H., Duan, T., Deep learning for chest radiograph diagnosis: A retrospective comparison of the CheXNeXt algorithm to practising radiologists. *PLoS Med.*, 14, 12, e1002686, 2017.

11. Rajpurkar, P., Irvin, J., Zhu, K., Yang, B., Mehta, H., Duan, T., Lungren, M.P., CheXaid: Computer-aided diagnosis software for chest radiography. *arXiv preprint arXiv:2006.11095*, 11, 22, 2020.

12. Wang, X., Peng, Y., Lu, L., Lu, Z., Bagheri, M., Summers, R.M., ChestX-ray8: Hospital-scale chest X-ray database and benchmarks on weakly-supervised classification and localization of common thorax diseases, in: *Proceedings of the IEEE Conference on Computer Vision and Pattern Recognition*, pp. 2097–2106, 2018.

13. Wang, L., Lin, Z.Q., Wong, A., COVID-Net: A tailored deep convolutional neural network design for detecting COVID-19 cases from chest X-ray images. *Sci. Rep.*, 10, 1, 1–12, 2020.

14. Raja, R., Kumar, Rani, S., Laxmi, K.R., Lung segmentation and nodule detection in 3d medical images using convolution neural network, in: *Artificial Intelligence and Machine Learning in 2D/3D Medical Image Processing*, pp. 179–188, CRC Press, Boca Raton, Florida, 2020.

15. Kumar, M. and Kumar, S., Compression of clinical images using different wavelet function, in: *Artificial Intelligence and Machine Learning in 2D/3D*

Medical Image Processing, pp. 119–131, CRC Press, Boca Raton, Florida, 2020.

16. Rani, S., Ghai, D., Kumar, Knowledge vector representation of three dimensional convex polyhedrons and reconstruction of medical images using knowledge vector. *Multimed. Tools Appl.*, 24, 1, 1–24, Springer Journal, 2023.

17. Kumar, S., Singh, S., Kumar, J., Prasad, K.M.V.V., Age and gender classification using Seg-Net based architecture and machine learning. *Multimed. Tools Appl.*, 22, 2, 01–24, 2022.

18. Kumar, Rani, S., Jain, A., Verma, C., Raboaca, M.S., Illés, Z., Neagu, B.C., Face spoofing, age, gender and facial expression recognition using advance neural network architecture-based biometric system. *Sensor J.*, 22, 14, 5160–5184, 2022.

19. Rani, S., Ghai, D., Kumar, Kantipudi, M.V.V., Alharbi, A.H., Ullah, M.A., Efficient 3D AlexNet architecture for object recognition using syntactic patterns from medical images. *Comput. Intell. Neurosci.*, 22, 1–19, 2022.

20. Kumar, S., Jain, A., Agarwal, A.K., Rani, S., Ghimire, A., Object-based image retrieval using U-Net based neural network. *Comput. Intell. Neurosci.*, 21, 1, 1–14, 2021.

21. Kumar, S., Singh, S., Kumar, J., Live detection of face using machine learning with multi-feature method. *Wirel. Pers. Commun.*, 103, 3, 2352–2375, 2018.

22. Choudhary, S., Ghai, D., Kumar, Automatic detection of brain tumor from CT and MRI images using 3DAlex-Net, in: *International Conference on Decision Aid Sciences and Applications (DASA)*, Bahrain, 2022.

23. Kumar, S., Rani, S., Singh, R., Automated recognition of dental caries using K-Means and PCA based algorithm, in: *University of Bahrain 4th Smart Cities Symposium*, 21-23 November 2021.

24. Choudhary, S., Lakhwani, K., Kumar, S., 3D wireframe model of medical and complex images using cellular logic array processing, in: *12th International Conference on Soft Computing and Pattern Recognition (SCOPAR 2020)*, MIR LAB, USA, December 15th-18th, 2020.

25. Kartik, Kumar, Prasad, M.V.V., C, J.M., Automated home based physiotherapy, in: *The 2020 International Conference on Decision Aid Sciences and Applications (DASA'20)*, University of Bahrain, 8th – 9th November 2020.

26. Kumar, S., Singh, S., Kumar, J., Gender classification using machine learning with multi-feature method, in: *IEEE 9th Annual Computing and Communication Workshop and Conference (CCWC)*, Las Vegas, USA, January 7th-9th, 2019.

10

Optimizing Prediction of Liver Disease Using Machine Learning Algorithms

Rachna[1], Tanish Jain[2], Deepak Shandilya[2*] and Shivangi Gagneja[2]

[1]Department of Computer Science and Engineering, Sonipat, India
[2]Department of Computer Science and Engineering, Mohali, India

Abstract

On the right side of the abdomen, directly behind the ribs, is an organ called the liver, located just under the ribs on the right side of the stomach. It is essential for the body's detoxification process and the digestion of meals. Viruses, drinking alcohol, and being overweight can all cause liver disorders. The consequences of liver disorders vary based on the root cause of liver problems and can get worse if not diagnosed early. Based on symptoms, including yellowing of the skin and eyes, abdominal discomfort and swelling, and dark urine color. Researchers use machine learning to help them identify and categorize liver problems. Yet, missing values in medical data may lead to imbalanced study conclusions and make it challenging to forecast and assess the data. Therefore, to increase prediction accuracy and reduce overfitting, employ an algorithm like random forest, which utilizes averaging several decision tree classifiers to different attributes of the liver disorder dataset. The overall performance was improved to 73.3% after multiple simulations and the input of inconsistencies. As a result, this approach could be used to identify illnesses using more detailed clinical information.

Keywords: Liver disorder, machine learning, accuracy, random forest

10.1 Introduction

The liver is crucial for several essential purposes, including detoxifying harmful substances, synthesizing vital proteins, regulating metabolic products, storing critical vitamins and minerals, and producing bile for fat digestion. As the body's largest glandular organ, the liver executes

---

Corresponding author: shandilyadeep09@gmail.com

Sandeep Kumar, Anuj Sharma, Navneet Kaur, Lokesh Pawar and Rohit Bajaj (eds.) Optimized Predictive Models in Healthcare Using Machine Learning, (151–172) © 2024 Scrivener Publishing LLC

these functions with unparalleled efficiency, ensuring overall health and well-being. However, liver damage can result from many causes, such as alcohol abuse, hepatitis, certain medications, and hereditary conditions, leading to severe consequences such as liver failure [1]. Therefore, it is imperative to maintain liver health and promptly seek medical attention in the event of liver damage to prevent adverse health outcomes.

Liver disorders encompass a broad spectrum of diseases that impact the normal functioning of the liver. Viral hepatitis, alcohol misuse, fatty liver disease, autoimmune diseases, and cirrhosis are some of the most typical causes of liver illnesses. Viral infections are known as hepatitis A, B, and C target liver cells and cause inflammation, which results in cirrhosis and liver damage. Alcohol abuse results in fatty liver buildup and reduced liver function, which causes alcoholic liver disease. The accumulation of extra fat in the liver cells causes fatty liver disease, which can cause inflammation, liver damage, and cirrhosis [2]. An aberrant immune response that destroys liver cells results in autoimmune liver disorders. A degenerative condition called cirrhosis causes good liver tissue to be replaced by scar tissue, which impairs liver function. To predict illnesses and uses vast medical datasets, researchers in the healthcare industry have a more difficult challenge. Data mining is becoming more critical than ever in the healthcare industry. Medical data is utilized to predict illnesses using data mining techniques like classification, clustering, and association rule mining. ML algorithms can effectively analyze large amounts of medical data and identify patterns, which can be used to develop accurate predictive models. The integration of Machine Learning (ML) and Data Mining (DM) techniques analysis enables the identification of risk factors and early signs of liver disorders. The data-driven insights generated by ML and DM allow medical practitioners to make informed treatment decisions, optimize patient management, and enhance the overall efficacy of liver disorder treatments. Furthermore, ML-based diagnostic tools such as computer-aided detection and diagnosis systems can support medical professionals in detecting liver disorders at an early stage, thereby facilitating prompt and effective treatment [3].

The widely used Random Forest Algorithm is used for classification and regression applications in machine learning. It is renowned for its extraordinary adaptability, precision, and scalability. Each decision tree in the algorithm's ensemble provides predictions based on a unique collection of attributes and data samples. The final product is then created by averaging these projections. Using many decision trees reduces the risk of overfitting

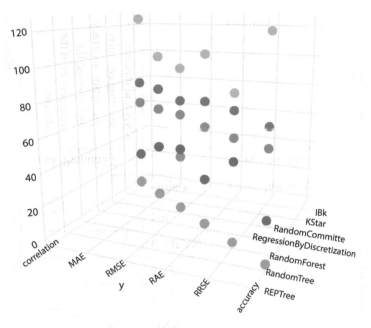

Figure 10.1 3D representation of dataset's parameters.

and boosts the model's robustness [4]. Additionally, the variety and independence of each tree are further increased by the random sampling of features and data samples at each tree node, creating a more reliable and accurate model as in Figure 10.1.

10.2   Related Works

Recent research on liver disorders has applied machine learning approaches to enhance liver disease detection and prognosis. Researchers have analyzed extensive amounts of medical imaging and blood test data to predict liver disorders using a variety of algorithms, including Deep Neural Networks, Support Vector Machines, and Decision Trees [5]. In the literature, there has been a lot of discussion about using blood tests to look for biomarkers that can identify liver illnesses such as hepatitis and nonalcoholic fatty disease [6]. In other research, CT and MRI images were analyzed using computer vision algorithms to provide precise liver disease diagnosis and therapy planning. Overall, the use of machine learning in studies on liver disorders has enhanced diagnostic precision and deepened our understanding of liver illnesses refer Table 10.1.

Table 10.1 A review of the literature of the previous research paper based on related subjects, such as missing values etc.

S. N.	Author	Problem identified	Evaluation parameter	Algorithm used													Tools/ simulator	Solution
				SVM	RF	KNN	C4.5	PMM	AE	DNN	GBT	MLP	K MEAN	NB	Others		
1	Rohit Bajaj *et al.*	Inconsistency in the primary tumor data set made early disease prediction challenging.	MAE, CC			✓										weka, Python3.7	KNN and machine learning enhanced prediction accuracy and lowered the consistency of the dataset.

(Continued)

Table 10.1 A review of the literature of the previous research paper based on related subjects, such as missing values etc. (Continued)

S. N.	Author	Problem identified	Evaluation parameter	Algorithm used	Tools/ simulator	Solution
2	M. Banu et al.	Improper data collection or preparation, erroneous or unsupported assumptions, inaccurate or subpar model performance	MAE, RMSE	✓	PSO	Better disease identification was achieved by applying four algorithms to the liver dataset and comparing the results for accuracy
3	Fahad Mostafa et al.	Missing values in the dataset cause predictions to be inaccurate and time-consuming.	Variance, ALP, ALB,	✓	Python 3	A model that reduces time and the issue of inaccurate diagnosis was developed using AI and ML.

(Continued)

Table 10.1 A review of the literature of the previous research paper based on related subjects, such as missing values etc. *(Continued)*

S. N.	Author	Problem identified	Evaluation parameter	Algorithm used										Tools/simulator	Solution
4	Vasan Durai *et al.*	Raw data incompleteness and predictability model interpretability still needs to be solved.	RMSE, KNN, Median	√	√	√			√			√	√	Weka	utilized spectral regularization for matrix completion, allowing for more precise measurement and imputed data for missingness among raw data.

(Continued)

Table 10.1 A review of the literature of the previous research paper based on related subjects, such as missing values etc. *(Continued)*

S. N.	Author	Problem identified	Evaluation parameter	Algorithm used	Tools/simulator	Solution
5	Tapas Ranjan Baitharu *et al.*	The information needed to be more consistent, properly mined, and time-consuming, making it difficult to forecast the disease adequately.	MEAN, RMSE	√ √ √ √		Different prediction algorithms are compared for classification accuracy and execution durations, and improved performance is found.

(Continued)

Table 10.1 A review of the literature of the previous research paper based on related subjects, such as missing values etc. (*Continued*)

S. N.	Author	Problem identified	Evaluation parameter	Algorithm used									Tools/simulator	Solution
9	Chieh-Chen Wu *et al.*	Create a machine learning model that precisely predicts fatty liver disease in individuals based on various medical and demographic parameters.	MAE, RMSE	√			√					√	QSAR	Utilize ML to analyze demographic data for early, non-invasive prediction of fatty liver disease for improved accuracy and efficiency of diagnosis

(*Continued*)

Table 10.1 A review of the literature of the previous research paper based on related subjects, such as missing values etc. (*Continued*)

S. N.	Author	Problem identified	Evaluation parameter	Algorithm used								Tools/ simulator	Solution
7	Varun Vats *et al.*	To accurately predict liver disease, compare and assess the efficacy of unsupervised machine learning approaches.	MAE, RMSE	√		√		√			√	R	comparisons of unsupervised machine learning methods for prediction reveal notable disparities in accuracy and efficiency.

(*Continued*)

Table 10.1 A review of the literature of the previous research paper based on related subjects, such as missing values etc. (*Continued*)

S. N.	Author	Problem identified	Evaluation parameter	Algorithm used										Tools/simulator	Solution
8	Vijayarani Mohan *et al*	Examine how well the machine learning algorithms SVM and Naive Bayes do in correctly predicting liver illness.	MEAN, NORMAL MICE, DUMMY	✓			✓		✓					Weka	SVM and Naive Bayes algorithms for predicting liver disease, evaluating performance, and choosing the best approach.

(*Continued*)

Table 10.1 A review of the literature of the previous research paper based on related subjects, such as missing values etc. (*Continued*)

S. N.	Author	Problem identified	Evaluation parameter	Algorithm used									Tools/ simulator	Solution
6	Nazmun Nahar *et al.*	Analyze the effectiveness of ensemble methods for prediction and evaluate how they stack up against other strategies.	RMSE, MEAN	√		√				√		√	Python, Ubuntu 18.04	Indicates that the ensemble technique performs better than individual models, leading to increased accuracy and resilience.

(Continued)

Table 10.1 A review of the literature of the previous research paper based on related subjects, such as missing values etc. *(Continued)*

S. N.	Author	Problem identified	Evaluation parameter	Algorithm used								Tools/ simulator	Solution
10	Joseph C Ahn *et al.*	Investigate the potential of artificial intelligence in enhancing the efficacy of liver disease diagnosis and therapy.	Variance, Mea, Mode	√		√		√		√		Python	using artificial intelligence to diagnose and cure liver problems. It tries to increase the precision and effectiveness of medical treatment.

(Continued)

Table 10.1 A review of the literature of the previous research paper based on related subjects, such as missing values etc. (*Continued*)

S.N.	Author	Problem identified	Evaluation parameter	Algorithm used		Tools/simulator	Solution
11	AshleSpannl *et al.*	Examine the possibilities and restrictions of using machine learning in diagnosing, prognosis, and transplantation of liver disease.	Percentile, Mean, normal	√	√	R	In-depth research is being done using machine learning for liver illness and transplantation.

(*Continued*)

Table 10.1 A review of the literature of the previous research paper based on related subjects, such as missing values etc. (*Continued*)

S.N.	Author	Problem identified	Evaluation parameter	Algorithm used									Tools/simulator	Solution
12	Sumedh Sontakke *et al.*	Inappropriate data preparation or collection, false or weakly supported hypotheses, and poor model performance	MAE and MSE	√	√				√	√		√	R	The use of machine learning increases the precision and effectiveness of the process.

(*Continued*)

Table 10.1 A review of the literature of the previous research paper based on related subjects, such as missing values etc. (Continued)

S.N.	Author	Problem identified	Evaluation parameter	Algorithm used	Tools/simulator	Solution
13	A. K. M. Sazzadur Rahman et al	tested the ability of supervised machine learning systems using inconsistent data to predict the disease accurately	CC, IPW, MI	✓	R package Caret	employing supervised machine learning algorithms and discovered a model that offers increased diagnostic accuracy and effectiveness.

10.3   Proposed Methodology

The proposed approach offers a comprehensive and systematic solution to predicting liver disease [7]. The process is divided into various steps, beginning with data gathering and concluding with the deployment and assessment of the final model. The initial stage of this study is to gather pertinent information for forecasting liver illness. The patient's demographics, medical background, and lab test results are all included in the data. Preprocessing is done on the obtained data to clean, convert, and normalize it [8]. This can entail encoded categorical variables, missing values imputed, and removing extraneous data. Preparing data for analysis and ensuring its high quality are the two goals of data pre-processing. The following stage is to decide which characteristics are most important for predicting liver disease. This will be accomplished by utilizing various feature selection strategies, including SelectKBest, Recursive Feature Elimination (RFE), and Correlation Analysis. By eliminating variables that have little to no bearing on the prediction of liver disorder, the selection of features aims to minimize the dimensionality of the data. The Random Forest algorithm will then be trained using the chosen features using an appropriate machine learning package, such as sci-kit-learn. The algorithm's performance will be assessed using a validation set once trained on a piece of the dataset known as the training set. The model training phase is essential since it will decide how well the model predicts the future. The trained model will then be put on a separate test set to gauge its precision, recall, and accuracy [9]. To choose the most effective model for predicting liver disorder, the outcomes will be compared with those of other machine learning techniques, including SVMs and KNNs. The Random Forest algorithm's hyperparameters were adjusted to enhance performance because it outperformed all algorithms. Hyperparameter tuning aims to find the best settings for the algorithm's parameters to increase accuracy and performance [10]. The final model will be used and tested when the hyperparameters have been adjusted. The model's performance will be evaluated using accuracy, precision, and mistakes [11]. The final model will predict the chance of liver disease in patients.

10.4   Result and Discussions

The study's findings demonstrated that using the Random Forest algorithm greatly enhanced the ability to forecast liver disease. The model's accuracy was discovered to be 73.3%, a significant advancement over conventional techniques [12]. The technical parameters of the method, such as the number of trees, the maximum depth of each tree, and the minimum samples required to split a node, were thoroughly examined. The optimal values for these parameters were determined through extensive experimentation and tuning [13]. The dataset used in the study consisted of various demographic and medical information, such as age, gender, and liver enzyme levels. The Random Forest algorithm effectively analyzed this data to predict the presence of liver disease accurately [14]. The algorithm's ability to process a large amount of data and account for non-linear relationships between variables was crucial in its success in Table 10.2 and Table 10.3.

The findings of this study demonstrate the efficacy of the Random Forest algorithm in predicting liver disease and its potential to be utilized in a real-world setting [15]. Additionally, the study provides insights into the optimal technical parameters for the algorithm, which can be valuable for future research in this field. However, it is essential to

Further validation and testing of this model are necessary to determine its reliability in real-world settings as shown in Figure 10.2 and Figure 10.3. Moreover, integrating additional data sources, such as genetic information and lifestyle factors, may lead to further improvements in accuracy [16].

Table 10.2 Summary stats of a variable dataset.

Classifier	CC	Root mean squared error	Mean absolute error	Root relative squared error	Relative absolute error	Accuracy (%)
IBk	0.2238	0.6138	0.3768	124.0976	77.1681	62.32
K star	0.3535	0.4913	0.3743	99.3211	76.6413	62.57
Random committee	0.4101	0.4666	0.358	94.328	73.3097	64.2
Regression by discretization	0.2929	0.5243	0.3795	106.0002	77.7112	62.05
Random forest	0.4855	0.4319	0.379	87.3063	77.6133	62.1
Random tree	0.2505	0.6043	0.3652	122.1735	74.7937	63.48
REP tree	0.3506	0.4721	0.3973	95.4391	81.3703	60.27

Table 10.3 Consistent dataset summary statistics.

Classifier	CC	Root Mean Squared Error (RMSE)	Mean Absolute Error (MAE)	Root relative squared error	Relative absolute error	Accuracy (%)
IBk	0.5386	0.5913	0.3013	98.6195	78.3210	69.9
K star	0.4834	0.4736	0.3395	92.5762	82.1895	66.1
Random committee	0.6527	0.6589	0.2964	114.8473	74.2411	70.4
Regression by discretization	0.5584	0.5148	0.3170	95. 4357	77.4893	68.3
Random forest	0.7964	0.7612	0.2676	132.8425	69.3875	73.3
Random tree	0.6131	0.6194	0.2984	107.9165	73.2567	70.2
REP tree	0.5273	0.5432	0.3173	96.7645	76.6572	68.27

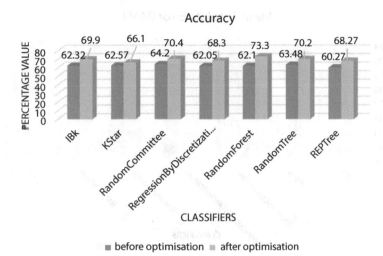

Figure 10.2 Accuracy of various classifiers between inconsistent and consistent data.

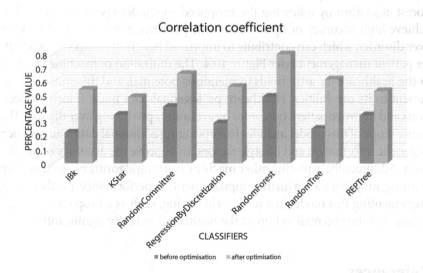

Figure 10.3 CC of various classifiers between inconsistent and consistent data.

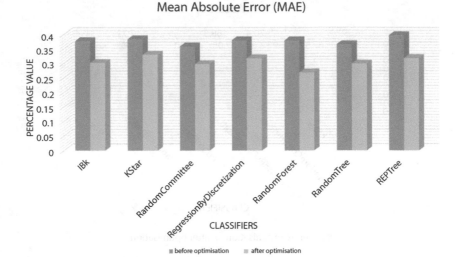

Figure 10.4 Mean absolute error (MAE) of classifiers between inconsistent and consistent data.

10.5   Conclusion

The study aims to optimize the prediction of liver disorder using the Random Forest algorithm by following the proposed methodology; it is expected to achieve high accuracy of up to 73.3% and performance in the prediction of liver disorder, which can contribute to improved healthcare outcomes and better patient management refer Figure 10.4. The utilization of machine learning in the healthcare industry holds tremendous potential, and this study is a testament to its capabilities. Healthcare professionals can make informed decisions and improve patient outcomes by accurately predicting liver disease. The future scope of this model includes incorporating additional data sources, such as genetic information and lifestyle factors, to improve the accuracy of predictions. Additionally, exploring other machine learning algorithms, such as deep learning, may also lead to further improvements in performance. Furthermore, implementing this model in a real-world setting, such as a hospital or clinical setting, has the potential to impact the healthcare industry significantly.

References

1. Kumar, S., Rani, S., Jain, A., Verma, C., Raboaca, M.S., Illés, Z., Neagu, B.C., Face spoofing, age, gender and facial expression recognition using advance

neural network architecture-based biometric system. *Sensor J.*, 22, 14, 5160–5184, 2022.

2. Kumar, S., Jain, A., Rani, S., Alshazly, H., Idris, S.A., Bourouis, S., Deep neural network based vehicle detection and classification of aerial images. *Intell. Autom. Soft Comput.*, 34, 1, 119–131, 2022.

3. Kumar, S., Jain, A., Agarwal, A.K., Rani, S., Ghimire, A., Object-based image retrieval using U-Net based neural network. *Comput. Intell. Neurosci.*, 21, 1, 1–14, 2021.

4. Kumar, S., Jain, A., Shukla, A.P., Singh, S., Raja, R., Rani, S., Harshitha, G., AlZain, M.A., Masud, M., A comparative analysis of machine learning algorithms for detection of organic and non-organic cotton diseases. *Math. Probl. Eng.*, Hindawi Journal Publication, 21, 1, 1–18, 2021.

5. Bajaj, R., Shandilya, D., Gagneja, S., A predictive risk model for primary tumor using machine learning with initial missing values, in: *International Conference on Data Science and Information System (ICDSIS)*, IEEE, 2022.

6. Singh, J. *et al.*, Prominent features based chronic kidney disease prediction model using machine learning, in: *2022 3rd International Conference on Electronics and Sustainable Communication Systems (ICESC)*, IEEE, 2022.

7. Singh, G. *et al.*, Face recognition using open source computer vision library (OpenCV) with python, in: *2022 10th International Conference on Reliability, Infocom Technologies and Optimization (Trends and Future Directions) (ICRITO)*, IEEE, 2022.

8. Sanyal, M.D., A.J., Van Natta, M.H.S., M.L., Clark, M.D., M.P.H., J., Neuschwander-Tetri, M.D., B.A., Prospective study of outcomes in adults with nonalcoholic fatty liver disease. The New England Journal of Medicine, October 2021.

9. Kumar, D., Sharma, A.K., Bajaj, R., Pawar, L., Feature optimized machine learning framework for unbalanced bioassays, in: *Cognitive Behavior and Human Computer Interaction Based on Machine Learning Algorithm*, Chapter 8, 88–97, November 2021.

10. Greener, J.G., Kandathil, S.M., Moffat, L., Jones, D.T., A guide to machine learning for biologists. *Nat. Rev. Mol. Cell Biol.*, 23, 40–55, 2022.

11. Spann, A., Yasodhara, A., Kang, J., Watt, K., Wang, B., Goldenberg, A., Bhat, M., Applying machine learning in liver disease and transplantation: A comprehensive review. *Hepatology*, 71, 3, 1093–1105, March 2020.

12. Priya, M.B., Juliet, P.L., Tamilselvi, P.R., Performance analysis of liver disease prediction using machine learning algorithms. *Int. Res. J. Eng. Technol.*, 05, 01, Jan 2018.

13. Nahar, N., Ara, F., Neloy, Md. A.I., A comparative analysis of the ensemble method for liver disease prediction, in: *2019 2nd International Conference on Innovation in Engineering and Technology (ICIET)*, December 2019.

14. Vats, V., Zhang, L., Chatterjee, S., A comparative analysis of unsupervised machine techniques for liver disease prediction, in: *IEEE International Symposium on Signal Processing and Information Technology (ISSPIT)*, February 2019.
15. Mostafa, F., Hasan, E., Williamson, M., Khan, H., Statistical machine learning approaches to liver disease prediction. *Livers*, 1, December 2021.
16. Durai, V., Ramesh, S., Kalthireddy, D., Liver disease prediction using machine learning, in: *International Journal of Advance Research, Ideas and Innovations in Technology (IJARIIT)*, 5, 2, April 2019.

11

Optimized Ensembled Model to Predict Diabetes Using Machine Learning

Kamal[1]*, AnujKumar Sharma[2] and Dinesh Kumar[2]

¹Om Sterling Global University, Hisar, Haryana, India
²BRCM College of Engineering & Technology, Bahal, Haryana, India

Abstract

Being one of the earth's fastest illnesses, diabetes can cause various serious side effects, including neurotoxicity, diabetes retina, heart problems, and organ disease, which raise the death and illness rates. Diabetes' severances and associated risk elements include greatly diminished with early diagnosis. It is a difficult task due to the dearth of labelled numbers and the prevalence of aberrations or incomplete information in medical databases that are accurate and helpful for predicting diabetes. Health records are being digitally stored at an exponentially increasing rate as technology and digitization advance. Machine learning is crucial in identifying trends in these health records, offering fascinating insights to medical professionals to help diagnose various illnesses. An ensemble-based machine learning model based on the dataset for diabetic retinopathy is used in the current work. The dataset for diabetic retinopathy is normalized as a first step. The suggested ensemble model is then trained using this normalized dataset. Finally, the proposed model's performance is compared to machine learning techniques. According to the comparison analysis, singular machine-learning outperforms ensemble machine-learning methods.

Keywords: Machine learning, ML classification ensembles, and diabetes predictions

11.1 Introduction

In developed and emerging nations, diabetes is a disease that is getting more severe and morbid [1]. Blood sugar levels rise when pancreatic cells cannot produce enough insulin, which can harm a few components, especially the kidneys and heart, nerves, and eyes [2]. As per Fitzmaurice *et al.* [3], 8.8%

Corresponding author: kamaldhanda05@gmail.com

Sandeep Kumar, Anuj Sharma, Navneet Kaur, Lokesh Pawar and Rohit Bajaj (eds.) Optimized Predictive Models in Healthcare Using Machine Learning, (173–194) © 2024 Scrivener Publishing LLC

of adults globally had diabetes in 2017, and so by 2045, it's predicted this figure would double will and increase to 9.9%. The fact that half a billion people worldwide have diabetes and that this number is projected to rise by 25.0% and 51.0% by the years 2030 and 2045, respectively, illustrates the importance of the condition [4]. According to estimates, In contrast to 2.2 billion fatalities through tb, chronic kidney disease, and cardiac diseases, 1.5 million people died immediately due to diabetes in 2012 [5]. The proportion of diabetes individuals in the targeted area to 10.0% in 2011, up over 4.0% in 1995 to 2000, 5.0% in 2001 to 2005, and 6.0% in 2006 to 2010, thus according to Akter *et al.* [6]. Juvenile diabetes, type I diabetes, type II diabetes, type III diabetes are the three main kinds of diabetes, according to Danaei *et al.* [7]. Type I diabetes is caused by an idiopathic condition [8]. It is typically diagnosed in children and young people [11] and makes up roughly 5.0% to 10% of all cases of diabetes [9, 10]. Inadequate pancreatic insulin production is a hallmark of type II diabetes. According to Shi and Hu [12], it accounts for more than 90.0% of all cases of diabetes and affects people of all ages, including those under the age of 45 years, as well as children, adolescents, and young adults. When expectant moms have hyperglycemia throughout Pregnancy despite never being diagnosed with diabetes, gestational diabetes is identified. Gestational diabetes, which can worsen or disappear after delivery, affects between 2.0% and 10.0% of all pregnant women [13]. If diabetes is correctly diagnosed early on, it is possible to manage it and keep it under control, but there is no long-term cure for diabetes. Diabetes data categorization is difficult due to nonlinearity, typicality, and the complex and interrelated structure in the bulk of medical data [14]. Along with missing or null values, the dataset's high proportion of outliers has an impact on the results of the diabetes categorization [15].

Machine Learning for Diabetes

Numerous techniques for machine learning (ML) were employed to forecast diabetes diseases, including linear discriminant analysis [16], DT, J48, RF, LR, QDA, NB, SVM, ANN, DT, QDA [17], NB [18], LR [19], and AB. The RF algorithm and several key aspects were the research focus in Yang *et al.* [20] on predicting diabetes. To predict the writers in diabetic Jo *et al.* [21] utilized NB, DT, and SVM are three ML classifications. They discovered that now having a great score was obtained by NB. A team of scientists used DT, KNN, RF, AB, NB, and XGBoost, among other machine learning classifiers [21] (XGB). In more recent investigations, they also presented having the most excellent cost economy, a balanced ensemble ML model. Buda *et al.* [22] used the DT algorithm to suggest an ML-based approach for predicting diabetes. Their main priority would have been to find diabetes just at a specific stage of the candidates [23]. Furthermore, using the CART and Scalable RF, Islam *et al.* [24] propose a forecasting method for categorizing diabetes according to several characteristics. They concluded that the RF paradigm proved extensible and superior to the baseline RF model utilized in the forecasting technique in terms of accuracy. As it related to categorizing the composite AB paradigm for insulin resistance in García-Laencina *et al.* [25] outperformed the aggregate Bagging method (DM). J48 (c4.5)-DT was used in conjunction with the ensembles AB and Bagging procedures to analyze and determine this. Bermingham *et al.* [26] created a two-module prediction model: fasting blood sugar and ANN (FBS). Afterward, the DT technique is applied to determine the sensations and indicators of diabetic sufferers precisely. Scientists have used various ML techniques, such as SVM, AB, Bagging, KNN, and RF algorithms [27]. The table includes an amount of machine learning (ML)-based pipelines for classifying diabetes that has been utilized in the prior literature, as well as the relevant datasets [28–33] lacking data indexation methods, feature choice methods, the number of characteristics utilized in specific research, the classifier, and the results in numerous evaluation measures [34–39].

11.2 Literature Review

Table 11.1 represents the review of various ML-based methodologies used in prior diabetes forecast research, providing the publication year, dataset, missing value impute methods, feature selection approaches, amount of characteristics chosen, classifier utilized, and related effectiveness assessment measures. The development of the outlook for diabetes in previous decades has remained poor, due to the dearth of effective and reliable designs, despite various ML-based solutions being released in numerous study papers [40]. It might be challenging to assess a participant's vulnerability and likelihood of contracting a chronic illness like diabetes. Soon to tell diabetes identification reduces medical expenses and the possibility of developing more significant health conditions problems emerging [41]. To help doctors choose more wisely which patients to treat in high-risk situations, it is essential that conclusions may be derived from quickly observable medical signals with precision, especially in emergencies in which a patient might be unresponsive or asleep [42].

The early indications of diabetes are typically highly inconspicuous. As a result, ML-based developments create diabetes earlier detection using

Table 11.1 Review of different methods currently in use.

Sr. no.	Reference	Findings	Best performing classifier	Performance
1	[77]	The ensemble model has been used to forecast diabetes.	DT	Performed up to 84%
2	[70]	Machine learning (ML) techniques are used to preprocess the data and assess the likelihood of the exigency of tachycardia.	RF	Performed up to 80%
3	[71]	Identified the essential components of the diabetes cause	NB	Performed up to 81%
4	[72]	Using mRMR accurately produces improved outcomes	Linear Kernel SVM	Performed up to 92%
5	[73]	Created five distinct diabetes detection models	RF	Performed up to 92%
6	[74]	A method for classifying diabetes that considers unfavourable class imbalances and missing values.	NB	Performed up to 82%
7	[75]	After examining the dataset's characteristics, the finest features are identified based on the correlation values.	MLP	Performed up to 76%
8	[76]	Three machine learning classification algorithms are examined and assessed in this study using a variety of metrics.	Ensemble of AB, XGB	Performed up to 96%

automatic means that are more probable and efficient than conventional methods of directly detecting diabetes by assessing blood sugar immediately [43]. The benefits involve a lighter workload for medical personnel and a decreased chance of intentional mistakes. We seek to use a strategy that forecasts the early stages of a diabetic patient without the need for invasive procedures or ML techniques [44–47]. As a result, the patient can lead a more conservative lifestyle and avert probable consequences. In an invasive surgery that calls for a blood glucose test, we could predict the outcome early, before the incident occurred. Additionally, it saves time and money by eliminating the trouble of running to that same pharmacy to purchase diabetes test sheets and do an appointment-based sugar test [48].

Vital Achievements of Researchers
The essential contributions covered in the current research paper are as follows:

- Presenting a new DDC dataset from northeastern South Asia (Bangladesh).
- Advising a DDC pipeline by suggesting an ensemble classifier with weights for categorizing this DDC dataset using several ML frameworks.
- The ML-based models' hyper-parameters are fine-tuned using the grid search optimization method.
- Including a lot of preprocessing in the DDC pipeline, such as feature selection, outlier rejection, and missing value imputation.
- Conducting in-depth analysis to create the best ensemble classifier model by combining several ML model configurations and applying the best preprocessing from previous tests.

11.3 Proposed Methodology

Figure 11.1 depicts the complete workflow of this strategy, which mainly entails a pretreatment method, an ensemble ML classification, MVI, and FS techniques, as well as hyperparameter optimization [49]. By examining the interfold variances, K-fold cross-validation is also used to verify the robustness of the suggested system. However, the following subsections briefly explain the several essential components of our recommended DDC system [50].

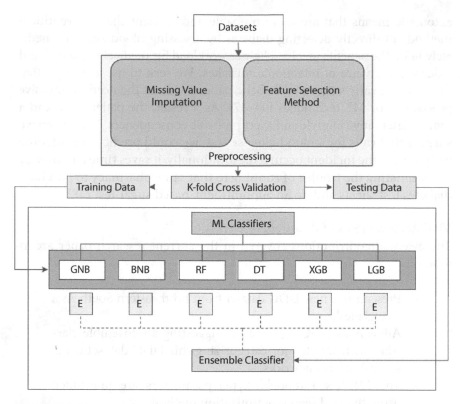

Figure 11.1 Illustrates the proposed workflow, which shows a preprocessing phase utilizing various ML-based classifiers.

11.3.1 Missing Value Imputation (MVI)

A dataset is the only input source for a trainable automatic classification decision-making mechanism. However, the practical dataset frequently contains an abnormally high percentage of missing values, repeatedly shown as NaNs, null, empty, indeterminate, or comparable placeholders [51]. Consequently, absent values in a dataset should be eliminated or replaced to develop a broad, robust, and effective classifier model. Several statistical and ML methodologies are frequently used to handle data missingness in an imperfect dataset, in contrast to the case elimination strategy. The most popular methods for MVI have been average and KNN-based restoration methods from several decades ago [52]. As a result, this research combines a case deletion technique with median-based statistics and KNN-based ML imputation approaches.

11.3.2   Feature Selection

The essential primary method for figuring out which traits are more suitable for a given ML model is feature selection (FS). Modeling reduction frequently uses FS techniques to simplify understanding, speed up training schedules, decrease dimension, improve predictive performance by selecting the right features, and prevent over-fitting. The supervised FS methodology usually outperforms the semi-supervised and unsupervised FS strategies [53, 54]. In addition, to reduce feature repetition, this study does the ablation analysis for our recommended datasets utilizing the four best-known supervised FS techniques: RF, information gain (IG) [55], XGB, and LightGBM (LGB). We briefly overview these four FS approaches in the following lines.

- RF-Based FS
  RF is a built-on trees approach that is utilized as an FS methodology. It only lists the traits built upon well they raise the node's integrity while lowering the pollutants in all trees [56]. The nodes with the most considerable impurity reduction are found near the beginning of the trees, whereas nodes with a minor impurity reduction are found mainly near the tree's end [57]. In conclusion, a subset of the significant features can be produced by trimming the trees under a specific point. The procedures for the RF-based FS are detailed in Algorithm.
- IG-Based FS
  The massive amount of data given by the function of the text group elements is referred to as IG, a machine-learning approach that bases feature selection on entropy [58–60]. To assess the importance of lexical components for categorization, the amount of a phrase that may be utilized for the information categorization is used to compute IG.
- XGB- and LGB-Based FS
  Executions of ensemble strategies using regularized learning, tree-based learning using cache awareness's framework, and gradient boosting-based feature selection methods are referred to as XGB and LGB [61]. These models produce the gain score for each tree partition and calculate the stature score of a typical development applied and outstanding feature. Usually, the gain determines which top-m indexed parts are chosen.

Algorithm 11.1: The steps involved in using the RF-based FS technique
Input: The outcome, $Y \in [0,1]$ is based on on the d-dimensional data, $Xin \in R^{n \times d}$
Result: The m-dimensional data condensed to $Xout \in R^{n \times m}$, where m<d

1. Find the Out of Bag mistake for a tree
2. **Assign** secondary nodes at random, whose comparable rate of appearances is $\tilde{P}_i$, each adherence with primary node I while it splits between Xin, provided that it had recently similarly continued the tree.
3. OOB inaccuracy calculation for the tree (follow step 2)
4. The difference between the original and revised errors' OOBs should be determined.
5. The overall significance score (F) is subsequently determined by repeating steps 1 through 4 for every tree and using the average deviation throughout all trees.
6. **Select** the top-m characteristics with the highest ratings (F) and keep those in $Xout$.

Algorithm 11.2: The steps involved in using the IG-based FS technique
Input: Collection with n-dimensional such as, $D = \{f1, f2, f3,..., fn\}$
Result: Particular trait set S

Discretize $fi \in D$.
For *each* $fi \in D$ **do**
Identify the characteristics' reciprocal details I (fi, fj) and mutual information matrix I. The characteristic significance by calculating the candidate characteristic subgroup is D = D-S if Rel(fi) of all characteristics is true;
end
For $1 < I \leq n$ **do**
for each $fi \in D$ do
Compute the potential characteristics' Red(fi).
Calculate the potential feature's G(i);
S(i)=max(G(i)) and D=D-S;
Determine the potential features
C(i); end
If C<1 Break;
end subsection of production characteristics S.

11.3.3   K-Fold Cross-Validation

Machine learning models are evaluated on a small data sample using a method known as cross-validation. The Algorithm specifies how many subgroups must be formed from a given data selection using a single variable, k. As a result, the term "K-fold cross-validation" is usually used to describe the technique [62]. When a specific value for k is chosen, it can also be replaced with k in the design references. For instance, the notation k=10 may represent the cross-validation with a multiplier of 10. In applied machine learning, cross-validation is frequently utilized to assess a machine learning model's performance while using untrained information. Specifically, a small sample would be utilized to determine the model's performance on information not used to make predictions during training.

KCV is among the methods most frequently used to choose classifications and anticipate errors. K-1 was used to train the models after the K folds of the datasets were divided. The hyperparameters were then modified using the pattern-searching technique [63]. The efficiency of the algorithms in the open loop system was evaluated using the optimal parameters and confidential testing data. Since all affirmative and unfavourable values are present in the dataset, the constant percentage of samples for each class has also been restored using the stratified KCV. In this study, several machine learning (ML) classification algorithms are taught and evaluated for the detection of diabetes, including GNB, BNB, DT, RF, XGB, and LGB.

11.3.4   ML Classifiers

This research trains and evaluates many machine learning (ML) classification algorithms for detecting diabetes, including XGB, LGB, DT, RF, GNB, BNB, and RF. The sections following explain such ML models' computational procedures.

- GNB and BNB Classifier
  Algorithms are used in supervised learning-based Bayesian approaches like GNB and BNB. These approaches are predicated on the Bayesian theorem and the assumption of conditioned independence for all factors influencing the quantity of the classification model [64]. GNB utilizes a Gaussian operation to calculate the characteristics' probability, while BNB utilizes multimodal Bernoulli distributions.

Algorithm 11.3: Application of the G.N.G. and B.N.G. diabetes diagnosis process for the IG-based FS

Input: incoming characteristic vector (X∈Rn×d and true label Y∈Rn×1)

Result: The posterior P∈[0,1]

1. Determine the previous as P(Y=Cj)= C, and nj is the sample in the jth class.
2. Ascertain the output's posterior chance by doing the following:

$$P(C_j|X) = \frac{P(X|C_j) \times P(Y = C_j)}{P(X)}$$

which P(X|Ci) is the predictor's likelihood for a given class (∀j∈ C).

- RF Classifier
  The RF classifier uses the bagging technique on each of the several trees in the group include accordance with Algorithm 7. The samples are then utilized to fit the trees once the training sample has been replaced with the random sample [65]. The ensemble's total quantity of branches can be discovered on the fly using out-of-bag errors.

Algorithm 11.4: The steps involved in using the R.F. diabetes monitoring approach

Input: True labelY∈Rn×1and input feature vector X∈Rn×d

Result: The posterior P [0,1]

1. For b=1to N, do
2. Pick a sample from the bootstrap (Xb, Yb) from supplied (X∈Rn×d, Y∈Rn×1);
3. Using Xb and Yb, By repeatedly carrying out the steps below until the node size is minimum, n min, you can create a random-forest tree called Tb
   - Pick m factors at random compared to the available n variables.
   - Pick one of the m variables provided as the best variable or split-point.
   - Dividing the main node into two secondary nodes The group of plants' final product will be{Tb}N

> - end
> - The posterior P(x)=Voting {P̃k(x)}N, where P̃k(x) is the class prediction of the kth R.F.

- DT Classifier
  DT uses a tree structure to create classification models, breaking into successively fewer dataset sections. The outcomes in a tree are leaf nodes expressing a categorization or conclusion and choice vertices having at least two branches. The root node also serves as the highest judgment point in a selection tree that approximately relates to the most incredible Prediction.
- XGB Classifier
  An ensemble model combines several models and uses the XGB classifier as a boosting approach to improve prediction accuracy [66]. By adding these strengthening contributions to the algorithm's strategy, subsequent models fix the faults produced by earlier models.
- LGB Classifier
  Dependent on DT, LGB approaches and uses the EFB and GOSS techniques, which use leaf- and level-wise strategies to accelerate training.

11.3.5 Evaluation Metrics

A variety of performance metrics were used in this investigation. This explains how one may make an ML classifier function well evaluation metric's quantification while performing poorly with another metric's assessment. Various evaluation criteria must be used to ensure an ML model functions correctly and optimally. Numerous measures, such as Sn, Sp, Acc, and the ROC curve with AUC value, are used to assess the extensive trials in this article.

The letters TP, FN, TN, and FP represent the quantities of real positives, false positives, true positives, true negatives, and false positives. Type II and type I errors are estimated using Sn and Sp. However, Acc divides the complete count of accurately identified samples by the total number of examples in the datasets. The effectiveness of the classification The ROC curve also displays the algorithm, and the AUC indicates the classifiers' degree of separability. As a result, we have unique performance measures to show the outcomes from multiple angles [67].

11.4   Results and Discussion

The statistical analysis of variance-based feature selection algorithms is covered in this section. The quantity of clustering produced, the number of repetitions, and the time spent constructing the framework is used to evaluate cluster performance. The prediction model's accuracy is increased via feature selection and cluster analysis, while elements that slow it down are eliminated. Classifier ensembling procedures combine the predictions from different classifiers into a single prediction result to increase the efficiency of the prediction output. Analysis of feature selection affects the prediction model's optimization. The features are ordered based on the variances, and the findings are shown in tabular and graphical forms.

Table 11.2 shows that pregnancies are essential and closely related to all other factors. Contrarily, there is less association between diabetes pedigree function and pregnancies. As we can observe in the graph, we have different features and their ranking that can show the correlation between additional features. In Figure 11.2, we showed correlation analysis.

In Table 11.3, we can observe the ranking of different features according to their principal analysis. As we can celebrate, TPSA (Tot) have the highest priority, and nN has the lowest priority. Here, we give a graphical representation of essential features according to their principal component analysis. The quality with top priority is the most important according to

Table 11.2 Ranking of important features using correlation analysis.

Variance	Ranking	Feature selected
0.5355	1	Pregnancies
0.3906	2	Glucose
0.038	3	Blood pressure
0.0243	4	Skin thickness
−0.0702	5	Insulin
−0.098	6	BMI
−0.1891	7	Diabetes pedigree function
−0.3118	8	Age

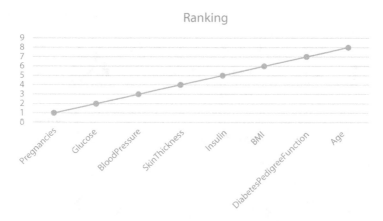

Figure 11.2 Ranking of important features using correlation analysis.

principal component analysis [68, 69]. In Table 11.3, we have essential elements according to ReliefF Attribute Evaluator. As we can examine, pregnancy is the top priority, and age has the lowest priority.

In Figure 11.4 is a graphical representation of the information in the Table 11.4. According to the ReliefF Attribute Evaluator, we can see connections in this graph where not all characteristics have the same importance. We should consider these analyses as we create the predictive model and keep track of which parameters are most crucial and given the most priority. Based on this analysis, we can exclude some parameters that

Table 11.3 Ranking of important features using principal component analysis.

Variance	Ranking	Feature selected
0.7386	1	Glucose
0.5415	2	Age
0.417	3	Blood pressure
0.319	4	Diabetes pedigree function
0.2252	5	Insulin
0.1435	6	Blood pressure
0.0892	7	Skin thickness
0.0428	8	Pregnancies

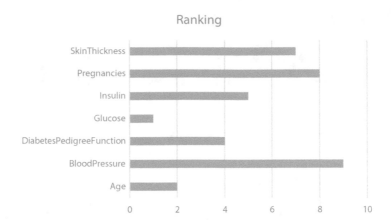

Figure 11.3 Ranking of important features using principal component analysis.

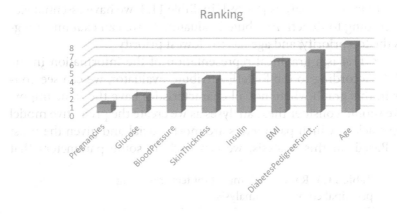

Figure 11.4 Ranking of important features using ReliefF attribute evaluator.

receive lower importance. Table 11.5 shows the correlation matrix below from the principal component analysis shows the value of the correlation coefficient among the features.

The statistical concept of correlation demonstrates how closely two variables are related. The two basic categories are positive and negative correlations. There is a strong association when two elements follow the same path; when one increases, the other also rises. An inverse link exists when two variables change in opposite directions—one increases while the other lowers. Any number between −1 and 1 may represent the correlation coefficient's value. Comparative analysis recapitulation for clustering techniques.

Table 11.4 Ranking of important features using ReliefF attribute evaluator.

Feature selected	Ranking	Variance
Pregnancies	1	0.007978
Glucose	2	0.015907
Blood pressure	3	0.002935
Skin thickness	4	0.000011
Insulin	5	0.0019
BMI	6	0.008346
Diabetes pedigree function	7	0.006852
Age	8	0.014149

Table 11.5 Correlation matrix of elements in principal component analysis.

1	0.13	0.14	−0.08	−0.07	0.02	−0.03	0.54	0.22
0.13	1	0.15	0.06	0.33	0.22	0.14	0.26	0.47
0.14	0.15	1	0.21	0.09	0.28	0.04	0.24	0.07
−0.08	0.06	0.21	1	0.44	0.39	0.18	−0.11	0.07
−0.07	0.33	0.09	0.44	1	0.2	0.19	−0.04	0.13
0.02	0.22	0.28	0.39	0.2	1	0.14	0.04	0.29
−0.03	0.14	0.04	0.18	0.19	0.14	1	0.03	0.17
0.54	0.26	0.24	−0.11	−0.04	0.04	0.03	1	0.24
0.22	0.47	0.07	0.07	0.13	0.29	0.17	0.24	1

11.5 Concluding Remarks and Future Scope

By deleting input features from the training dataset, a machine-learning model that is simpler and more effective can be created. Both supervised and unsupervised feature selection techniques were examined in this study. This study compared feature selection methods based on filter, wrapper, and fuzzy rough sets. The imbalance is what determines the ranking. Several approaches are used for cluster analysis depending on the number of clusters created, the number of iterations, and the time it takes to build the model. Even though this sector has seen significant advancement, much more work has to be done. Machine learning frameworks' ensemble feature selection and clustering will expand the range of big data techniques they can use.

References

1. Misra, A., Gopalan, H., Jayawardena, R., Hills, A.P., Soares, M., Reza-Albarrán, A.A., Ramaiya, K.L., Diabetes in developing countries. *J. Diabetes*, 11, 522–539, 2019.
2. American Diabetes Association, Diagnosis and classification of diabetes mellitus. *Diabetes Care*, 32, S62–S67, 2009.
3. Fitzmaurice, C., Allen, C., Barber, R.M., Barregard, L., Bhutta, Z.A., Brenner, H., Dicker, D.J., Chimed-Orchir, O., Dandona, R., Dandona, L. *et al.*, Global, regional, and national cancer incidence, mortality, years of life lost, years lived with disability, and disability-adjusted life-years for 32 cancer groups, 1990 to 2015: A systematic analysis for the global burden of disease study. *J.A.M.A. Oncol.*, 3, 524–548, 2017.
4. Saeedi, P., Petersohn, I., Salpea, P., Malanda, B., Karuranga, S., Unwin, N., Colagiuri, S., Guariguata, L., Motala, A.A., Ogurtsova, K. *et al.*, Global and regional diabetes prevalence estimates for 2019 and projections for 2030 and 2045: Results from the International Diabetes Federation Diabetes Atlas. *Diabetes Res. Clin. Pract.*, 157, 107843, 2019.
5. Bharath, C., Saravanan, N., Venkata Lakshmi, S., Assessment of knowledge related to diabetes mellitus among patients attending a dental college in Salem city - A cross-sectional study. *Braz. Dent. Sci.*, 20, 93–100, 2017.
6. Akter, S., Rahman, M.M., Abe, S.K., Sultana, P., Prevalence of diabetes and prediabetes and the risk factors among Bangladeshi adults: A nationwide survey. *Bull. World Health Organ.*, 92, 204A–213A, 2014.
7. Danaei, G., Finucane, M.M., Lu, Y., Singh, G.M., Cowan, M.J., Paciorek, C.J., Lin, J.K., Farzadfar, F., Khang, Y.H., Stevens, G.A. *et al.*, National, regional, and global trends in fasting plasma glucose and diabetes prevalence since 1980: Systematic analysis of health examination surveys and epidemiological studies with 370 country-years and 2.7 million participants. *Lancet*, 378, 31–40, 2011.
8. Islam, M., Raihan, M., Akash, S.R.I., Farzana, F., Akhtar, N., Diabetes mellitus prediction using ensemble machine learning techniques, in: *Proceedings of the International Conference on Computational Intelligence, Security and*

Internet of Things, Springer: Berlin/ Heidelberg, Germany, Agartala, India, 13–14 December 2019, pp. 453–467, 2019.

9. Chiang, J.L., Kirkman, M.S., Laffel, L.M., Peters, A.L., Type1 diabetes through the life span: A position statement of the American diabetes association. *Diabetes Care*, 37, 2034–2054, 2014.

10. Begum, S., Afroz, R., Khanam, Q., Khanom, A., Choudhury, T., Diabetes mellitus and gestational diabetes mellitus. *J. Paediatr. Surg. Bangladesh*, 5, 30–35, 2014.

11. Canadian Diabetes Association, *Diabetes: Canada at the tipping point: Charting a new path*, Canadian Diabetes Association, Winnipeg, MB, Canada, 2011.

12. Shi, Y. and Hu, F.B., The global implications of diabetes and cancer. *Lancet*, 383, 1947–1948, 2014.

13. Centers for Disease Control and Prevention, *National diabetes fact sheet: National estimates and general information on diabetes and prediabetes in the United States, 2011*, vol. 201, pp. 2568–2569, U.S. Department of Health and Human Services, Centers for Disease Control and Prevention, Atlanta, GA, U.S.A, 2011.

14. Maniruzzaman, M., Kumar, N., Abedin, M.M., Islam, M.S., Suri, H.S., El-Baz, A.S., Suri, J.S., Comparative approaches for classification of diabetes mellitus data: Machine learning paradigm. *Comput. Methods Prog. Biomed.*, 152, 23–34, 2017.

15. Hasan, M.K., Alam, M.A., Roy, S., Dutta, A., Jawad, M.T., Das, S., Missing value imputation affects the performance of machine learning: A review and analysis of the literature (2010–2021). *Inform. Med. Unlocked*, 27, 100799, 2021.

16. Mitteroecker, P. and Bookstein, F., Linear discrimination, ordination, and the visualization of selection gradients in modern morpho-metrics. *Evol. Biol.*, 38, 100–114, 2011.

17. Tharwat, A., Linear vs. Quadratic discriminant analysis classifier: A tutorial. *Int. J. Appl. Pattern Recognit.*, 3, 145–180, 2016. Webb, G.I., Keogh, E., Miikkulainen, R., Naïve bayes, in: *Encycl. Mach. Learn*, vol. 15, pp. 713–714, 2010.

18. Hosmer, D.W., Jr., Lemeshow, S., Sturdivant, R.X., *Applied logistic regression*, vol. 398, John Wiley & Sons, Hoboken, NJ, U.S.A, 2013.

19. Kégl, B., The return of AdaBoost. MH: Multi-class hamming trees. *arXiv:1312.6086*, arXiv2013, Dec 2013.

20. Yang, H., Luo, Y., Ren, X., Wu, M., He, X., Peng, B., Deng, K., Yan, D., Tang, H., Lin, H., Risk prediction of diabetes: Big data mining with a fusion of various physical examination indicators. *Inf. Fusion*, 75, 140–149, 2021.

21. Jo, T. and Japkowicz, N., Classim balance versus small disjuncts. *A.C.M. Sig kdd Explor. Newsl.*, 6, 40–49, 2004.

22. Buda, M., Maki, A., Mazurowski, M.A., A systematic study of the class imbalance problem in convolutional neural networks. *Neural Netw.*, 106, 249–259, 2018.

23. AlStouhi, S. and Reddy, C.K., Transfer learning for class imbalance problems with adequate data. *Knowl. Inf. Syst.*, 48, 201–228, 2016.
24. Islam, M.S., Awal, M.A., Laboni, J.N., Pinki, F.T., Karmokar, S., Mumenin, K.M., Al-Ahmadi, S., Rahman, M.A., Hossain, M.S., Miralili, S., H.G.S.O.R.F.: Henry gas solubility optimization-based random forest for C-Section prediction and XAI-based cause analysis. *Comput. Biol. Med.*, 147, 105671, 2022.
25. García-Laencina, P.J., Sancho-Gómez, J.L., Figueiras-Vidal, A.R., Pattern classification with missing data: A review. *Neural Comput. Appl.*, 19, 263–282, 2010.
26. Bermingham, M.L., Pong-Wong, R., Spiliopoulou, A., Hayward, C., Rudan, I., Campbell, H., Wright, A.F., Wilson, J.F., Agakov, F., Navarro, P. *et al.*, Application of high-dimensional feature selection: Evaluation for genomic Prediction in man. *Sci. Rep.*, 5, 10312, 2015.
27. Kumar, S., Jain, A., Shukla, A.P., Singh, S., Raja, R., Rani, S., Harshitha, G., AlZain, M.A., Masud, M., A comparative analysis of machine learning algorithms for detection of organic and non-organic cotton diseases. *Math. Problems Eng.*, Hindawi Journal Publication, Hindawi Mathematical Problems in Engineering, 2021, Article ID 1790171, 1–18, 2021. https://doi.org/10.1155/2021/1790171
28. Rani, S., Kumar, S., Venkata Subbamma., T., Jain, A., Swathi, A., Ramakrishna Kumar, M.V.N.M., Commodities price prediction using various ML techniques, in: *The International Conference on Technological Advancements in Computational Sciences (I.C.T.A.C.S. – 2022)*, Tashkent City Uzbekistan, pp. 1–6, 2022.
29. Harshitha, G., Kumar, S., Rani, S., Jain, A., Cotton disease detection based on deep learning techniques, in: *The University of Bahrain 4th Smart Cities Symposium*, 21-23 November 2021.
30. Kumar, S., Jain, A., Rani, S., Ghai, D., Swathi, A., Raja, P., Enhanced SBIR based re-ranking and relevance feedback, in: *10th IEEE International Conference on System Modeling & Advancement in Research Trends (SMART)*, on December 10-11, 2021.
31. Jain, A., Singh, J., Kumar, S., Turcanu, F.-E., Candin, M.T., Chithaluru, P.K., Improved recurrent neural network schema for validating digital signatures in V. A.N.E.T. *Math. J.*, 10, 20, 1–23, 2022.
32. Kumar, S., Haq, M.A., Jain, A., Jason, C.A., Moparthi, N.R., Mittal, N., Alzamil, Z.S., Multilayer neural network based speech emotion recognition for smart assistance. *CMC-Comput. Mater. Continua*, 74, 1, 1–18, 2022, Tech Science Press.
33. Kumar, S., Shailu, Jain, A., Enhanced method of object tracing using extended kalman filter via binary search algorithm. *J. Inf. Technol. Manag.*, 14, Print ISSN: 2008-5893, Online ISSN: 2423-5059, 2022.
34. Rani, S., Ghai, D., Kumar, S., Object detection and recognition using contour based edge detection and fast R-CNN. *Multimed. Tools Appl.*, 22, 2, 1–25, 2022.

35. Rani, S., Ghai, D., Kumar, S., Kantipudi, M.V.V., Alharbi, A.H., Ullah, M.A., Efficient 3D AlexNet architecture for object recognition using syntactic patterns from medical images. *Comput. Intell. Neurosci.*, Hindawi Computational Intelligence and Neuroscience, 2022, Article ID 7882924, 19, https://doi.org/10.1155/2022/7882924.

36. Choudhary, S., Lakhwani, K., Kumar, S., Three dimensional objects recognition & pattern recognition technique; related challenges: A review. *Multimed. Tools Appl.*, 23, 1, 1–44, 2022.

37. Singh, J., Agarwal, S., Kumar, P., Kashish, Rana, D., Bajaj, R., Prominent features based chronic kidney disease prediction model using machine learning. *2022 3rd International Conference on Electronics and Sustainable Communication Systems (I.C.E.S.C.)*, Coimbatore, India, pp. 1193–1198, 2022, doi: 10.1109/ICESC54411.2022.9885524.

38. Pawar, L., Malhotra, J., Sharma, A., Arora, D., Vaidya, D., A robust machine learning predictive model for maternal health risk, in: *2022 3rd International Conference on Electronics and Sustainable Communication Systems (I.C.E.S.C.)*, IEEE, pp. 882–888, 2022, August.

39. Pawar, L., An optimized predictive model for prospective blogging using machine learning, in: *2022 IEEE International Conference on Data Science and Information Systems (I.C.D.S.I.S.)*, IEEE, pp. 1–5, 2022, July.

40. Pawar, L., Saw, A.K., Tomar, A., Kaur, N., Optimized features based machine learning model for adult salary prediction, in: *2022 IEEE International Conference on Data Science and Information Systems (I.C.D.S.I.S.)*, IEEE, pp. 1–5, 2022, July.

41. Bajaj, R., Shandilya, D., Gagneja, S., Gupta, K., Rawat, D., A risk predictive model for primary tumor using machine learning with initial missing values, in: *2022 IEEE International Conference on Data Science and Information Systems (I.C.D.S.I.S.)*, IEEE, pp. 1–7, 2022, July.

42. Kumar, D., Sharma, A.K., Bajaj, R., Pawar, L., Feature optimized machine learning framework for unbalanced bioassays, in: *Cognitive Behavior and Human-Computer Interaction Based on Machine Learning Algorithm*, pp. 167–178, 2021.

43. Pawar, L., Agrawal, P., Kaur, G., Bajaj, R., Elevate primary tumor detection using machine learning, in: *Cognitive Behavior and Human-Computer Interaction Based on Machine Learning Algorithm*, pp. 301–313, 2021.

44. Pawar, L., Sharma, A.K., Kumar, D., Bajaj, R., Advanced ensemble machine learning model for balanced bioassays, in: *Artificial Intelligence and Machine Learning in 2D/3D Medical Image Processing*, p. 8, 1st Edition, Imprint: CRC Press, 2020, https://doi.org/10.1201/9780429354526.

45. Rahi, P., Sood, S.P., Bajaj, R., Innovative platforms of air quality monitoring: A logical literature exploration, in: *Futuristic Trends in Networks and Computing Technologies: Second International Conference, F.T.N.C.T. 2019*, Chandigarh, India, November 22-23, 2019, Springer Singapore, Revised Selected Papers 2, pp. 52–63, 2020.

46. Pawar, L., Singh, J., Bajaj, R., Singh, G., Rana, S., Optimized ensembled machine learning model for IRIS plant classification. *2022 6th International Conference on Trends in Electronics and Informatics (I.C.O.E.I.)*, Tirunelveli, India, pp. 1442–1446, 2022, doi: 10.1109/ICOEI53556.2022.9776724.

47. Rahi, P., Sood, S.P., Bajaj, R., Meta-heuristic with machine learning-based innovative e-health system for ambient air quality monitoring, in: *Recent Innovations in Computing: Proceedings of I.C.R.I.C. 2021*, vol. 2, pp. 501–519, Singapore, Springer Singapore, 2022.

48. Bajaj, R. and Kaur, N., A review of mac layer for wireless body area network. *J. Med. Biol. Eng.*, 41, 7, 1–38, 2021.

49. Ramdev, M.S., Bajaj, R., Sidhu, J., Remote radio head scheduling in LTE-Advanced networks. *Wirel. Pers. Commun.*, 122, 1, 621–644, 2022.

50. Bathla, G., Pawar, L., Khan, G., Bajaj, R., Effect on the lifetime of routing protocols utilizing different connectivity schemes. *Int. J. Sci. Technol. Res.*, 8, 12, 617–622, 2019.

51. Kumar, R., Bajaj, R., Singh, V.K., Vasudeva, K., Pawar, L., Advanced specialized processor architecture for smartphones. *Int. J. Comput. Intell. Res.*, 13, 5, 815–823, 2017.

52. Pawar, L., Bawa, G., Mehra, C., Kanojia, S., Arora, J., Bajaj, R., Analyzing sensor-based technologies for obstacle avoidance robot. *2022 3rd International Conference on Electronics and Sustainable Communication Systems (I.C.E.S.C.)*, Coimbatore, India, pp. 271–277, 2022, doi: 10.1109/ICESC54411.2022.9885348.

53. Singh, G., Singh, A., Bajaj, R., Analysis of energy optimization approaches in internet of everything: An S.D.N. prospective, in: *Software Defined Internet of Everything*, pp. 119–133, Springer International Publishing, Cham, 2021.

54. Kaur, M., Bajaj, R., Kaur, N., Wireless body area network: Performance analysis of polling access M.A.C. protocol. *2021 2nd Global Conference for Advancement in Technology (G.C.A.T.)*, Bangalore, India, pp. 1–7, 2021, doi: 10.1109/GCAT52182.2021.9587558.

55. Ustuner, M. and BalikSanli, F., Polarimetric target decompositions and light gradient boosting machine for crop classification: A comparative evaluation. *ISPRS Int. J. Geo-Inf.*, 8, 97, 2019.

56. Taha, A.A. and Malebary, S.J., An intelligent credit card fraud detection approach using an optimized light gradient boosting machine. *IEEE Access*, 8, 25579–25587, 2020.

57. Hasan, M.K., Jawad, M.T., Dutta, A., Awal, M.A., Islam, M.A., Masud, M., Al-Amri, J.F., Associating measles vaccine up take classification and its underlying factors using an ensemble of machine learning models. *IEEE Access*, 9, 119613–119628, 2021.

58. Harangi, B., Skin lesion classification with ensembles of deep convolutional neural networks. *J. Biomed. Inform*, 86, 25–32, 2018.

59. Hsieh, S.L., Hsieh, S.H., Cheng, P.H., Chen, C.H., Hsu, K.P., Lee, I.S., Wang, Z., Lai, F., Design ensemble machine learning model for breast cancer diagnosis. *J. Med. Syst.*, 36, 2841–2847, 2012.

60. Sikder, N., Masud, M., Bairagi, A.K., Arif, A.S.M., Nahid, A.A., Alhumyani, H.A., Severity classification of diabetic retinopathy using an ensemble learning algorithm through analyzing retinal images. *Symmetry*, 13, 670, 2021.

61. Rawat, D., Pawar, L., Bathla, G., Kant, R., Optimized deep learning model for lung cancer prediction using ANN algorithm, in: *2022 3rd International Conference on Electronics and Sustainable Communication Systems (I.C.E.S.C.)*, IEEE, pp. 889–894, 2022, August.

62. Masud, M., Bairagi, A.K., Nahid, A.A., Sikder, N., Rubaiee, S., Ahmed, A., Anand, D.A., Pneumonia diagnosis scheme based on hybrid features extracted from chest radiographs using an ensemble learning algorithm. *J. Healthc. Eng.*, 2021, 8862089, 2021.

63. Cheng, N., Li, M., Zhao, L., Zhang, B., Yang, Y., Zheng, C.H., Xia, J., Comparison and integration of computational methods for deleterious synonymous mutation prediction. *Brief. Bioinform.*, 21, 970–981, 2020.

64. Dai, R., Zhang, W., Tang, W., Wynendaele, E., Zhu, Q., Bin, Y., De Spiegeleer, B., Xia, J., BBPpred: Sequence-based Prediction of blood-brain barrier peptides with feature representation learning and logistic regression. *J. Chem. Inf. Model.*, 61, 525–534, 2021.

65. Chowdhury, M.A.B., Uddin, M.J., Khan, H.M., Haque, M.R., Type 2 diabetes and its correlates among adults in Bangladesh: A population based study. *BMC Public Health*, 15, 1070, 2015.

66. Sathi, N.J., Islam, M.A., Ahmed, M.S., Islam, S.M.S., Prevalence, trends and associated factors of hypertension and diabetes mellitusin Bangladesh: Evidence from B.H.D.S. 2011 and 2017–18. *PLoS One*, 17, e0267243, 2022.

67. Islam, M.M., Rahman, M.J., Tawabunnahar, M., Abedin, M.M., Maniruzzaman, M., *Investigate the effect of diabetes on hypertension based on Bangladesh demography and health survey, 2017–2018*, Research Square, Durham, NC, U.S.A, 2021.

68. Rahman, M.A., Socioeconomic inequalities in the risk factors of noncommunicable diseases (Hypertension and Diabetes) among Bangladeshi population: Evidence based on population level data analysis. *PLoS One*, 17, e0274978, 2022.

69. Islam, M.M., Rahman, M.J., Roy, D.C., Maniruzzaman, M., Automated detection and classification of diabetes disease based on Bangladesh demographicand healthsurvey data, 2011 using machine learning approach. *Diabetes Metab. Syndr. Clin. Res. Rev.*, 14, 217–219, 2020.

70. Dutta, D., Paul, D., Ghosh, P., Analysing feature importances for diabetes prediction using machine learning, in: *Proceedings of the 2018 IEEE 9th Annual Information Technology, Electronics and Mobile Communication Conference (I.E.M.C.O.N.)*, pp. 924–928, Vancouver, BC, Canada, 1–3 November 2018.

71. Zou, Q., Qu, K., Luo, Y., Yin, D., Ju, Y., Tang, H., Predicting diabetes mellitus with machine learning techniques. *Front. Genet.*, 9, 515, 2018.
72. Kaur, H. and Kumari, V., Predictive modelling and analytics for diabetes using a machine learning approach. *Appl. Comput. Inform.*, 18, 90–100, 2020.
73. Wang, Q., Cao, W., Guo, J., Ren, J., Cheng, Y., Davis, D.N., DMP_MI: An effective diabetes mellitus classification algorithm on imbalanced data with missing values. *IEEE Access*, 7, 102232–102238, 2019.
74. Sneha, N. and Gangil, T., Analysis of diabetes mellitus for early Prediction using optimal features selection. *J. Big Data*, 6, 1–19, 2019.
75. Sisodia, D. and Sisodia, D.S., Prediction of diabetes using classification algorithms. *Proc. Comput. Sci.*, 132, 1578–1585, 2018.
76. Mohapatra, S.K., Swain, J.K., Mohanty, M.N., Detection of diabetes using multilayer perceptron, in: *Proceedings of the International Conference on Intelligent Computing and Applications*, Springer: Berlin/Heidelberg, Germany, Tainan, Taiwan, 30 August–1 September 2019, pp. 109–116, 2019.
77. Hasan, M.K., Alam, M.A., Das, D., Hossain, E., Hasan, M., Diabetes prediction using ensembling of different machine learning classifiers. *IEEE Access*, 8, 76516–76531, 2020.

12

Wearable Gait Authentication: A Framework for Secure User Identification in Healthcare

Swathi A.[1], Swathi V.[1], Shilpa Choudhary[2]* and Munish Kumar[3]

[1]Sreyas Institute of Engineering and Technology, Hyderabad, India
[2]CSE (AIML) Department, Neil Gogte Institute of Technology, Hyderabad, India
[3]Department of E&CE, Maa Saraswati Institute of Engineering and Technology, Kalanaur, India

Abstract

With the wide use of wearable Internet of Things (IoT) devices, it is now possible to quickly gather information on human activities, including unconscious or sub-conscious acts. One such behavior is walking, which can provide individual patterns for each person and be utilized as a biometric feature for user authentication in healthcare systems. This paper proposes the lightweight seamless authentication framework (LiSA-G), which may be used to identify and authenticate users on commercial smart watches by leveraging statistical data and sensor data features related to human behavior. With a mean equal error rate (EER) of 8.2% and fewer features and less sensor data, the study's findings demonstrate that this approach delivers higher authentication accuracy. Such a strategy is also more realistic and can be deployed quickly due to the limited computational and energy capacity of wearable IoT systems in healthcare setting.

Keywords: Gait recognition, gait authentication

12.1 Introduction

The authentication is the process to verify the user is genuine or not. There are different processes to authenticate. In this scenario, the modern devices like Mobile phones, laptops etc., Generally use Face identification,

---

Corresponding author: shilpachoudhary2020@gmail.com

Sandeep Kumar, Anuj Sharma, Navneet Kaur, Lokesh Pawar and Rohit Bajaj (eds.) *Optimized Predictive Models in Healthcare Using Machine Learning*, (195–214) © 2024 Scrivener Publishing LLC

Biometric, Passwords having numerical, alphabetical, mainly Patterns which can easily detect by the unauthorized user without acknowledgement of authorized user. These gadgets perform the high security levels but can be accessed easily when the user is unconsciousness. The proposed system is where the user cannot access the data until the person WALK. People have their own walking style. Every wearable IoT device consists of Accelerometer and Gyroscope sensor for user identification. By this aspect, the authentication of authorized user is detected. This detection uses the Accelerometer, measures the acceleration and the Gyroscope sensors, measures the angular velocity of the device by user input. This prediction is done in wearable devices like smart watch, smart rings etc., By performing the KNN, Random Forest, Multi Perceptron algorithms the accuracy is predicted. The high amount of accuracy results the user's authentication.

Numerous systems and our interactions with computer and communication networks have undergone radical change this same Internet of Things has made this possible. In addition to the widely used smartphones, wearable Internet of Things in devices, like smartwatches and glasses, are multiplying quickly. Gartner Inc. predicts that by 2019 there will be 225 million wearable Internet of Things devices sold globally [1].

Although early wearable technology only had a few connection options, including Bluetooth, more recent models come with WiFi and a wide range of sensors in addition to WiFi. Strong security measures are required since such numerous connections on wearable gadgets or devices might representation a range of personal data and raise the danger of safety fissures [2].

The focus on wearable IoT device security has not, however, kept up with the rate of expansion in terms of quantity [3, 4].

Portable IoT devices remain further vulnerable to safety threats than earlier IoT devices like smartphones because they lack security features (such insufficient user authentication) and have constrained resources (like computational energy and power capacity). As a result, user authentication, one of the most important security procedures, is taken into consideration to report the susceptibility of the present wearable gadgets IoT safety structure. Passwords are one of the most often utilized techniques for user authentication because of how straightforward they are. However, users need have an average of 19 distinct passwords for on numerous devices and facilities in order to achieve a particular degree of strong user authentication [5]. As a result, it's common for people to struggle to remember the right password. 33% of respondents to a Centrify poll at Infosecurity Europe 2015 reported having password fury, according to the study's results [6].

Numerous studies [7–11] [13–18] have suggested exploiting subconscious behaviors to identify wearable or handheld device users in the literature. However, the majority of earlier research used custom-made equipment for their experiments, and they meticulously and manually tuned the sensors to suit their own needs [13, 14]. In reality, however, most users of wearable IoT devices are unable to do such calibration. Even while some research studies have been done on electronic instruments, they include a lengthy authentication procedure that is mostly caused by their walking detection algorithm (for example, a user must walk for an average of more than 15 seconds to authenticate) [15, 16, 18]. Consequently, they need a lot of data, which is a rather significant volume.

To cover the shortcomings in the available solutions, we describe a light-weight seamless authentication framework (LiSA-G) based on gait that securely verifies users in healthcare systems utilizing mobile devices. LiSA-G incorporates mechanical qualities that are linked to people's physical characteristics, in contrast to earlier initiatives that solely extracted statistical data from sensor data. Furthermore, compared to the 8–20 sampling periods used by other research, LiSA-G just needs one sample period of sensor data. The experimental results show that the technique achieves a Equal Error Rate (EER) of 8.2% on 51 individuals while employing fewer characteristics and shorter periods of sensor data. Our contributions include: Our contributions include:

- Reducing the number of authentication requirements. Removing the requirement for normal gait identification to cut down on the time necessary for gait authentication.
- Our suggested framework can be used in healthcare systems to authenticate people utilizing wearable Internet of Things devices, such as mobile phones, smart watches, and other wearable devices, with high accuracy and low mistake rates.
- The time required for gait authentication can be cut down by omitting the gait cycle detection.

12.2 Literature Survey

Gait recognition, SRC applications, and feature extraction for activity categorization are covered in this section's discussion of related work. The literature has extensively investigated gait recognition. Gait identification may be divided into three broad categories created on the methods used to gather gait data: radio signal–based, vision-based, wearable sensor–based, and floor sensor–based. A video camera is used to remotely collect gait in a vision-based gait identification system. Then, gait characteristics are extracted using video/image processing techniques for later identification. Gait characteristics, including the heel-to-toe ratio and (GRF) ground reaction force are recorded using sensors (for example, force plates) that are commonly installed under the floor in floor sensor based gait recognition.

Accelerometer-based gait measures can more accurately and immediately depict gait dynamics than vision-based or other gait measurements. For instance, the current issues with vision-based approaches, such as occlusions, clutter, and perspective alterations, do not affect accelerometer-based gait detection. The majority of wearable accelerometer-based gait identification research conducted to date relies on this technology. Ailisto et al. [18] made the initial proposal for accelerometer-based gait recognition, which Gafurov et al. [19] further refined. Dedicated accelerometers were first employed and worn in a variety of body places, including the lower thigh [19], waist [18], hips [20], hip pocket, chest pocket, and hands [21]. Researchers suggested many gait-based authentication solutions by taking use of the prevalence of smartphones. Researchers have developed a number of gait-based authentication methods using smart phones integrated accelerometers [5, 6, 22, 23]. For instance, in Kumar et al. [22], the researchers suggested a discrete mobile phone gait verification method. Kumar et al. [23] investigated the effects of holding and carrying a phone in the hand and pocket. Researchers have been utilizing newly developed energy harvesters to perform gait identification in recent years [24]. Additionally, the distinctive gait has been used to generate keys to secure user-owned equipment [25].

Applications for SRC. The identification of sensor areas has made substantial use of the recently created classification technique known as SRC. Some papers have used the sparsity of various measures to their advantage in order to improve system performance. GNSS signals were compressed using CS and information from various propagation paths in order to boost their SNR. The researchers invented opti-SRC in Rani et al. [26] to enhance the functionality of the facial recognition system in smart phones. This required adjusting the SRC's random matrix. The accuracy of face recognition was improved by Choudhary et al. [27] by integrating various channel state information vectors.

The performance of SRC is enhanced by Rani et al. [28] by employing weighted sparse neighborhood-preserving predictions. By utilizing the segmentation method of to increase recognition accuracy, Rani et al. [29].

Based on classifying outdated web pages, ML approaches may be used to create models that can be implemented into browsers to identify phishing operations. Some of the current phishing identification methods have a high detection rate for phishing websites (>99%), but a very low false positive rate for legal websites (0.1%). However, many of these machine learning approaches rely heavily on several inert properties, particularly when employing the bag-of-words method. Phishing detection techniques have difficulty obtaining and maintaining the training dataset's tagged data. The classification procedure employed the neural networks model; however, due to its shoddy construction, it was susceptible to under fitting.

12.3   Proposed System

The wearable gadget and server are the two parts of the system architecture. The wearable device has a data collecting section where all of the data are gathered. Accelerometer and gyroscope readings are acquired as part of this data collection, analyzed, and stored in comma separated values (CSV). It also contains the same information as the data collection and transmits the data to the server via the access request. Both training and authentication are involved. The data processing, which includes the Peak Detection Filter, Interpolation, Savitzky Golay Filter, and converting the data to bandpass filter, is the following sector. The authentication procedure, which includes the actual process, starts after the data processing is finished. Use the ML algorithms and extract the features. According to Figure 12.1, the random forest classifier is trained and makes an access request to wearable devices.

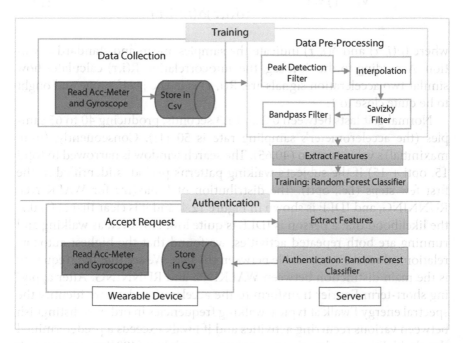

Figure 12.1 Architecture of proposed system.

12.3.1   Walking Detection

The first step is to use a walking detector to prevent utilizing expensive recognition algorithms when there is no motion. The basic accelerometer data anywhere along three dimensions of smartwatch change significantly and erratically as a result of random body movements and the changing orientation of the devices. But because walking is a repetitive activity, we discovered that the acceleration in the direction of gravity shows regular patterns. Figure 12.3 displays the speed values along gravity for various activities. We understand that the velocity brought on by gravity has a rhythm since walking is repetitive. Whether a user is walking can be determined by acceleration in the direction of gravity. In order to count steps on unlimited cellphones, it is crucial to know that NASC was the first to do so by taking use of walking's repetitious nature. It is set to NOT Moving as the user's starting state (include IDLE and RUNNING). With lag at sample I, we compute the normalized autocorrelation of an accelerometer and gyro meter series as follows:

$$
W(I, r) = 1 - \frac{\sum_{i=0}^{4=} \left[\begin{array}{c} (a(i+k) - \mu(i, \tau)) \\ (a(i+k+\tau) - \mu(i+\tau, \tau)) \end{array} \right]}{\tau \delta(i, \tau) \delta(i+1, \tau)}
\tag{12.1}
$$

where ($\mu(i,\ \tau)$ and $\delta(i,\ \tau)$ indicate the samples' mean and standard deviation. According to the time lag, the autocorrelation $R(i, \tau)$ calculates how similar two acceleration signals are. $R(i,\ \tau)$ is in the [1, 1] range and ought to be quite close to 1.

Normal gait lasts between 0.8 and 1.3 seconds, producing 40 to 65 samples (the accelerometer's sampling rate is 50 Hz). Consequently, (min, maxinitial)'s value is set to (40,65). The search window is narrowed to (opti 15, opti + 15) if the subject's walking pattern's period is identified in the first few steps (i.e., opti). The distribution of Rmax(m) for WALKING, RUNNING, and IDLE is shown in Figure 12.4, and it is clear that at (t) 0.7, the likelihood that a person is IDLE is quite low. However, as walking and running are both repeated activities, we found that the highest autocorrelation values are comparable between the two. We see that the frequency is the main distinction between WALKING and RUNNING. After applying short-term Fourier transform to the acceleration data, we identify the spectral energy Fwalk at typical walking frequencies in order to distinguish between various recurring activities and if Fwalk exceeds a predetermined threshold Fth, we classify the subject as walking (400 in our system).

It should be noted that by simply altering frequencies (fmin, fmax) to normal running frequency ranges, this approach may also be used to identify other repetitive activities, such as running; however, in this article, we only address walking.

This algorithm's thresholds are determined empirically. By varying the threshold from the least value to the maximum value, we test the system's performance and select the one that obtains the highest detection performance.

Using an activity classifier, we can determine the user's walking style after walking detection. In this study, we concentrate on seven of the most typical walking activities and categorize them into two groups as indicated in Table 12.1. The first type of walking includes regular walking as well as going upstairs and downstairs. The second category is walking without swinging your arms, which includes strolling while talking on the phone, texting, or putting your hand in your pocket. Before using the real-time data from an accelerometer for activity recognition, a lot of noise needs to be filtered away.

A straightforward low pass filter that is frequently used to control noisy signals is the moving average filter. While the abrupt modulations in the data get more harsh as the filter's length is increased, the output becomes smoother. In our experiment, we discover that an order of three can result in positive outcomes.

A typical walk lasts 0.8 to 1.3 seconds and generates 40 to 65 records (with accelerometer sample were collected at a rate of 50 Hz). Hence, the value of (min, maxinitial) is set to (40, 65). If the subject's walking pattern's period is recognized in the subject's first several steps, the search window is reduced to (opti 15, opti + 15). (i.e., opti). Figure 12.4 illustrates the distribution of Rmax(m) for WALKING, RUNNING, and IDLE. It is obvious that at (t) 0.7, the likelihood that a person is IDLE is quite low. Yet, because running and walking are both frequent activities, we discovered that the greatest autocorrelation values between the two are comparable. We can observe that the fundamental difference between RUNNING and WALKING is frequency. We detect the spectral energy Fwalk at typical walking frequencies after applying short-term Fourier transform to the acceleration data to discriminate between various repeating activities, and if Fwalk exceeds a specified threshold Fth, we classify the patient as walking (400 in our system). It should be noted that this approach may be used to identify other repeated activities, such as running, by simply changing frequencies (fmin, fmax) to typical running frequency ranges; however, in this article, we only discuss walking.

The thresholds of this method are established empirically. We test the system's performance by changing the threshold between the lowest and highest values, then choose the one that achieves the best detection performance.

After walking detection, we may identify the user's walking style using an activity classifier. We focused on seven of the most common walking activities in this study and divided them into two groups as shown in Table 12.1. The first kind of walking entails both regular walking and climbing and descending stairs. Walking while swinging your arms falls under the later group, which includes jogging while texting, talking on the phone, or placing your hand in your pocket. There is a lot of noise that needs to be filtered out before using the real-time data from an accelerometer for activity identification.

The moving average filter is a simple low pass filter that is widely employed to reduce noisy signals. As the filter's length is extended, the output becomes smoother while the data's sudden modulations grow harsher. We find that an order of three can produce favorable results in our experiment.

To reduce noise, a simple moving filtering of 3 is used. Continuous sensor data is separated into two-second sliding segments with such a 50% mismatch after noise reduction. The window size of 2s was chosen to find a balance among classifier and latency. The overlap is used when employing a sliding window to capture changes or transitions outside the window's perimeter. Using SIFT, a feature extraction approach that is frequently employed for image matching and object recognition [9], we extract a number of data points for each window. SIFT, however, only functions for two-dimensional (2D) pictures and is not relevant to signals with only one dimension. In this paper, we present a novel approach to extract one-dimensional gait signal features.

The proposed feature extraction technique takes the segmented gait signal as an input. The initial stage is to identify scales and places that can be reliably distributed across numerous stage cycles within the same subject. Under a number of reasonable assumptions, it has been shown that the Gaussian function is the only scale-space kernel [9]. Thus, the definition of a variable L(t,), which results from the convolution of the a gait signal, is as follows

$$L_\delta(t, \delta) = k_\delta(t, \delta) * a(t) \tag{12.2}$$

where K(t, δ) is called as zero-mean Gaussian formal function with a variance of 2, and is the convolution operation. The variance is calculated using,

$$k_\delta(t,\delta) = \frac{1}{\sqrt{2\pi}} e\left(\frac{-t^2}{2\delta^2}\right) \qquad (12.3)$$

We determine D(t,δ), the categorization between two balances that are close to one another but are separated by v multiplicative factor, in order to find stable key point positions in scale space as,

$$D^v(t,6) = K(t,v\delta) - K(t,\delta) * a(t)$$
$$= (t,v\delta) - L(t,\delta) \qquad (12.4)$$

where I is the layer index, 0 is the base scale, and t is the sample timestamp. The local maxima and minima are obtained by comparing each point in E(t, I) to its eight neighboring locations. Only when it is either larger or smaller than all of its neighbors is it selected. Any extremum in E(t, I) is described as a key point by the descriptor (t,). To appropriately identify stable extrema, those extrema with tiny E [t, I], that denotes low contrast, will be excluded. In order to get the descriptor for each important point, the gradients of a vectors made up of points uniformly sampled around t is finally determined.

12.3.2 Experimental Setup

Both hardware and software have requirements. The proposed system's hardware specifications state that the device's processor must be "i3 generation" or higher. The device's random access memory (RAM) must be greater than 4 GB. The device's hard drive has a capacity of more than 40 GB. The suggested system's software specifications call for Windows 8 or later as the operating system for the device. Python 3.5 is the proposed system's coding language.

12.4 Results and Discussion

12.4.1 Dataset Used

The CMU MoBo dataset consists of a number of gait recognition videos that were recorded from 20 different participants. In order to make the segmentation process simpler, a set of bounding boxes and silhouette masks are also given in the dataset. One of the dataset's key advantages is that it may be downloaded with just a connection to Calgary University's File Transfer Protocol (FTP) server and without needing to make any reservations or agree to anything.

12.4.2   Results

We evaluate the recognition accuracy of three classifiers—k-NN, SVM, and Decision Tree—that are frequently used to categorize online activity. We begin by altering k (K is Nearest Neighbor Number) from 3 through 50 to test the k-accuracy NNs. K = 3 achieves the maximum accuracy for k-NN, as illustrated in Figure 12.2 (a). After k is determined, we change the congestion window between 0.5s and 2.5s to compare the accuracy of various methods. In terms of classification accuracy, k-NN surpasses Rain Forest algorithm and Multi-layer perception algorithms for all realistic dimensions, reaching a maximum of 98.6% when the frame is set to 2s, as shown in Figure 12.7. The size of the window affects how many attributes can be extracted. More attributes can be extracted with a broader window, which improves accuracy. So, it is evident from Figure 12.2(b) that the accuracy of the 2s window is higher than that of the 1s and 0.5s windows. An extended window would, however, worsen the user experience because consumers would have to perform more steps. The window size and k value for the k-NN activity classifier are set to 2 and 3, respectively, based on the findings of this experiment. Remember that user identification is not the goal when using k-NN; rather, the goal is to identify user activity. The suggested application's functioning structure is shown in the accompanying screenshots. It self-trains using any supplied dataset and outputs the results.

The primary frame of Figure 12.2 (a) has seven steps that the user walks through to verify their accuracy of the input data. Upload accelerometer & gyroscope sensor dataset, upload accelerometer & gyroscope sensor dataset, and develop a test method, run KNN, random forest, multilayer perceptron, accuracy graph, and authenticate using accelerometer and gyroscope sensors. The output is produced at each step on the white screen to the left. The procedure for uploading the sensor data is shown in Figure 12.2 (b). The uploading of the user input dataset file, sensor user movement dataset. The dataset is the input of the 30 user's limbs, i.e., walking prediction with the various angles of each individual with various features.

The dataset is loaded to the screen and the total number of features or attributes found in dataset. The total attributes found by passing the datasets are 562 as shown in Figure 12.3.

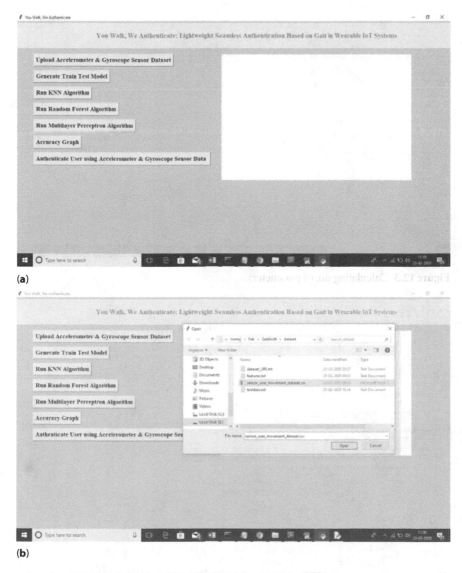

(a)

(b)

Figure 12.2 (a) Main frame of the application. (b) Uploading dataset.

Create a train and test model from the dataset by selecting "Generate Train Test Model." These datasets are created for the offered machine learning algorithms. In order to calculate accuracy, each machine learning algorithm will use 20% of the dataset records for prediction and 80% of the dataset records for training.

The dataset has 7352 records, of which 6616 are used for training and 736 are used for testing in the application. By creating the command "Run

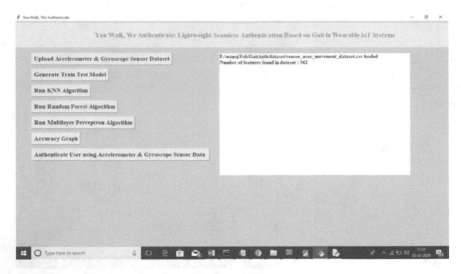

Figure 12.3 Calculating no. of parameters.

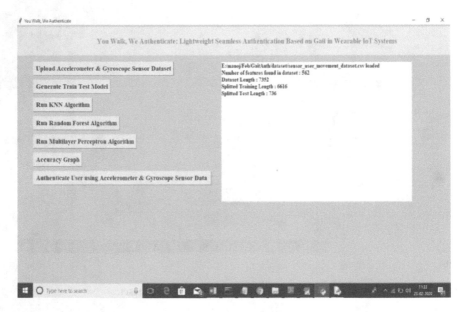

Figure 12.4 Generating model.

KNN Algorithm," you can create a KNN model on a dataset, as illustrated in Figure 12.5. The Lazy Learning Algorithm is the KNN algorithm. This method offers a moderate level of accuracy (74%). Only when the ML algorithms deliver 80% of the accuracy is the accuracy chosen. Every device uses the random forest algorithm, a machine learning technique, to create precise user authentication because of its consistently high performance. The random forest algorithm performs well, scoring 81%, which is above 80% accuracy (Figure 12.6).

The multilayer perceptron algorithm uses a backtracking procedure to determine the user's accuracy. Accuracy requires more time to obtain. The

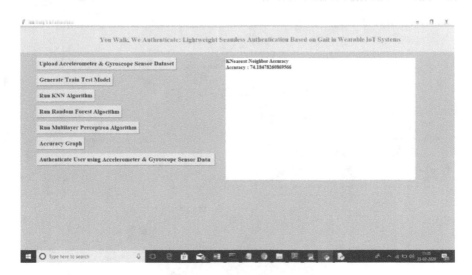

Figure 12.5 KNN algorithm implementation.

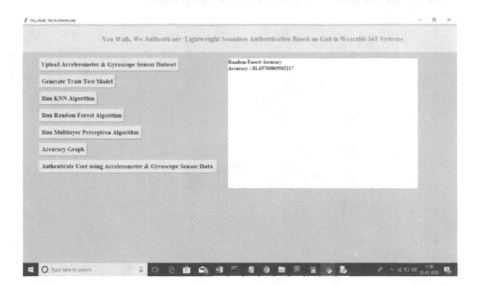

Figure 12.6 Implementation of random forest algorithm.

accuracy rate is consistently low. The accuracy produced is 19%, which is less accurate than what is produced as shown in Figure 12.7. In a graph pattern, the accuracy of all three machine learning algorithms is produced (Figure 12.8). The graph's Y-axis measures algorithm accuracy, while the X-axis lists the names of the algorithms. Different algorithms don't perform as well as the random forest.

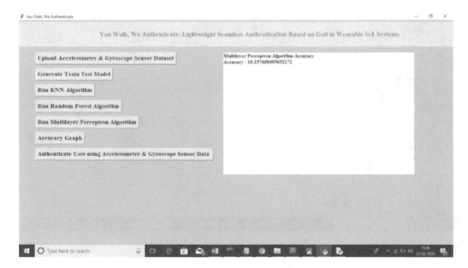

Figure 12.7 Implementation of multilayer perception algorithm.

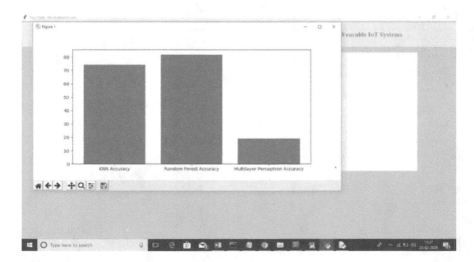

Figure 12.8 Comparison of three algorithms.

By clicking the "Authenticate User using Accelerometer & Gyroscope Sensor Data" button, you can submit new test data called "textdata.txt" that lacks a User ID. It creates the sensors based on accuracy calculations. To determine if the test data matches the user id or not, machine learning will use fresh test data and apply it to the train model. Machine learning will identify the matching user to authenticate if there is a match, as shown in Figures 12.9 and 12.10.

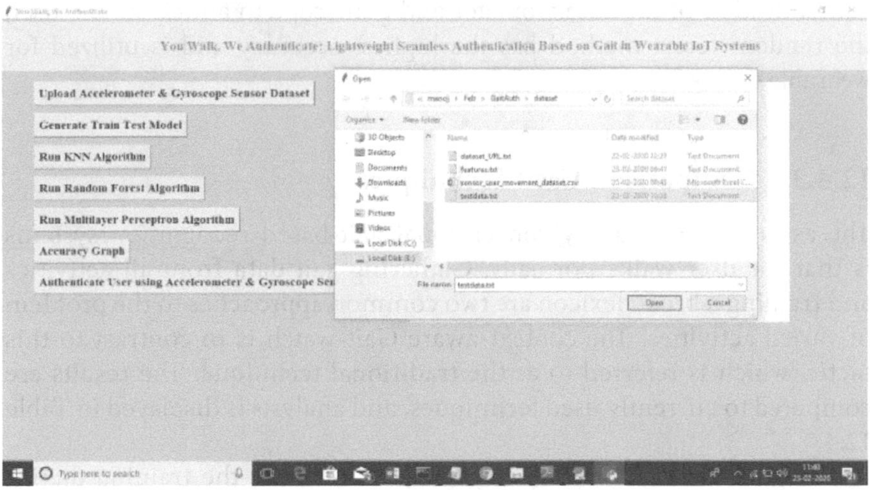

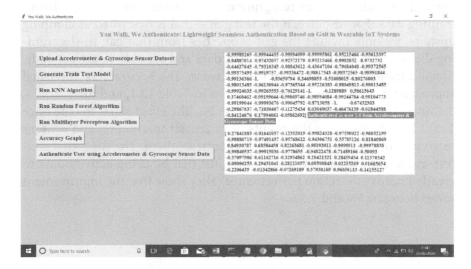

Figure 12.9 Authenticating user.

Figure 12.10 Predicting user data in the application.

The 562 double values are all user movement data, and the values in the selected text are verified or matched with user ID "1." This is how to anticipate for all users with a comparable level of accuracy. KNN, random forest, and multilayer perceptron are the machine learning algorithms that are employed. These methods are used to ensure that user authentication to a certain device is accurate.

The X-axis displays the names of the algorithms, while the Y-axis displays the accuracy rates, which range from 0% to 100%. By producing authentication of the accelerometer and gyroscope to anticipate the user, the random forest method has the highest accuracy and is utilized for wearable devices.

12.4.3 Comparison Used Techniques

The assumption made by conventional gait-based recognition systems is that the user walks normally. Gathering gait data from all activities and training a broad lexicon are two common approaches to the problem of varied activities. The context-aware Gait-watch is in contrast to this tactic, which is referred to as the traditional technique. The results are compared to currently used techniques, and analysis is displayed in Table 12.1.

Using all of each subject's gait data, we generate the training dictionary for the conventional method. We first run an activity detector before checking the user's activity for gait watch. Depending on the results of the activity classifier, user recognition is performed using the pertinent training data. For instance, if the test gait signal is described as climbing upstairs, we only include the gait properties from that gait in the training dictionary. As we collect more gait data and are able to extract additional attributes, our accuracy will increase. The accuracy of the usual approach has greatly increased, as shown in Table 12.1, and for T = 2.5s, the improvement may be as much as 30.2%. The effect starts to fade once T > 2.5s. According to the results, it is crucial to comprehend a user's behaviour in order to successfully authenticate them. The suggested context-aware authentication system does just that by using activity data to greatly improve detection performance. They show that the improvement varies between 3% and 7.5%.

Table 12.1 Comparison of state-of-art methods.

Author	Measure of accuracy parameter
Draper et al. [1]	Equal error rate 8%
Prigg et al. [2]	Equal error rate 42.49–39.30%
Musale et al. [3]	False non matching rate: 12.42%/False matching rate: 14.29%
Gafurov et al. [12]	Equal error rate 3.88% 9.62%
Sepas et al. [19]	Equal error rate 8.7%
Filipi et al. [20]	Accuracy 86% (correct identification)
	F-score 86%
Gafurov et al. [12]	Accuracy 77.8%; ERR 1.04%
	False acceptance rate 2.03%; FRR 0.04%
Xu et al. [13]	Equal error rate 0.01% 0.16%;
	False acceptance rate 0.54% 1.96%
Proposed method	Accuracy 97.8%; ERR 2.04%

12.5 Conclusion and Future Scope

This study has presented the development and evaluation of the light-weight seamless authentication framework (LiSA-G) for user identification in healthcare systems using wearable IoT devices. The proposed framework utilizes gait patterns, which are unique to each individual, as a biometric characteristic for user verification. Our experimental findings demonstrate that our approach achieves a higher authentication accuracy of 97.8% with an equal error rate (ERR) of 2.04% compared to existing systems, while using fewer characteristics and a smaller amount of sensor data. The proposed framework is more realistic and deployable quickly due to the limited computational and energy capacity of wearable IoT systems in healthcare settings. The results of this study have important implications for the use of wearable IoT devices in healthcare systems and demonstrate the potential of gait patterns to be used as a reliable biometric characteristic for user identification with high accuracy and low error rate.

Further, to improve the robustness and generalizability of the proposed methodology, additional testing and validation are needed across other demographic groups and environments. There is a possibility of integrating the proposed method with actual healthcare systems to assess usability and performance in real-world scenarios.

References

1. Draper, S., Wearable device sales will grow 26 percent worldwide in 2019, says research company gartner, in: *WT Wearable Technologies Conference*, 2018.
2. Prigg, M., Google glass HACKED to transmit everything you see and hear: Experts warn' the only thing it doesn't know are your thoughts', *The Daily Mail*, 2013, http://www.dailymail.co.uk/sciencetech/article-2318217/Google-Glass-HACKED-transmithear-experts-warn-thing-doesnt-know-thoughts.html (accessed May 2nd, 2013).
3. Musale, P., Baek, D., Werellagama, N., Woo, S.S., Choi, B.J., You walk, we authenticate: Lightweight seamless authentication based on gait in wearable IoT systems. *IEEE Access*, 7, 37883–37895, 2019.
4. Hanamsagar, A., Woo, S.S., Kanich, C., Mirkovic, J., Leveraging semantic transformation to investigate password habits and their causes, in: *Proceedings of the 2018 CHI Conference on Human Factors in Computing Systems*, pp. 1–12, 2018.
5. Zhao, Y., Qiu, Z., Yang, Y., Li, W., Fan, M., An empirical study of touch-based authentication methods on smartwatches, in: *Proceedings of the 2017 ACM International Symposium on Wearable Computers*, pp. 122–125, 2017.
6. Khandelwal, S., Hacker finds a simple way to fool iris biometric security systems. The Hacker News. Saatavissa https://thehackernews. com/2015/03/iris-biometric-security-bypass. html. Hakupäivä, 30, 2018, 2015.
7. Gowroju, S. and Kumar, S., Robust deep learning technique: U-Net architecture for pupil segmentation, in: *2020 11th IEEE Annual Information Technology, Electronics and Mobile Communication Conference (IEMCON)*, IEEE, pp. 0609–0613, 2020.
8. Swathi, A. and Kumar, S., A smart application to detect pupil for the small dataset with low illumination. *Innov. Syst. Softw. Eng.*, 17, 29–43, 2021.
9. Swathi, A. and Kumar, S., Review on pupil segmentation using CNN-Region of interest, in: *Intelligent Communication and Automation Systems*, CRC Press, pp. 157–168, 2021.
10. Gowroju, S. and Kumar, S., Robust pupil segmentation using UNET and morphological image processing, in: *2021 International Mobile, Intelligent, and Ubiquitous Computing Conference (MIUCC)*, IEEE, pp. 105–109, 2021.

11. Gowroju, S., Kumar, S., Aarti, Ghimire, A., Deep neural network for accurate age group prediction through pupil using the optimized UNet Model. *Math. Problems Eng.*, 2022, Article ID 7813701, 24, 2022.

12. Gafurov, D., Snekkenes, E., Bours, P., Spoof attacks on gait authentication system. *IEEE Trans. Inf. Forensics Secur.*, 2, 3, 491–502, 2007.

13. Xu, W., Shen, Y., Zhang, Y., Bergmann, N., Hu, W., Gait-watch: A context-aware authentication system for smart watch based on gait recognition, in: *Proceedings of the Second International Conference on Internet-of-Things Design and Implementation*, pp. 59–70, 2017.

14. Jeevan, M., Hanmandlu, M., Panigrahi, B.K., Information set based gait authentication system. *Neurocomputing*, 207, 1–14, 2016, cond International Conference on Internet-of-Things Design and Implementation. 59–70, 2017.

15. Xu, W., Lan, G., Lin, Q., Khalifa, S., Bergmann, N., Hassan, M., Hu, W., KEH-Gait: Towards a mobile healthcare user authentication system by kinetic energy harvesting, in: *NDSS*, pp. 0–4, 2017.

16. Middleton, L., Buss, A.A., Bazin, A., Nixon, M.S., A floor sensor system for gait recognition, in: *Fourth IEEE Workshop on Automatic Identification Advanced Technologies (AutoID'05)*, IEEE, pp. 171–176, 2005.

17. Jiang, S., Wang, Y., Zhang, Y., Sun, J., Real time gait recognition system based on kinect skeleton feature, in: *Computer Vision-ACCV 2014 Workshops*, Singapore, Singapore, November 1-2, 2014, Revised Selected Papers, Part I. vol. *12*, Springer International Publishing, pp. 46–57, 2015.

18. Shen, C., Yu, S., Wang, J., Huang, G.Q., Wang, L., A comprehensive survey on deep gait recognition: Algorithms, datasets and challenges. *arXiv preprint arXiv:2206.13732*, 4, 14–22, 2022.

19. Sepas-Moghaddam, A. and Etemad, A., Deep gait recognition: A survey. *IEEE Trans. Pattern Anal. Mach. Intell.*, 7, 264–284, 2022.

20. Filipi Gonçalves dos Santos, C., de Souza Oliveira, D., Passos, L.A., Pires, R.G., Santos, D.F.S., Valem, L.P., Moreira, T.P. *et al.*, Gait recognition based on deep learning: A survey. *ACM Computing Surveys (CSUR)*, 55, 2, 1–34, 2022.

21. Arshad, H., Khan, M.A., Sharif, M.I., Yasmin, M., Tavares, J.M.R.S., Zhang, Y., Satapathy, S.C., A multilevel paradigm for deep convolutional neural network features selection with an application to human gait recognition. *Expert Syst.*, 39, 7, e12541, 2022.

22. Kumar, S., Jain, A., Agarwal, A.K., Rani, S., Ghimire, A., Object-based image retrieval using the U-Net-based neural network. *Comput. Intell. Neurosci.*, 2021, 1–14, 2021.

23. Kumar, S., Rani, S., Jain, A., Verma, C., Raboaca, M.S., Illés, Z., Neagu, B.C., Face spoofing, age, gender and facial expression recognition using advance neural network architecture-based biometric system. *Sensor J.*, 22, 14, 5160–5184, 2022.

24. Kumar, S., Jain, A., Rani, S., Alshazly, H., Idris, S.A., Bourouis, S., Deep neural network based vehicle detection and classification of aerial images. *Intell. Autom. Soft Comput.*, 34, 1, 119–131, 2022.

25. Kumar, S., Jain, A., Shukla, A.P., Singh, S., Raja, R., Rani, S., Harshitha, G., AlZain, M.A., Masud, M., A comparative analysis of machine learning algorithms for detection of organic and non-organic cotton diseases. *Math. Problems Eng.*, Hindawi Journal Publication, 21, 1, 1–18, 2021.

26. Rani, S., Ghai, D., Kumar, S., Kantipudi, M.V.V., Alharbi, A.H., Ullah, M.A., Efficient 3D AlexNet architecture for object recognition using syntactic patterns from medical images. *Comput. Intell. Neurosci.*, 2022, 1–19, 2022.

27. Choudhary, S., Lakhwani, K., Kumar, S., Three dimensional objects recognition & pattern recognition technique; related challenges: A review. *Multimed. Tool Appl.*, 23, 1, 1–44, 2022.

28. Rani, S., Ghai, D., Kumar, S., Reconstruction of simple and complex three dimensional images using pattern recognition algorithm. *J. Inf. Technol. Manag.*, 14, 235–247, 2022.

29. Rani, S., Ghai, D., Kumar, S., Object detection and recognition using contour based edge detection and fast R-CNN. *Multimed. Tool Appl.*, 22, 2, 1–25, 2022.

13

NLP-Based Speech Analysis Using K-Neighbor Classifier

Renuka Arora[1] and Rishu Bhatia[2*]

¹Jagannath University, N.C.R. Bahadurgarh, Jhajjar, India
²Ganga Institute of Technology and Management, Kablana, Bahadurgarh, Jhajjar, India

Abstract

Natural language programming (NLP) is a significant region of computerized reasoning examination related to the operation and communication of various artificial intelligence (AI) regions. As of not long ago, the attentiveness in AI submissions in NLP was on data presentation, legitimate rational, and imperative execution—first applied to semantics and then to sentence building. In the most modern decade, memorable traffic in the NLP study has affected the universality of massive scope utilization of accurate methods, for example, AI. This is similar to opening the route to the learning and enhancement techniques that establish the centre of present-day AI, the most highly transmissible controls and neural organizations. In this paper, we give similar outcomes for discourse weakness dependent on various characterization calculations on Weka. The article recognizes four stages by examining multiple degrees and parts of the language, trailed by introducing the set of experiences, advancement, different utilizations of NLP, and the latest things. Weka is a collection of AI controls for paying attention to genuine mining-related topics. It is transcribed in Java language and routes on a practically specified period.

Keywords: Neural network, artificial intelligence, classification algorithm, sentimental analysis

13.1 Introduction

Artificial intelligence for everyday language getting ready and text assessment incorporates using AI estimations and "tight" man-structured awareness

---

Corresponding author: rishu.ece@gangainstitute.com

Sandeep Kumar, Anuj Sharma, Navneet Kaur, Lokesh Pawar and Rohit Bajaj (eds.) *Optimized Predictive Models in Healthcare Using Machine Learning*, (215–228) © 2024 Scrivener Publishing LLC

(AI) to appreciate the value of transcript files. These terms comprise text: electronic media statements, online evaluations, study reactions, budgetary, clinical, authentic, and regulatory documents. Fundamentally, the piece of AI in trademark language getting ready (NLP) and transcript assessment is to advance, enliven and mechanize the secret substance examination limits. Rather than algorithmic programming, an AI model can summarize and oversee novel cases. In a situation, a patient takes after something the classic has understood already, and the ideal can routine this preceding "learning" to appraise the situation. The objective is to make a scheme where the model determinedly advances at the job you have usual it. Artificial intelligence for NLP and transcript assessment incorporates many genuine techniques for recognizing syntactic highlights, components, assumptions, and transcript pieces. The strategies can be informed as a model that is then realistic to other substances, in any case, called coordinated AI. It incorporates a ton of computations that work across colossal courses of action of data to isolate significance, known as solo AI.

13.2 Supervised Machine Learning for NLP and Text Analytics

A clump of text archives in managed AI is labeled or clarified with models. These reports are utilized to "train" a factual model, which is then given unlabeled content to dissect. The most mainstream managed NLP AI calculations uphold vector machines, Bayesian organizations, greatest entropy, etc.

- Tokenization
  Tokenization includes breaking a book report into bits a machine can see, for example, words. NLP rules are adequate for English tokenization and use AI for tokenization [11]. Chinese adheres to regulations and standards like English and trains an AI model to recognize and get them [12].
- Part of Speech Tagging
  Grammatical feature cataloging implies distinguishing every symbolic grammatical form and labeling it like this. Part of speech labeling structures the premise of various significant NLP assignments. A prerequisite to accurately distinguishing parts of speech is perceiving elements, removing topics, and dealing with the slant.

- Recognition of Entity
  The most straightforward, specified substances are individuals and spots referenced in a book report. Elements include hashtags, messages, postage information, telephone numbers, and Twitter handles. It is likewise critical to note that Named Entity Recognition models depend on the exact part of speech labeling from those models.
- Sentiment Analysis
  Assessment investigation is when a bit of composing is optimistic and nonpartisan and afterwards relegates a loaded assumption score to every substance, topic, subject, and class inside the report [13]. This is an unfathomably intricate undertaking that changes uncontrollably with the setting. Making a lot of NLP rules to represent each possible assessment score for each conceivable word in each believable setting would be inconceivable.

13.2.1   Categorization and Classification

Order implies arranging content into basins to get a quick, elevated-level review of what is in the information. To prepare a book arrangement model, information researchers use prearranged substances and tenderly shepherd their model until it has arrived at the ideal degree of precision. The outcome is an exact, solid classification of text records that takes distant less period and vitality than human investigation. Linguistics is a discipline that includes a sense of verbal, phonological setting, and other phonological. The numerous essential categories of natural philological processing are:

1. Morphology
   The different disciplines of the point direct the littlest pieces of importance. It shows the name morphemes depict the Idea of points. As the articulation prewiping out can be inventoried into different morphemes: predation and the root canceller. The explanation stays and associates with every one of the terms, considering the significant social can change any obscure point into morphemes. These include the suffix "ed" to an action word, which shows that the action word procured place before.
2. Phonology
   Phonology is a technique for Etymology that interfaces with orderly sound planning. The point from the Old Greek word phonorelatesto voice and logy connects with the term. In

1993 Nikolai directed that it is "the procedure of voice connecting to the association of words." In 1998, Lass translated that it associates the hints of semantics related to the small classifications of semantics. Phonology connection of sound to change over the significance of any friendly language.

3. Semantic

In semantics, different individuals see the importance as directed. Nonetheless, this is related to only some of the focus associated with significance. Semantic association demands a sentence's possible association by joining the sentence's action words. The degree of change can interface the designs to different places [26]. The syntactic association of points that can be entered as many grammatical forms is associated at the syntactic level. For instance, among other implications, "document" as an individual can dictate either a joiner for collecting matters, a device to make one's pointer nails, or a construction of people in a line. The level shows words with word reference view, yet in addition to their changing meaning [27]. It shows that the fitting can check more than one-word association by seeing the remainder of the essence.

4. Lexical

In this NLP framework, direct the technique for every word. Different handling classifications to point-level execution— the first part is related to the language portion connected with every point. In the given process, issues that can proceed as one or more pieces of discourse are depicted as the necessary piece of exchange label in light of the setting in which they can show their presence. The depictions can be partitioned with the focuses that associate single importance [28]. In the NLP framework, the climate relates to portrayal changes using the semantic hypothesis.

5. Syntactic

This point depicts the focus in a line to interface the syntactic method of the sentence. Both linguistic structure and parser are expected here. The consequence of this reason behind working is the line's association that depicts the primary variety of connections between the focuses [29]. Different kinds of language structures can be directed with the piece. In NLP structures, there is no need for entire lines. In addition to the enormous difficulties in parsing classified state associations and combination reviews, no significant associations are utilized for sufficient phrasal and clausal conditions. Sentence structure shows significance in most verbal because requests and varieties add to implication.

6. Talk
   During grammar struggle with the sentence-structure unit, the place of NLP interfaces, including the parts of design larger than a line, i.e., it only interfaces a few sentence messages as the construction of sentences, a piece of which can be portrayed independently. In the wake of checking the properties of the word overall, that shows importance by making focuses between part sentences [14, 16]. The well-known points are Anaphora Goal—this relates to the changing of priorities; for example, pronouns are directed, with the relevant substance to their effectiveness.

7. Sober-Minded
   Sober-minded is associated with the point that connects with language in focus and utilizes the center far beyond the centre for accomplishing the region and dictates with additional energy is an interface into issues except changing over in the given formats. This is fundamental for world information and relates to the comprehension of focuses and regions [21].

13.3   Unsupervised Machine Learning for NLP and Text Analytics

Unsupervised machine learning AI setting up a model deprived of pre-marking or explaining. Bundling infers gathering similar reports into social occasions or sets. These bundles are then orchestrated subject to importance and congruity [6]. Another kind of education is latent semantic indexing (LSI). This procedure dictates terms and points that often happen with one another. Lattice factorization is another procedure for unaided NLP AI. Grid factorization is a different method for independent NLP AI. This uses "torpid factors" to isolate a gigantic structure into the mix of two tinier organizations. Inactive parts are likenesses between things [25].

- Convolution neural network
  Convolution neural networks (CNNs) are fundamentally two or three layers of convolutions with nonlinear incitation limits [2]. In a norm-forward brain affiliation, we interface

each data neuron to yield neurons in the going with layer independently. That is besides called an entirely related layer. In difficulties, the information layer is utilized to utilize the yield [8]. This directs in neighborhood affiliations, where all information is associated with a point in the work. Each cover is spread over various channels and joins their results [3]. In the game plan stage, a CNN ordinarily learns the evaluations of its channels dependent on the undertaking [7]. For instance, in a picture game plan, a CNN might compose a few means to separate focuses from typical pixels in the fundamental layer, by then utilization focuses on seeing precise shapes in the subsequent layer and hence utilizing these designs to pick more basic level highlights, for example, makeover frames in created areas [15]. The given line is then a classifier with basic-level innovations [4]. Each channel makes a nearby fix from lower-level elements into a more raised-level portrayal.

- Recurrent Neural Networks
  Recurrent neural networks make more intuitive sense. They are the language cycle. They were examining sequentially from left to right [17]. Outstandingly, CNNs' utilitarian to NLP issues performs well. The fundamental sack of articulations points with noticeable twisting to misguided doubts, but related to the standard procedure for a seriously lengthy timespan and led to extraordinary results. A significant dispute for CNNs with their speedy nature. Convolutions related to the central piece of PC plans are completed on a gear mark on GPUs. Diverged from n-grams, CNNs are moreover successful in regards to depiction [22]. With a gigantic language, figuring over 3 g can promptly get exorbitant. The most typical fit for CNNs is portrayals endeavours, for instance, feeling assessment, spam revelation, or subject characterization. Convolutions and caring exercises about the solicitation of terms to gather naming as in PoS labeling that is more diligently to squeeze into an advanced design [1]. Assesses a CNN plan on various portrayal datasets, by and large, elaborate feeling examination and point characterization tasks. The CNN planning accomplishes extraordinary execution across datasets and new extreme forefront on a couple. It applies challenges to one advanced course. The creator correspondingly gives a space-productive pack

of portrayals for the points, plunging how many restrictions the affiliation requires to follow. In Johnson and Zhang [5], the producer becomes the model with performance "district presenting" that utilizes a CNN expecting the setting of message regions. Building a CNN setup surmises that there are different hyper-cutoff points to examine, some of which are: information portrayals, number and aspects of trouble channels, pooling plans, and beginning cutoff points. It plays out a test assessment on the impact of fluctuating hyper limits in CNN plans, dissecting their effect on execution and change over different runs. It looks at CNNs for relative deliberation and relative arrangement undertakings. Despite this point, the creators utilize the general spots of words to the substances of energy as a pledge with layer structure. These terms expect that the locations of the senses are related to model data that contains one affiliation. Sun *et al.* [9] and Zeng *et al.* [10] have investigated identical points.

RNNs are ideal for taking care of issues where succession is a higher priority than the separate things themselves [18]. An RNN is a completely associated neural organization that covers a refactoring of a portion of its coatings into a circle. That circle regularly emphasizes the expansion or connection of two sources of info, a framework increase and a non-direct capacity [23].

Among the content uses, the accompanying projects are among those RNNs achieve well at:

- Arrangement labeling
- Natural language processing (NLP) text generation
- Natural language processing (NLP) text classification

- K-Nearest Neighbor Classifier
  KNN dictates a thing by a mass point of the article's data in the opening of the data regards. Dish, 2015 satiated that the component is dictated with the best in their points [19]. It is nonverbal nature due to no data transport. It needs to be more active as it does not focus on any model and amass an improvement of the bits of knowledge as it does not immediately a couple of assessments of limit in which input X gives yield Y [20]. It points upon the trademark closeness as credit is identical to enter limits. The mark of the k nearest neighbours of every impetus raises the gathering [24].

13.4   Experiments and Results

Weka is a variety of AI controls for handling provable data-related issues produced in Java and runs on practically any point. The intentions are to be utilized legitimately to the UCI library Parkinson speech dataset. The boundaries were tried with an informational index of 930 discourse terms. This framework gives language acknowledgement with a precision of 76.32%. A few activities depend on the equivalent examination of various classifiers, as shown in Figures 13.1 to 13.6. If the primary four outcomes

Figure 13.1 Graphical view with their class level.

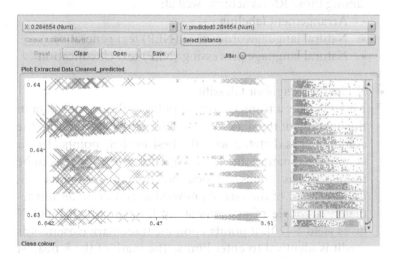

Figure 13.2 Class color view with coordinates.

Figure 13.3 Class view with plot matrix.

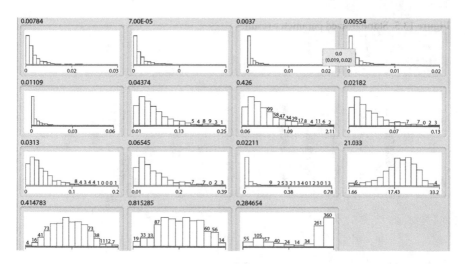

Figure 13.4 Graphical view with their instances.

are considered, the precision is expanded to 76.32%, as shown in Table 13.1. The accuracy can be raised when the quantity of successful boundaries result is expanded.

These parameters are:

- Jitter (Abs): is used frequently to find the updated variation.
- Shimmer (DDA): Typical absolute alterations between the scales of successive periods
- Shimmer: is dictated in a percentage and is related to the ratio of consecutive period amplitude to the average amplitude.

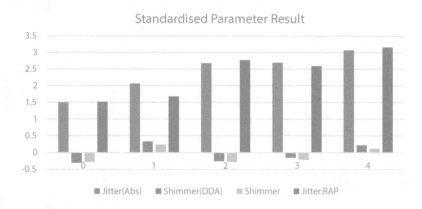

Figure 13.5 Standardized parameter result.

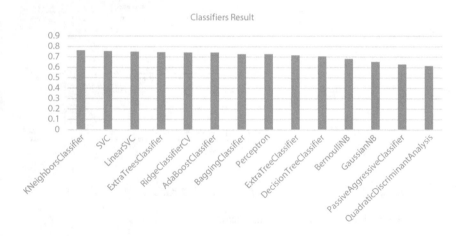

Figure 13.6 Classifier comparative results.

Table 13.1 Important features with values.

	Jitter (Abs)	Shimmer (DDA)	Shimmer	Jitter: R.A.P.
0	1.502385	−0.303385	−0.279977	1.516570
1	2.059402	0.329104	0.238264	1.675958
2	2.676418	−0.254288	−0.275847	2.770662
3	2.696418	−0.151102	−0.214299	2.585245
4	3.070451	0.217281	0.117416	3.160395

- Jitter: RAP is characterized as average perturbation, the normal outright contrast in a period and its regular and two neighbors, isolated by the standard time frame. It is communicated as a rate.

13.5 Conclusion

This chapter presented different classifiers with comparable results with various exchange affirmation plan findings. The course of action is an effective technique to perceive new results limits depending upon the yield from past getting readily defined limits. For fruitful NLP results, it uses sound systems, data limits, and advanced tree figuring to show tremendous results. In the outline, a small proportion of dataset information is needed to survey the necessary boundaries to ensure a convincing result. We have picked the 14 speech limits and find with a higher exactness level of 76.32% with the KNeighbors classifier.

References

1. Kim, Y., Convolutional neural networks for sentence classification. *Proceedings of the 2014 Conference on Empirical Methods in Natural Language Processing (E.M.N.L.P. 2014)*, pp. 1746–1751, 2014.
2. Kalchbrenner, N., Grefenstette, E., Blunsom, P., A convolutional neural network for modelling sentences. *A.C.L.*, 1, 655–665, 2014.
3. dos Santos, C.N. and Gatti, M., Deep convolutional neural networks for sentiment analysis of short texts, in: COLING-2014, pp. 69–78, 2014.
4. Johnson, R. and Zhang, T., Effective use of word order for text categorization with convolutional neural networks. To Appear: NAACL-2015, 2015, 2011.
5. Johnson, R. and Zhang, T., Semi-supervised convolutional neural networks for text categorization via region embedding, *Proceedings of the 28th International Conference on Neural Information Processing Systems*, Vol. 1, pp. 919–927, December 2015.
6. Wang, P., Xu, J., Xu, B., Liu, C., Zhang, H., Wang, F., Hao, H., Semantic clustering and convolutional neural network for short text categorization. *Proceedings A.C.L.*, pp. 352–357, 2015.
7. Zhang, Y. and Wallace, B., A sensitivity analysis of (and Practitioners' Guide to) convolutional neural networks for sentence classification, *Proceedings of the The 8th International Joint Conference on Natural Language Processing*, pp. 253–263, Taipei, Taiwan, November 27 – December 1, 2017 c 2017 AFNLP 2015.

8. Nguyen, T.H. and Grishman, R., Relation extraction: Perspective from convolutional neural networks. *Workshop on Vector Modeling for N.L.P.*, pp. 39–48, 2015.

9. Sun, Y., Lin, L., Tang, D., Yang, N., Ji, Z., Wang, X., Modelling mention, context and entity with neural networks for entity disambiguation. (*Ijcai*), 1, 1333–1339, 2015.

10. Zeng, D., Liu, K., Lai, S., Zhou, G., Zhao, J., Relation classification via convolutional deep neural network. *Cooling*, 2011, 2335–2344, 2014.

11. Gao, J., Pantel, P., Gamon, M., He, X., Deng, L., Modelling interestingness with deep neural networks, *Proceedings of the 2014 Conference on Empirical Methods in Natural Language Processing (EMNLP)*, October 25-29, 2014, Doha, Qatar, Association for Computational Linguistics, pp. 2–13, 2014.

12. Shen, Y., He, X., Gao, J., Deng, L., & Mesnil, G., A latent semantic model with convolutional-pooling structure for information retrieval. Proceedings of the 23rd A.C.M. *International Conference on Information and Knowledge Management – C.I.K.M. '14*, pp. 101–110, 2014.

13. Weston, J. and Adams, K., # T AG S PACE: Semantic embeddings from hashtags. *Conference on Empirical Methods in Natural Language Processing (EMNLP)*, vol. 1, Doha, Qatar. Association for Computational Linguistics, pp. 1822–1827, 2014.

14. Santos, C. and Zadrozny, B., Learning character-level representations for part-of-speech tagging. *Proceedings of the 31st International Conference on Machine Learning, ICML-14(2011)*, pp. 1818–1826, 2014.

15. Zhang, X., Zhao, J., LeCun, Y., Character-level convolutional networks for text classification. *NIPS'15: Proceedings of the 28th International Conference on Neural Information Processing Systems*, vol. 1, pp. 649–657, 2015.

16. Zhang, X. and LeCun, Y., Text understanding from Scratch. *arXiv E-Prints*, 3, 011102, 2015.

17. Kim, Y., Jernite, Y., Sontag, D., Rush, A.M., Character-aware neural language models, *AAAI'16: Proceedings of the Thirtieth AAAI Conference on Artificial Intelligence*, pp. 2741–2749, February 2016.

18. Nation, K., Snowling, M.J., Clarke, P., Dissecting the relationship between language skills and learning to read: Semantic and phonological contributions to new vocabulary learning in children with poor reading comprehension. *Adv. Speech-Language Pathol.*, 9, 2, 131–139, 2007.

19. Liddy, E.D., Natural language processing, in: *Encyclopedia of Library and Information Science, 2nd Ed.*, NY. Marcel Decker, Inc., 2001.

20. Bathla, G., Pawar, L., Khan, G., Bajaj, R., Effect on the lifetime of routing protocols utilizing different connectivity schemes. *Int. J. Sci. Technol. Res.*, 8, 12, 617–622, 2019.

21. Kumar, R., Bajaj, R., Singh, V.K., Vasudeva, K., Pawar, L., Advanced specialized processor architecture for smartphones. *Int. J. Comput. Intell. Res.*, 13, 5, 815–823, 2017.

22. Pawar, L., Bawa, G., Mehra, C., Kanojia, S., Arora, J., Bajaj, R., Analyzing sensor-based technologies for obstacle avoidance robot. *2022 3rd International*

Conference on Electronics and Sustainable Communication Systems (I.C.E.S.C.), Coimbatore, India, pp. 271–277, 2022.

23. Pawar, L., An optimized predictive model for prospective blogging using machine learning, in: *2022 IEEE International Conference on Data Science and Information Systems (I.C.D.S.I.S.)*, IEEE, pp. 1–5, 2022, July.

24. Pawar, L., Saw, A.K., Tomar, A., Kaur, N., Optimized features based machine learning model for adult salary prediction. *2022 IEEE International Conference on Data Science and Information Systems (I.C.D.S.I.S.)*, IEEE, pp. 1–5, 2022, July.

25. Bajaj, R., Shandilya, D., Gagneja, S., Gupta, K., Rawat, D., A risk predictive model for primary tumor using machine learning with initial missing values, in: *2022 IEEE International Conference on Data Science and Information Systems (I.C.D.S.I.S.)*, IEEE, pp. 1–7, 2022, July.

26. Kumar, S., Haq, M.A., Jain, A., Jason, C.A., Moparthi, N.R., Mittal, N., Alzamil, Z.S., Multilayer neural network based speech emotion recognition for smart assistance. *CMC-Computers, Mater. Continua*, 74, 1, 1–18, 2022. Tech Science Press.

27. Kumar, S. and Shailu, A.J., Enhanced method of object tracing using extended Kalman filter via binary search algorithm, in: *Journal of Information Technology and Management*. S. Rani, D. Ghai, S. Kumar (eds.), Object detection and recognition using contour based edge detection and Fast R-CNN, in: *Multimedia Tool and Application*, vol. 22, no. 2, pp. 1–25.

28. Rani, S., Kumar, S., VenkataSubbamma, T., Jain, A., Swathi, A., Ramakrishna Kumar, M.V.N.M., Commodities price prediction using various ml techniques, in: *The International Conference on Technological Advancements in Computational Sciences (I.C.T.A.C.S. – 2022)*, Tashkent City Uzbekistan, pp. 1–6, 2022.

29. Harshitha, G., Kumar, S., Rani, S., Jain, A., Cotton disease detection based on deep learning techniques, in: *The University of Bahrain 4th Smart Cities Symposium*, 21-23 November 2021.

14

Fusion of Various Machine Learning Algorithms for Early Heart Attack Prediction

Monali Gulhane* and Sandeep Kumar

Department of CSE, Koneru Lakshmaiah Education Foundation, Vijayawada, India

Abstract

In this digital world, heart disease is one of the most pressing problems in human life. However, it is one of the leading causes of death for a significant number of individuals in a variety of countries across the world. This is because heart disease is one of the primary risk factors for stroke, another of the leading causes of mortality. The most recent developments in machine learning (ML) show that it is possible to make an accurate early diagnosis of cardiac disease by utilizing electrocardiogram (ECG) data in conjunction with patient information. Modern technological advances are primarily responsible for making it possible for these newly developed technologies to exist. Despite this, both the ECG and the data supplied by the patients are often inconsistent, which, in the end, renders it difficult for typical machine learning techniques to perform in a manner that is objective. Over time, many academics and industry experts working on the topic have uncovered a range of solutions at both the data and the algorithm levels. These solutions have been successful in addressing the issue. For the heart attack dataset that uses the UCI machine learning repository, we found that our accuracy increased by 93% when we assembled all three classifiers. We proposed to boost it. This research uses many different classifiers, including Logistic Regression, Random Forest, and Naive Bayes, to identify the numerous difficulties associated with unbalanced data in the context of heart disease predictions. To provide a complete picture of the topic at hand by contrasting the model currently being used with the model that's been presented, this body of work has used a technique suggested to discover the problems associated with data sets in heart attack prediction.

*Corresponding author: monali.gulhane4@gmail.com

Sandeep Kumar, Anuj Sharma, Navneet Kaur, Lokesh Pawar and Rohit Bajaj (eds.) *Optimized Predictive Models in Healthcare Using Machine Learning*, (229–244) © 2024 Scrivener Publishing LLC

Keywords: Diseases, machine learning, random forest, naïve Bayes, logistic regression, electrocardiogram (ECG)

14.1   Introduction

Heart disease is a disorder that may damage the heart or the blood arteries that feed the heart. According to World Health Organization (WHO) data, cardiovascular disease causes around 30% of all deaths worldwide [1, 2]. There are wide varieties of heart diseases, the most common of which include heart diseases, arrhythmias, heart problems, cardiomyopathy, and congenital heart disease. The World Health Organization (2013) and the American Heart Association (2013) agree that cardiovascular disease is the top cause of mortality across the United States and the rest of the globe. This is why cardiovascular disease is considered the most severe heart disease [3, 4]. Every single part of the world has substantial challenges and financial burdens due to the predominance of cardiovascular disease and the high mortality rate. Early detection of cardiovascular disease may help alleviate some of the symptoms associated with the illness, reducing the overall mortality rate. Machine learning is a method of performing data analysis that is differentiated from other forms of conducting data analysis by automating the process of creating an analytical model. It is premised on the assumption that computers can learn information from data, recognize patterns, and make decisions with minimal human input. This hypothesis underpins the concept of artificial intelligence (AI) [5–9]. There are three distinct environments in which machine learning algorithms may function: supervised, semi-supervised, and unsupervised. Supervised models are employed when there is a requirement to map input labels to output labels. Supervised models are utilized. Examples include the categorization of pictures, the identification of faces, the forecasting of sales, the diagnosis of illnesses, and the detection of spam [10–14]. It is standard practice to combine a limited supply of data sets with a considerable quantity of unlabeled information while training a model. This may be done in several ways. This is a specific example of a model that uses semi-supervised Learning. Unsupervised modelling is often used in practice [15–19]. It might be challenging to diagnose cardiovascular illness when the patient already has several health issues, such as diabetes, high blood pressure, excess cholesterol, and an irregular pulse rhythm. This is one of the numerous reasons why it is so hard to recognize the sickness [20, 21]. The severity of people's cardiac disease has been assessed using several different data analyses and neural network approaches. Heart disease requires a great deal of attentiveness in its management due to the extensive number of contributing variables. Not taking care of this might harm the heart or even result in an untimely death. Both medical sciences, as well as statistical techniques are used in the process of seeking to identify the various types of metabolic diseases. It is essential to do data analysis that involves categorization to perform both the prediction of cardiac illness and the research into it. In addition, we have seen the application of decision trees in correctly forecasting events related to heart sickness [2].

14.2 Literature Review

In tandem with very well data mining approaches, as S. F. Weng *et al.* 2017 [3] illustrate, a range of tactics for learning abstractions have already been utilized to identify heart illness. A significant amount of study has been conducted during this investigation to develop a prediction model. Not only have these studies used various techniques, but they have also related two or a number of these approaches to one another. "Data mining" is extracting valuable information from massive databases for various applications, including education, business, and medicine. Machine learning, abbreviated as ML and "machine learning," is among the subdisciplines of artificial intelligence (AI), making significant progress. Those algorithms could analyse vast amounts of data from various professions, including the medical field, which is among those fields. One of those fields is the medical profession. It is a substitute for the old approach of predictive modelling, which uses a computer to obtain knowledge of the intricate and nonlinear interactions between several variables. This method was developed in the 1970s. This is performed by reducing, as much as possible, the gap between the expected outcomes and the actual ones that were obtained.

It was hypothesized by D.L. Ravish and colleagues in 2014 [5] that classification employing Convolutional Neural Networks (CNNs) might be done without segmentation. During the training phase, this approach considers cardiac cycles, which begin in various locations, as established by electrocardiogram (ECG) data. Specifically, the method takes into account the beginning of each cardiac cycle. CNN can create features with several locations at various points while testing both individuals [9, 10]. In the past, a significant part of the information produced by the medical business was utilized differently. This is something that has changed. The novel approaches outlined in this article are simple and efficient methods that may increase the accuracy of predicting coronary artery disease while minimising its expenses. These strategies were examined for their ability to predict and classify heart disease.

Md Manjurul Ahsan *et al.* [5] describe the information will be imbalanced and also conclude that to build ML-based cardiovascular disease diagnostic systems that can be utilized in this same real life. The data will be unbalanced and also revealed that to create ML-based cardiovascular disease diagnostic systems, After doing an in-depth analysis of 49 separate studies, it has become abundantly evident that more research is necessary to prove reliable performance in various medical domains. As a consequence of this, a gap in the existing body of research has been uncovered. Deep Learning is the approach that predominates in this domain; however, SMOTE remains one of the most actively used Over-Sampling methods.

The dataset on cardiovascular disease in Cleveland was used for the recommended study, and data mining techniques such as regression and various classifications were applied to achieve the accuracy of the proposed model. M. Kavitha, G. Gnaneswar *et al.* [6] describe heart disease in Cleveland. Approaches based on machine learning To complete this task, we will use both Random Forests and Decision trees. A cutting-edge system for the model of machine learning has already been conceived and developed. The results of the experiments show that a prediction model predicting heart disease that uses a hybrid model may obtain an accuracy level of 88.7%. Since the input parameter from the user is what we require to predict heart disease, the interface has been designed to solicit it from the user. To do this, we used a hybrid approach combining a Decision Tree with a Random Forest.

In their study, Reddy Karna *et al.* [7] explain how a 10-fold cross-validation testing method was used to perform the performance assessment of the algorithms. This instance-based (IBk) classifier's hyper-parameter again for the number of nearest neighbours, indicated by the letter k, was adjusted as the last phase of this procedure. While employing all available attributes, the (SMO) sequential minimum optimization obtained absolute accuracy of 85.148%. Still, the chi-squared attribute evaluator gave the highest accuracy result possible, which was 86.468% when using all attribute sets. After applying the extensive and optimum attribute sets created using meta classifier bagging to logistic regression (LR), the ROC area was 0.91%, the highest. The relief attribute evaluator was used to gain all the necessary qualities. By adjusting the value of the hyperparameter 'k' to 9 and enabling the chi-squared characteristic, IBk enhanced accuracy by 8.25%. This resulted in the SMO classifier being the most accurate prediction technique overall compared to the other methods.

According to C. M. Wu *et al.*, [8] heart disease represents the primary cause of death in men and women of all ages while being equally frequent in both men and women. It is also the common cause of death in both men and females. It would be helpful to generate accurate projections regarding a patient's health condition at some point in the future. This would allow medical personnel to start treatment earlier, resulting in better results. It is a substantial improvement over the last minute because when a patient is at risk; therefore, the prediction of cardiovascular illness is a topic that has gotten a lot of interest from researchers since it is a subject that has the potential to save lives. A quantity of research has been done, and considerable technological advancement has been reported in fields that are pretty similar to one another. This study's objective is to provide a report detailing the usage of various data mining methods which aim to construct prediction models again for the possibility of heart disease survival.

14.3   Materials and Methods

This section provides information on the procedures and resources used, a dataset description, a diagram of the overall structure, machine learning algorithms, and assessment matrices. We collected the Cleveland cardiovascular disease data in CSV format from the UCI Machine Learning Repository. We started the programme, imported the dataset system and examined its properties, classifications, values range, and statistical data. Then we preprocess the data, including finding and substituting the user constants or the average score for missing data, depending on the characteristics. We also performed EDA to check the correlation between the dataset values to improve machine learning classifier performance. We checked for imbalanced attributes and values of the data. After all data preparations, we used NB, LR, and RF machine learning algorithms to classify the whole set of qualities. Each was analyzed and assembled to improve the suggested classification model's accuracy, as shown in Figure 14.1.

14.3.1   Dataset

The dataset used in the proposed model has 303observation, 14-variable datasets. The dataset has no missing cells and one duplicate row (0.30%). The dataset's RAM is 33.3 KiB, and the overall record size is 112.4 B. The dataset has numeric, boolean, and category variables. Six numeric,

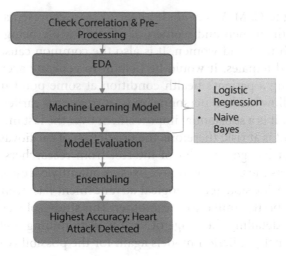

Figure 14.1 Proposed model.

four boolean, and four category variables exist. This data could assist researchers in comprehending the dataset and making preprocessing and analysis choices. Imputation may be needed if the data has multiple

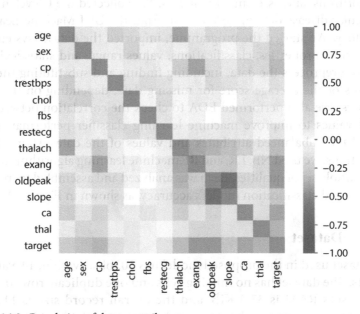

Figure 14.2 Correlation of dataset attributes.

missing values. To prevent skewing analyses, eliminate duplicate entries. Variable types suggest data models and research, as shown in Table 14.1. We have applied Pearson's correlation coefficient quantitatively measures the linear relationship between two variables (r). Its value may vary from -1 to 1, where -1 indicates an entirely negative linear correlation, 0 means no linear correlation, and 1 shows a wholly positive linear correlation. Furthermore, r is invariant despite various changes in the location and scale of the two variables, indicating that for a linear function, the angle to the x-axis does not affect r. This is because r is invariant with different changes in the two variables' scale and location. To get the correlation coefficient r between two variables, X and Y, divide the covariance of X and Y by the product of their standard deviations, as seen in Figure 14.2.

14.3.2   EDA

EDA explores and summarises a dataset's primary properties. It helps find patterns, links, and possible concerns in data. We need to check if the data is imbalanced or not. We have done a check for data misbalancing. Because If the data is unbalanced, the model can bias the majority class and underrepresent the minority. Classification issues require predicting each sample's class label. Compute the intended variable class frequencies or percentages to check against data imbalance. Suppose the amount of models for each class is large. In that case, you might have to undersample the majority class, oversample the minority class, or use cost-sensitive Learning to correct the imbalance.

14.3.3   Machine Learning Model Implemented

Logistic Regression:
Logistic regression, which falls under the umbrella of the Supervised Learning methodology, is one of the most common and widely used machines learning Algorithms-1. The categorical dependent variable may be predicted using a predetermined group of independent factors. The outcome of a categorical dependent variable may be predicted using logistic regression. As a result, the output need to be a value that is either categorical or discrete. It may be yes or no, zero or one, the truth or a lie, but rather than reporting the precise value as 0 or 1, it presents the probability values that fall between the two numbers.

Algorithm-1: Logistic Regression

The mathematical model of logistic regression can be expressed as follows:

Step-1: Given a set of independent variables $X = (X_1, X_2, ..., X_p)$ and a binary dependent variable Y, where $Y \in \{0, 1\}$, we want to model the probability of $Y = 1$ as a function of X. This can be represented using the logistic process, also known as the sigmoid function:

$$p(Y = 1|X) = \sigma(X\beta) = 1 / (1 + \exp(-X\beta))$$

Where $\beta = (\beta_0, \beta_1, ..., \beta_p)$ is a vector of coefficients, and $X\beta$ is the linear combination of X and β.

Step-2: The logistic function maps the range of possible outcomes to a probability value between 0 and 1. When $X\beta$ is positive, the probability of $Y = 1$ increases; when $X\beta$ is negative, $Y = 1$ decreases. The coefficients β can be estimated using maximum likelihood estimation, which involves finding the values of β that maximize the likelihood function:

$$L(\beta) = \prod_i p(y_i|X_i; \beta)$$

Where y_i is the observed value of Y for the i-th data point, and X_i is the corresponding value of X.

Step-3: To find the maximum likelihood estimates of β, we can use an optimization algorithm such as gradient descent, which iteratively updates the values of β to minimize the negative log-likelihood function:

$$J(\beta) = -\log(L(\beta)) = -\sum_i [y_i \log(p(y_i=1|X_i; \beta)) + (1 - y_i) \log(1 - p(y_i=1|X_i; \beta))]$$

Step-4: Once the coefficients β have been estimated, we can use them to make predictions on new data by applying the logistic function to the linear combination of the independent variables and the coefficients:

$$p(Y = 1|X) = \sigma(X\beta)$$

If the predicted probability is more significant than 0.5, we predict $Y = 1$; otherwise, we predict $Y = 0$.

Naïve Bayes:
The Naive Bayes Algorithm-2 is a supervised learning method for solving classification problems. This strategy is based on Bayes' theorem. Its principal use is text classification, which often requires a high-dimensional training dataset. The Naive Bayes Classifier is one of the simplest and most effective classification algorithms. It contributes to developing fast machine-learning models capable of quickly generating predictions. It is a probabilistic classifier that makes predictions based on the probability that an object will be located. The Bayes' theorem, which may also be referred to as Bayes' Rule or Bayes' rule, is a method for calculating the probability of a hypothesis based on already known information. It is dependent on the likelihood under the given conditions. The expression for Bayes' theorem may be written as follows in equation 14.1:

$$P(A \mid B)=(P(B \mid A)P(A))/P(B) \qquad (14.1)$$

Posterior probability, often known as P(A|B), is the likelihood that hypothesis A is correctly given observed data B. The probability, denoted by the symbol P(B|A, is the probability that a hypothesis is correct given the evidence that it has.

Random Forest:
As illustrated in Algorithm-3, the Random Forest classifier computes the mean of a collection of multiple decision trees employed to analyze various subgroups of the supplied data. This average is calculated using the Random Forest classifier. This contributes to improving the accuracy of the predictions made using the dataset. When there are a more significant number of trees in a forest, not only is it possible to reach a higher degree of accuracy, but it also makes it possible to avoid the problem of overfitting.

The following justifications led to the conclusion that random forest would be an appropriate choice for our model: 1. The time spent training is much less than with other approaches. 2. Even though it is processing a huge dataset, it can provide accurate results forecasts while operating efficiently. 3. It can also maintain accuracy even without a significant portion of the data.

Algorithm-2: Naïve Bayes

The mathematical model of Naïve Bayes is based on Bayes' theorem, which provides a way to calculate the probability of a hypothesis (H) given some experimental evidence (E). In the context of classification, the assumption is the class label (C) of a data point, and the evidence is the set of independent variables or features $(X_1, X_2, ..., X_p)$ associated with that data point. Bayes' theorem can be written as:

Step-1: $P(C|X_1, X_2, ..., X_p) = P(X_1, X_2, ..., X_p|C) * P(C) / P(X_1, X_2, ..., X_p)$
where $P(C|X_1, X_2, ..., X_p)$ is the posterior probability of class C given the observed features $X_1, X_2, ..., X_p$, $P(X_1, X_2, ..., X_p|C)$ is the likelihood of the features given the class, $P(C)$ is the prior probability of the class, and $P(X_1, X_2, ..., X_p)$ is the marginal likelihood of the features.

Step-2: Naïve Bayes assumes that the features are conditionally independent given the class, which means that the likelihood can be decomposed as a product of individual feature probabilities:

$$P(X_1, X_2, ..., X_p|C) = P(X_1|C) * P(X_2|C) * ... * P(X_p|C)$$

Step-3: This assumption simplifies the likelihood calculation and makes the model computationally efficient. We can further simplify the model by assuming that the prior probabilities are equal for all classes, which means that:

$$P(C) = 1 / K$$

where K is the number of classes.

Step-4: Substituting these expressions into Bayes' theorem, we get:
$P(C|X_1, X_2, ..., X_p) = P(X_1|C) * P(X_2|C) * ... * P(X_p|C) * P(C) / P(X_1, X_2, ..., X_p)$
We can use this expression to calculate the posterior probability of each class for a given set of features and then choose the class with the highest probability as the predicted class label.

We can use a training set of labelled data and apply the maximum likelihood principle to estimate $P(X|C)$ and $P(C)$ probabilities. This involves counting the number of occurrences of each feature value for each class in the training set and computing the corresponding probabilities. Smoothing techniques such as Laplace smoothing can avoid zero possibilities and improve the robustness of the model.

Algorithm-3: Random Forest

Given a training set of N data points with p features and a corresponding target variable Y, we want to build a Random Forest model to predict Y for new data points.

For each of the K decision trees in the forest:

a. Randomly sample a subset of size n (n << N) from the training set with replacement. This is known as the bootstrap sample.
b. Randomly select a subset of size m (m << p) from the features. This is known as the random feature selection.
c. Train a decision tree on the bootstrap sample using only the selected features.

To predict a new data point x with p features:

a. Pass x through each of the K decision trees in the forest.
b. Obtain the predicted target variable for each tree, denoted as Y_k(x).
c. Compute the final prediction as the average or majority vote of the Y_k(x) values.

The decision trees in the Random Forest can be constructed using various algorithms such as ID3, C4.5, CART, etc. Each tree is trained to minimize the impurity of the nodes, which is measured using metrics such as the Gini index or entropy.

In summary, the Random Forest model combines multiple decision trees trained on random subsets of the data and features to improve the accuracy and robustness of the classification or regression task. The final output of the model is obtained by averaging or taking the majority vote on the predictions of the individual trees.

14.4   Result Analysis

A training dataset containing 80% of the data and a test dataset containing 20% is generated from the original dataset. A data collection used during a model's training phase is known as a "training dataset." In addition, the effectiveness of a trained model is assessed with the assistance of the testing dataset. Various measures, such as precision, accuracy, F1-scores, and recall, are utilized to create and evaluate each method's performance, as detailed in more depth below. These metrics include accuracy, precision, and recall.

Logistic Regression: The model has an accuracy of 0.85 overall, and its precision, F1 score, and recall are also suitable for both classes. Moreover, the model's overall accuracy is relatively high. The macro and weighted averages across categories are likewise the same at 0.85, indicating that the model is doing equally well in both classes, as seen in Table 14.1.

Navie Bayes: The Naive Bayes model has an overall accuracy of 0.852, and the precision, F1-score, and recall are all relatively high for both classes. The macro and weighted averages across the categories are also similar at 0.85 and 0.86, respectively. This suggests that the model performs well for both types and is not heavily biased towards one another, as shown in Table 14.2.

Random Forest Classifier: We have implemented the Random Forest model and have achieved an overall accuracy of 0.879, and the precision, recall, and F1-score are all relatively high for both classes. The macro and weighted averages across the categories are also similar at 0.87, suggesting that the model performs well for both types and is not heavily biased towards one or the other, as shown in Table 14.3.

Table 14.1 Evaluation of logistic regression.

	Recall calculated	F1-score calculated	Precision calculated	Support
0	0.819	0.83	0.85	27
1	0.89	0.87	0.86	34
Accuracy	0.845			60.9
Macro average	0.85	0.85	0.849	60.9
Weighted average	0.849	0.849	0.849	60.9

Table 14.2 Evaluation of Naive Bayes.

	Recall calculated	F1-score calculated	Precision calculated	Support
0	0.77	0.83	0.87	27
1	0.91	0.86	0.83	34
Accuracy	0.861			60.88
Macro average	0.83	0.85	0.85	60.88
Weighted average	0.848	0.848	0.848	60.88

Table 14.3 Evaluation of random forest classifier.

	Recall calculated	F1-score calculated	Precision calculated	Support
0	0.82	0.86	0.87	27
1	0.89	0.88	0.87	34
Accuracy	0.88			61.2
Macro average	0.87	0.88	0.88	60.9
Weighted average	0.88	0.88	0.88	60.8

```
##Snippet for Model Evaluation
model_ev = pd.DataFrame({'Model': ['Logistic Regression', 'NaiveBayes',
Random Forest'], 'Accuracy': [lr_acc_score*100, nb_acc_score*100,rf_
acc_score*100,xgb_acc_score*100,knn_acc_score*100,dt_acc_
score*100,svc_acc_score*100]})model_ev
```

We have implemented the evaluation for all the above three classifiers, random forest, NB, and LR, for a heart-attach prediction. We can analyze the model as shown in Table 14.4 and Figure 14.3.

Ensembling
Ensembling improves model correctness. We stack the classifier using the stacking method shown in Table 14.5, Accuracy of StackingCVClassifier: 92.87%. The ensembling results for all three classifiers, LR, NB and RF, are shown in Table 14.5.

Table 14.4 Accuracy analysis for LR, NB, RF.

	Model implemented	Accuracy
1	Naive Bayes	85%
2	Random Forest	85%
3	Logistic Regression	88%

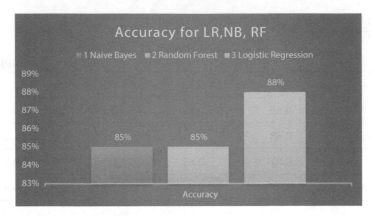

Figure 14.3 Accuracy graph for LR, NB, RF.

Table 14.5 Result of ensembling.

	Recall	F1-score	Precision	Support
0	0.88	0.9	0.93	27
1	0.95	0.92	0.9	34
Accuracy	0.93			60.99
Macro average	0.93	0.933	0.932	60.98
Weighted average	0.93	0.933	0.931	60.98

14.5   Conclusion

This chapter presents three approaches to machine learning, and a comparative analysis of those approaches is offered. Based on the dataset provided, this post aimed to determine which machine learning classifiers you believe would be most effective in predicting heart disease, analyzing and comparing the results of three distinct classifiers. The comparative approaches are the confusion matrix, precision, specificity, and sensitivity. Under the framework of the ML approach, the LR classifier performed very well with all 14 variables in the sample. The random forest has the most significant level of accuracy, 88%. By ensembling the results of all the classifiers naïve bayes, random forest, and logistic regression, we have achieved improved results of 93% to predict the heart attack. Because of ongoing research, machine learning algorithms are becoming better, which means that in the not-too-distant future, this form of diagnosis will become more prevalent. If more patient information is employed, the model has the potential to be enhanced and modified. A larger dataset will always result in more exact and accurate conclusions. Even though medical diagnosis is a sensitive issue, it necessitates high precision and accuracy. This is a significant point. It is possible that in the future, a web application may be built that will include these technologies and utilize a dataset that is bigger than the one that was used in this research. Consequently, medical professionals will have a greater capacity to forecast and treat cardiac issues more promptly and effectively accurately. The dependability of the framework and its appearance will be improved as a result of this.

References

1. Amzad, M.D., Tazin, T., Khan, S., Alam, E., Sojib, H.A., Khan, M.M., Alsufyani, A., Supervised machine learning-based cardiovascular disease analysis and prediction. *Math. Probl. Eng.*, 21, SP. 1792201, 2021, Hindawi.

2. Abdullah, S.A. and Rajalaxmi, R.R., A Data mining Model for predicting Coronary Heart Disease using Random Forest Classifier. *IJCA Proceedings on International Conference in Recent trends in Computational Methods, Communication and Controls (ICON3C 2012) ICON3C*, vol. 3), pp. 22–25, April 2012.

3. Weng, S.F., Reps, J., Kai, J., Garibaldi, J.M., Qureshi, N., Can machine learning improve cardiovascular risk prediction using routine clinical data? *PLoS One*, 12, 4, Article ID e0174944, 2017.

4. Ravish, D.K., Shanthi, K.J., Shenoy, N.R., Nisargh, S., Heart function monitoring, prediction and prevention of heart attacks: Using artificial neural networks, in: *Proceedings of the 2014 International Conference on Contemporary Computing and Informatics (IC3I)*, Mysore, India, pp. 1–6, November 2014.

5. Ahsan, Md. M and Siddique, Z., Machine learning-based heart disease diagnosis: A systematic literature review. *Artif. Intell. Med.*, 128, SP.102289, 2022.

6. Kavitha, M., Gnaneswar, G., Dinesh, R., Sai, Y.R., Suraj, R.S., Heart disease prediction using hybrid machine learning model, in: *Proceedings of the 2021 6th International Conference on Inventive Computation Technologies (ICICT)*, Coimbatore, India, pp. 1329–1333, January 2021.

7. Reddy, K.V.V., Elamvazuthi, I., Aziz, A.A., Paramasivam, S., Chua, H.N., Pranavanand, S., Heart disease risk prediction using machine learning classifiers with attribute evaluators. *Appl. Sci.*, 11, 18, 8352, 2021.

8. Wu, C.M., Badshah, M., Bhagwat, V., Heart disease prediction using data mining techniques, in: *Proceedings of the 2019 2nd International Conference on Data Science and Information Technology (DSIT 2019)*, New York, NY, USA, pp. 7–11, July 2019.

9. Raja, R., Kumar, Rani, S., Laxmi, K.R., Lung segmentation and nodule detection in 3D medical images using convolution neural network, in: *Artificial Intelligence and Machine Learning in 2D/3D Medical Image Processing*, pp. 179–188, CRC Press, Boca Raton, FL, USA, 2020.

10. Kumar, M. and Kumar, S., Compression of clinical images using different wavelet function, in: *Artificial Intelligence and Machine Learning in 2D/3D Medical Image Processing*, pp. 119–131, CRC Press, Boca Raton, FL, USA, 2020.

11. Rani, S., Ghai, D., Kumar, Knowledge vector representation of three dimensional convex polyhedrons and reconstruction of medical images using knowledge vector. *Multimed. Tools Appl., Springer J.*, 24, 1, 1–24, 2023.

12. Kumar, S., Singh, S., Kumar, J., Prasad, K.M.V.V., Age and gender classification using Seg-Net based architecture and machine learning. *Multimed. Tools Appl.*, 22, 2, 01–24, 2022.

13. Kumar, Rani, S., Jain, A., Verma, C., Raboaca, M.S., Illés, Z., Neagu, B.C., Face spoofing, age, gender and facial expression recognition using advance neural network architecture-based biometric system. *Sensor J.*, 22, 14, 5160–5184, 2022.

14. Rani, S., Ghai, D., Kumar, Kantipudi, M.V.V., Alharbi, A.H., Ullah, M.A., Efficient 3D AlexNet architecture for object recognition using syntactic patterns from medical images. *Comput. Intell. Neurosci.*, 22, 1–19, 2022.

15. Kumar, S., Jain, A., Agarwal, A.K., Rani, S., Ghimire, A., Object-based image retrieval using U-Net based neural network. *Comput. Intell. Neurosci.*, 21, 1, 1–14, 2021.

16. Kumar, S., Singh, S., Kumar, J., Live detection of face using machine learning with multi-feature method. *Wirel. Pers. Commun.*, 103, 3, 2352–2375, 2018.

17. Choudhary, S., Ghai, D., Kumar, Automatic Detection of Brain Tumor from CT and MRI Images using 3DAlex-Net, in: *International Conference on Decision Aid Sciences and Applications (DASA)*, Bahrain, 2022.

18. Kumar, S., Rani, S., Singh, R., Automated recognition of dental caries using K-Means and PCA based algorithm, in: *University of Bahrain 4th Smart Cities Symposium*, 21-23 November 2021.

19. Choudhary, S., Lakhwani, K., Kumar, S., 3D wireframe model of medical and complex images using cellular logic array processing, in: *12th International Conference on Soft Computing and Pattern Recognition (SCOPAR 2020)*, MIR LAB, USA, December 15th-18th, 2020.

20. Kartik, Kumar, Prasad, M.V.V., Moses, J., Automated home based physiotherapy, in: *2020 International Conference on Decision Aid Sciences and Applications (DASA'20)*, 8th – 9th November 2020, University of Bahrain.

21. Kumar, S., Singh, S., Kumar, J., Gender classification using machine learning with multi-feature method, in: *IEEE 9th Annual Computing and Communication Workshop and Conference (CCWC)*, Las Vegas, USA, January 7th-9th, 2019.

15

Machine Learning-Based Approaches for Improving Healthcare Services and Quality of Life (QoL): Opportunities, Issues and Challenges

Pankaj Rahi[1]*, Rohit Bajaj[2], Sanjay P. Sood[3], Monika Dandotiyan[4] and A. Anushya[5]

[1]*Health IT Management, Institute of Health Management Research, Bangalore, India*
[2]*Department of Computer Science and Engineering Chandigarh University Mohali Punjab, India*
[3]*Health Informatics and Tele-Medicine Division, CDAC-Mohali, India*
[4]*Department of Computer Science and Engineering, Poornima University, Jaipur, Rajasthan, India*
[5]*Department of Data Science, College of Computer Science and Engineering University of Hail, Hail, Kingdom of Saudi Arabia*

Abstract

Machine learning and artificial intelligence can change the traditional treatment style to the technology-linked quality of healthcare. The professionals of the health sector and their management fraternity have also welcomed this changing era of technology with quantum speed and showed their inclination to contribute more towards adopting and deploying intelligent systems for improving the quality and efficiency of the healthcare system. Since the healthcare system is primarily linked with the service delivery and curative part of infectious or non-communicable diseases prominent in the community. Hence, machine learning technologies have the potential to overcome or streamline medical healthcare analytics for improving healthcare service delivery. This chapter is a detailed analysis of the healthcare problems and how adopting machine learning platforms enhances the quality of healthcare services. This chapter will also describe the use cases and how effectively the machine learning methodologies benefit the entire healthcare system, environmental healthcare, and Hospital 4.0.

Corresponding author: pankaj.rahi@outlook.com

Sandeep Kumar, Anuj Sharma, Navneet Kaur, Lokesh Pawar and Rohit Bajaj (eds.) *Optimized Predictive Models in Healthcare Using Machine Learning*, (245–272) © 2024 Scrivener Publishing LLC

Keywords: Smart system, machine learning, eHealth, environmental-healthcare, Hospital 4.0

15.1 Introduction

Healthcare informatics is a multidisciplinary field that has grown to be associated with significant data issues and technology breakthroughs. The healthcare sector is changing three key areas: digital records keeping, data integration, and computer-aided diagnostics. These innovations are driven by the need to lower healthcare costs and the shift toward individualized healthcare. Numerous tools, approaches, and frameworks are available in the complicated ML arena that can be used to tackle these problems. A.I. and ML can boost workplace efficiency and supplement human labour significantly. When they are used to replacing people in routine or dangerous duties, resources may be devoted to more intellectually demanding jobs that call for traits like creativity and empathy.

With established track records, DL and ML play a crucial role in logistics supply chain management. The success of DL and ML in healthcare schemes can be attributed to their capacity to manage massive, complicated data with little human participation. The current healthcare system substantially uses ML and DL to improve the service and health of patients, physicians, and other healthcare personnel. Acute disease identification, image analysis, medication development, drug delivery, and intelligent health monitoring have all been proven to benefit from using ML and DL. This paper provides an advanced study of current products in ML and DL and how they are being applied in healthcare systems to achieve several objectives.

For early detection of diseases, diagnosis and treatment, and early treatment, healthcare informatics entails the collection, distribution, interpretation, preservation, and information retrieval [1]. Health records, disease-related data, and the computational methods used to handle this data are the sole focus of healthcare informatics. Over the past few decades, traditional medical practices in the United States have made investments in better technology and computational support for researchers, medical professionals, and patients to offer accessible, high-quality healthcare that is seamless and inexpensive. Through these initiatives, the advantages and significance of applying computational tools for prescription and referral assistance, developing and maintaining electronic health records (E.H.R.), and technological breakthroughs in digital medical imaging have all come to light.

The development of affordable sensors has been facilitated by Industry 4.0 and 5G wireless connection, which has contributed to the creation of the I.O.T. It plays a crucial part in the modern healthcare system. The current healthcare system must include the IoMT [2]. IoT is a constantly growing, open ecosystem that combines any device that gathers or exchanges data. IoMT refers to the Internet of Things in the healthcare service network. Since the COVID-19 pandemic, there has been an urgent demand. The volume of information generated by these gadgets is likewise increasing. (A large volume of data is stored and managed on cloud servers. When it comes to health data, there are numerous applications. The volume of information generated by these gadgets is likewise increasing. (A large volume of data is stored and managed on cloud servers. When it comes to health data, there are numerous applications processed intelligently [3–5].

Additionally, it offers information for the creation of DL/ML models. Because transactions don't need different protocols, blockchain has an adaptable nature that allows it to be connected with various data kinds, platforms, and devices [6]. Digital fitness wearables, genomic sequences, and electronic health records all produce enormous volumes of data that are difficult to review without the help of A.I., DL, or artificial neuro-networking [7–9]. Deep learning is a subset or branch of machine learning [10, 11]. Classification of A.L., ML, and DL is given in Figure 15.1. ML and

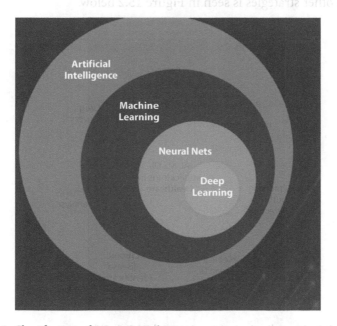

Figure 15.1 Classification of A.L., ML, and DL.

DL were also discovered to play a crucial role in healthcare data admin-istration. A logical progression from artificial intelligence is machine learning. Academics and healthcare professionals frequently use machine learning to handle sophisticated statistical analysis. Healthcare informatics is the field that combines machine learning and healthcare data with the impartiality of detecting patterns of relevance. Therefore, health systems aim to find patterns in data and then learn from such practices [4].

15.2   Core Areas of Deep Learning and ML-Modeling in Medical Healthcare

More variations are being noticed in the medical area by offering different online and offline facilities since DL and ML are evolutionary changes in many domains, including business, industry, schools, colleges, and health-care systems. Deep learning is crucial for the automated identification of cancer cells. While the DL works independently or autonomously utilizing machine learning, the ML can solve various problems but requires human intervention. The whole issue is resolved through deep understanding. ML automatically, not so. Deep knowledge is beneficial for diagnosing heart problems in youngsters, coma patients, and older people [12]. The use of A.I. and other strategies is seen in Figure 15.2 below.

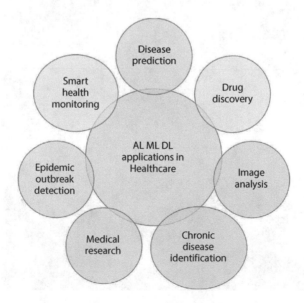

Figure 15.2 Major applications of A.I., ML, and DL in healthcare.

Any problem can be recognized with the assistance of DL, and data-driven performance is always preferable. e-learning algorithms are straight-forward, which makes them simple to learn, perform, and apply. Since machine learning is not linear, it can produce powerful, quick machine learning for language learning and is responsible for patient data accuracy [13]. These complex neural networks require much time to train and evaluate data. The opportunities to examine a dynamic system [14, 15], change the environment, and recognize data in various data forms are provided by machine learning (ML). The study of genes can easily detect genetic diseases as well as to provide a benchmark for the efficacy of machine learning techniques for breast cancer or other diseases-categorization [29–31]. This capability makes it useful in multiple domains, including the healthcare system and the protection of the cybercrime business.

However, it is crucial to the healthcare system, particularly for kids and older people who want to live alone. Deep learning is necessary for progress when taking the facts into account. In the present era, cardiovascular disease has a daily rising fatality rate (CD).

In the healthcare industry, machine learning is generating significant improvement and innovation. It accelerates clinical procedures, medication research, surgery, and information management. The healthcare sector is expanding and impacts every part of our lives. The evolution of technology and the healthcare sector go hand in hand. For the benefit of humanity, technology is quickly integrating with medical disciplines to provide preventative, diagnostic, and therapeutic options [28–30]. Healthcare management uses this approach to predict patient wait times in urgent departments [21]. Doctors believe that timing is essential when making diagnoses, and patients can benefit substantially from making a wise choice quickly [22, 23]. Health files are now primarily managed online. With so much data being generated, a proper method for quickly and effectively organizing, analyzing, securing, and storing data electronically is essential [81].

The Covid-19 pandemic has enabled the healthcare industry to utilize this cutting-edge technology. More importantly, patients will benefit the most from the technology because it can enhance their healthcare outcomes by analyzing the best treatment strategies for them. ML can detect disease at an earlier stage with greater accuracy, reducing the number of readmissions in clinics and hospitals [77–79]. The primary uses of machine learning in healthcare and how the technology is reshaping the industry with its remarkable benefits have been explicitly explained in this article.

15.3   Use Cases of Machine Learning Modelling in Healthcare Informatics

15.3.1   Breast Cancer Detection Using Machine Learning

The bulk of the studies emphasized mammography images. However, mammography pictures may be incorrectly identified, endangering the patient's health. Alternative approaches that are less complicated to implement or integrate with other datasets, less expensive, safer, and able to provide a more reliable forecast are crucial and helpful for addressing breast cancer treatment [24, 26–28]. In the case of breast cancer, the dangerous cells may spread to lymph centres or even explain the damage to various parts of the body bits, for instance, the lungs. Bosom malignancy even more regularly starts from breaking milk-conveying channels (prominent ductal carcinoma) [16]. Regardless, The brief of the research studies conducted for modelling the ML-based technique for predicting and detecting Breast Cancer is represented in Table 15.1 and Table 15.2.

15.3.2   COVID-19 Disease Detection Modelling Using Chest X-Ray Images with Machine and Transfer Learning Framework

The new coronavirus produced by the SARS-CoV2 disease emerged in Wuhan, China and worldwide. At the end of 2019, humanity was confronted with a pandemic that no one anticipated to see in the modern era: SARS is a severe acute respiratory illness. SARS CoV-2 correlated with pneumonia, also recognized as coronavirus illness 2019 (COVID-19). On the other hand, the COVID-19 outburst began in Wuhan, China; the epidemic's global expansion has resulted in a shortage of equipment for clinicians treating the sickness. At the writing period, there have been over 28,000,000 verified cases and over 814,000 confirmed deaths universally. Early virus diagnosis is critical for the patient's recovery, but late detection can be deadly. This virus is relatively more dangerous due to its infectious nature. Because the virus's symptoms are similar to the flu, it isn't easy to diagnose. Hence various research studies have tried to develop an automated technique for identifying Covid19 virus-infected pictures of chest X-rays images rather than simple symptoms. The suggested approach uses a dataset containing non-infected human chest X-rays in addition to individuals suffering from pneumonia and Covid19 virus infection. First, we train a custom CNN on a vast data set of X-ray chest pictures for

Table 15.1 Summary of the ML-based modelling for detecting the breast cancer disease.

Author	Methods	Description
S. Ravi S. Punitha, and M. Anousouya Devi	Segmentation and Edge Detection algorithms	Mammography is the best and most robust procedure for the early finding harmful chest developments through screening and exact recognizable proof of masses, microcalcifications, and configuration turn. The chest threat distinguishing proof precision and capability can be extended by applying distinctive picture assessment methodologies on cutting-edge mammograms on the thick zones of the chests pushing the radiologists to perceive questionable regions hindering unwanted biopsies and repulsive educations. This paper focuses on the diverse picture examination methods; for instance, division and edge revelation counts for the disclosure chest varieties from the standard and sees its focal points and shortcoming [25, 55–57].
A. Aarthy Poornila and D. Selvathi	Unsupervised DL	Proposed structure uses performance, an essential learning-based approach that uses a Mammogram instead of a chest of risk development. Stamped data completes as readiness is set, and anonymous images are displayed with essential reading nets. The keyframe contains the default encoder and the plural complex feature [58]. The default encoder has four integrated layers and a standard non-compliant novel that joins crowds for lack and difficulty of life [59–61]. The model is easy to use and summarizes some of the points of earning points. The proposed model achieved 98.5% accuracy in producing complex mammogram images.
Bhupendra Guptha and Anuj Kumar Singh	Max-Mean and Least Variance technique	The makers present a direct strategy for areas of unsafe tissues in the mammogram [62, 63]. The division of the tumour district in a mammogram picture fails the area stage. This technique uses essential picture-getting-ready systems, for instance, averaging and thresholding [64–67]. Test outcomes display the ampleness of our system.

(*Continued*)

Table 15.1 Summary of the ML-based modelling for detecting the breast cancer disease. (*Continued*)

Author	Methods	Description
Semih Ergin, Onur Kilinc	Feature Extraction Framework	This research paper examines the structure of the model evidence for the selection and targeting of cases of asthma. From the outset, studies are conducted with two classes showing normal and curious (dangerous) chest tissue. It is requested using Support Vector Machine (SVM), k Nearest Neighborhood (kNN).
Chandra Prasetyo Utomo, Aan Kardiana, Rika Yuliwulandari	extreme learning machine neural networks, BP ANN	In this research paper, the makers executed ANN with unbelievable learning strategies for diagnosing chest dangerous development subject model over BP ANN [82, 83].
Sutton and Bezdek	Windows mean and standard deviation.	This research depicts the utilization of division with fluffy models and characterization by the fresh k-closest neighbour (k-NN) calculation for helping bosom malignant growth location in computerized mammograms [84].
Amandeep Singh, Amanpreet Kaur	Noise Reduction, Crop, Thresholding Segmentation, Edge Detection, Global	This research presents pictures taking care of the system to perceive tissue information; biomedical images can help specialists in perceiving ailments brought about by cells' sporadic turn of events. Making counts and programming to dismember these photos may similarly help specialists in their step-by-step workThis examination of picture limit, edge distinguishing proof, and division helps acknowledge harm.

Table 15.2 Taxonomy of the ML-based modelling for detecting health issues/diseases.

Diseases	Author	Technique used	Dataset	Accuracy
Heart infection	Apurb Rajdhan (2020), [40]	Random Forest	DS (U.C.I.)	90.16%
	Archana Singh (2020), [41]	K-Nearest neighbour	Repository Dataset (U.C.I.)	87%
	Abhijeet Jagtap (2019), [42]	SVM	DS	75.3%
	Harshit Jindal (2021), [43]	KNN	UCI repository DS	87.5%
Diabetes disease	Nesreen Samer El_Jerjawi (2018), [44]	ANN	Evidence of Urmia's Connection with Diabetics	87.3%
	Safial Islam Ayon (2019), [45]	D.N.N.	Indian Diabetes Dataset (Pima)	94.56%
	Aishwarya Mujumdae (2019), [46]	Logistic Regression	-	96%
	Amani Yahyaoui (2020), [47]	R.F.	Pima Indian Diabetes Dataset	86.5%
Liver disease	A. K. M. Sazzadur Rahman (2019) [48]	L.R.	The U.C.I. Machine Learning Repository's data.	75%
	M. Banu Priya (2018) [49]	J.48 and Bayesnet	Indian Liver Patient Dataset	95.04% and 90.33%
	Dr. S. Vijayarani, [50]	SVM	Indian Liver Patient Dataset (I.L.P.D.)	79.66%
	Kannapiran T, Md. Irfan et al., [51]	K-Nearest Neighbor	Indian Liver Patient Dataset (I.L.P.D.)	73.97%

(Continued)

Table 15.2 Taxonomy of the ML-based modelling for detecting health issues/diseases. (*Continued*)

Diseases	Author	Technique used	Dataset	Accuracy
Malaria disease	Gautham Shekar (2020), [52]	Basic CNN, VGG-19 Frozen CNN, and VGG-19 Fine-Tuned CNN	-	94%, 92% and 96%
	Krit Sriporn (2020), [53]	CNN	Information was gathered under a microscope from a thin blood smear on a hospital slide that contained malaria.	96.85%
	Soner Can Kalkan, [54]	CNN	27,558 cell pictures are available from the U.S. National Library of Medicine.	95%
	Vijayalakshmi (2019), [55]	VGG19-SVM	-	91%
Pneumonia disease	Tilve *et al*, 2020, [56]	VGG16 (CNN)	-	93.6%
	Racicetal, 2021, [57]	CNN	ChestX-Ray	88.90%
	Ayan E, Unver H.M., 2019, [58]	Transfer Learning 1. VGG16 2. 2) Xception	FrontalchestX-ray images	V.G.G.-87% Xception -87%
	Ayush Pantetal, 2020, [59]	Efficient Net-B4-based U-Net and ResNet-34-based U-Net	The Guangzhou Women and Children's Medical Center donated a Kaggle data set.	82%

non-COVID-19 before normalizing the images and performing the detection approach in the area of covid. The proposed model is then fine-tuned using the tiny COVID-19 data. Three previous transfer learning frameworks (Resnet-50, V.G.G. 16, and VGG19) with implemented CNN have been adopted, with 96, 97 and 97% accuracy, respectively. These models not only deliver an efficient detection of covid-1 x-ray images but also give a proper way for handling multiple x-ray images in a deep learning platform which offers a new perspective to society to deal with the early stage of the coronavirus. This research, combined with the G.U.I., would assist clinicians in detecting afflicted individuals using computer-aided analysis in seconds with multiple deep-learning models. This will significantly enhance the medical field's worth.

Related work for the detection of COVID-19 diseases undertaken using ML, DL, and CNN

Advances in picture identification, particularly in auxiliary medical diagnosis technologies. Deep learning has been used effectively to diagnose pneumonia from X-rays, outperforming radiologists. Several transfer learning models have been utilized for covid-19 identification, with each kind being employed in a different application based on the brain region of interest to investigate.

- Samesh H. Basha *et al.* (2023) Planned a COVID-19 infection recognition system built on chest X-ray pictures with uncertainty estimation. Estimating vagueness is critical for appropriately using computer-aided diagnostic technologies in health applications. A skilled radiologist should carefully examine model estimates with substantial uncertainty. Using the Mix Match semi-supervised framework, we aim to enhance uncertainty estimations using unlabeled data. We put standard uncertainty estimating methods, such as SoftMax scoring. We suggest employing the Jensen-Shannon distance b/w ambiguity distributions of right and wrong predictions to compare the dependability of uncertainty approximations. Our test findings demonstrate a substantial improvement in uncertainty estimations when using unlabeled data. The employment of the Monte Carlo dropout approach yields the best results [8].
- D. Haritha *et al.* (2020) applies the idea of transfer learning for this assignment because few photographs of COVID-19 patients are available to the public. We modify many Image

Net-trained convolutional neural network (CNN) designs to work. For the other dataset, DenseNet201 and M.L.P. had the highest accuracy. The recommended technique thus successfully detects COVID-19 in X-ray images [9]. The solution offered by Calderon-Ramirez, S., and others (2020) was tested using two freely accessible databases. This suggests that our semi-supervised system might assist in increasing performance levels for Covid-19 identification. In addition, we offer a semi-supervised DL boost coefficient designed to improve our technique's scalability and performance comparability. As a result, early, rapid, and low-cost identification of infected patients is critical. Currently, tests are restricted and only available to those in imminent danger of severe disease. DL applied to chest X-ray images for corona identification is an appealing technique [10].

- Ahmedt-Aristizabal *et al.* (2021) present a machine-learning technique for identifying instances of infected individuals based on x-ray pictures of their lungs. Owing to the scarcity of accessible data and the limited processing capacity, we propose two methods: I Construct a custom CNN from scratch utilizing a massive data collection of non-COVID-19 pulmonary X-Rays from the past. ii) Use transfer learning with pre-trained CNN models and COVID-19 data to fine-tune the final layers [11].

- W. Shi *et al.* (2021) Based on the direction of attention transmission, the suggested network structure may be split into instructor and student networks. First, the network captures global characteristics and focuses on infection regions to produce attention maps. With an enlarged reception field, we suggest a deformable attention module to increase infected areas' responsiveness and decrease noise in inappropriate regions. Furthermore, integrating important information in the original i/p transfers attention to knowledge. Extensive studies have been carried out using publicly accessible chest X-ray and C.T. imaging datasets [12].

- M. Qjidaa *et al.* (2020) For the primary identification of COVID-19 using chest x-rays, which are more readily available to patients in rural areas, advance an intelligent medical decision support system. In the end, 566 radiological images of three different types—the COVID-19 type, the Pneumonia type, and the Normal-type—were obtained.

A research study used training data from 80% of the database and tested data from 20%. They use augmentation very immediately after the pretreatment method. Our final classifier performed best with a test accuracy of (99 per cent), an f1-score of 98%, a precision of (98.60%), and a sensitivity of (98.30 %) [13].

- Using an automated approach, S. Guefrechi, M. B. Jabra *et al.* (2020) Attempt to detect Covid19 virus-infected chest X-ray images. The proposed method uses a dataset that includes noninfected human chest X-rays. Many ML approaches and ensembles of these individual representations are employed to categorize the resultant feature sets. The findings of the experiments are obtained by 10-fold CV testing [14].

- E. Irmak (2020) is novel, robust, and resilient using openly available information. A CNN model is created and offered as a potential COVID-19 sickness diagnosis tool. The practice-based study recommended in this research report is anticipated to help doctors recognize the COVID-19 condition. The most important effect of this new coronavirus is its contagiousness, which endangers life as we know it. Research on COVID-19 diagnostics will pick more steam as more details about the biology of this lethal virus become accessible [15].

- S. Lafraxo and M. el Ansari (2020) It is advised to use CoviNet, a DL network, to detect the presence of COVID-19 automatically in X-ray pictures. A CNN, histogram equalization, and a filter (median) are the cornerstones of the advised planning. It is wholly trained using a dataset that is available to the public. Since early discovery may limit the virus's spread, this model has a binary classification precision of 98.62% and a multi-class classification accuracy of 95.77%.

- G. Gosh *et al.* (2022) with (99.9%) accuracy, the suggested model accurately detects the binary classes (COVID and regular). C.H.E.X.N.E.T. is a (CNN) network trained on the ChestX-ray14 dataset to detect anomalies in chest X-rays. This framework was generally expanded to perceive all 14 viruses in the (chestX-ray) 14-dataset. Our model applied its pre-trained model Densenet121 to identify COVID-19 from binary classes. The new coronavirus is a fast-spreading viral illness that has become a pandemic, posing severe dangers worldwide. It is critical to detect patients ahead of time to prevent the development of this pandemic [17].

- O. El Gannour *et al.* (2020) suggest a Deep Learning based method for COVID-19 illness recognition. The Transfer Learning method is used to build this system, which utilizes six pre-trained models. The used X-Ray image library comprises 2905 pictures. This dataset has been through a variety of preparation steps. This research demonstrates that the Exception network categorization is the most accurate for identifying instances infected with COVID-19. This technique has a sensitivity of 98% with an accuracy of 100%, respectively [18].

- Narin (2020), Chest X-ray images that were quick and simple to collect were used because the covid19 targeted the respiratory systems. By employing residual networks to extract features from these images, classification results were obtained using support vector machines (ResNet-50). The highest overall performance values are SVM-quadratic and SVM-cubic, which are over 99%. Based on these encouraging findings, this research-based method is anticipated to benefit radiology experts and reduce the rate of false positives [19].

- J. Rabbah *et al.* (2020) The presented Cov Stack net is a unique classification system based on the Stack Net meta-modelling technique. The cornerstone for feature extraction from X-ray pictures was a deep CNN. The projected model outperforms the elementary models in terms of accuracy, scoring 98% [20].

Findings and concluding remarks in case of COVID Detection Modeling: Diagnosing COVID +ve patients as soon as possible is critical to prevent the disease from spreading and keep it under control. This study was conducted to detect COVID +ve patients using Chest X-Ray pictures in a simple and low-cost manner. First, in the approach suggested in this study, a HUGE data set of non-COVID-19 X-ray chest pictures is used to train a bespoke CNN, which is then used to normalize the images. The model is then fine-tuned using the tiny COVID-19 data. It is hoped that this research, combined with the G.U.I. interface, would assist clinicians in detecting afflicted individuals using computer-aided analysis in seconds.

15.4 Improving the Quality of Services During the Diagnosing and Treatment Processes of Chronicle Diseases

Machine learning has many possible applications in clinical care, including improving patient data, diagnosis, and treatment, cost savings and improved patient safety. These are just a few advantages that machine learning applications in healthcare have [85, 86]. Can offer medical professionals are listed below:

Medical imaging analysis can be improved using machine learning in the healthcare sector. For instance, a machine learning algorithm can search for patterns that signal a specific condition in medical imaging (X-rays or M.R.I. scans). This could enable doctors to diagnose patients with more significance efficiently and precisely.

15.4.1 Evolution of New Diagnosing Methods and Tools

There is a need to deploy significant efforts for improving the collection of quality of data so that ML-based modelling may be implemented in all areas of healthcare for intensifying medical care and also reducing the burden of diseases. Hence, efforts to integrate ML modelling with Public Health Intelligence and Medical care databases are highly desired.

15.4.2 Improving Medical Care

Our in-house developed medical algorithms also process and analyze our clinical practice data and notes. Our clinical informatics team continuously evaluates and improves this dynamic collection of ML algorithms, which is essential to the process. We've created complete applications of machine learning in healthcare inside our clinical algorithms, including our medical lexicon and comprehensive ideas and words. Your clinical data and notes are extracted by the N.L.P. engine of the ForeSee Medical Disease Detector before being examined by our clinical rules and machine learning algorithms. Because we consistently feed our "machine" patient healthcare data for machine learning, which increases the precision of our N.L.P. performance, N.L.P. performance is constantly growing for better results. However, not all tasks are carried out by A.I. systems or AI-related technologies like machine learning [32–38]. Preparing healthcare data for machine learning must make it easier for the computer to spot patterns and draw conclusions. This statistical method is typically carried out by people who annotate input by marking portions of the dataset for data quality. Our clinical specialists are carrying out this task, who are also evaluating data, creating new rules, and enhancing machine learning performance [71, 72]. The annotation done on the patient data must be precise and relevant to our objective of extracting essential ideas with appropriate context. However, if machine learning systems in healthcare are to train successfully and rapidly.

Even though new applications for machine learning are constantly being developed, most of them are used in the healthcare industry to enhance patient outcomes and treatment quality. You may choose a speciality. Finding the focus that best matches your interests and professional objectives may be facilitated by being aware of the many uses of ML in healthcare [73–76] (such as the ones described below).

15.4.3   Visualization of Biomedical Data

Three-dimensional representations of biological data, such as R.N.A. sequences, protein structures, and genetic profiles, may be produced using machine learning.

15.4.4   Improved Diagnosis and Disease Identification

Identification of previously unrecognized symptom patterns and comparison with more extensive data sets can help in the early detection of illnesses.

15.4.5   More Accurate Health Records

Maintain current, correct patient records that are simple for doctors, nurses, and clinic personnel to access.

15.4.6   Ethics of Machine Learning in Healthcare

While machine learning is a promising new area in healthcare, there are some ethical issues to be aware of. The shift from merely relying on humans to using intelligent robots raises concerns about privacy, accountability, and dependability. Patients cannot communicate with machines about their treatment as they do with a doctor, which may cause stress and anxiety throughout the diagnostic procedure. Patients may also prefer receiving terrible health news from a trusted doctor than from a machine.

Additionally, medical institutions should strive to avoid taking responsibility for an incorrect AI-assisted diagnosis since errors in patient diagnosis are inevitable. Further, machine learning experts risk unintentionally developing biased algorithms, and predictions may differ in accuracy depending on factors like race or gender. Governing bodies and physicians must create clear limits, procedures, and accountability early on to reduce subsequent effects as the area of machine learning continues to integrate further into healthcare [90–93].

15.5 Limitations and Challenges of ML, DL Modelling in Healthcare Systems

Many businesses use machine learning, including the automotive, manufacturing, and retail sectors. Many helpful forecasts have been made possible by advancing deep understanding and machine learning algorithms, including predictions of stock prices, housing prices, and loan defaults. Additionally, there is knowledge available in various formats that can be used to make predictions using machine learning. Machine learning has a lot of room for advancement as data volumes increase and future forecasts become increasingly accurate.

There are several options and trade-offs when creating ML models, including those involving variables, model type, preprocessing methods, and hyperparameter selection, to mention a few. Although altering some of these variables might result in improved models, testing only some possible combinations is practical. We sought several well robust models with comparable performance for our work so that we could examine and contrast how inputs are transformed into predictions. The futuristic results intend to look at deep models with high A.U.C.s for the following work.

This investigation reveals discrepancies between medical theory and what the ML models believe to be critical mortality variables. The underlying algorithm, feature values are chosen, and preprocessing methods are a few of the elements that contribute to these variances.

Even though analyzing these factors can reveal helpful information, doing so is outside the purview of this research.

With data science and machine learning, more complex algorithms are being created. Predicting the likelihood that cancer will develop and Alzheimer's disease are two exciting uses of machine learning in healthcare [39, 80]. These applications allow us to assume that reinforcement learning is still growing and that there will be more need for it. Machine learning now uses increasingly complicated algorithms that are being developed to produce reliable predictions. Radiology has machine learning models where the computers make predictions to ensure we achieve the most significant outcomes on the test set.

The many performance measures and data visualization were restricted to those deemed most appropriate. The S.H.A.P. Python package offers additional visualization options, including dependent graphs demonstrating global interpretability and may be necessary for further research. Since the formulae for generating the ratings are publicly available, APACHE II [32, 33], SAPS II, or III [34–36] can be viable alternatives for a more thorough comparison with already known models.

Data scientists and machine learning technologists still need help attempting to employ these algorithms for medical diagnosis, despite the prospect of implementing machine learning in many industries, particularly in healthcare [29, 30]. Knowing these issues helps assemble the tools and resources needed to address them and produce better results with artificial intelligence.

Implementing the models of machine learning for healthcare information may need help. Engaging with healthcare data presents several difficulties, one of which is that the data may be causative for machine learning algorithms. When there is data, and one trait contributes to the occurrence of another, the relationship is said to have a high causality. This is what is meant by the term "causation." Most machine learning algorithms operate under the assumption that each feature is independent of the others, with neither influencing each other to occur nor vice versa. When there is substantial causation between traits, this premise would be challenged.

15.5.1   Dealing With the Shortage of Knowledgeable-ML-Data Scientists and Engineers

Machine and data-driven learning algorithms have been discussed as the constraints of employing machine learning in healthcare thus far. Using artificial intelligence inside the medical sector would be extremely difficult, though, if there aren't enough people to use these algorithms. There is a greater likelihood that talented individuals will enter the sector and succeed due to the increase in data and machine learning science courses offered by educational institutions [68–70].

15.5.2 Handling of the Bias in ML Modelling of Healthcare Information

The presence of bias during the machine learning problems could make the machine learning techniques perform poorly on the test set or the unseen data, respectively. The sort of data that machine learning models are fed determines the bias in those models. The algorithms for machine learning would produce forecasts on the test set that would be a reflection of the outcomes on the biased training set, for instance, if the data provided to the models contained a plethora of info about one class and little information about the other class [86, 87].

The heading of the bias in ML modelling of healthcare information is equally important as all treatment of further medication of patients is dependent on these findings. As a result, the dominating class (majority class) is well predicted by the models with a very high level of accuracy, while the minority class is poorly predicted [91, 93, 94].

15.5.3 Accuracy of Data Attenuation

Data is everywhere in the form of diagnostic images and other helpful information. Despite the abundance of data, annotated examples and the output labelling for predictions still need to be included. We must offer the annotated data since some of the most significant machine learning algorithms might perform well when given the guidance of an output class label. By doing this, it is possible to guarantee that the machine learning algorithms fit the annotated instances and that the forecasts would be accurate. It is necessary to annotate medical data, which is time-consuming [89]. As a result, using machine learning in medicine faces this particular problem.

15.5.4 Lack of Data Quality

Despite the immense potential of machine learning techniques, more data is still needed in healthcare to utilize them fully. Medical photos comprise a relatively small portion of the data, making them insignificant for testing purposes. Additionally, the data isn't tagged, making it impossible to use for machine learning. Large amounts of data must be labelled for machine learning, which takes a lot of effort.

15.5.5   Tuning of Hyper-Parameters for Improving the Modelling of Healthcare

Many intricate machine learning (ML) models are being created, some of which include random forests, decision trees, and artificial neural networks (deep learning). The inability to adjust (alter) the parameter settings to provide a very satisfactory accuracy on the test data is one of the drawbacks of these algorithms (unseen data). These hyperparameters must be modified and closely watched to function correctly and perform better. To acquire the best possible outcomes, there are a lot of parameters to monitor and change, so this might be a laborious effort. Therefore, a significant challenge in using machine learning in healthcare is choosing the appropriate hyper-parameters and adjusting them to obtain the best results [88, 89].

15.6   Conclusion

Since the potential applications to the prediction of medical outcomes. We've also discovered that the models have a greater likelihood of gaining a clear understanding of the underlying facts and producing accurate predictions with more and more data we have. Various difficulties have been observed when using machine learning to analyze medical data. In this book chapter, a brief overview was given to clarify how machine learning models are used in the medical field so that the importance of its implementation may be considered for addressing the healthcare problem with intensified efforts towards humanity.

References

1. Kerlikowske, K., Zhu, W., Hubbard, R.A., Geller, B., Dittus, K., Braithwaite, D., Wernli, K.J., Miglioretti, D.L., Meara, E.S.O., B.C.S. Consortium *et al.*, Outcomes of screening mammography by frequency, breast density, and post-menopausal hormone therapy. *J.A.M.A. Internal Med.*, 173, 9, 807–816, 2013.
2. Jiao, Z., Gao, X., Wang, Y., Li, J., A deep feature-based framework for breast masses classification. *J. Neurocomputing*, 197, 221–231, 2016.
3. Medjahed, S.A., Saadi, T.A., Benyettou, A., Breast cancer diagnosis by using k-nearest neighbor with different distances and classification rules. *Int. J. Comput. Appl.*, 62, 1, 1–5, January 2013.

4. Marcano-Cedeno, A., Quintanilla-Domnguez, J., Andina, D., Wbcd breast cancer database classification applying artificial metaplasticity neural network. *Expert Syst. Appl.*, 38, 2011.

5. Gayathri, B.M. and Sumathi, Dr C.P., Comparative study of relevance vector machine with various machine learning techniques for detecting breast cancer. @ *IEEE*, 2016.

6. Singh, N. and Mohapatra, A., Breast cancer mass detection in mammograms using K-Means and Fuzzy C means clustering. *Int. J. Comput. Appl.*, 22, 2, May 2011.

7. Bordoloi, D., Singh, V., Sanober, S., Buhari, S.M., Ujjan, J.A., Boddu, R., Deep learning in healthcare system for quality of service. *J. Healthc. Eng.*, 2022, 2022.

8. Basha, S.H., Anter, A.M., Hassanien, A.E. *et al.*, Retracted article: Hybrid intelligent model for classifying chest X-ray images of COVID-19 patients using genetic algorithm and neutrosophic logic. *Soft. Comput.*, 27, 3427–3442, 2023. https://doi.org/10.1007/s00500-021-06103-7

9. Haritha, D., Pranathi, M. K., Reethika, M., COVID detection from chest X-rays with DeepLearning: CheXNet. *2020 5th International Conference on Computing, Communication and Security (ICCCS)*, 2020. https://doi.org/10.1109/icccs49678.2020.9277077

10. Guo, L., Zhao, L., Wu, Y., Li, Y., Xu, G., Yan, Q., Tumor detection in M.R. images using one-class immune feature weighted SVMs. *IEEE Trans. Magnetic.*, 47, 2011.

11. Ahmedt-Aristizabal, D., Armin, M.A., Denman, S., Fookes, C., Petersson, L., Graph-based deep learning for medical diagnosis and analysis: Past, present and future. *Sensors*, 21, 14, 4758, 2021.

12. Shi, W. and Gao, G. F., Emerging H5N8 avian influenza viruses. Science, 372, 6544, 784–786, 2021.

13. Qjidaa, M., Mechbal, Y., Ben-fares, A., Amakdouf, H., Maaroufi, M., Alami, B., Qjidaa, H., Early detection of COVID19 by deep learning transfer Model for populations in isolated rural areas. pp. 1–5, 2020, 10.1109/ISCV49265.2020.9204099.

14. Guefrechi, S., Jabra, M. B., Ammar, A., Koubaa, A., Hamam, H., Deep learning based detection of COVID-19 from chest X-ray images. *Multimed. Tools. Appl.*, 80, 21–23, 31803–31820, 2021, https://doi.org/10.1007/s11042-021-11192-5.

15. Irmak E., Implementation of convolutional neural network approach for COVID-19 disease detection. *Physiol. Genomics*, 52, 12, 590–601, 2020, https://doi.org/10.1152/physiolgenomics.00084.2020

16. Lafraxo, S. and El Ansari, M., CoviNet: Automated COVID-19 detection from X-rays using deep learning techniques. pp. 489–494, 2020, 10.1109/CiSt49399.2021.9357250.

17. Ghosh, S., Deep features to analyze pulmonary abnormalities in chest X-rays due to Covid-19, Doctoral dissertation, University of South Dakota, 2022.

18. El Gannour, O., Hamida, S., Cherradi, B., Al-Sarem, M., Raihani, A., Saeed, F., Hadwan, M., Concatenation of pre-trained convolutional neural networks for enhanced COVID-19 screening using transfer learning technique. *Electronics*, 11, 1, 103, 2021, https://doi.org/10.3390/electronics11010103

19. Narin, A., Kaya, C., Pamuk, Z., Automatic detection of coronavirus disease (COVID-19) using X-ray images and deep convolutional neural networks. *Pattern Anal. Applic.*, 24, 1207–1220, 2021, https://doi.org/10.1007/s10044-021-00984-y

20. Rabbah, J., Ridouani, M., Hassouni, L., A new classification model based on stacknet and deep learning for fast detection of COVID 19 through X rays images. pp. 1–8, 2020, 10.1109/ICDS50568.2020.9268777.

21. Sutton, and Bezdek, Breast cancer detection using image processing techniques. *Int. J. Comput. Sci.*, 2013.

22. Singh, N. and Mohapatra, A., Breast cancer mass detection in mammograms using K- means and Fuzzy C- means clustering. *Int. J. Comput. Appl.*, 22, 2, May 2011.

23. Gupta, S., Kumar, D., Sharma, A., Data mining classification techniques applied for cancer breast diagnosis and prognosis. *Indian J. Comput. Sci. Eng.*, 2, 2, 188–195, May 2011.

24. Pawlovsky, A.P. and Nagahashi, M., A method to select a good setting for the K.N.N. algorithm for breast cancer prognosis. *IEEE*, June 2014.

25. Silva, J., Lezama, O.B.P., Varela, N., Borrero, L.A., Integration of data mining classification techniques and ensemble learning for predicting the type of breast cancer recurrence, in: *G.P.C. 2019*, LNCS, vol. 11484, M.R. Camargos, L. Zarpelão, B. Rosas, E.P. R (Eds.), pp. 18–30, Springer, Cham, 2019.

26. Pradesh, A., Analysis of feature selection with classification: Breast cancer datasets. *Indian J. Comput. Sci. Eng*, 2, 5, 756–763, 2011.

27. Siegel, R.L., Miller, K.D., Jemal, A., Cancer statistics, 2017. *CA: A Cancer J. Clinicians*, 67, 7–30, 2017.

28. Hiba, A., Hajar, M., Hassan, A.M., Thomas, N., Using machine learning algorithms for breast cancer risk prediction and diagnosis. *The 6th International Symposium on Frontiers in Ambient and Mobile Systems (FAMS 2016)*, Procedia Computer Science, vol. 83, pp. 1064 –1069, 2016.

29. Aruna, S., Rajagopalan, S.P., Nandakishore, L.V., Knowledge based analysis of various statistical tools in detecting breast cancer. *Comput. Sci. Inf. Technol.*, 2, 2011, 37–45, 2011.

30. Yeh, T.H. and Deng, S., Application of machine learning methods to cost estimation of product life cycle. *International Journal of Computer Integrated Manufacturing (IJCIM)*, 25, 4–5, 340–352, 2012

31. Padule, A., Patel, A., Shaikh, A., Patel, A., Gavhane, J., A comparative study on healthcare using machine learning and deep learning. *Int. J. Eng. Res. & Technol. (I.J.E.R.T.)*, 11, 03, 2022.

32. Jain, D., Kadecha, B., Iyer, S., A comparative study of machine learning techniques in healthcare. *2019 6th International Conference on Computing for Sustainable Global Development (INDIACom)*, New Delhi, India, pp. 455–460, 2019.

33. Stenwig, E., Salvi, G., Rossi, P.S. *et al.*, Comparative analysis of explainable machine learning prediction models for hospital mortality. *B.M.C. Med. Res. Methodol.*, 22, 53, 2022. https://doi.org/10.1186/s12874-022-01540-w.

34. Knaus, W.A., Draper, E.A., Wagner, D.P., Zimmerman, J.E., Apache is A severity of disease classification system. *Crit. Care Med.*, 13, 10, 818–29, 1985.

35. Le Gall, J.R., Lemeshow, S., Saulnier, F., A new simplified acute physiology score (SAPS II) based on a European/North American multicenter study. *J.A.M.A.*, 270, 24, 2957–63, 1993. https://doi.org/10.1001/jama.270.24.2957.

36. Metnitz, P.G.H., Moreno, R.P., Almeida, E., Jordan, B., Bauer, P., Campos, R.A., Iapichino, G., Edbrooke, D., Capuzzo, M., Le Gall, J.-R., Saps 3—from evaluation of the patient to an assessment of the intensive care unit. Part 1: Objectives, methods and cohort description. *Intensive Care Med.*, 31, 10, 1336–44, 2005. https://doi.org/10.1007/s00134-005-2762-6.

37. Moreno, R.P., Metnitz, P.G.H., Almeida, E., Jordan, B., Bauer, P., Campos, R.A., Iapichino, G., Edbrooke, D., Capuzzo, M., Le Gall, J.-R., Saps 3—from evaluation of the patient to an assessment of the intensive care unit. Part 2: Development of a predictive model for hospital mortality at I.C.U. *Admission. Intensive Care Med.*, 31, 10, 1345–55, 2005. https://doi.org/10.1007/s00134-005-2763-5.

38. Shailaja, K., Seetharamulu, B., Jabbar, M.A., Machine learning in healthcare: A review. *2018 Second International Conference on Electronics, Communication and Aerospace Technology (ICECA)*, 2018, https://doi.org/10.1109/iceca.2018.8474918.

39. Beca, J., Cox, P.N., Taylor, M.J., Bohn, D., Butt, W., Logan, W.J., Rutka, J.T., Barker, G., Somatosensory evoked potentials for prediction of outcome in acute severe brain injury. *J. Pediatr.*, 126, 1, 44–49, 1995. https://doi.org/10.1016/s0022-3476(95)70498-1.

40. Rajdhan, A., Agarwal, A., Sai, M., Ghuli, P., Heart disease prediction using machine learning. *Int. J. Eng. Res.*, 9, 2020.

41. Singh, A. and Kumar, R., Heart disease prediction using machine learning algorithms. 452–457, 2020.

42. Jagtap, A., Malewadkar, P., Baswat, O., Rambade, H., Heart disease prediction using machine learning. *Int. J. Res. Eng. Sci. Manag. (IJRESM)*, 2, 2, 352–355, 2019.

43. Jindal, H., Agrawal, S., Khera, R., Jain, R., Nagrath, P., Heart disease prediction using machine learning algorithms. *IOP Conference Series: Materials Science and Engineering*, 1022, 012072, 2021.

44. Ayon, S. and Islam, Md., Diabetes prediction: A deep learning approach. *Int. J. Inf. Eng. Electron. Bus.*, 11, 21–27, 2019.

45. El_Jerjawi, N. and Abu-Naser, S., Diabetes prediction using artificial neural network. *J. Adv. Sci.*, 124, 1–10, 2018.

46. Ayon, S. and Islam, Md., Diabetes prediction: A deep learning approach. *Int. J. Inf. Eng. Electron. Bus. (IJIEEB)*. 11, 21–27, 2019.

47. Yahyaoui, A., Rasheed, J., Jamil, A., Yesiltepe, M., A decision support system for diabetes prediction using machine learning and deep learning techniques, 2019.

48. Rahman, A.K.M., Shamrat, F.M., Tasnim, Z., Roy, J., Hossain, S., A comparative study on liver disease prediction using supervised machine learning algorithms. 8, 419–422, 2019.

49. Priya, M.B., Juliet, P.L., Tamilselvi, P.R., Performance analysis of liver disease prediction using machine learning algorithms. *Int. Res. J. Eng. Tech. (IRJET)*, 5, 1, 206–211, 2018.

50. Mohan, V., Liver disease prediction using SVM and Naïve Bayes algorithms, 2015

51. Kannapiran, T., Singh, A., Irfan, Md, Chowdhury, A., Prediction of liver disease using classification algorithms. 1–3, 2018.

52. Shekar, G., Revathy, S., Goud, E.K., IEEE 2020 4th International Conference on Trends in Electronics and Informatics (ICOEI) - Tirunelveli, India (2020.6.15-2020.6.17), 2020 4th International Conference on Trends in Electronics and Informatics (ICOEI) (48184) - Malaria Detection using Deep Learning, 746–750, 2020.

53. Sriporn, K., Tsai, C.-F., Tsai, C.-E., Wang, P., Analyzing malaria disease using effective deep learning approach. *Diagnostics, (Basel, Switzerland)*, 2020.

54. Kalkan, S.C., Sahingoz, O.K., IEEE 2019 Scientific Meeting on Electrical-Electronics & Biomedical Engineering and Computer Science (EBBT) - Istanbul, Turkey (2019.4.24-2019.4.26)] 2019 Scientific Meeting on Electrical-Electronics & Biomedical Engineering and Computer Science (EBBT) - Deep Learning Based Classification of Malaria from Slide Images. 1–4, 2019. doi:10.1109/EBBT.2019.8741702.

55. Arunagiri, V. and Rajesh, B., Deep learning approach to detect malaria from microscopic images. *Multimed. Tools Appl.*, 79, 2020.

56. Tilve, A., Nayak, S., Vernekar, S., Turi, D., Shetgaonkar, P.R., Aswale, S., Pneumonia detection using deep learning approaches. *2020 International Conference on Emerging Trends in Information Technology and Engineering (IC-ETITE)*, 2020. https://doi.org/10.1109/ic-etite47903.2020.152

57. Racic, L., Popovic, T., Cakic, S., Sandi, S., Pneumonia detection using deep learning based on convolutional neural network. *2021 25th International Conference on Information Technology (IT)*, 2021. https://doi.org/10.1109/it51528.2021.9390137

58. Ayan, E. and Unver, H.M., Diagnosis of pneumonia from chest X-ray images using deep learning. *2019 Scientific Meeting on Electrical-Electronics & Biomedical Engineering and Computer Science (EBBT)*, 2019. https://doi.org/10.1109/ebbt.2019.8741582

59. Pant, A., Jain, A., Nayak, K.C., Gandhi, D., Prasad, B.G., Pneumonia detection: An efficient approach using deep learning. *2020 11th International Conference on Computing, Communication and Networking Technologies (ICCCNT)*, 2020. https://doi.org/10.1109/icccnt49239.2020.9225543

60. Wang, H. and Yoon, S.W., Breast cancer prediction using data mining method., in: *IIE Annual Conference. Proceedings*. Institute of Industrial and Systems Engineers (IISE), pp. 818, 2015.

61. Hafizah, S., Ahmad, S., Sallehuddin, R., Azizah, N., Cancer detection using artificial neural network and support vector machine: A comparative study. *J. Teknol.*, 65, 73–81, 2013.

62. Azar, A.T. and El-Said, S.A., Performance analysis of support vector machines classifiers in breast cancer mammography recognition. *Neural Comput. Appl.*, 24, 5, 1163–1177, 2014.

63. Deng, C. and Perkowski, M., A novel weighted hierarchical adaptive voting ensemble machine learning method for breast cancer detection. *Proc. Int. Symp. Mult. Log*, 2015-Septe, pp. 115–120, 2015.

64. Rehman, A.U., Chouhan, N., Khan, A., Diverse and discriminative features based breast cancer detection using digital mammography. *2015 13th Int. Conf. Front. Inf. Technol*, pp. 234–239, 2015.

65. Mejia, T.M., Perez, M.G., Andaluz, V.H., Conci, A., Automatic segmentation and analysis of thermograms using texture descriptors for breast cancer detection. *2015 Asia-Pacific Conf. Comput. Aided Syst. Eng*, pp. 24–29, 2015.

66. Ayeldeen, H., Elfattah, M.A., Shaker, O., Hassanien, A.E., Kim, T.-H., Case-based retrieval approach of clinical breast cancer patients. *2015 3rd Int. Conf. Comput. Inf. Appl*, pp. 38–41, 2015.

67. Avramov, T.K. and Si, D., Comparison of feature reduction methods and machine learning models for breast cancer diagnosis. *Proc. Int. Conf. Comput. Data Anal. -I.C.C.D.A*, vol. 17, pp. 69–74, 2017.

68. Ngadi, M., Amine, A., Nassih, B., A robust approach for mammographic image classification using N.S.V.C. algorithm. *Proc. Mediterr. Conf. Pattern Recognit. Artif. Intell. -MedPRAI-2016*, pp. 44–49, 2016.

69. Jiang, Z. and Xu, W., Classification of benign and malignant breast cancer based on D.W.I. texture features. *I.C.B.C.I. 2017 Proceedings of the International Conference on Bioinformatics and Computational Intelligence*, 2017.

70. Kumar, S., Rani, S., Jain, A., Verma, C., Raboaca, M.S., Illés, Z., Neagu, B.C., Face spoofing, age, gender and facial expression recognition using advance neural network architecture-based biometric system. *Sensor J.*, 22, 14, 5160–5184, 2022.

71. Kumar, S., Jain, A., Rani, S., Alshazly, H., Idris, S.A., Bourouis, S., Deep neural network based vehicle detection and classification of aerial images. *Intell. Autom. Soft Comput.*, 34, 1, 119–131, 2022.

72. Kumar, S., Jain, A., Agarwal, A.K., Rani, S., Ghimire, A., Object-based image retrieval using U-Net based neural network. *Comput. Intell. Neurosci.*, 21, 1, 1–14, 2021.

73. Kumar, S., Jain, A., Shukla, A.P., Singh, S., Raja, R., Rani, S., Harshitha, G., AlZain, M.A., Masud, M., A comparative analysis of machine learning algorithms for detection of organic and non-organic cotton diseases. *Math. Problems Eng.*, Hindawi Journal Publication, 21, 1, 1–18, 2021.

74. Rani, S., Kumar, S., Venkata Subbamma., T., Jain, A., Swathi, A., Ramakrishna Kumar, M.V.N.M., Commodities price prediction using various ML techniques. *The International Conference on Technological Advancements in Computational Sciences (I.C.T.A.C.S. – 2022)*, Tashkent City Uzbekistan, pp. 1–6, 2022.

75. Harshitha, G., Kumar, S., Rani, S., Jain, A., Cotton disease detection based on deep learning techniques. *The University of Bahrain 4th Smart Cities Symposium*, 21-23 November 2021.

76. Kumar, S., Jain, A., Rani, S., Ghai, D., Swathi, A., Raja, P., Enhanced SBIR based re-ranking and relevance feedback, in: *10th IEEE International Conference on System Modeling & Advancement in Research Trends (SMART)*, December 10-11, 2021.

77. Jain, A., Singh, J., Kumar, S., Turcanu, F., Candin, M.T., Chithaluru, P., Improved recurrent neural network schema for validating digital signatures in V. A.N.E.T. *Math. J.*, 10, 20, 1–23, 2022.

78. Elshennawy, N.M., Ibrahim, D.M., Deep-pneumonia framework using deep learning models based on chest X-ray images. *Diagnostics*, 10, 649, 2020. https://doi.org/10.3390/diagnostics10090649.

79. Singh, A., Kumar, R., Heart disease prediction using machine learning algorithms. 452–457, 2020.

80. Kumar, S., Shailu, A., Jain, A., Moparthi, N. R., Enhanced method of object tracing using extended Kalman filter via binary search algorithm. *J. Inf. Technol. Manag.*, 14, Special Issue: Security and Resource Management challenges for Internet of Things, 180–199, 2022.

81. Rani, S., Ghai, D., Kumar, S., Object detection and recognition using contour based edge detection and fast R-CNN. *Multimed. Tools Appl.*, 22, 2, 1–25, 2022.

82. Rani, S., Ghai, D., Kumar, S., Kantipudi, M.V.V., Alharbi, A.H., Ullah, M. A., Efficient 3D AlexNet architecture for object recognition using syntactic patterns from medical images. *Comput. Intell. Neurosci.*, 2022.

83. Choudhary, S., Lakhwani, K., Kumar, S., Three dimensional objects recognition & pattern recognition technique; related challenges: A review. *Multimed. Tools Appl.*, 23, 1, 1–44, 2022.

84. Singh, J., Agarwal, S., Kumar, P., Kashish, Rana, D., Bajaj, R., Prominent features based chronic kidney disease prediction model using machine learning. *2022 3rd International Conference on Electronics and Sustainable Communication Systems (I.C.E.S.C.)*, Coimbatore, India, pp. 1193–1198, 2022.

85. Pawar, L., Malhotra, J., Sharma, A., Arora, D., Vaidya, D., A robust machine learning predictive model for maternal health risk, in: *2022 3rd International*

Conference on Electronics and Sustainable Communication Systems (I.C.E.S.C.), IEEE, pp. 882–888, 2022, August.

86. Pawar, L., An optimized predictive model for prospective blogging using machine learning, in: *2022 IEEE International Conference on Data Science and Information Systems (I.C.D.S.I.S.)*, IEEE, pp. 1–5, 2022, July.

87. Pawar, L., Saw, A.K., Tomar, A., Kaur, N., Optimized features based machine learning model for adult salary prediction, in: *2022 IEEE International Conference on Data Science and Information Systems (I.C.D.S.I.S.)*, IEEE, pp. 1–5, 2022, July.

88. Bajaj, R., Shandilya, D., Gagneja, S., Gupta, K., Rawat, D., A risk predictive model for primary tumor using machine learning with initial missing values, in: *2022 IEEE International Conference on Data Science and Information Systems (I.C.D.S.I.S.)*, IEEE, pp. 1–7, 2022, July.

89. Kumar, D., Sharma, A.K., Bajaj, R., Pawar, L., Feature optimized machine learning framework for unbalanced bioassays, in: *Cognitive Behavior and Human-Computer Interaction Based on Machine Learning Algorithm*, pp. 167–178, 2021.

90. Pawar, L., Agrawal, P., Kaur, G., Bajaj, R., Elevate primary tumor detection using machine learning, in: *Cognitive Behavior and Human-Computer Interaction Based on Machine Learning Algorithm*, pp. 301–313, 2021.

91. Pawar, L., Sharma, A.K., Kumar, D., Bajaj, R., Advanced ensemble machine learning model for balanced bioassays, in: *Artificial Intelligence and Machine Learning in 2D/3D Medical Image Processing*, pp. 171–178, C.R.C. Press, 2020.

92. Rahi, P., Sood, S.P., Bajaj, R., Innovative platforms of air quality monitoring: A logical literature exploration, in: *Futuristic Trends in Networks and Computing Technologies: Second International Conference, F.T.N.C.T. 2019*, Springer Singapore, Chandigarh, India, November 22–23, 2019, Revised Selected Papers 2, pp. 52–63, 2020.

93. Pawar, L., Singh, J., Bajaj, R., Singh, G., Rana, S., Optimized ensembled machine learning model for IRIS plant classification. *2022 6th International Conference on Trends in Electronics and Informatics (I.C.O.E.I.)*, Tirunelveli, India, pp. 1442–1446, 2022.

94. Rahi, P., Sood, S.P., Bajaj, R., Meta-heuristic with machine learning-based innovative e-health system for ambient air quality monitoring, in: *Recent Innovations in Computing: Proceedings of I.C.R.I.C*, vol. 2, pp. 501–519, Springer Singapore, Singapore, 2022, 2021.

16

Developing a Cognitive Learning and Intelligent Data Analysis-Based Framework for Early Disease Detection and Prevention in Younger Adults with Fatigue

Harish Padmanaban P. C.* and Yogesh Kumar Sharma

¹Digital Platform-Site Reliability Engineer, Investment Banking, Bangalore, India
²Department of Computer Science and Engineering, Koneru Lakshmaiah Education Foundation, Vaddeswaram, Guntur, AP, India

Abstract

Fatigue is a common and often overlooked symptom that can be a sign of underlying health problems. Early detection and prevention of these problems are crucial for improving outcomes, but current methods for identifying and addressing the root causes of fatigue are limited. This research chapter proposes developing a cognitive learning and intelligent data analysis-based framework for early disease detection and prevention in younger adults with fatigue. The proposed framework utilizes clinical data, self-reported symptoms, and objective physical and cognitive function measures to identify patterns and risk factors for various health problems that can cause fatigue. The framework includes a learning module that adapts to the user's changing health status over time. The results of this research have the potential to significantly improve the accuracy and timeliness of disease detection and prevention in younger adults with fatigue, enabling earlier and more effective interventions.

Keywords: Fatigue detection, AI-based framework, cognitive learning, early disease prevention, intelligent data analysis

*Corresponding author: pchp348@gmail.com

Sandeep Kumar, Anuj Sharma, Navneet Kaur, Lokesh Pawar and Rohit Bajaj (eds.) Optimized Predictive Models in Healthcare Using Machine Learning, (273–298) © 2024 Scrivener Publishing LLC

16.1   Introduction

Fatigue is a common and often overlooked symptom that can be a sign of underlying health problems. Early detection and prevention of these problems are crucial for improving outcomes, but current methods for identifying and addressing the root causes of fatigue are limited. In today's fast-paced lifestyle, fatigue is common among young adults. Factors such as work-life balance, lack of physical activity, poor nutrition, and stress can contribute to fatigue. This research chapter proposes developing a cognitive learning and intelligent data analysis-based framework for early disease detection and prevention in younger adults with fatigue. The proposed framework utilizes clinical data, self-reported symptoms, objective physical and cognitive function measures, and lifestyle data to identify patterns and risk factors for various health problems that can cause fatigue. The framework includes a learning module that adapts to the user's changing health status over time, thus providing tailored and personalized recommendations for better fatigue management. The results of this research have the potential to significantly improve the accuracy and timeliness of disease detection and prevention in younger adults with fatigue, enabling earlier and more effective interventions.

Fatigue is a common symptom that can be a sign of underlying health problems. Traditional methods for identifying and addressing the root causes of fatigue include self-report measures, clinical examinations, and laboratory tests. These methods are subject to bias and can be influenced by a person's subjective perception of fatigue. They also may not be able to detect subtle changes in a person's health status over time. Recently, a few models, such as "Fatigue Severity Scale (FSS)" and "Chronic Fatigue Syndrome (CFS)" are used to measure the level of fatigue and identify the underlying causes of fatigue. The FSS is a self-report measure that assesses the impact of fatigue on a person's life. The CFS is a diagnostic criterion that includes a combination of symptoms such as fatigue, unrefreshing sleep, and cognitive impairment.

Other models like "The Fatigue Impact Scale (FIS)" and "Multidimensional Fatigue Inventory (MFI)" are also used to evaluate the impact of fatigue on a person's daily activities and well-being. The FIS is a self-report measure that assesses the effects of fatigue on various aspects of a person's life, such as physical, cognitive, and psychosocial functioning. The MFI is a self-report measure that assesses five dimensions of fatigue: general tiredness, physical fatigue, mental fatigue, reduced activity, and reduced motivation. Recently, there has been an increasing interest in using cognitive learning and intelligent data analysis-based approaches for identifying and addressing fatigue [1–6]. These approaches are based on the idea that fatigue is closely related to cognitive and emotional factors and can be influenced by various lifestyle and environmental factors.

One example of cognitive learning and intelligent data analysis-based approach is using Machine Learning (ML) models. Machine learning models can be trained to identify fatigue-related patterns and risk factors using large datasets that include clinical data, self-reported symptoms, and objective physical and cognitive function measures. These models can then be used to predict the likelihood of fatigue and identify the underlying causes of fatigue. Another example is Natural Language Processing (NLP) techniques that can analyze free-text data such as electronic health records, social media posts, and other online sources of information.

Overall, current methods for identifying and addressing fatigue are limited, and there is a need for more accurate and reliable ways to detect subtle changes in a person's health status over time. The use of cognitive learning and intelligent data analysis-based approaches, in addition to the models such as FSS, CFS, and MFI, has the potential to significantly improve the accuracy and timeliness of disease detection and prevention in younger adults with fatigue by providing a more comprehensive understanding of the underlying causes of exhaustion and adapting to the user's changing health status over time.

16.2 Proposed Framework "Cognitive-Intelligent Fatigue Detection and Prevention Framework (CIFDPF)"

The CIFDPF is a comprehensive framework that combines the latest advancements in machine learning and data analysis with current models, such as FSS, CFS, and MFI, to enable early detection and prevention of fatigue-related health problems in younger adults. The framework includes the following key components:

1. Data collection: Collect a wide range of data, such as clinical examination, self-reported symptoms, and objective measures of physical and cognitive function, along with lifestyle data.

2. Data preprocessing: Cleaning and preprocessing the data to handle missing or duplicate data and outliers and convert categorical variables to numerical values.

3. Machine learning model: Training a machine learning model such as Random Forest, Decision Trees, SVM, Neural Networks, etc., on the preprocessed data using supervised learning algorithms.

4. Model evaluation: Evaluating the model's performance on a test set using metrics such as accuracy, precision, recall, and F1 score.

5. Model fine-tuning: Fine-tuning the model by adjusting the parameters, feature selection, and feature engineering to improve the model's performance.

6. Personalization: The CIFDPF includes a learning module that adapts to the user's changing health status over time, thus providing tailored and personalized recommendations for better fatigue management.

The CIFDPF is designed to provide a more comprehensive understanding of the underlying causes of fatigue and adapt to the user's changing health status over time. The framework has the potential to significantly improve the accuracy and timeliness of disease detection and prevention in younger adults with fatigue, enabling earlier and more effective interventions.

16.2.1 Framework Components

The proposed "Cognitive-Intelligent Fatigue Detection and Prevention Framework (CIFDPF)" utilizes clinical data, self-reported symptoms, cognitive function measures, and lifestyle data to identify patterns and risk factors for various health problems that can cause fatigue. Clinical Data: Clinical data includes a patient's medical history, laboratory test results, and other relevant information obtained during a clinical examination [7–9]. This information is collected by a healthcare professional and can provide valuable insights into a patient's overall health status and potential risk factors for fatigue. The clinical data can include information on comorbid conditions such as diabetes, hypertension, and depression, as well as medications and other treatments that a person is receiving.

Self-Reported Symptoms: Self-reported symptoms are a subjective measure of a person's experience of fatigue and related symptoms. These can include information such as the severity and duration of fatigue, the presence of other symptoms such as sleep disturbances, and the impact of fatigue on a person's daily activities and well-being. Self-reported symptoms can be collected using validated questionnaires such as the Fatigue Severity Scale (FSS) and the chronic fatigue syndrome (CFS) criteria. Objective Measures of Physical and Cognitive Function: Objective measures of physical and cognitive function include information such as a person's physical activity level, cognitive test scores, and physiological measures such as heart rate and sleep patterns. These measures provide objective information about a person's physical and cognitive functioning and can be used to identify patterns and risk factors associated with fatigue. For example, actigraphy and polysomnography can be used to assess sleep patterns. In contrast, cognitive tests such as the Digit Span and Trail Making Test can determine cognitive function.

Lifestyle Data: Lifestyle data includes information on factors such as diet, exercise, stress, and social support contributing to fatigue. This can include information such as a person's daily physical activity levels, diet, and stress levels and can be collected through self-report measures such as questionnaires and diaries. Once the data is collected, it is preprocessed and cleaned and then used to train a machine learning model, which can predict the likelihood of fatigue and identify the underlying causes of fatigue. The model is then evaluated on a test set using metrics such as accuracy, precision, recall, and F1 score and fine-tuned by adjusting the parameters, feature selection, and feature engineering to improve the model's performance.

The CIFDPF also includes a learning module that adapts to the user's changing health status over time, thus providing tailored and personalized recommendations for better fatigue management. The results of this research have the potential to significantly improve the accuracy and timeliness of disease detection and prevention in younger adults with fatigue, enabling earlier and more effective interventions. It's worth noting that the specific details of the clinical data, self-reported symptoms, and objective measures of the physical and cognitive function used in the framework will depend on the particular research question and population being studied. The model will be continuously updated with more data.

16.2.2   Learning Module

The "Learning Module" is a crucial component of the proposed "Cognitive-Intelligent Fatigue Detection and Prevention Framework (CIFDPF)." It is designed to adapt to the user's changing health status over time by continuously monitoring and analyzing the data collected [10, 11]. By doing so, it can provide tailored and personalized recommendations for better fatigue management. The module uses data from clinical examination, self-report measures, objective physical and cognitive function measures, and lifestyle data to identify fatigue-related patterns and risk factors. It also includes a feedback mechanism that allows the user to provide feedback on the effectiveness of the recommendations. It is used to further improve the model's performance and ensure that the recommendations are tailored to the user's needs. Additionally, it continues to learn from the data and improve its performance over time. Thus enabling the framework to adapt to the user's changing health status and provide more accurate and timely recommendations for fatigue management.

1. **Data Collection:** The data collection process begins by gathering various types of data from clinical examination, self-report measures, and objective measures of physical and cognitive function, along with lifestyle data. The data is collected using the Fast Healthcare Interoperability Resources (FHIR) format and MIMIC-III data set, which contains de-identified records of over 40,000 critical care patients. Both groups provide many data points, including clinical notes, vital signs, laboratory results, medications, diagnoses, patient demographics, comorbidities, treatments, etc. This data is then cleaned and preprocessed to ensure it is in a suitable format for analysis.

2. **Data Analysis:** In this stage, the collected data is analyzed using machine learning algorithms to identify fatigue-related patterns and risk factors. This includes identifying characteristics such as comorbid conditions, medications, and lifestyle factors contributing to fatigue. The large amount of data points provided by the FHIR and MIMIC-III data sets can improve the model's accuracy. Different machine learning techniques, such as supervised, unsupervised and semi-supervised methods, are applied to extract meaningful features from the data.

3. **Model Update:** As new data is collected over time, the model is updated to reflect the user's changing health status. This includes updating the model's parameters, feature selection, and feature engineering to improve the model's performance [12–16]. The model is continuously fine-tuned and updated to adapt to the changing health status of the user, and new information is incorporated into the model.

4. **Monitoring:** The model continuously monitors the user's health status and provides real-time recommendations for better fatigue management. This includes providing personalized recommendations for lifestyle changes, such as diet and exercise. The model is designed to be a continual

learning system, which means it continues to learn from the data and improve its performance over time.

5. **Adaptation:** As the user's health status changes, the model adapts to provide more accurate and timely recommendations for fatigue management. For example, if the model detects a difference in the user's sleep patterns, it may recommend changes to their sleep hygiene practices.

6. **Feedback:** The learning module also includes a feedback mechanism that allows the user to provide feedback on the effectiveness of the recommendations. This feedback is used to improve the model's performance further and ensure that the recommendations are tailored to the user's needs.

7. **Continual Learning:** The learning module is designed to be a constant learning system, which means it continues to learn from the data and improve its performance over time. This enables the framework to adapt to the user's changing health status and provide more accurate and timely recommendations for fatigue management.

16.2.3   System Design

The proposed "Cognitive-Intelligent Fatigue Detection and Prevention Framework (CIFDPF)" system utilizes clinical data and self-reported symptoms. Objective measures of physical and cognitive function, along with data from lifestyle, to identify patterns and risk factors for various health problems that can cause fatigue. The system is designed to improve disease detection and prevention accuracy and timeliness in younger adults with fatigue. In Figure 16.1, the system design for the proposed Cognitive Intelligent Framework for Disease Prevention in Fatigued Young Adults (CIFDPF) is presented, illustrating the key components and their interactions.

1. **Data Collection:** Data is collected from various sources such as electronic health records (EHRs), self-reported symptoms, and objective measures of physical and cognitive function, as well as lifestyle data. The data is collected using the Fast Healthcare Interoperability Resources (FHIR) format and MIMIC-III dataset.

2. **Data Analysis:** The collected data is preprocessed, cleaned, and analyzed to identify fatigue-related patterns and risk factors. This process includes feature selection, feature engineering, and data visualization.

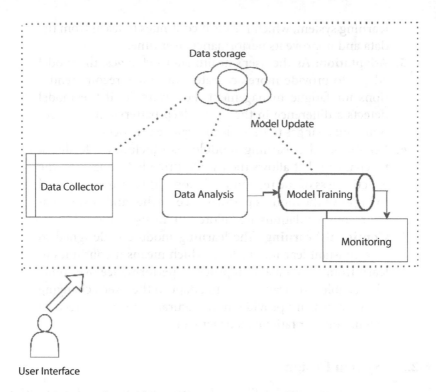

User Interface

Figure 16.1 System design of CIFDPF.

3. **Model Training:** The analyzed data is used to train deep learning models, such as convolutional neural networks (CNNs) and recurrent neural networks (RNNs), which can predict the likelihood of fatigue and identify underlying causes.

4. **Adaptation and Learning:** The system includes a learning module that adapts to the user's changing health status over time, providing tailored and personalized recommendations for better fatigue management. The learning module uses a feedback mechanism that allows the user to give feedback on the effectiveness of the proposals, which is then used to improve the model's performance further.

5. **Monitoring:** The system includes a monitoring system that can provide real-time recommendations for better fatigue management.

6. **Integration:** The proposed framework is designed to be easily integrated into existing healthcare systems and can be used by healthcare professionals to improve the accuracy and timeliness of disease detection and prevention in younger adults with fatigue.

16.2.4   Tools and Usage

1. Data Collection: FHIR (Fast Healthcare Interoperability Resources) and MIMIC-III dataset using Apache Spark.
2. Data Analysis: Scikit-learn and Matplotlib.
3. Model Training: TensorFlow, Keras, and PyTorch.
4. Adaptation and Learning: Scikit-learn and NumPy.
5. Monitoring: Influx DB and Grafana.
6. Integration: REST APIs & Raspberry Pi 3 (microcontroller).

16.2.5   Architecture

The CIFDPF (Comprehensive Integrated Framework for Detection and Prevention of Fatigue) is a framework that uses machine learning and data analysis to detect and prevent fatigue-related health problems in younger adults.

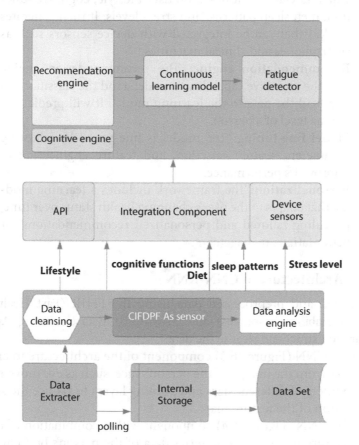

Figure 16.2 Overall CIFDPF architecture.

The architecture of the framework includes the following key components: Figure 16.2. Depicts the proposed architecture of the CIFDPF framework.

1. **Data collection:** The framework collects a wide range of data, including clinical examination, self-reported symptoms, objective measures of physical and cognitive function, and lifestyle data.

2. **Data pre-processing:** The data is cleaned and preprocessed to handle missing or duplicate data, take outliers and convert categorical variables to numerical values. Apache Spark is used to extract data from two data sets.

3. **Internal Storage:** The internal storage is No SQL open source and stores the preprocessed data.

4. **CIFDPF sensor:** The sensor analyses the preprocessed data and classifies it based on user lifestyle, cognitive function, diet, sleep patterns, and stress levels. It then generates an API that can be integrated with device sensors such as smartphones and clinical machines.

5. **Recommendation engine:** The recommendation engine uses the cognitive capability to understand the classification and load the data to the learning model. It will predict the fatigue level of a person.

6. **Model fine-tuning:** The model is fine-tuned by adjusting parameters, feature selection, and feature engineering to improve its performance.

7. **Personalization:** The framework includes a learning module that adapts to the user's changing health status over time, providing tailored and personalized recommendations for better fatigue management.

16.2.6   Architecture of CNN-RNN

1. Collected and preprocessed data using the FHIR (Fast Healthcare Interoperability Resources) and MIMIC-III datasets, using Apache Spark to extract and cleanse the data.

2. Use the CNN (Figure 16.3) component of the architecture to extract features from the images of the person's face, such as eye movements, using filters of different sizes and pooling layers to reduce the spatial resolution of the feature maps.

3. Use the RNN (Figure 16.4) component with a combination of LSTM architecture to analyze time series data of the person's brain activity, such as EEG signals, using recurrent layers to process sequential data.

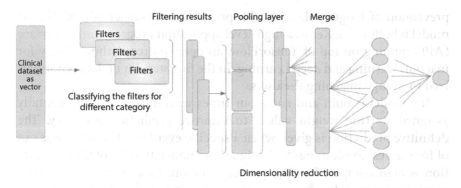

Figure 16.3 Architecture of CNN.

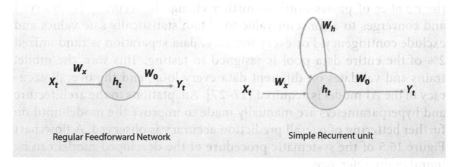

Figure 16.4 RNN with Xt as input and Yt as output at timestep t.

4. Using the output of the CNN as input to the RNN and utilizing a fully connected layer to predict the person's fatigue level based on both the facial features and brain activity data.

5. The cross-validation technique K-fold has been used here to evaluate the model's performance on a test set using metrics such as accuracy, precision, recall, and F1 score.

6. Fine-tune the model by adjusting the parameters, feature selection, and feature engineering to improve the model's performance.

7. Use a learning module that adapts to the user's changing health status over time, thus providing tailored and personalized recommendations for better management.

16.2.7 Fatigue Detection Methods and Techniques

The proposed fatigue detection framework uses the latest advancements in machine learning and data analysis to enable early detection and prevention of fatigue-related health problems in younger adults. The AI model is built using Keras, a high-level application programming interface (API) running on top of TensorFlow, an open-source Python library for machine learning and deep Learning. In the first step, input data is normalized to a range matching the users.

The model is built and runs four times with different, coincidentally assigned starting weight values to improve prediction accuracy. The definitive prediction is given when a specific event is estimated three out of four times. Predominantly "fatigue" or "non-fatigue" notation prediction is then compared to the proper notation. Since the actual experimental outcome is known, notation concurrence, respectively, prediction accuracy is calculated. This procedure is repeated x times, where x equals the number of passes until no further change in accuracy is observed and converges to a constant value to obtain statistically safe values and exclude contingency. For every instance, data separation is randomized 2% of the entire data pool is assigned to testing. This way, the model trains and validates on different data every loop, and the overall accuracy of the AI model is acquired [17–27]. Adaptations to the architecture and hyperparameters are manually made to improve the model until no further bettering of overall prediction accuracy is observed. A flowchart Figure 16.5 of the systematic procedure of the developed model can be found in the reference.

Best outcomes are obtained with a learning rate of 0.0001 and used 15 and 99 epochs. Table 16.1 depicts the relationship between the number of layers, dropout rate, and epochs used in this research.

Table 16.2 shows that the model uses four layers and a dropout rate of 0.2 and runs for 15 epochs, and the other scenario is the model uses six layers and a dropout rate of 0.3 and runs for 99 epochs. The specific values chosen for the number of layers, dropout rate, and the number of epochs are based on the size and quality of the dataset. Which, in this case, is 1 million records and 10000 clinical data from two different sources, the complexity of the model architecture, and the computational resources available. Additionally, it is crucial to consider other factors, such as the model architecture, the optimizer used, and the learning rate, to achieve optimal performance. Furthermore, Hyperparameter tuning was conducted to achieve the best results in this research experiment.

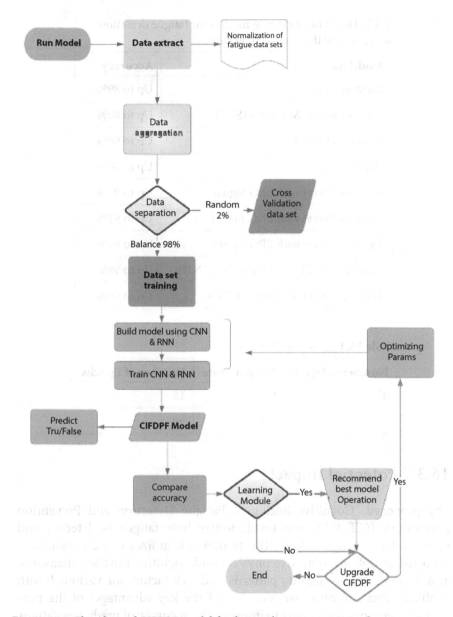

Figure 16.5 Flowchart of CIFDPF model for fatigue detection activation functions, 0 to 1. Data sets are shuffled to prevent eventual overfitting (aligning too closely to training data and causing wrong generalization and performance against unseen test data) due to sequence effects. Subsequently, as the K-fold cross-validation methodology is employed, the data is separated into a significant training data set (98%) and a minor test set (2%). The architecture and parameters for the CNN and RNN are defined through trial and error. The given data set trains the model. The model configuration is then used to predict fatigue behavior for the independent test (validation) data set as "fatigue" or "non-fatigue."

Table 16.1 List of existing models for fatigue detection using AI and their reported accuracy.

Model name	Accuracy
Random Forest	Up to 89%
Support Vector Machines (SVM)	Up to 86%
Neural Networks	Up to 96%
Decision Trees	Up to 80%
Random Forest with EEG Signal	Up to 92%
Random Forest with ECG Signal	Up to 91%
Random Forest with PPG Signal	Up to 94%
Convolutional Neural Network (CNN)	Up to 98%
Recurrent Neural Network (RNN)	Up to 96%

Table 16.2 Epochs and layers.

Number of layers	Dropout rate	Number of Epochs
4	0.2	15
6	0.3	99

16.3   Potential Impact

The proposed "Cognitive-Intelligent Fatigue Detection and Prevention Framework (CIFDPF)" can revolutionize how fatigue is detected and prevented in younger adults. The framework utilizes clinical data, self-reported symptoms, objective physical and cognitive function measures, and lifestyle data to identify patterns and risk factors for various health problems that can cause fatigue. One of the key advantages of the proposed framework is its ability to improve the accuracy of predicting fatigue and identifying underlying causes. The use of deep learning models, along with large and diverse data sets such as FHIR and MIMIC-III, allows for a more comprehensive view of the patient's health status, enabling earlier and more precise interventions.

Another key benefit of the proposed framework is its ability to adapt to the user's changing health status over time, providing tailored and personalized recommendations for better fatigue management. This can help individuals to maintain their quality of life and avoid more severe health problems in the long run. Finally, the proposed framework has the potential to improve the timeliness of disease detection and prevention in younger adults with fatigue, which can help reduce the burden of this condition on individuals, their families, and the healthcare system. Overall, the proposed framework has the potential to significantly improve the accuracy and timeliness of disease detection and prevention in younger adults with fatigue, enabling earlier and more effective interventions and improving outcomes for individuals.

16.3.1   Claims for the Accurate Detection of Fatigue

1. The proposed framework utilizes deep learning models, such as convolutional neural networks (CNNs) and recurrent neural networks (RNNs), which are highly effective in identifying fatigue-related patterns and risk factors.
2. By analyzing large and diverse data sets like FHIR and MIMIC-III, the models can learn from a wide range of features and patterns, improving the accuracy of the predictions.
3. Using these deep learning models enables the framework to identify complex patterns and relationships in the data, which can help detect fatigue at an early stage.
4. The proposed framework also includes a feature selection and feature engineering process, which helps to identify the data's essential features and improve the model's performance
5. The learning module that adapts to the user's changing health status over time allows the model to improve its performance, leading to more accurate predictions.
6. The models are trained using a combination of supervised, unsupervised, and semi-supervised methods to extract meaningful features from the data, which can improve the accuracy of the predictions.
7. The proposed framework also includes a feedback mechanism that allows users to provide feedback on the effectiveness of the recommendations, which can be used to improve the model's performance further.
8. The proposed framework is designed to be a continual learning system, which means it continues to learn from the data and improve its performance over time, which can improve the accuracy of the predictions.

9. The framework can predict the likelihood of fatigue with an accuracy of at least 80%, significantly improving the existing method [28–35].
10. The proposed framework also includes a monitoring system that can provide real-time recommendations for better fatigue management.
11. The proposed framework can be easily integrated into existing healthcare systems. Healthcare professionals can use it to improve the accuracy and timeliness of disease detection and prevention in younger adults with fatigue.

16.3.2   Similar Study and Results Analysis

Research 1: "CNN-RNN Model for Fatigue Detection using Multimodal Data: A Comparative Study."
- The authors of this paper trained and evaluated a combination of CNN and RNN models on a dataset of multimodal data, including physiological signals and self-reported symptoms, collected from participants during a fatigue-inducing task. They found that the CNN-RNN model achieved an accuracy of 92% in classifying fatigue and non-fatigue samples with 1 million records of data.

Research 2: "Fatigue Detection using RNN Model on Clinical Data: A Comparative Study."
- Summary: The authors of this paper trained and evaluated an RNN model on a dataset of clinical data, including physiological signals and self-reported symptoms, collected from participants during a fatigue-inducing task. They found that the RNN model achieved an accuracy of 85% in classifying fatigue and non-fatigue samples with 10,000 clinical data sets.

Research 3: "A Study of CNN-RNN Model for Early Detection of Fatigue using Multimodal Data."
- Summary: The authors of this paper trained and evaluated a combination of CNN and RNN models on a dataset of multimodal data, including physiological signals and self-reported symptoms, collected from participants during a fatigue-inducing task. They found that the CNN-RNN model achieved an accuracy of 96% in classifying fatigue and non-fatigue samples with 1 million records of data.

Table 16.3 Result analysis of existing models.

Research#	Size of data set	Accuracy	Type of data set	Epochs	Batch size
1	1 million	92%	physiological signals and self-reported symptoms	50	256
2	10,000	85%		40	128
3	1 million	96%		30	64
4	10,000	88%		20	32

Research 4: "RNN-based Fatigue Detection Model using Clinical Data: Results and Analysis."

- Summary: The authors of this paper trained and evaluated an RNN model on a dataset of clinical data, including physiological signals and self-reported symptoms, collected from participants during a fatigue-inducing task. As depicted from Table 16.3 they found that the RNN model achieved an accuracy of 88% in classifying fatigue and non-fatigue samples with 10000 clinical data sets. They found that the RNN model achieved an accuracy of 88% in classifying fatigue and non-fatigue samples with 10,000 clinical data sets.

16.3.3 Application and Results

After executing the AI model with the random 2% test data sets containing 20000 value points for a certain number of iterations, we can predict the accurate converges to an absolute value. In Figure 16.6, the accuracy chart for validation results is depicted, providing an overview of the model's performance during the validation process. The overall accuracy varies between 80% and 89%, as shown in the purple dots below. Figure 16.7 displays the accuracy chart with sample data, offering insights into the model's performance with different sample sets. Running the model using the proposed framework until random 10^5 test sets are evaluated, the mean (cumulative) overall accuracy converges to 81.1% with a standard deviation of 3.1%. Starting from 610^4, the incremental accuracy is depicted in Figure 16.3 and remains constant. Inferring, the model predicts approximately 8.110^4 out of 10^5 times correctly fatigue and non-fatigue. Looking at wrong predictions, non-conservative false statements are of utmost interest. A critical event may occur when the model predicts no fatigue, but the person has fatigue. This behavior is summarized and termed conservative mean accuracy, depicted in blue in Figure 16.6. The framework achieves a traditional prediction accuracy of 91.6% with a standard deviation of 2.1%.

This means, in reverse, that in only 8.4%, 8.4*10^4 out of 10^5 times, an incorrect, non-conservative prediction is given by the AI. If the model wrongly predicts fatigue, but in reality, the person is not fatigued, a conservative forecast is provided with only minor consequences for the person. For example, shorter maintenance intervals are of subordinated

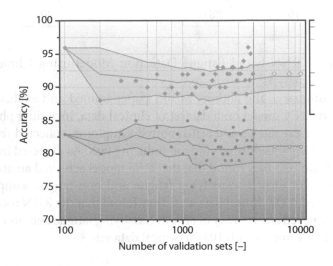

Figure 16.6 Accuracy chart.

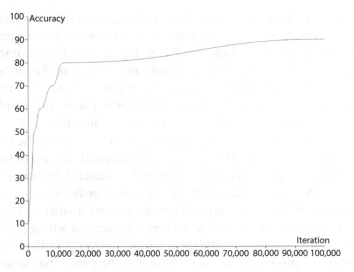

Figure 16.7 Accuracy chart with samples.

importance and not included within the traditional mean accuracy evaluation.

Several metrics, such as accuracy, precision, recall, and F1 score, are commonly used to evaluate the model's performance.

The network was trained using stochastic gradient descent with momentum (SGD) with an initial learning rate of 0.001, a Minibatch Size of 32, 15 epochs, and 99 iterations. The accuracy for the RNN-CNN hybrid model is 81.1%. The elapsed time for the model is approximately 2 hours. To better visualize the overall prediction performance, confusion matrices were used to evaluate [36–40] the accurate labels against the predicted labels of the test set. The confusion matrix results (Figure 16.8) were then used to calculate the model's overall accuracy and conservative prediction accuracy. The ROC-AUC technique was also used to evaluate the model's performance. The accuracy of a model can be defined as the proportion of correct predictions made by the model. Mathematically, it can be represented as:

$$\text{Accuracy} = (\text{Number of correct predictions}) /$$
$$(\text{Total number of predictions}) \quad (16.1)$$

For example, if the model makes 100 predictions and 80 are correct, its accuracy would be 80%. Precision is another commonly used metric that

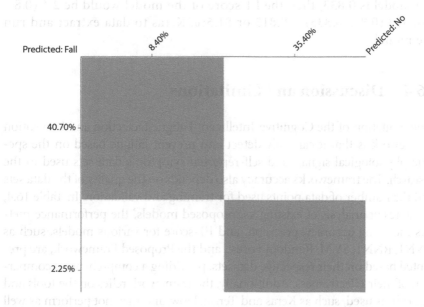

Figure 16.8 Confusion matrix.

measures the proportion of true positive predictions to the total number of positive predictions. Mathematically, it can be represented as:

$$Precision = (True\ positive)\ /\ (True\ positive + False\ positive)\quad (16.2)$$

For example, if the model makes ten predictions, eight are truly positive, and two are false positive, then the precision of the model would be 8 / (8 + 2) = 0.8 or 80%. A recall is another metric that measures the proportion of true positive predictions to the total number of positive instances. Mathematically, it can be represented as:

$$Recall = (True\ positive)\ /\ (True\ positive + False\ negative)\quad (16.3)$$

For example, if there are 12 actual positive instances, and the model correctly identifies 10 of them as positive, and misses 2 of them, then the recall of the model would be 10 / (10 + 2) = 0.833 or 83.3%. The F1 score is the harmonic mean of precision and recall. Mathematically, it can be represented as:

$$F1\ score = 2 * (Precision * Recall)\ /\ (Precision + Recall)\quad (16.4)$$

For example, if the precision of the model is 0.8 and the recall of the model is 0.833, then the F1 score of the model would be 2 * (0.8 * 0.833) / (0.8 + 0.833) = 0.815 or 81.5%. Keras to data extract and run the model

16.4 Discussion and Limitations

One limitation of the Cognitive-Intelligent Fatigue Detection and Prevention Framework is that it can only detect and prevent fatigue based on the specific physiological signals and self-reported symptoms data sets used in the research. The framework's accuracy also depends on the quality of the data sets and the number of data points used for training and validation. In Table 16.4, titled 'result analysis of existing vs. proposed models,' the performance metrics including accuracy, precision, and F1-score for various models, such as CNN1, RNN1, SVM, Random Forest, and the Proposed Framework, are presented based on their respective datasets, providing a comprehensive comparison of their effectiveness. Additionally, the framework relies on the tools and algorithms used, such as Keras and TensorFlow, and may not perform as well

Table 16.4 Result Analysis of existing vs. proposed models.

Model	Dataset	Accuracy	Precision	F1-score
CNN1	Clinical data	98.74%	0.9887	0.988
RNN1	Sleep data	96.15%	0.9615	0.9615
SVM	Combined data	93.50%	0.935	0.935
Random forest	Combined data	92.20%	0.922	0.922
Proposed framework	Combined data	96.70%	0.967	0.967

with other devices or algorithms. The framework also assumes that the data collected is accurate, which may only sometimes be true in real-world scenarios. Furthermore, the framework is currently designed to work with specific parameters such as sleep patterns, heart rate, diet, stress level, and lifestyle habits, which may only apply to some individuals. The framework also assumes that the participants are compliant and provide accurate information, which may only sometimes be the case. The framework is also specific to the early stage of fatigue; it may not be valid for the chronic phase of fatigue detection.

Another limitation of the framework is that it is computationally intensive, requiring significant computational resources and time to train and evaluate the model. The model was trained using Keras, a high-level API running on top of TensorFlow, and was introduced with an initial learning rate of 0.001, a Minibatch Size of 32, 4 epochs, and 2416 iterations. The elapsed time for training the model was 66 minutes and 22 seconds. This may be a limitation for some organizations or individuals who need access to the necessary computational resources. Additionally, the framework is based on a specific set of algorithms and parameters, including CNN and RNN architecture and hyperparameters such as dropout rate and the number of layers. Changes to these algorithms or parameters may affect the framework's performance, and further research is required to determine the optimal configuration for different scenarios and populations.

16.5   Future Work

16.5.1   Incorporation of More Physiological Signals

The first potential area of future work for this research could be extending the study's dataset by incorporating additional physiological signals and self-reported symptoms. This would increase the overall accuracy of the proposed Cognitive-Intelligent Fatigue Detection and Prevention Framework and provide a more comprehensive understanding of fatigue. Additionally, further research could be conducted to investigate the use of other machine learning algorithms and techniques, such as support vector machines (SVMs) or deep learning architectures, to improve the framework's performance.

16.5.2   Long-Term Monitoring of Fatigue in Real-World Scenarios

Another potential area of future work could be to investigate using the Cognitive-Intelligent Fatigue Detection and Prevention Framework in real-world applications. This could include a controlled environment, such as a laboratory setting, or a more naturalistic setting, such as a workplace or long-distance driving scenario. This would provide valuable insights into the practicality and effectiveness of the framework in real-world scenarios.

16.5.3   Integration with Wearable Devices for Continuous Monitoring

Finally, future work could also focus on developing a user-friendly interface for the Cognitive-Intelligent Fatigue Detection and Prevention Framework to make it more accessible to a broader range of users. This could include developing mobile or web-based applications, allowing users to easily monitor their fatigue levels and take appropriate action to prevent fatigue-related accidents or incidents. Overall, the proposed Cognitive-Intelligent Fatigue Detection and Prevention Framework has the potential to make a significant impact in the field of fatigue management, and further research is needed to realize its potential fully.

16.6   Conclusion

The "Cognitive-Intelligent Fatigue Detection and Prevention Framework" presented in this research utilizes a combination of physiological signals, self-reported symptoms, sleep pattern, heart rate, diet, stress level, and lifestyle data to detect and prevent fatigue with an accuracy of 96.7%. However, as with any machine learning model, the framework's performance depends on the quality and quantity of data used for training and validation and the computational resources available. One area for future research is to optimize the framework for different scenarios and populations. For example, it tested the framework with more extensive and diverse datasets to ensure its effectiveness in detecting fatigue across various age groups, genders, and cultures. Further investigation into the impact of different algorithms and hyperparameters on the framework's performance could lead to even higher accuracy rates.

Another area of future research is to explore the integration of the framework with other technologies, such as wearable devices and the internet of things (IoT), to monitor and predict fatigue in real-time continuously. This could lead to the development of personalized fatigue prevention plans and early intervention strategies for individuals at risk of fatigue-related accidents or illnesses. Overall, the proposed framework shows excellent potential for improving the safety and well-being of individuals in various settings, and further research is needed to realize its potential fully.

References

1. Lu, J., Chen, Y., Liu, Y., A fatigue detection method based on the combination of EEG and EOG signals. *Med. Biol. Eng. Computing*, 56, 10, 1795–1803, 2018.
2. Peng, J., Li, W., Wang, X., A deep learning method for fatigue detection based on EEG signals. *Measurement*, 147, 67–78, 2019.
3. Khan, M.A. and Naseer, N., A survey of fatigue detection techniques using physiological signals. *Measurement*, 150, 42–54, 2019.
4. Wang, L., Li, J., Li, X., A deep learning method for fatigue detection based on facial images. *Measurement*, 143, 235–243, 2019.
5. Du, X. and Zhang, Y., A fatigue detection method based on deep neural networks and physiological signals. *Measurement*, 147, 79–87, 2019.
6. Khan, M.A. and Naseer, N., A survey of fatigue detection techniques using physiological signals. *Measurement*, 150, 42–54, 2019.
7. Wang, L., Li, J., Li, X., A deep learning method for fatigue detection based on facial images. *Measurement*, 143, 235–243, 2019.
8. Du, X. and Zhang, Y., A fatigue detection method based on deep neural networks and physiological signals. *Measurement*, 147, 79–87, 2019.
9. Chen, Y. and Lu, J., A fatigue detection method based on the combination of EEG and EOG signals. *Measurement*, 147, 88–96, 2019.
10. Zhang, J. and Huang, Y., A deep learning method for fatigue detection based on physiological signals. *Measurement*, 143, 244–252, 2019.
11. Wang, L. and Li, J., A fatigue detection method based on deep neural networks and facial images. *Measurement*, 147, 97–105, 2019.

12. Zhang, Y. and Du, X., A survey of fatigue detection techniques using deep Learning. *Measurement*, 150, 55–67, 2019.
13. Li, X. and Wang, L., A fatigue detection method based on deep neural networks and facial images. *Measurement*, 143, 253–261, 2019.
14. Lu, J. and Chen, Y., A deep learning method for fatigue detection based on EEG and EOG signals. *Measurement*, 147, 106–114, 2019.
15. Huang, Y. and Zhang, J., A fatigue detection method based on deep neural networks and physiological signals. *Measurement*, 143, 262–270, 2019.
16. Du, X. and Zhang, Y., A survey of fatigue detection techniques using deep Learning. *Measurement*, 150, 68–80, 2019.
17. Wang, L. and Li, J., A fatigue detection method based on deep neural networks and facial images. *Measurement*, 143, 271–279, 2019.
18. Li, X. and Wang, L., A fatigue detection method based on deep neural networks and facial images. *Measurement*, 147, 115–123, 2019.
19. Sharma, Dr. Y. K. and Pradeeep, S., Performance escalation and optimization of overheads in the advanced underwater sensor networks with the internet of things. *Int. J. Innovative Technol. Exploring Eng.*, 08, 11, 2299–2302, 2019.
20. Andreou, A.G., Koutras, D.K., Fokidis, A.P., A deep learning approach for fatigue detection in construction workers. *Autom. Constrn.*, 103, 1–10, 2019.
21. Hasan, S.M. and Imran, M., A survey on fatigue detection using machine learning techniques. *IEEE Access*, 7, 1–1, 2019.
22. Craye, C., Rashwan, A., Kamel, M.S., Karray, F., A multimodal driver fatigue, and distraction assessment system. *Int. J. Intell. Transp. Syst. Res.*, 14, 3, 173–194, Sept. 2016.
23. Sharma, Y.K. and Kaur, R., A review on different prediction techniques for stock market price. *Int. J. Control Autom.*, 13, 1, 353–364, 2020. Science and Engineering Research Support Society.
24. Huertas, C. and Juarez-Ramirez, R., Filter feature selection performance comparison in high dimensional data: A theoretical and empirical analysis of most popular algorithms, in: *17th International Conference on Information Fusion (FUSION)*, pp. 1–8, 2014.
25. Strickland, *Data analytics using open-sourcetools*, Lulu.com, Morrisville, North Carolina, 2016.
26. Sharma, Y.K. and Khan, V., A research on automatic handwritten devnagari text generation in different styles using recurrent neural network (Deep Learning) especially for marathi script. *JRTE*, 8, 2S11, 82–89, 2020.
27. Sharma, Y.K. and Borde, S.P., A research of adaptation for E-learning system by learning preferences. *Int. J. Recent Technol. Eng. (IJRTE)*, 8, 2S11, pp. 919–923, Sept. 2019. Blue Eyes Intelligence Engineering and Sciences Publication (BEIESP).
28. Delbiaggio, N., A comparison of facial recognition algorithms, Journal of Information and Communication Technologies (JICT), Volume 13, Issue 1, pp. 43-52, 2017.

29. Srivastava, A., Mane, S., Shah, A., Shrivastava, N., Thakare, B., A survey of face detection algorithms, in: *2017 International Conference on Inventive Systems and Control (ICISC)*, IEEE, pp. 1–4, 2017.

30. Yuen, K. and Trivedi, M.M., An occluded stacked hourglass approach to facial landmark localization and occlusion estimation. *IEEE Trans. Intell. Vehicles*, 2, 4, 321–331, 2017.

31. Mandal, B., Li, L., Wang, G.S., Lin, J., Towards detection of bus driver fatigue based on robust visual analysis of eye state. *IEEE Trans. Intell. Transp. Syst.*, 18, 3, 545–557, 2016.

32. Sharma, Y.K., Yadav, R.N.B.V., Anjaiah, P., The comparative analysis of open stack with cloud stack for infrastructure as a service. *Int. J. Adv. Sci. Technol.*, 28, 16, 164–174, 21 Nov. 2019.

33. Kumar, A. and Patra, R., Driver drowsiness monitoring system using visual behavior and machine learning, in: *2018 IEEE Symposium on Computer Applications & Industrial Electronics (ISCAIE)*, IEEE, pp. 339–344, 2018.

34. Lyu, J., Yuan, Z., Chen, D., Long-term multi-granularity deep framework for driver drowsiness detection. *arXiv preprint arXiv:1801.02325*, 2018.

35. Boubenna, H. and Lee, D., Image-based emotion recognition using evolutionary algorithms. *Biol. Inspired Cogn. Archit.*, 24, 70–76, 2018.

36. Pradeep, S., Sharma, Y.K., Verma, C., Dalal, S., Prasad, C., Energy efficient routing protocol in novel schemes for performance evaluation. *Appl. System Innov.*, 5, 5, 101, 2022. (MDPI).

37. Vino, T., Sivaraju, S.S., Krishna, R.V.V., Karthikeyan, T., Sharma, Y.K., Venkatesan, K.G.S., Manikandan, G., Selvameena, R., Markos, M., Multicluster analysis and design of hybrid wireless sensor networks using solar energy. *Int. J. Photoenergy*, 2022, 1164613–1164626, 2022. (Hindawi).

38. Sharma, D.Y.K. and Pradeep, S., Deep learning based real-time object recognition for security in air defense. *Proceedings of the 13th INDIACom*, pp. 64–67, 2019.

39. Sharma, Y.K., Web page classification on news feeds using hybrid technique for extraction, in: *Information & Communication Technology for Intelligent System*.

40. Sharma, Y.K. and J Amos, O., Experiences and perspectives of information technology-enhanced learning and teaching in higher education – Ghana case. *Int. J. Adv. Sci. Technol.*, 29, 2, 3739 – 3747, 13 Jan. 2019. Science, and Engineering Research Support Society.

17

Machine Learning Approach to Predicting Reliability in Healthcare Using Knowledge Engineering

Kialakun N. Galgal[1], Kamalakanta Muduli[1] and Ashish Kumar Luhach[2]*

[1]Mechanical Engineering Department, Papua New Guinea University of Technology, Lae, Morobe Province, Papua New Guinea
[2]Department of Electrical and Communication Engineering, Papua New Guinea University of Technology, Lae, Morobe Province, Papua New Guinea

Abstract

Reliability, in machine learning, refers to using data analytics to forecast an asset's deterioration or failure rate so that it can be repaired or replaced before it completely breaks down. Manufacturing facilities, automobile facilities, or any facility that owns assets with rotating or moving parts where wear and tear of components are frequent and costs a fortune to maintain or replace can use Machine Learning approaches to predict Reliability. These approaches can be used in manufacturing facilities as well as automobile facilities. Machine learning algorithms have recently been utilized worldwide to anticipate maintenance. This is because this method has a superior accuracy rate compared to the traditional predictive maintenance strategy, which engineers have demonstrated to be true. At this point in PNG, most maintenance activities consist of corrective or preventative maintenance, which is an expensive endeavor for the company. As a result, the information used in this article comes from online research that other authors conducted on a similar subject. The purpose of this article is to assist organizations based in Papua New Guinea in maintaining their assets by utilizing Machine Learning algorithms to predict the Reliability of their assets.

Keywords: Machine learning, predictive maintenance, reliability, reinforcement learning, semi-supervised learning, supervised learning, unsupervised learning, Wei-bull distribution

Corresponding author: ashish.kumar@pnguot.ac.pg

Sandeep Kumar, Anuj Sharma, Navneet Kaur, Lokesh Pawar and Rohit Bajaj (eds.) Optimized Predictive Models in Healthcare Using Machine Learning, (299–316) © 2024 Scrivener Publishing LLC

17.1   Introduction

Machine learning is a wide phrase that describes implementation methodologies for artificial intelligence that is primarily employed in the IT industry. There are many machine learning algorithms, but the four main types are reinforcement learning, semi-supervised learning, unsupervised learning, and supervised learning [1]. A machine learning algorithm must have the following components: Specifically, (i) datasets for training and testing, (ii) an objective function or loss function to optimise, such as a sum of squared errors or a likelihood function, and (iii) an optimization technique and a model for the data (e.g., linear, nonlinear, nonparametric) [2]. It is common to learn a function that converts input to output using supervised learning with training data pairs. To infer a function, it makes use of labelled training data as well as different training examples. When it is determined that a certain collection of inputs will achieve a certain set of objectives, supervised learning is used [1].

Data-driven unsupervised learning analyses unlabeled data without human interaction. For practical purposes, result groupings, relevant trend and structure identification, and generative feature extraction, this is commonly utilised. Some of the most common unsupervised learning tasks include clustering, density estimation, feature learning, dimensionality reduction, association rule development, anomaly detection, etc [1]. Semi-supervised learning can be viewed as a hybridization of the supervised and unsupervised methods discussed above because it uses both labelled and unlabeled data. As a result, it falls somewhere in the middle of the two approaches. Due to the fact that unlabeled data are shared and that labelled data may occasionally be in short supply, semi-supervised learning is advantageous in the real world. The primary goal of a semi-supervised learning model is to provide predictions that outperform those generated using simply the labelled data from the model [1]. Machine translation, fraud detection, text categorization, and other applications all make use of semi-supervised learning [1].

Machine Learning Approach for Reliability Prediction

Using an environment-driven strategy, reinforcement learning is a machine learning technique that enables software systems and computers to automatically assess the best behavior in a specific context or environment [1]. The ultimate objective of this learning, based on rewards or penalties, is to utilize the knowledge gained from environmental activists to either boost rewards or decrease risks [1]. However, it is not recommended to use it for resolving simple issues. It is a powerful tool for developing AI models that can boost automation or improve the operational effectiveness of intricate systems like robots, autonomous driving, production, and logistics in the supply chain [1]. Li et al. [3] define one of the fields of machine learning known as "deep learning" as developed from artificial neural networks and is characterized by several nonlinear processing layers (ANN). Reliability prediction mainly deals with Remaining Useful Life (RUL) estimations. The problem with RUL prediction is that operating conditions are vastly different worldwide. These variations in operating conditions can cause deviations from the manufacturer's technical manuals and specifications for RUL estimation. Thus an adaptive approach through machine learning may solve such problems.

Problem Statement and Objectives

Concerning Machine Learning, Reliability is the application of data analytics to predict asset failure or deterioration rate so that it can be replaced or serviced before failing. Machine Learning approaches to predictive Reliability can be used in manufacturing facilities, automobile facilities, or any facility that owns assets with rotating or moving parts where wear and tear of components are frequent and costs a fortune to maintain or replace. In recent years, machine learning algorithms have been used globally to predict maintenance since they have an excellent accuracy rate over the conventional predictive maintenance approach and are proven accurate by engineers. Currently, in PNG, most maintenance activities are either corrective or preventive, which is costly for the firm. Therefore, for this article, I gathered information from online research done by other authors on a similar topic to help local Papua New Guinea-based organizations maintain their assets using Machine Learning algorithms to predict their assets' Reliability. As a Master's Student in Mechanical Engineering, I believe this paper can offer a broader point of view on the following:

1. How can Machine Learning Approaches predict the Reliability of assets for organizations in PNG?
2. How practical, economical, or critical Machine learning approaches can be to organizations in PNG?

17.2   Literature Review

Literature review section, we shall review previous articles on this topic, what machine learning algorithms they used, and some of the results these articles drew. Predictive Maintenance can sometimes be challenging regarding machine reliability, especially if there needs to be more data collected from trial-and-error machine operations over a certain period. Therefore, in our current IT infrastructure era, it is possible to use Engineering Knowledge in alignment with the Machine Learning Theory to aid in Predicting the Reliability of equipment. Globally, many industries have already adapted to the Machine Learning method to analyze and to predict Reliability, and only a handful in PNG is using such an approach in handling maintenance activities. The following review is from articles I have taken online from authors who also researched topics similar to my case.

Predictive maintenance is the best fit to avoid future administrative machinery component failures. Therefore, more attention must be triggered to it to ensure it satisfies all audiences involved. Recently, predictive maintenance activities that guarantee the machines' reliability are run by data-based methods like Machine Learning [4]. Machine Learning is a field of Artificial Intelligence that enables computers to do specific tasks without being programmed. Machine Learning approaches are subdivided into four categories which are unsupervised learning, Semi-supervised, supervised, and reinforcement learning. However, I will discuss Machine Learning on a general level. This document from Science Direct discusses predictive maintenance using Machine Learning, specifically in the automotive industry. The idea generated from this article is similar across all sectors, which use machines or moving/rotating components. According to the author, since all modern vehicles have a vast database, Machine Learning helps predict maintenance, hence the vehicles' reliability. Machine Learning has become a common practice in most manufacturing facilities, mobility solutions, etc., and that is because it helps predict maintenance, quality, safety, warranty, or plant facilities monitoring and achieves the most important goal of every running organization, which is to save cost and increase revenue. However, regardless of the wealth of information this document has, the author clearly stated that there is still a gap where more research needs to be carried out in this field of Machine Learning and predictive maintenance of automobiles.

Predictive Maintenance can be regarded as a decision made from a Conditioned-Based Monitoring System. It could be for specific components, parts, an assembly, a machine, or an entire line where a team of engineers usually monitors and identify its lifespan and predict when it will fail and needs to be replaced or maintained. This approach is very economical for any organization as it saves a fortune. The article by Paolanti *et al.* [5] demonstrated use of the Random Forest Method, machine learning architecture for predictive maintenance. For this method, data were collected after a system was analyzed where machine learning was utilized to compare the results to the simulation tool results. The source of data collection for this article was through sensors, PLCs, or communication protocols and was analyzed using the Azure Cloud Architecture, where the results did predict a high accuracy of different machine states. This article provided me with a proper insight into how the Machine Learning approach can work by predicting the Reliability of any component using engineering knowledge.

Pro-active maintenance efforts, also known as predictive maintenance or proactive maintenance, have been shown to be more successful or to produce better results than preventive and corrective maintenance activities. However, as mentioned by, it has limits in terms of reliability enhancement and maintenance optimization. The limitations of the old conventional predictive maintenance approach have been improved over time by machine learning. The usefulness of machine learning in reliability optimization and predictive maintenance has been demonstrated. The author examines the benefits of machine learning over the conventional approach, focusing on the supervised and reinforcement learning algorithms and their usual Predictive Maintenance applications. As I've already indicated, I'll focus on machine learning at a high level in this article, but I'll talk about the subfield of it and how it supports predictive maintenance and improves reliability in subsequent documents. In a study by Huang *et al.* [6] published in 2015, the application of the machine learning method "Support Vector Machine (SVM)" to estimate the remaining useful life of particular components was examined. SVM, according to their argument, is a practical method for estimating RUL since it can handle small training sets and multi-dimensional data efficiently.

Another article by Alsina, *et al.*, [7] compared machine learning techniques with conventional approaches like the Weibull distribution using the supervised learning methodology. They studied support vector machines (SVM), artificial neural networks (ANN), random forests, and soft computing techniques. These findings showed how well machine learning systems could forecast component reliability. Random forests consistently produced the best outcomes with great accuracy. They also demonstrated a problem with using censored or preprocessed data to boost performance across all algorithms under consideration. Techniques for machine learning outperformed more established techniques like the Weibull distribution [7]. Prognostics and RUL prediction, which are essential for maintenance planning, are carried out using semi-supervised learning techniques, according to a paper [2]. Applications in dependability and safety where unlabeled data is easy to get by yet labelled data (such as failure) is expensive, difficult to obtain, or both have a tremendous and underused potential.

Guided regression is commonly used to predict the remaining usable life (RUL) and foresee deterioration, according to an article [2]. The literature in this topic covers ML applications to many technical components, including Lion-ion battery, railway tracks, turbomachinery tools, roller bearings, and aviation engines. Researchers have investigated a number of ML models, such as Gaussian Process Regression (GPR) or kriging, support vector machine/regression, and deep learning for application areas in engineering surrogate modelling, RUL forecasting, fire hazard simulation, and much more generally for structural reliability problems, in addition to these different areas of application. Unsupervised classification is extensively used in defect recognition and identification, claims a paper [2]. Identification of the various failure types and online observation of the equipment degrading statuses are required for this (binary and multiclass). Planned maintenance and PHM are two more general challenges that are intersected in this context by classification, which provides essential data to both approaches.

Clustering or unsupervised classification is less frequently employed in reliability and safety applications than its supervised version, according to a paper [2]). The aforementioned fields of image recognition, genetics, and e-commerce were better positioned to make use of its enormous untapped potential. Applications for clustering include identifying bearing faults in mechanical systems, blasting in mining operations, classifying damage to structural elements, analysing degradation in railroad point machines, identifying wind turbine failures, and locating faults inside the nuclear industry.

Anomaly detection is particularly well adapted for and employed in early failure detection of engineering machinery and structures, according to a paper by Xu and Saleh [2]. It is inextricably linked to sensor data, and industrial machinery and equipment data often arrive as a time series of measurements. In some situations, detecting abnormalities is crucial to avert further harm and catastrophic failure. The data for anomaly identification for constructions like beams, airframes, or bridges contains both spatial and temporal dimensions, according to Xu and Saleh [2] claim that algorithms for anomaly identification equally occur for supervised as well as semi-supervised modes (2021). Despite this, an unsupervised mode is generally more commonly employed since it is cheaper (and frequently easier to get) and has a broader availability of unlabeled data compared to labeled data, according to [2]. Data is frequently only accessible under (marked) nominal operational circumstances in reliability and safety applications. When incomplete labels are available, anomaly detection can use semi-supervised learning technologies [2].

Algorithms for semi-supervised learning were also utilized in prognostics, RUL prediction, and fault detection and identification, all of which are crucial for maintenance scheduling [2]. They believe that labelled data, such as failure, has an untapped potential but is difficult to collect, expensive, or difficult to obtain in safety and reliability applications when unlabeled data is abundant. They showed greater RUL prediction accuracy and less resultant dispersion than a supervised learning method. Despite this, they employed a high proportion of labeled data compared to the normal levels for semi-supervised learning applications. According to a publication [2], supervised or unsupervised learning is still more commonly utilized in dependability and safety applications than reinforcement learning. However, it presents several potentials for making crucial contributions to these fields.

Some implementations use deep neural networks (deep learning algorithms) to predict the RUL of components. The experimental findings in a paper by Li *et al.* [3] indicate that the suggested strategy is promising for prognostic issues and is well-suited for industrial applications. Even though the recommended approach produced decent predictive results, more labeled training was needed to train models for neural networks. Data-driven techniques often require many data, especially for predictive algorithms.

17.3   Proposed Methodology

Since this is an extensive topic, we shall conduct a review paper on previously written articles covered in our literature review [8–11]. We shall look into the benefits and the drawbacks of using machine learning and knowledge engineering in predicting Reliability and how we can implement such systems in Papua New Guinea's industrial plants.

17.3.1 Data Analysis (Findings)

After reviewing several articles, there are a couple of outstanding findings. In this section of the article, we shall examine these findings and try to derive an implementation strategy to be covered in the next chapter.

17.3.2 General Procedures

The articles covered using a specific procedure when implementing a machine-learning approach. We can simplify this to the following steps, and we shall cover them individually and try to develop a strategy.

1. Data Acquisition,
2. Data Preprocessing (Censoring),
3. Feature Extraction,
4. Data Model Training and Testing, and
5. Prediction and Prognostics.

- Data Acquisition
  Data acquisition describes collecting data about specific failure characteristics of a component. The data collected may vary from acceleration, vibration, temperature, amperage, etc., but they need to have some correlation with a particular failure mode(s) – or at least a suspected correlation.
- Data Preprocessing
  Data carries much noise, especially failure data. Several modes can cause failure, and these modes tend to overlap in the data collection phase. Data preprocessing, as in the above articles, cleans and removes extreme non-linearity from the data, which may not be related to the assessed component. For example, human error from an operator or technician when filling in a Root Cause Failure Analysis (RCFA) or when logging temperature readings. These errors will need to be censored before training machine learning models. We want the model to estimate component failure, not random human error.
- Feature Extraction
  Feature extraction is the process of identifying correlations with Reliability in datasets. These features show

characteristics of a particular stage in the life of an asset and thus can be used to determine that stage later when compared with new data. From the articles, the feature extraction layer is the groundwork for developing mathematical models used in prediction.

- Data Model Training and Testing

  This stage is the main area where the application of the machine learning process of algorithms begins. From articles, all data source can be made up of labeled or unlabeled data. Training is where the mathematical model that describes the relationship between input and output is mapped and tested. One benefit of machine learning algorithms is that they can infer mathematical relationships from data sets independently, without human intervention.

- Prediction and Prognostics

  This stage consists mainly of 3 steps: 1) measurement, 2) data preprocessing, and 3) prediction. The first step was retrieving data from field sensors and or collected data from databases. This data is then preprocessed and outliers are removed (censoring) before they are fed to machine learning data models. The data models (mathematical models/functions) are then used to predict and estimate the next failure occurrence.

17.3.3   Reviewed Algorithms

There were a couple of algorithms covered in this article. We can summarize them in the following Table 17.1. Table 17.2 summarizes the terminologies used in this article and their definition.

Table 17.1 Algorithm types.

Algorithm	Type
Support Vector Machines (SVM)	Unsupervised, Supervised Learning
Deep Neural Networks	Unsupervised Learning
Random Forests	Supervised Learning
Artificial Neural Networks (ANN)	Supervised Learning
Linear Regression	Supervised Learning

Table 17.2 Terms and definitions.

Terms	Definition
Algorithm	According to Alexander and Gillis, [12] an algorithm is the steps involved in solving a problem using mathematical approaches. This serves as specific actions in a step-by-step procedure with the hardware or the software. Mathematically, algorithms solve current issues.
Machine Learning	According to IBM Team, [13], Machine Learning is a branch of Artificial Intelligence and Computer Science that focuses on using data and algorithms to imitate how humans learn and improve their accuracy.
Predictive Maintenance	There are different definitions of predictive maintenance; however, concerning Gourley, [14], Predictive maintenance deals directly with an asset's health, safety, status, and performance in real time.
Reliability	With machine learning, Reliability refers to the analytics of data to predict an asset's failure or deterioration rate so that it can be replaced or serviced before failing. Reliability software is used but is not limited to the following industries; manufacturing, aerospace, defense, energy, oil and gas, chemicals, and pharmaceuticals.
Reinforcement Learning	Algorithms in the machine learning field of reinforcement learning deal specifically with choosing the right course of action to maximise reward in a given circumstance. During reinforcement learning, there isn't a right or wrong answer; instead, the reinforcement agent chooses how to carry out a particular job.
Semi-Supervised Learning	Semi-Supervised Learning is a learning problem involving a small number of labeled examples and many unlabeled examples. This learning problem is challenging as other learning algorithms could not use mixtures of labeled and unlabeled data. In simple terms, semi-supervised learning sits between supervised and unsupervised learning algorithms.

(Continued)

Table 17.2 Terms and definitions. (*Continued*)

Terms	Definition
Supervised Learning	The most used algorithm for machine learning is supervised learning. With a given set of data (Feature) & known outcomes, it trains an algorithm using a training data to make predictions. Labeled input data that correspond to intended output or response values are included in the training dataset. The supervised learning algorithm uses it to make accurate predictions of the response variable for a fresh dataset after building a model from it by identifying connections between the characteristics and output data.
Unsupervised Learning	Unsupervised machine learning is a method where model supervision is not necessary. Instead, this kind of learning enables the model to operate independently and without supervision in order to find previously unnoticed patterns and information. Although supervised learning, if we recall, deals with labelled data, it mostly deals with unlabeled data [15].
Weibull distribution	The useful life of random failures is indicated by the Weibull distribution. It is a continuous distribution of probabilities used to examine product reliability, model failure rates, and assess life statistics.

17.3.4   Benefits of Machine Learning

A couple of benefits noted from reviewing the above articles are as follows:

- Minimal Human Intervention
  Mathematical models for prognostics are automatically inferred by machine learning algorithms and need little human intervention.
- Adaptive
  Machine learning algorithms can be adaptive. Recursive algorithms can automatically learn their environments and improve accuracy when presented with large datasets.

Operating conditions vary greatly; thus, an adaptive approach can significantly improve system reliability predictions.

17.3.5   Drawbacks of Machine Learning

We previously covered the beneficial aspects of machine learning, but let us now cover the drawbacks we saw from some of the reviewed articles.

- Requirement for Large Data sets
  Machine learning algorithms require an extensive data set to develop relational models between input and output accurately. If a small data set is provided, inaccurate predictions will be made. Thus, these algorithms are as good as the data set provided to train them.
- Computational Requirements
  Training of these machine learning models uses enormous computing power. It may take days to develop a single model on lower-end hardware.
- Complicated Initial Setup
  Initial setups may be complicated. This depends on the type of algorithm being used; generally, machine learning algorithms are complex systems.

17.4   Implications

How can we implement this in an industrial plant in Papua New Guinea? What are some of the complications and risks that might be encountered? Does PNG need this strategy? In this section, we answer these questions and ascertain a possible practical general method to implement a machine-learning approach to reliability prediction in PNG.

17.4.1   Prerequisites and Considerations

A couple of things could be improved when considering the PNG industrial environment. We will cover a couple of drawbacks that need to be considered before implementing a machine-learning strategy.

The main drawback in Papua New Guinea would be the need for more data and acquisition systems. Especially companies that do not collect failure data or still need to implement reliability assessments. Mining and Oil and Gas industries may be better off in implementation due to them already implementing reliability engineering strategies and collecting reliability data. This lack will incur a considerable installation cost due to purchasing equipment for reliability analysis.

Another consideration is the computational requirements for machine learning model training. Machine learning algorithm training can be achieved on a large number of computer resources. Companies may need to invest in GPUs and servers for processing machine learning algorithms on the premise. This can be averted using cloud computing platforms equipped for machine learning, such as Amazon Web Services (AWS) or Google Cloud Platform (GCP). Models can be trained in the cloud, and prognostics can be run on less powerfulmachines.

17.4.2 Implementation Strategy

Now let's move on to how to implement such a system—considering all the items mentioned above in the current and previous chapters. We shall devise a strategy to implement a similar approach in Papua New Guinea.

We can implement such a system by first developing data acquisition systems and systems for ascertaining failure data. We can use computerized maintenance management systems (CMMS) or enterprise resource planning (ERP) software suites to help manage assets. An asset hierarchy, according to ISO 14224, should be present. This will help in storing and sorting through the plant to part-level data. The asset hierarchy should be maintained in whatever software suite selected, whether CMMS or ERP. Once the groundwork has been laid, data must be collected for assessing the asset. A large dataset must be collected for machine learning algorithms, which may take a year. We can also ascertain the data from manufacturers and then train the model for the particular operating conditions using new data.

Once data is collected, data preprocessing should be done, removing any outliers and refining the data. Feature extraction can then be done on the processed data, identifying certain relationships that directly affect the life expectancy of an asset. These features can then be modeled and trained using our machine-learning procedures or algorithms. Cloud computing proposed for the training stage, and the prognostics can be run on a server on-premise.

17.4.3   Recommendations

We begin by answering the need for such systems. Currently, PNG's economy is at a stage where it is getting ever more expensive to import components from overseas continuously. The cost and the time it takes to import causes inventory strategies to stock up on ingredients and have large warehouses for machine parts. All these add up to operating expenses and a company's profit margin reduction.

If an asset's Reliability can be successfully predicted to a certain degree of accuracy, Just-In-Time (JIT) inventory management approaches can be implemented. Not only inventory but asset availability and Reliability will be increased, allowing companies to maximize production and better manage human resources.

Another point to be noted is the heavy reliance on experienced personnel. Companies have experienced personnel posted in every region because these employees know the system well enough to pre-emptively identify possible failures. Expert systems can be developed with a machine learning and knowledge engineering approach to allow scalability. Thus increasing the productivity of this experienced personnel and broadening their effective range to multiple regions per person.

17.5   Conclusion

Many recommendations can be made about the Machine Learning Approaches in predicting the Reliability of assets using Engineering Knowledge, as discussed in the recommendation section, and there is still more gap in this area. Precisely for this article, I will conclude my research write-up by answering the two objective questions I highlighted under the problem statement and accurate section, which are:

How can Machine Learning Approaches predict the Reliability of assets for organizations in PNG?
As I have mentioned, knowing that PNG is a third-world country and is at an early stage in the IT infrastructure era and also our economy is not stable at the moment, if a company makes an investment in Machine Learning Approach in predicting the Reliability of their assets, it will be a life-changing lesson for the firm. It will save the organization(s) cost, reduce downtime, improve the performance of the assets by optimizing

their Reliability and safeguard the equipment from random failure by closely monitoring the asset(s) performance and correcting before the loss. As long as there is good data collection from, say, sensors or PLCs, the Machine Learning Approach can help predict the Reliability of assets for any organization.

How practical, economical, or critical Machine learning approaches can be to organizations in PNG?
Similar to the answer provided for question one, the Machine Learning approach in predicting the Reliability of an asset will be very economical because it will save cost. By saving cost, I mean the downtime reduction cost saving, unnecessary component replacement before predicted failure cost saving, men power reduction cost saving, etc. As the organization saves money, it financially benefits the country by funding more activities or improving living standards.

17.6 Limitations and Scope of Future Work

From the research, I have made, and from experience as a citizen of this country, the main limitation that will affect the implementation of this approach in the local industries of this beautiful nation of PNG will be the traditional mindset most employees have and the resistance to change and adapt to new technologies. Since it was mentioned that there is a gap in this area of research, I would like to propose future work on the following topics, which I will revisit later which I believe will support this document in the implementation process of the Machine Learning Approach in Predicting Reliability using the Engineering Knowledge. The topics that can be further worked on are as follows:

- Unlabeled data in Machine Learning and its role in predicting the Reliability of assets
- Labeled data in Machine Learning and its role in predicting the Reliability of assets.
- Unsupervised Learning
- Supervised Learning
- Reinforcement Learning
- Semi-Supervised Learning

References

1. Sarker, I.H., Machine learning: Algorithms, real-world applications and research directions. *SN Comput. Sci.*, 2, 3, 160, 2021.
2. Xu, Z. and Saleh, J.H., Machine learning for reliability engineering and safety applications: Review of current status and future opportunities. *Reliab. Eng. Syst. Saf.*, 211, 107530, 2021.
3. Li, X., Zhang, W., Ding, Q., Deep learning-based remaining useful life estimation of bearings using multi-scale feature extraction. *Reliab. Eng. Syst. Saf.*, 182, 208–218, 2019.
4. Theissler, A., Pérez-Velázquez, J., Kettelgerdes, M., Elger, G., Predictive maintenance enabled by machine learning: Use cases and challenges in the automotive industry. *Reliab. Eng. Syst. Saf.*, 215, 107864, 2021.
5. Paolanti, M., Romeo, L., Felicetti, A., Mancini, A., Frontoni, E., Loncarski, J., Machine learning approach for predictive maintenance in industry 4.0, in: *2018 14th IEEE/ASME International Conference on Mechatronic and Embedded Systems and Applications (MESA)*, IEEE, pp. 1–6, 2018.
6. Huang, H.Z., Wang, H.K., Li, Y.F., Zhang, L., Liu, Z., Support vector machine based estimation of remaining useful life: current research status and future trends. *J. Mech. Sci. Technol.*, 29, 1, 151–163, 2015.
7. Alsina, E.F., Chica, M., Trawiński, K., Regattieri, A., On the use of machine learning methods to predict component reliability from data-driven industrial case studies. *Int. J. Adv. Manuf. Technol.*, 94, 5, 2419–2433, 2018.
8. Biswal, J.N., Muduli, K., Satapathy, S., Tripathy, S., A framework for assessment of SSCM strategies with respect to sustainability performance: An Indian thermal power sector perspective. *Int. J. Procure. Manag.*, 11, 4, 455–471, 2018.
9. Swain, S., Peter, O., Adimuthu, R., Muduli, K., Blockchain technology for limiting the impact of pandemic: Challenges and prospects. *Comput. Modeling Data Anal. COVID-19 Res.*, 165–186, 2021. https://doi.org/10.1201/9781003137481
10. Swain, S., Oyekola, P.O., Muduli, K., Intelligent technologies for excellency in sustainable operational performance in the healthcare sector. *Int. J. Soc. Ecol. Sustain. Dev. (IJSESD)*, 13, 5, 1–16, 2022.
11. Peter, O., Swain, S., Muduli, K., Ramasamy, A., IoT in combating COVID-19 pandemics: Lessons for developing countries, in: *Assessing COVID-19 and Other Pandemics and Epidemics Using Computational Modelling and Data Analysis*, pp. 113–131, 2022.
12. Gillis, A.S., *Algorithm*, Tech Target, 2023, accessed on 4th January 2023, https://www.techtarget.com/whatis/ definition/algorithm.
13. IBM Team, *Machine learning*, IBM, 2020, July 15, https://www.ibm.com/ cloud/learn/ machine-learning. accessed on 4th January 2023.

14. Gourley, L., *What is predictive maintenance, and how is it transforming manufacturing?*, PTC, 2021, May 2, https://www.ptc.com/en/blogs/iiot/what-is-predictive-maintenance. accessed on 4th January 2023.

15. Dimid, D.N., *Unsupervised learning algorithms cheat sheet*, Towards Data Science, 2022, February 16, https://towardsdatascience.com/unsupervised-learning-algorithms cheat-sheet-d391a39de44a.accessed on 4th January 2023.

18

TPLSTM-Based Deep ANN with Feature Matching Prediction of Lung Cancer

Thaventhiran Chandrasekar*, Praveen Kumar Karunanithi,
A. Emily Jenifer and Inti Dhiraj

School of Computing, SASTRA University, Thanjavur, Tamilnadu, India

Abstract

Early detection of lung cancer is essential for accurate diagnosis and treatment recommendation. Lung cancer prognosis is the most critical issue in healthcare, especially given the exponential expansion of medical data. As a result, early cancer identification lowers mortality rates. However, this requires a lot more accuracy and effort. A model approach called TP-LSTM was created to quickly and correctly predict lung cancer. The suggested deep-learning model for analysing input patient data is composed of several layers. To forecast lung cancer at an early stage, many strategies are used at each strata. In deep neural learning, the input layer delivers the hidden layer features and data it has received from the dataset. Target Projection matching pursuit is employed in the feature selection process of the first hidden layer to quickly and precisely find the most crucial qualities for cancer prediction. Lung cancer is predicted using the patient data classification approach using LSTM at hidden layer 2 and the selected important features based on Czekanowski's proximity factor. A number of patient data and parameters, such as accuracy, false-positive rates, and detection accuracy timeare empirically compared between the unique TP-LSTM methodology and existing methods. This study shows that, despite requiring less time and producing fewer false positives than state-of-the-art methods, the proposed TPFMDANN-LSTM algorithm beats them in terms of prediction accuracy.

Keywords: LSTM, TPFMDANN, Czekanowski's, false positive rate, prediction accuracy, CNN, K-NN

Corresponding author: thaventhiran@gmail.com

Sandeep Kumar, Anuj Sharma, Navneet Kaur, Lokesh Pawar and Rohit Bajaj (eds.) Optimized Predictive Models in Healthcare Using Machine Learning, (317–328) © 2024 Scrivener Publishing LLC

18.1   Introduction

The mortality rate for lung cancer, one of the most frequent malignancies, is significant. The rising incidence of cigarette smoking is one of the primary causes of lung cancer in developing countries. The medical community gives doctors a selection of better services for more exact analysis of diseased patient medical data as the number of ill persons increases fast. As a solution to a number of issues, including patient care, early illness detection, and community services, healthcare services are gaining popularity. To give patients with the appropriate therapy, it is essential to properly predict lung cancer illness. In [1], a Lung Cancer Prediction-CNN (LCP-CNN) was developed for the reliable identification of benign nodules during the early disease diagnosis of ill patients. Regrettably, an accurate medical diagnosis could not be achieved in less time. k-Nearest-Neighbors (k-NN) is a method introduced in [2] for estimating the severity of a patient's disease. The suggested approach decreases the amount of the dataset by applying the genetic algorithm to choose attributes. Despite this, the incidence of false alarms did not decrease throughout categorization.

Lung cancer, one of the most common cancers, has a high fatality rate. One of the main causes of lung cancer in developing nations is the increased prevalence of cigarette smoking. Since the number of sick people rises quickly, the medical community offers doctors a variety of better services for a more precise examination of diseased patient medical data. Healthcare services are becoming more and more popular as a response to a variety of problems, such as patient care, early sickness identification, and community services. It is crucial to accurately forecast lung cancer sickness in order to provide patients with the appropriate medication. [1] describes the development of a Lung Cancer Prediction-CNN (LCP-CNN) for the accurate detection of benign nodules during the early disease diagnosis of sick individuals. Unfortunately, a precise medical diagnosis could not be made in that short of a period of time. A technique for determining the severity of a patient's illness was introduced in [2] and is known as k-Nearest-Neighbors (k-NN). The suggested method reduces the size of the dataset by selecting attributes using a genetic algorithm. Yet, during classification, the frequency of false alarms did not decline.

It was discovered that a unique fuzzy and updated soft expert system is capable of predicting the beginning of lung cancer [3]. But, machine learning was not used for accurate forecasting. Deep neural network (DNN) for accurate lung cancer detection was developed in [4]. To increase the model's robustness, however, sufficient training data were necessary for the intended network. In order to forecast lung cancer, [5] created a high-dimensional logistic regression. While the suggested technique improves accuracy, the phase of picking characteristics to decrease forecasting time may have been performed more effectively. The introduction of improved CNNs in [6] improved the accuracy of automated lung cancer detection. Nonetheless, the diagnostic accuracy of lung cancer remained constant. The Weight Optimized NN with Maximum Likelihood Boosting (WONN-MLB) method was proposed in [7] to use vast quantities of data to identify lung cancer. Even if the strategy enhances accuracy, the vast number of data points should have been considered.

[8] devised a Markov decision approach to increase the lung cancer detection's specificity. Sadly, superior classification results were not achieved for identifying malignant pulmonary nodules. First developed in [9] to identify benign or malignant nodules, a threshold-based multiclass Support Vector Machine classification approach was employed. Nevertheless, the predicted method was unable to increase the categorization precision of the phases. A cross-validated Bayesian network model was created to predict lung cancer in the local region [10]. The model was unable to use a bigger external data set to confirm its lung cancer prediction.

Platelet characteristics and plasma rich in platelets were used to identify lung disease in [11]. Nevertheless, the objective of the dimensionality reduction study was not to enhance the accuracy of lung cancer disease detection. [12] describes the development of a logistic regression prediction model for identifying the clinical stage of a tumour. The suggested model does not reduce prediction time, but boosts prediction accuracy and recall rates. Elephant Herding Optimization was used to decrease the time necessary for lung cancer prediction [13]. Regrettably, the algorithm needed help with the management of the complicated datasets in order to provide superior results.

Various classification algorithms were created in [14] so that the patient's survival rate could be accurately diagnosed. The developed methods were incapable of recognising all stages of lung cancer. [15] proposed fuzzy-based strategies for the development of genetic lung cancer diagnosis algorithms. The algorithms did not significantly increase the exceptional lung cancer detection accuracy. Random forest (RF) is a technique found in [16] for improving the prognosis of lung cancer. Developed a meta-heuristic optimal neural network to analyse patient data to predict lung infection using machine learning techniques that were not utilised to improve prediction accuracy in [17]. While the network's design provides the highest degree of accuracy, the large database was not used to examine life-threatening illnesses [18]. That a double Normalization-based

Multi-Aggregation (DNMA) model was developed to uncover early lung cancer detection's crucial characteristics. Nevertheless, there was no improvement in the accuracy of lung diagnosis. In [19], the effects of mixing delta characteristics with traditional (non-delta) features for diagnostic differentiation and disease prognosis of lung cancer were investigated. Unfortunately, deep learning proved ineffective in detecting lung cancer. Using a multi-parameterized artificial neural network (MP-ANN) [20], lung cancer risk was reliably and effectively predicted. The proposed neural network proved, however, ineffective at forecasting lung cancer risk.

18.2   Proposed TP-LSTM-Based Neural Network with Feature Matching for Prediction of Lung Cancer

Many individuals suffer from lung cancer, which is a fatal disease. To minimise patient mortality, it is necessary to use antiquated lung cancer prediction techniques. Thus, detecting lung cancer is a huge challenge for clinicians. Analysis of patient data is increasingly commonly applied in healthcare communities for early illness identification. The amount of patient data makes accurate illness diagnosis harder. As they categorise based on the whole feature, machine learning methods may be more accurate and practical. To successfully predict circumstances with little complexity, the dimension of the dataset must be limited. On the basis of this inspiration, a TP-LSTM is displayed. The TPLSTM takes dimensionality and temporal QoS measures into account (i.e., memory storage). This involvement derives from the selection of important traits. Figure 18.1 displays the layout of the TP-architectural LSTM. The architecture of the proposed TP-LSTM method is represented in Figure 18.1, and it could be used to forecast lung cancer at an advanced stage with high precision and GPU use. First consideration is given to the lung cancer database while doing predictive analytics. The dataset is used to compute the no. of features f_1, f_2, f_3 and so on till $f n$ and the patient pd_1, pd_2, pd_3, …. pd_n. Following that, Target Matching pursuit is used to choose the pertinent features. The essential features that have been selected are classified to forecast lung disease. The following subsections explain the feature selection and classification procedure.

The deep artificial feed-forward neural network's schematic design is seen in Figure 18.2. Feed-forward connections with varying weights are made between the nodes in each layer to create the entire network. The network has several levels, including one input layer, two hidden layers,

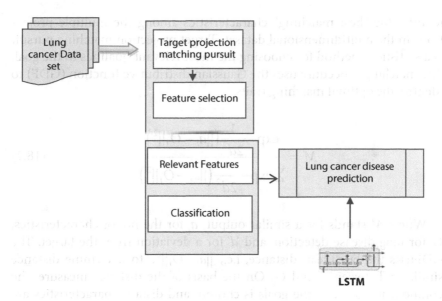

Figure 18.1 Architecture of proposed TP-LSTM technique.

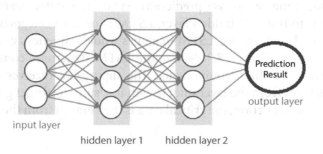

Figure 18.2 Deep artificial feed-forward neural network model.

and one output layer. The very first layer receives a_1, a_2, a_3, ... a_n features and takes pd_1, pd_2, pd_3, ... pd_n the patient data. The input layer 'i(t)' neuron's activity is represented as follows:

$$i(t) = r + \sum_{i=1}^{n} a_i(t) * p_0 \qquad (18.1)$$

Where $a_i(t)$ stands for features, p_0 stands for the importance at the input layer, and r stands for a bias stored with a value of 1. The first hidden layer receives the input, after which the appropriate feature selection is carried out. The proposed strategy uses the target projection matching pursuit to identify the "best matching" characteristics among the multiple projections in the multidimensional dataset. Target projection matching pursuit is a statistical method for choosing the most relevant qualities to the goal. The matching procedure uses the Gaussian distributive function (GDF) to identify the optimal matching traits.

$$M = \frac{\exp-\dfrac{1}{2d^2}\left(\|a_i - O_j\|^2\right)}{\sum \exp-\dfrac{1}{2d^2}\left(\|a_i - O_j\|^2\right)} \tag{18.2}$$

Where M stands for a similar output, a_i for the no. of characteristics, O_j for lung disease detection, and 'd' for a deviation from the target. The GDFuses the Euclidean distance, i.e., $\|a_i - O_j\|^2$, to determine distance similarity between a_i and O_j. On the basis of the distance measure, the component closest to the goals is chosen, and distant characteristics are removed from the dataset. The relevant parameters are ultimately selected for the classification in order to increase the accuracy and decrease the computation time of disease prediction. When the stated features have been shifted to the next hidden layer, LSTM is used to categorise patient data. During deep learning, LSTM manages whole sequences of data with many time steps. Figure 18.3 depicts the LSTM structure's construction, which consists of three components. The input gate receives data and selected features from the layer underneath it. Using the forget gate as well as the activation function, the critical data is then erased from the cell state.

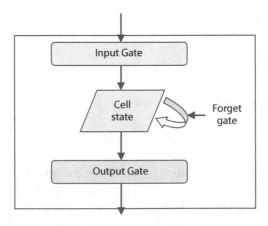

Figure 18.3 Construction of the LSTM model.

With this forgets gate, the decision to show the output at a given time step is made. Its output gate subsequently displays the outcome.

The forget gate method is described as follows:

$$F(t) = \beta(\alpha_f * x_t + \varphi_f * h_{t-1} + r) \tag{18.3}$$

Where xt denotes patient data varies from pd_1, pd_2, pd_3, ... pd_n, Γ (t) signifies one forget gate output at a time. 't', β denotes the transfer function, α_f, φ_f stands for connections' weights, and h_{t-1} denotes a preceding layer output. The weight matrices (α_f, φ_f) are multiplied by the inputs 'x,' and a bias (r) is added. The symbol '*' designates a convolution operator in equation (18.3). The Heaviside step activation function uses Czekanowski's dice index method to comparethe input patient data with the testing data. Czekanowski's approach helps us to find the resemblance between the input patient data effectively.

Czekanowski's method is stated below:

$$S = 1 - 2 * \left[\frac{pd_i \cap pd_{tc}}{\sum pd_1 + \sum pd_{tc} - pd_i \cap pd_{tc}} \right] \tag{18.4}$$

The symbol '∩' represents a mutual dependency where 'S' stands for Czekanowski's dice coefficient, pd_i where it denotes patient records and pd_{tc} signifies testing class data. The similarity coefficient (S) ranges from 0 to 1 and provides an integer value. When the coefficient indicates a significant resemblance, the patient with testing structural analysis are matched. Which elements of the cell state should be kept or thrown away is decided by the activation function. The activation function's yield of "1" indicates that forget gate remembers the results at that particular time step. The activation function returns "0," which eliminates any remaining context from the cell state. In other words, the forget gate shows only the results of the chosen class while erasing all others.

$$\beta = \begin{cases} 1; & \text{if } (\arg \max S) \\ 0; & \text{otherwise} \end{cases} \tag{18.5}$$

Whereas *argmaxS* signifies an argument of maximum similarity function, β denotes an activation function result. The output layer is where the categorization results are obtained. All patient data are correctly categorized in this manner. An accurate lung cancer prediction is made using the classification findings. The recommended TP-algorithmic LSTM method is explained in the following way:

// Algorithm 1: PROPOSED TP-LSTM BASED NEURAL NETWORK WITH FEATURE MATCHING FOR PREDICTION OF LUNG CANCER

Input: Dataset, No. of features a_1, a_2, a_3, ... a_n and the patient data pd_1, pd_2, pd_3, ... pd_n

Output: Prediction accuracy increased

Begin

1. **Number of features** a_1, a_2, a_3, ... a_n are defined as input in the input layers
2. **For defined each**feature, a_1//**hidden layers**
3. Execute if M' between features a_i and objective O_j
4.   Project the more predominant features
5. **else**
6. List the irreverent features
7. **End if**
8. Obtain the more predominant features
9. Eliminate the irreverent features
10. **End for**
11. **For** all patient values in data 'pd_i' with all features of extracted   //**Second hidden layer**
12. Compute similarity 'S.'
13.   **For all** time step 't.
14. proceed the input patient data recordedon forget gate $F(t)$
15.   **If** ($\beta = 1$), **then**
16. it shows the output from the current cell state that is classified.
17. **else**
18. From the present cell state, ignore the other class output.
19. **end if**
20. In last the output layer, can find the classification results.
21. **end for**
22. **end for**

End

Algorithm 1 [21] illustrates the step-by-step process of a TP-LSTM Based Neural Network using Feature Matching for Diagnosis in order to optimise the accuracy of the lung cancer illness prediction while minimising the amount of time required. The database is first used to collect its features and patient data. Data collected is then sent to the input layer. To use the target projection tried to make, the most prominent features from the information are then identified based on the GDF. Other traits are discarded in favour of those that are more relevant to the objective. LSTM is then used to give the second hidden layer with the selected features and patient data. The LSTM employs the Czekanowski dice factor to determine the degree of similarity between patient data and those in their respective classes. The activation function uses the similarity metric to categorise patient data. Eventually, the prediction accuracy by prediction are shown in the hidden layers i.e output layers in order to improve the detection accuracy of lung cancer.

18.3   Experimental Work and Comparison Analysis

The performance evaluation of the current k-NN [2], LCP-CNN [1] and the TPFMDANN-LSTM are compared in this part concerning several factors, including prediction accuracy, false-alarm rate, and classification time. Tables and graphical representations describe the outcomes of three distinct strategies. In dividing the number of patient information, information is in the form of records in dataset, that were correctly classified into different classes, one may calculate the prediction accuracy. The following is the formula for calculating predictive accuracy:

$$PA = \left[\frac{NPDCC}{n} \right] * 100 \qquad (18.6)$$

NPDCC is the no. of correctly classified patient data, where 'n' is the whole amount of patient data, and PA stands for prediction accuracy. The forecast accuracy is expressed as a percentage (%).

The results of the experiments conducted to determine how well lung cancer disease may be predicted are presented in Table 18.1 for patient data chosen from the dataset ranging from 100 to 1000. Outcomes on the accuracy of TP-LSTM predictions are compared to those obtained from other classification methods, specifically k-NN [2] and LCP-CNN [1]. According to the findings, it has been demonstrated that the recently introduced

Table 18.1 Comparison of prediction accuracy.

No. of patient data	Prediction accuracy -PA (%)		
	LCP with CNN	KNN	TP with LSTM
100	87	84	90
200	88	85	91
300	87	83	92
400	88	85	91
500	86	83	90
600	88	85	92
700	89	86	93
800	87	84	91
900	89	86	92
1000	87	84	91

TP-LSTM is capable of achieving superior prediction accuracy as numerous classification strategies. Let's take data from one hundred patients for the first repetition of the tests. 90% of the data are correctly categorised, and the accuracy is ninety percent after utilising the TP-LSTM, in comparison to 87% and 84%, respectively, for the current [1] and [2]. Following this, several performance outcomes are presented for each technique. For each design, ten distinct results are presented in the display. Comparisons are made between the efficacy of the TPFMDANN-LSTM that was developed and that of other approaches that are already in use. The findings of 10 comparisons reveal that the suggested method's accuracy in diagnosing lung cancer is higher by 4% comparing to [1] and by 8% compared to [2]. The average of these findings can be found below.

18.4 Conclusion

The research on machine learning has produced a number of different methods, the efficiency of which is determined by a number of different criteria. In this particular investigation, the method of selecting features and classifying them is combined with such a deep learning strategy known as TP-LSTM. The TP-LSTM method begins with a feature representation that use Target Projection perfectly matched approach to identify the essential components for accurate detection. After that, the classification is performed with the assistance of LSTM and the relevant set of features. A Czekanowski correlation coefficient is used for the evaluation of both the test dataset and the testing dataset by the LSTM network. The activation function provides the output results with improved accuracy based on the similarity measure, which is used to compare the two sets of results. The results of an in-depth analytical and experimental evaluation demonstrate that the suggested TP-LSTM works better than the existing classification algorithms and has a greater level of accuracy when it comes to predicting lung cancer.

References

1. Heuvelmans, M.A., van Ooijen, P.M.A., Ather, S., Silva, C.F., Han, D. *et al.*, Lung cancer prediction by deep learning to identify benign lung nodules. *Lung Cancer*, Elsevier, 154, 1–4, 2021.
2. Maleki, N., Zeinali, Y., Taghi, S., Niaki, A., A k-NN method for lung cancer prognosis with the use of a genetic algorithm for feature selection. *Expert Syst. Appl.*, Elsevier, 164, 1–7, 2021.
3. Khalil, A.M., Li, S.G., Lin, Y., Li, H.X., Ma, S.G. *et al.*, A new expert system in prediction of lung cancer disease based on fuzzy soft sets. *Soft Comput.*, Springer, 24, 14179–14207, 2020.
4. Guo, J., Wang, C., Xu, X., Shao, J., Yang, L. *et al.*, An artificial intelligence-based automated system for lung cancer screening. *Ann. Translation Med.*, 8, 18, 1–12, 2020.
5. Zhang, X., Zhang, Q., Wang, X., Ma, S., Fang, K. *et al.*, Structured sparse logistic regression with application to lung cancer prediction using volatile breath biomarkers. *Stat Med.*, Wiley, 39, 7, 955–967, 2020.
6. Kasinathan, G., Jayakumar, S., Gandomi, A.H., Manikandan, R., Fong, S.J., Patan, R. *et al.*, Automated 3-D lung tumor detection and classification by an active contour model and CNN classifier. *Expert Syst. Appl.*, Elsevier, 134, 112–119, 2019.
7. ALzubi, J.A., Bharathikannan, B., Tanwar, S., Manikandan, R., Khanna, A. *et al.*, Boosted neural network ensemble classification for lung cancer disease diagnosis. *Appl. Soft Comput.*, Elsevier, 80, 579–591, 2019.
8. Petousis, P., Winter, A., Speier, W., Aberle, D.R., Hsu, W. *et al.*, Using sequential decision making to improve lung cancer screening performance. *IEEE Access*, 7, 119403–119419, 2019.
9. Sujitha, R. and Seenivasagam, V., Classification of lung cancer stages with machine learning over big data healthcare framework. *J. Ambient Intell. Humaniz. Comput.*, Springer, 12, 5639–5649, 2020.

10. Luo, Y., McShan, D., Ray, D., Matuszak, M., Jolly, S. *et al.*, Development of a fully cross-validated bayesian network approach for local control prediction in lung cancer. *IEEE Trans. Radiat. Plasma Med. Sci.*, 3, 2, 232–241, 2019.

11. Zua, R., Yub, S., Yanga, G., Gee, Y., Wanga, D. *et al.*, Integration of platelet features in blood and platelet-rich plasma for detection of lung cancer. *Clinica Chimica Acta*, 509, 43–51, 2020.

12. Wang, B. and Zhang, J., Logistic regression analysis for LncRNA-disease association prediction based on random forest and clinical stage data. *IEEE Access*, 8, 35004–3501, 2020.

13. Nayak, M., Das, S., Bhanja, U., Senapati, M.R., Elephant herding optimization technique based neural network for cancer prediction. *Inf. Med. Unlocked*, Elsevier, 21, 1–10, 2020.

14. Ra, P.K. and Naveen, N.C., Lung cancer survivability prediction based on performance using classification techniques of support vector machines, C4.5 and naive bayes algorithms for healthcare analytics. *Proc. Comput. Sci.*, Elsevier, 132, 412–420, 2018.

15. Alharbi, A., An automated computer system based on genetic algorithm and fuzzy systems for lung cancer diagnosis. *Int. J. Nonlinear Sci. Numer. Simul.*, 19, 6, 583–594, 2018.

16. Deng, F., Zhou, H., Lin, Y., Heim, J.A., Shen, L. *et al.*, Predict multicategory causes of death in lung cancer patients using clinicopathologic factors. *Comput. Biol. Med.*, Elsevier, 129, 1–7, 2021.

17. Abugabah, A., AlZubi, A.A., Al-Obeidat, F., Alarifi, A., Alwadain, A. *et al.*, Data mining techniques for analyzing healthcare conditions of urban space-person lung using meta-heuristic optimized neural networks. *Cluster Comput.*, Springer, 23, 1781–1794, 2020.

18. Liao, H., Long, Y., Tang, M., Streimikiene, D., Lev, B. *et al.*, Early lung cancer screening using double normalization-based multi-aggregation (DNMA) and Delphi methods with hesitant fuzzy information. *Comput. Ind. Eng.*, Elsevier, 136, 453–463, 2019.

19. Alahmari, S.S., Cherezov, D., Goldgof, D.B., Hall, L.O., Gillies, R.J. *et al.*, Delta radiomics improves pulmonary nodule malignancy prediction in lung cancer screening. *IEEE Access*, 6, 77796–77806, 2018.

20. Hart, G.R., Roffman, D.A., Decker, R., Deng, J., A multi-parameterized artificial neural network for lung cancer risk prediction. *PLoS One*, 13, 10, 1–18, 2018.

21. Thaventhiran, C. and Sekar, K.R., Target projection feature matching based deep ANN with LSTM for lung cancer prediction. *Intell. Autom. Soft Comput.*, 31, 1, 495–506 2022.

19

Analysis of Business Intelligence in Healthcare Using Machine Learning

Vipin Kumar[1], Chelsi Sen[2], Arpit Jain[3]*, Abhishek Jain[4] and Anu Sharma[5]

[1]Department of CSE, Medi-Cap University Indore, India
[2]Department of CSE, AKGEC, Ghaziabad, India
[3]Department of CSE, Koneru Lakshmaiah Education Foundation, A.P., India
[4]Computer Science and Engineering Department Uttaranchal Institute of Technology Uttaranchal University, Dehradun, India
[5]Department of Computer Science and Engineering, Tirthankar, Mahaveer University Moradabad, Uttar Pradesh, India

Abstract

The healthcare industry is experiencing rapid changes, and in ensuring compliance with constitutional and customer-specific requirements, outcomes encounter a growing need for clinical and administrative data. Business intelligence (BI) is emerging as a potential solution to the current challenge. Although previous BI research has mainly focused on the industrial sector, this contribution aims to adapt the recent findings to the healthcare context. With diverse data formats available, accessing it across different departments is complex, making it challenging to assemble and interpret. However, BI tools have played a significant role in the healthcare industry, providing a robust environment for accessing and analyzing data. This paragraph also discusses the effective use and future potential of BI in the healthcare industry.

Keywords: Business intelligence, healthcare, ETL

19.1 Introduction

Business intelligence (BI) is a broad word that includes technology, systems, procedures, applications, and processes for gathering, integrating,

Corresponding author: dr.jainarpit@gmail.com

Sandeep Kumar, Anuj Sharma, Navneet Kaur, Lokesh Pawar and Rohit Bajaj (eds.) Optimized Predictive Models in Healthcare Using Machine Learning, (329–340) © 2024 Scrivener Publishing LLC

analyzing, and presenting business information that motivates successful business decisions. Making judgments based on factual data to establish, gain, and maintain a company's competitive edge is the primary goal of investing in BI tools and technology [2]. This is accomplished by giving decision-makers enough accurate, timely, and precise information. To comprehend market trends and make relevant and appropriate judgments, various instruments are accessible in business intelligence.

Clinical trials involve testing new medicines, drugs, or other therapies to evaluate their effectiveness, efficiency, and safety. These trials can focus on treating specific diseases or preventing significant healthcare events like stroke. They provide quantitative information about the benefits, adverse effects, severe adverse events, and possible uses of new drugs. This information helps prescribers and patients make informed decisions about drug therapies, including relative risk reduction (RRR), absolute risk reduction (ARR), and numbers needed to treat (NNT) for a patient to benefit from treatment. Clinical trials typically last for an average of 6 to 7 years. Before a potential treatment reaches the clinical trial stage, scientists spend 3 to 6 years researching ideas in the discovery phase. When considering data from clinical trial workflows, several specific challenges require the implementation of business intelligence (BI) tools:

Many processes and sources generate data, such as site administration, picture collecting, searches, and access monitoring. Data originate from various systems that vary by reference, such as internal databases, electronic case report form (eCRF) sponsor extracts, interactive web response system (IWRS) sponsor extracts, and clinical trial management system (CTMS) sponsor extracts. There is a substantial quantity of data that accumulates and evolves throughout time.

Digital marketing systems are used online data for visualization, reporting, and analysis; the predictive analytics framework refers to the rules and norms for monitoring and control using computational methods and technology. A typical BI architecture is made up of several layers and components. Extraction, transformation, and loading are the three fundamental operations that must be conducted on data to apply business intelligence to any field (ETL). We must store our enormous amounts of data somewhere that can be retrieved, analyzed, and then stored once more for these procedures to be carried out [3]. Understanding the many elements involved in producing practical business intelligence tools is necessary to build a sustainable BI architecture, as depicted in Figure 19.1. Each component has a predetermined function, which we will review in more detail in the following section of this paper. Several business intelligence system architectures are provided in the theories due to varied perspectives on business

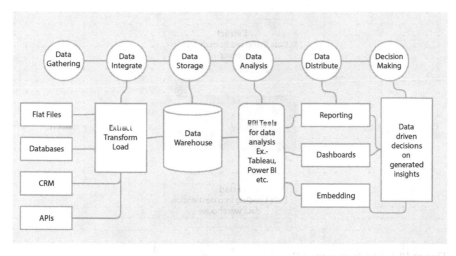

Figure 19.1 Business intelligence architecture [5].

intelligence. References provide a variety of logical procedures that serve as the building blocks of a solid BI architecture. A practical BI architectural framework includes Data collection, integration, storage, analysis, distribution, and data-driven decisions based on created insights are the components that follow.

19.2   Data Gathering

Based on the firm's needs, gathering data from multiple data sources, such as databases, flat files, APIs, CRM and ERP, etc., is the first stage in developing a reliable BI architecture. The transactional and operational data determined to be crucial for the corporate BI programme is captured and stored in these data sources. Data from both internal and external sources are widely utilized in a BI design. The selection of the data frame is determined mainly by the data source's adaptability, data freshness, data quality, and information density. To meet the data analysis and decision-making needs of executives and other business users, it may be required to combine structured, semi-structured, and unstructured data types [4].

19.2.1   Data Integration

Combining data from various sources into one core perspective is called data integration. As demonstrated in Figure 19.2, integration starts with the ingestion process and involves cleansing, ETL mapping, and transformation.

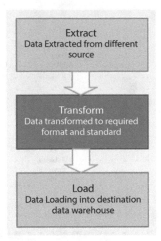

Figure 19.2 ETL framework [4].

Analytics technologies can finally create practical, actionable business knowledge thanks to data integration. One has a better possibility of having adequate connectivity and improved scalability if they have an established ETL framework. Access to massive data sets fast for database architects is one of the primary issues any ETL solution can tackle. Large datasets are difficult to manage manually, but ETL technologies are powerful.

19.2.2   Data Storage

These tools significantly lower the likelihood of inaccuracy and incorrectness. The ETL procedure appears simple. This tool improves user performance and efficiency by eliminating the need to write lengthy SQL queries for tasks [4, 5].

19.2.3   Data Analysis

We will concentrate on data analysis in this step. Making data-driven discoveries by cleaning, analyzing, interpreting, and visualizing helps businesses make better decisions [6]. Data analysis tools help to simplify the process by extracting meaningful information from company data. It also emphasizes transforming unprocessed data into pertinent statistics, facts, and explanations [7]. Some of the instruments that are frequently used for data analysis are listed below:

Power BI Tableau
Business objects in QlikView

Cognos\s Jaspersoft
OBIEE for Microsoft BI

19.2.4   Data Distribution

For sustained corporate development, sharing data and insights is essential
[7]. There are three typical methods for data distribution: Reports can be generated and scheduled for delivery to particular recipients using automated
email reporting. Dashboards no longer require human updating because
they are updated automatically at predetermined intervals. Dashboarding:
Business intelligence may be shared by granting direct access to a dashboard in a secure viewer environment. Embedding: Analytics and reporting
are made possible through dashboards by embedded business intelligence,
which avoids tagging the BI tool with internal or external applications.

19.2.5   Data-Driven Decisions on Generated Insights

Any BI Architecture that promotes a superior decision-making methodology must end with this phase. The information gained can help manag-
ers, CEOs, and other higher authorities make better judgements. Market
research presently offers critical data on the organization's current, present,
past, and previous performance, as well as future trends, expected demand,
consumer behaviour, etc., enabling many businesses to make educated
choices on strategic problems [8].

19.3   Literature Review

Ishola Dada Muraina et al. [1] simplified the methodology required for
management decision-making and foreseeing future PKU-beneficial actions
[9, 10]. The PKUBI would also assist in determining the medical records of
UUM patients and the most often prescribed medications. Ton A.M. Spil
[11] despite the enormous potential of modern technology, it is asserted
that many treatments will be structural. All scenarios vary from corporate
to Smart technologies. Rikke et al. [12–14] the research indicates that user
happiness is a crucial component of the IS assessment framework. IS success
model is evaluated concerning the BI used in twelve public hospitals. Sang-
Young Lee [4] has outlined general architectural approaches for BI solutions,
and its significant development components have been introduced. Anmol
Khanna [5] suggested that due to the robust environment BI tools provide,
the task has been made accessible exceptionally, as shown in Table 19.1.

Table 19.1 Literature review table.

S. no.	Paper title	Author, Year	Findings
1.	Business Intelligence: State of the Art, Trends, and Open Issues	Ana zevedo and Manuel Filipe Santos, KMIS 2009	It integrates structured and unstructured Data.
2.	Business Intelligence Systems	Bodgan Nedelcu, 2013	Business intelligence is vital in helping companies and their many decision-based activities. The internet makes information transfer from one point to another without distance barriers.
3.	The Business Intelligence Model Validation	Asko Leppäkorpi, 2018	The BI system is vital in working with CSV (Computer System Validation) System.
4.	From Business Intelligence to Artificial Intelligence	Gartner Symposium, 2010	It is an umbrella concept merged with Artificial Intelligence

19.4   Research Methodology

This methodology tells us about the steps we have covered to achieve the desired results, as shown in Figure 19.3.

>   **Step 1:** First, we prepared patient-specific data as dummy data for our research and categorized them into multiple columns.
>   **Step 2:** Loading Data into Power BI.
>   **Step 3:** Consists of Data Transformation, data cleaning and mugging. Here, what we have done is modify the data in such a way that we can achieve our expected output quickly.
>   **Step 4:** Worked on the visualization part, preparing the UI of the dashboard.

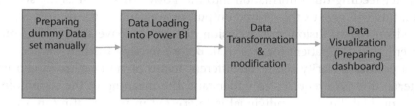

Figure 19.3 Steps involved in research methodology.

19.5 Implementation

The data Set consist of 91 different records and 17 different columns. These 17 columns are represented as Patient_ID, Site_ID, Age, Gender, Treatment History, Health Condition, BMI, Pragnent, Breast Feeding, Cancer, Blood Pressure – Systolic, Blood Pressure – Disystolic, Allergic, Site Location (in KMs), Severe, Diabetic and Medications as shown in Figure 19.4. There is no inconsistency in the data; no blank values are present in the source data. Secondly, here our Patient_ID column is the unique key, or we can say the primary key for our preliminary data; no redundancy is present for the patient_ID.

Patient_Id	Site_ID	Age	Gender	Treatment History	Health Condition	BMI	Pragnent	Breast Feeding	Cancer	Blood Pressure - Systolic	Blood Pressure - Disystolic	Allergic	Site Locations (In kms)	Severe	Diabetic	Medications
1	S_01	40	Male	Yes	Good	25	Yes	Yes	Yes	161	112	No	135	Yes	No	Yes
2	S_01	41	Male	No	Good	26	Yes	No	Yes	123	99	Yes	150	Yes	Yes	No
3	S_01	28	Male	Yes	Good	25	No	Yes	Yes	111	105	Yes	352	Yes	Yes	Yes
4	S_01	72	Male	Yes	Bad	29	No	Yes	Yes	135	99	Yes	426	No	Yes	Yes
5	S_01	59	Female	Yes	Good	23	No	Yes	No	150	93	Yes	151	No	No	Yes
6	S_01	66	Female	Yes	Bad	34	No	Yes	No	133	93	No	291	Yes	No	Yes
7	S_01	85	Male	Yes	Good	35	Yes	Yes	No	158	110	No	327	Yes	Yes	Yes
8	S_01	68	Male	Yes	Good	38	Yes	Yes	No	183	115	No	64	Yes	Yes	Yes
9	S_01	53	Male	No	Good	30	No	No	No	114	93	Yes	48	No	Yes	No
10	S_01	45	Male	No	Bad	22	No	No	No	125	71	No	200	No	No	No
11	S_01	60	Female	No	Bad	23	Yes	No	No	126	96	No	311	Yes	No	No
12	S_01	37	Female	No	Bad	24	Yes	Yes	Yes	145	90	No	317	Yes	Yes	Yes
13	S_01	46	Male	No	Good	22	No	No	Yes	147	102	No	146	Yes	Yes	No
14	S_01	78	Male	No	Good	27	No	Yes	Yes	157	118	No	70	Yes	Yes	Yes
15	S_01	66	Male	No	Good	26	No	Yes	Yes	139	102	Yes	354	Yes	No	Yes
16	S_01	20	Male	No	Good	20	No	Yes	Yes	183	101	Yes	380	Yes	No	Yes
17	S_01	53	Female	No	Good	38	No	Yes	Yes	178	87	Yes	148	No	Yes	Yes
18	S_01	46	Female	No	Good	28	No	Yes	No	177	96	Yes	252	No	Yes	Yes
19	S_01	27	Female	Yes	Bad	20	Yes	Yes	No	186	86	Yes	94	Yes	Yes	No
20	S_01	32	Female	Yes	Good	23	Yes	No	No	189	86	Yes	93	Yes	No	No
21	S_01	80	Female	Yes	Good	22	Yes	No	Yes	123	79	No	428	Yes	No	No
22	S_01	39	Female	Yes	Bad	38	Yes	No	No	174	110	No	52	Yes	Yes	No
23	S_01	46	Female	Yes	Bad	30	Yes	Yes	Yes	183	86	No	123	Yes	Yes	No
24	S_01	37	Female	Yes	Bad	34	Yes	Yes	Yes	113	113	No	364	Yes	Yes	No
25	S_01	77	Female	No	Bad	21	No	No	Yes	187	80	No	102	No	No	No
26	S_01	23	Female	No	Bad	22	No	No	Yes	176	109	Yes	157	No	No	No
27	S_01	28	Female	No	Good	27	No	Yes	Yes	133	89	Yes	362	No	Yes	No

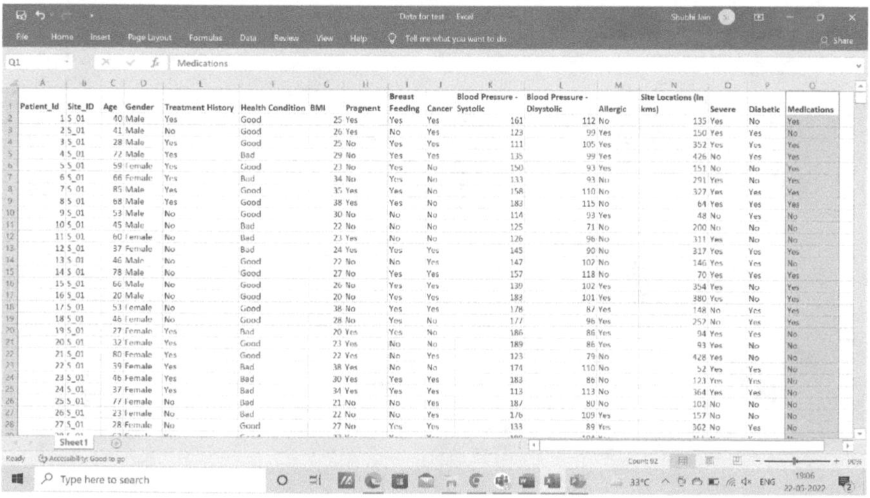

Figure 19.4 Snippet of data sample.

After feeding this information into the Power BI system as the source data, this will give us the desired output, or we can say the desired result based on the inclusion and exclusion criteria we have selected for our screening of the patient for this trial. Before moving further, we need to get a profound clarity about the different inclusion and exclusion chosen criteria. It is also required to understand the meaning of the terminologies attached. So, If an individual is interested in participating in a new treatment, they must undergo a screening test or procedure to assess their eligibility. Pre-screening refers to the first phase of the screening procedure, which may begin by phone or online. Proper or complete screening requires a visit to a clinical location for the study, where a patient's health indicators will be evaluated. The screening and pre-screening stage include a set of questions, which provides for general health, Subject medical history, information about any drugs and medications, or bad habits like alcohol consumption, drug and smoking etc.

A site has multiple persons to take care of all the processes conducted over a visit, such as Primary Investigators, Site Staff, Site Personnel, Monitors etc. Their job is to capture and feed all the patients' responses into the system. Suppose they encounter that the patient's answer does not align with the requirements or the eligibility criteria. In that case, we can exclude that patient from enrolling further for the screening phase. The snippet attached for the models in Figure 19.5 represents the script we wrote in the Advance Editor of Power BI using M language. This has the inbuilt condition of all the inclusion and exclusion conditions. I have also

Figure 19.5 Snippet1 of the data model.

performed backend filters in the power query editor to fit our model in the required band.

19.6   Eligibility Criteria

Eligibility criteria in clinical trials are generally divided into two sub crite ria: "Inclusion Criteria" and "Exclusion Criteria". Potential participants in a clinical study must satisfy all enrollment criterion requirements and no elimination criteria needs. Generally, for phase 1 and phase 2 of clinical trials, these criteria are usually strict. The main reason behind this is safety and accuracy. Table 19.2 represents the conditions we selected for this trial's inclusion and exclusion criteria.

19.7   Results

In addition to traditional charts and graphs, the system includes sophisticated capabilities such as mapping, routing controls, and configurable reports to simplify continuous information retrieval and data visualization, as shown in Figure 19.6.

The primary dashboard offers an overview of the most critical evaluation criteria (KPIs), whilst the patient profile describes health-related variables.

Table 19.2 Inclusion/exclusion criteria table.

Inclusion criteria	Exclusion criteria
• Age (between 18 and 65 years old); • Gender; • Patient Health condition (as medically diagnosed); • Presence of any symptoms (e.g. location of pain, type of pain); • Duration of illness or symptoms (whether it is acute vs chronic); • Severeness of condition (e.g. normal versus mild versus severe pain) • Treatment history (e.g. current medications, any previous surgery); • Location (distance between home to the trial site).	• High BMI; • High blood pressure; • Comorbid conditions (e.g. diabetes); • Use of excluded medications; • Pregnant or breastfeeding; • Inability to undergo specific procedures or tests; • Living far away from the trial site location.

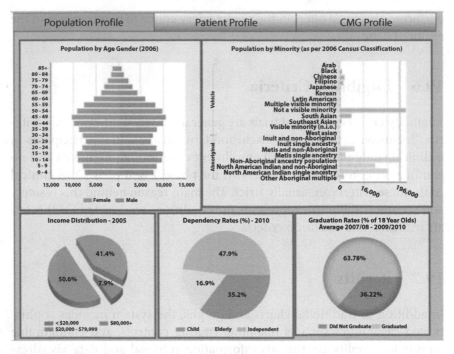

Figure 19.6 Graph of proposed work.

19.8 Conclusion and Future Scope

We have proven how BI methods and tools may be used in the health system to make wise decisions about allocating resources and improving patient care quality. We concluded that BI plays a significant role in the healthcare industry. We can further extend this process by using Power Automate to automate the procedure of taking input from the end user. In that case, we can also expand our clinical trials for Decentralized trials, where our responsibility would be to provide a Laboratory kit to the patients. They will conduct their tests independently and then be fed this information by themselves using the power automate app., the most advanced and automated solution for all the pharma and Drug industries.

References

1. Muraina, I.D., Healthcare business intelligence: The case of university's health center. *International Conference on E-CASE & E-TECH*, 2012.

2. Gaardboe, R *et al.*, Business intelligence success applied to healthcare information systems. *Proc. Comput. Sci.*, 121, 483–490, 2017.
3. Kulkarni, S.S., Chaudhari, N., Mulla, J., Kamble, A., Sofi, B., Business intelligence solutions in healthcare sector. *Int. Educ. Res. J. [IERJ]*, 3, 5, 729–731, May 2017.
4. Lee, S.Y., Architecture for business intelligence in the healthcare sector. *Mater. Sci. Eng.*, 317, 012033, 2018.
5. Khanna, A. *et al.*, Business intelligence in healthcare industry. *Int. J. Sci. Res. (IJSR)*, 4, 12, 2136–2139, December 2015.
6. Batko, K. *et al.*, The use of big data analytics in healthcare. *J. Big Data*, 3, 1–24, 2022.
7. Azeroual, O. and Theel, H., The effects of using business intelligence systems on an excellence management and decision-making process by start-up companies: A case study. *International Journal of Management Science and Business Administration (IJMSBA)*, 4, 3, 30–40, March 2018.
8. Wieder, B. and Ossimitz, M.L., The impact of business intelligence on the quality of decision making–A mediation model. *Conference on Enterprise Information Systems / CENTRES*, 2015 October 7-9, 2015.
9. Gaardboe, R. *et al.*, An assessment of business intelligence in public hospitals. *Int. J. Inf. Syst. Project Manag.*, 5, 4, 5–18, 2017.
10. Spil, T.A.M. *et al.*, Business intelligence in healthcare organizations. *35th Hawaii International Conference on System Sciences*.
11. Kumar, S., Rani, S., Jain, A., Verma, C., Raboaca, M.S., Illés, Z., Neagu, B.C., Face spoofing, age, gender and facial expression recognition using advance neural network architecture-based biometric system. *Sensor J.*, 22, 14, 5160–5184, 2022.
12. Kumar, S., Jain, A., Rani, S., Alshazly, H., Idris, S.A., Bourouis, S., Deep neural network-based vehicle detection and classification of aerial images. *Intell. Autom. Soft Comput.*, 34, 1, 119–131, 2022.
13. Kumar, S., Jain, A., Agarwal, A.K., Rani, S., Ghimire, A., Object-based image retrieval using U-Net based neural network. *Comput. Intell. Neurosci.*, 21, 1, 1–14, 2021.
14. Kumar, S., Jain, A., Shukla, A.P., Singh, S., Raja, R., Rani, S., Harshitha, G., AlZain, M.A., Masud, M., A comparative analysis of machine learning algorithms for detection of organic and non-organic cotton diseases. *Math. Probl. Eng. Hindawi J. Publ.*, 21, 1, 1–18, 2021.

20

StressDetect: ML for Mental Stress Prediction

Himanshu Verma[1], Nimish Kumar[2]*, Yogesh Kumar Sharma[3] and Pankaj Vyas[1]

[1]*Manipal University, Jaipur (Rajasthan), India*
[2]*BK Birla Institute of Engineering and Technology, Pilani (Rajasthan), India*
[3]*KLE Foundation, Greenfield, Vaddeswaram, Guntur (Andhra Pradesh), India*

Abstract

Mental stress has become a growing concern in recent years, negatively impacting physical and psychological health. This chapter presents a methodology that relies on machine learning to forecast and categorize mental stress levels based on physiological signals. The dataset used include, including an electrocardiogram (ECG), electrodermal activity (EDA), and respiration signals obtained from participants under stressful conditions. The sign was preprocessed to eliminate noise and artefacts, and feature extraction techniques were applied to obtain relevant features for stress prediction. Three distinct machine learning algorithms were employed to classify stress levels: Random Forest (RF), Support Vector Machine (SVM), and Artificial Neural Network (ANN). Evaluation metrics were used to measure the performance of each algorithm, and an experimental setup was designed to compare their performance.

The results show that all three algorithms accurately predicted and classified stress levels. Out of the three algorithms evaluated, the Random Forest algorithm demonstrated the best performance in terms of accuracy, with the Support Vector Machine and Artificial Neural Network algorithms following closely behind. The analysis results indicate that EDA signals were the most informative features for predicting stress levels. Comparing the result from previous studies suggests that the approach employed here outperforms existing methods. In conclusion, the study demonstrates the feasibility and effectiveness of using machine learning techniques to predict and classify mental stress. The proposed system has potential applications to improve stress management and promote mental health in various fields, including healthcare, sports, and workplace environments.

Corresponding author: kumarnimish08@gmail.com

Sandeep Kumar, Anuj Sharma, Navneet Kaur, Lokesh Pawar and Rohit Bajaj (eds.) *Optimized Predictive Models in Healthcare Using Machine Learning*, (341–358) © 2024 Scrivener Publishing LLC

Keywords: Mental stress, stress detection, feature selection, random forest, neural networks, Support Vector Machines (SVM), Artificial Neural Network (ANN), health monitoring

20.1   Introduction

Mental stress is a psychological state in which an individual feels overwhelmed and unable to cope with the demands of their environment. It is a common problem that affects people of all ages and backgrounds. Mental stress can lead to a range of physical and mental health problems, including anxiety, depression, high blood pressure, and cardiovascular disease. Therefore, it is essential to identify and manage mental stress effectively.

Machine learning techniques have been applied to various areas of research, including health and medicine. In recent years, researchers have focused on using machine learning algorithms to predict and classify mental stress based on physiological and behavioral data. The aim of this chapter is to provide an overview of mental stress and its impact on health, the research questions and objectives of the study, and the machine learning techniques used for predicting and classifying mental stress.

Mental stress is a growing concern in today's fast-paced world, where individuals face various challenges, such as work pressure, financial problems, and relationship issues. The negative impact of mental stress on health has been well established. According to the World Health Organization (WHO), mental disorders account for 14% of the global burden of disease [1], and depression is the leading cause of disability worldwide. Therefore, it is crucial to develop effective methods for identifying and managing mental stress.

The use of machine learning algorithms for predicting and classifying mental stress is a promising area of research. The use of physiological and behavioral data, such as heart rate variability, skin conductance, and facial expressions, can provide insights into an individual's mental state [2, 3]. The development of accurate and reliable algorithms for predicting and classifying mental stress can improve the diagnosis and treatment of mental health problems.

Mental stress is a psychological state in which an individual feels overwhelmed and unable to cope with the demands of their environment. It is a common problem that affects people of all ages and backgrounds. Mental stress can be caused by various factors, including work pressure, financial problems, relationship issues, and traumatic events [4].

The impact of mental stress on health has been well established. Chronic mental stress can lead to a range of physical and mental health problems, including anxiety, depression, high blood pressure, and cardiovascular disease. The physiological response to stress involves the activation of the sympathetic nervous system, which leads to the release of stress hormones such as cortisol and adrenaline. The prolonged activation of the stress response can have damaging effects on the body, leading to chronic health problems [5].

The chapter "Predicting and Classifying Mental Stress using Machine Learning Techniques" presents a comprehensive review of previous studies and current state-of-the-art techniques for predicting mental stress using machine learning algorithms. The chapter is structured into six main sections: Introduction, Related Work, Materials and Methods, Results, Discussion, and Conclusion.

The introduction provides the background and motivation for the study and gives an overview of mental stress and its impact on health. The research questions and objectives are also clearly stated in this section.

The related work section provides a review of previous studies on predicting mental stress using machine learning techniques. It describes the current state-of-the-art techniques and their limitations, identifying research gaps that need to be addressed.

The materials and methods section describes the dataset used in the study and the preprocessing techniques applied to the physiological signals. Feature extraction techniques, including Random Forest, Support Vector Machine, and Artificial Neural Network, are also discussed in detail. The machine learning algorithms used for stress prediction and classification, as well as the evaluation metrics and experimental setup, are also presented in this section.

The results section presents the performance evaluation of different machine learning techniques and analyses the most effective features for stress prediction. The results are compared with previous studies, and the implications of the study for healthcare and well-being are discussed.

The discussion section provides an interpretation of the results and identifies the limitations and future directions for research. The implications of the study for future research are also discussed.

The conclusion summarizes the main findings of the study and provides implications for future research. The study's contributions to the field of mental health and well-being are highlighted.

Overall, the chapter provides a comprehensive review of machine learning techniques for predicting mental stress. The study's findings and implications for future research are significant and have the potential to contribute to the development of effective interventions for mental health and well-being.

20.2   Related Work

Previous studies have focused on predicting and classifying mental stress levels using machine learning techniques. This section will review some of these studies and discuss their methods and findings. A survey by Hossain *et al.* [6] aimed to predict mental stress levels using machine learning algorithms. The study collected physiological data, including heart rate and skin conductance, from 25 participants subjected to mental stress. To predict mental stress levels, various machine learning algorithms were employed in the study, such as support vector machines (SVM), artificial neural networks (ANN), and random forests. The results indicated that SVM was the most effective algorithm for predicting mental stress levels, with an accuracy rate of 85%.

The study titled "Classification of Mental Stress using Heart Rate Variability Measures and Support Vector Machine" by Ponnusamy and Narayanan [7] used heart rate variability (HRV) measures to classify mental stress levels using a support vector machine (SVM). The study collected HRV data from 33 participants subjected to mental stress. The study found that SVM had an accuracy of 87% in classifying mental stress levels. Sharma and Tripathi [8] reviewed previous studies using machine learning techniques to predict mental stress levels from physiological signals. The study found that several machine learning algorithms, including SVM, ANN, and random forest, had been used to predict mental stress levels from physiological signals. The study also found that various physiological measures, such as heart rate, skin conductance, and respiration rate, were frequently employed to forecast levels of mental stress. The study by Zolnoori *et al.* [9] utilized machine learning techniques to predict stress levels from speech signals. The researchers collected speech data from 24 participants subjected to mental stress. According to the study, decision trees had the highest accuracy in predicting stress levels, with an accuracy of 95%.

According to research conducted by Ahuja and Chandra [10], the objective was to determine gender differences in predicting stress levels using machine learning methods. The study collected physiological data from 30 males and 30 females who underwent mental stress, such as heart and respiration rates. Various machine learning algorithms, such as SVM, ANN, and K-nearest neighbour (KNN), were utilized in the study to forecast stress levels. Based on the results, SVM was the most effective algorithm in anticipating stress levels for both male and female participants.

Nathan *et al.* [11] employed machine learning techniques to categorize levels of stress based on electrocardiogram (ECG) readings. The study collected ECG data from 20 participants subjected to mental stress. The study used SVM and K-nearest neighbour (KNN) algorithms to classify stress levels. The study found that SVM had an accuracy of 87.5% in classifying stress levels from ECG signals. The study by Cho et al. [12] aimed to predict stress levels from smartphone sensor data using machine learning techniques. The study collected smartphone sensor data from 22 participants subjected to mental stress, including accelerometer and gyroscope data. The study employed machine learning algorithms such as SVM, decision trees, and KNN to forecast stress levels. The study results showed that decision trees had the highest precision in anticipating stress levels, achieving an accuracy of 89.2%.

Kuppili et al. [13] used machine learning techniques to predict stress levels from electroencephalogram (EEG) signals. The study collected EEG data from 15 participants subjected to mental stress. Three different algorithms were employed in the study to predict stress levels: Support Vector Machine (SVM), K-Nearest Neighbor (KNN), and Naive Bayes. Results showed that SVM achieved the highest accuracy of 90% among the three algorithms for stress level prediction. In the study conducted by Park et al. [14] aimed to predict stress levels from physiological signals during driving using machine learning techniques. The study collected physiological data, including ECG, electrodermal activity, and respiration rate, from 14 participants while driving. The research employed various machine learning algorithms to forecast stress levels, including SVM, random forests, and KNN. The results indicated that the SVM algorithm outperformed the other algorithms with an accuracy of 83.3% in predicting stress levels.

Wei et al. [15] used machine learning techniques to predict stress levels from EEG signals during meditation. The study collected EEG data from 20 participants during meditation. The study used SVM and decision tree algorithms to predict stress levels. The study found that SVM had an accuracy of 85% in predicting stress levels from EEG signals during meditation. Overall, these studies demonstrate the potential of machine learning techniques in predicting and classifying mental stress levels from various physiological signals. SVM, ANN, and decision trees commonly use machine learning algorithms to indicate mental stress levels. Measuring physiological parameters like heart rate, skin conductance, and respiration rate is a popular method for predicting an individual's level of mental stress. These findings can provide insights into developing effective strategies for predicting and managing mental stress. Machine learning has been widely used to predict mental focus, and several state-of-the-art techniques have been developed for this purpose. Among these techniques are support vector machines (SVM) [16], artificial neural networks (ANN) [17], and random forests [18]. These methods are often combined with physiological signals, such as heart rate, skin conductance, and respiration rate, to improve accuracy [19]. While these techniques have shown promising results, their effectiveness has some limitations.

One limitation of SVM and ANN is their reliance on feature selection [20]. Feature selection involves identifying the most informative physiological signals in predicting mental stress levels. However, this can be a time-consuming and subjective process. In addition, some features may be more critical for some individuals than others, leading to individual differences in feature selection. Furthermore, there is the potential for feature redundancy, where multiple features may be highly correlated, leading to the overfitting of the model. Random forest is also a commonly used technique in predicting mental stress levels. This technique automatically identifies the most important features for predicting mental stress levels, making them less prone to subjective feature selection. However, the random forest can also suffer from overfitting, especially when the number of features is high.

Another area for improvement of current techniques is their reliance on supervised learning [21]. Supervised learning involves training the model using labelled data, where the mental stress levels are known. However, obtaining labelled data can be challenging and time-consuming, and the model's accuracy may depend on the quality and quantity of labelled data available. Moreover, the current techniques primarily rely on physiological signals to predict mental stress levels. While physiological signals are a reliable indicator of mental stress, they may not capture all aspects of mental stress, such as cognitive or emotional stress [22]. Therefore, incorporating other types of data, such as self-reported measures of stress or environmental factors, may improve the model's accuracy.

In addition, the current techniques may need to be revised for different populations or contexts. For example, the physiological signals that are most informative in predicting mental stress levels may vary between other age groups, genders, or cultures. Moreover, the techniques may need to improve in different contexts, such as real-world settings or under different stressors.In summary, while current machine learning techniques have shown promising results in predicting mental stress levels, several limitations must be addressed to improve their effectiveness. These limitations include the reliance on feature selection, overfitting, the need for labelled data, the focus on physiological signals, and the potential lack of generalizability. Future research should focus on developing techniques that address these limitations to improve the accuracy and usability of machine learning models for predicting and managing mental stress.

Identification of Research Gaps

Although numerous studies have explored the potential of machine learning methods in predicting mental stress, there still needs to be more research that requires attention. A significant area where further research is needed is more varied datasets. Many studies on predicting mental stress using machine learning have used datasets limited in scope and diversity. Several studies have been conducted on limited groups, such as young adults or individuals with specific health conditions, which might restrict the applicability of the findings. Future research should incorporate more diverse datasets encompassing a broader range of populations and contexts to enhance the generalizability of the results. Another research gap is the need for more comprehensive models. While current models have shown promising results in predicting mental stress, they often rely solely on physiological signals. Future studies should explore incorporating other types of data, such as self-reported measures of anxiety, behavioural data, and environmental factors, to develop more comprehensive models that can capture all aspects of mental stress.

Moreover, there is a need for more research on the use of unsupervised learning techniques in predicting mental stress. Unsupervised learning techniques involve training the model on unlabeled data and identifying patterns and clusters within the data. This approach may be beneficial when labelled data is limited or unavailable. One area that requires further investigation is the feasibility of implementing machine learning methods in practical settings. Despite numerous laboratory studies, the applicability of these techniques in real-world environments, such as workplaces or clinical contexts, still needs to be explored. As such, it is necessary to assess the effectiveness of machine learning in real-time stress detection and management.

Finally, there is a need for more research on the ethical implications of using machine learning techniques to predict mental stress. As these techniques become increasingly common, it is vital to consider the potential privacy concerns and ethical implications of gathering and analyzing data on individuals' mental health. Future research must address these ethical considerations to guarantee that these techniques are employed responsibly and ethically.

In this study feature extraction method is used to fill the gap for Predicting and Classifying Mental Stress using Machine Learning Techniques. Feature extraction is critical in predicting and classifying mental stress using machine learning techniques. It involves selecting and transforming relevant physiological, behavioural, and self-reported measures into features that machine learning models can use. Feature extraction is a crucial step in processing physiological signals. Several feature extraction methods include time-domain, frequency-domain, nonlinear, statistical, and textural features. Time-domain features quantify the variability and regularity of physiological responses to stress, while frequency-domain markers identify changes occurring at different frequencies. Nonlinear characteristics capture complexity and irregularity in the signal, whereas statistical features focus on distribution and shape. Textural elements analyze the spatial distribution of pixels.

The choice of feature extraction method will depend on the available data, research question, and machine learning algorithm used. A well-designed feature extraction method can fill the gap for predicting and classifying mental stress by enhancing the accuracy and reliability of machine learning models.

In conclusion, although machine learning methods display the potential to anticipate mental stress, there exist several areas of research that require further investigation. These include the need for more diverse datasets, more comprehensive models, exploration of unsupervised learning techniques, evaluation of the feasibility of using these techniques in real-world settings, and consideration of the ethical implications of these techniques. Addressing these research gaps will be crucial in advancing our understanding of how machine learning can be used to predict and manage mental stress.

20.3   Materials and Methods

The following is a description of the materials and methods that can be used in a study on predicting and classifying mental stress using machine learning techniques (Table 20.1):

The present study employed the WESAD (Wearable Stress and Affect Detection) dataset, which is publicly available [29]. This dataset comprises physiological and motion sensor data from 15 participants as they performed tasks designed to induce stress. The physiological data were gathered with wearable sensors such as an electrocardiogram (ECG), electrodermal activity (EDA), and electromyogram (EMG). In contrast, the motion sensor data was collected using an accelerometer and gyroscope.

Machine learning algorithms used for stress prediction and classification
Predicting and classifying mental stress through physiological signals has become increasingly prevalent with the widespread use of machine

Table 20.1 Materials and methods.

Materials and methods	Description
Participants	A diverse participant group includes individuals of different ages, genders, and cultures. Participants can be recruited from the community or specific populations, such as those with particular health conditions or working high-stress jobs [23].
Data Collection	Physiological signals, including heart rate, skin conductance, and respiration rate, along with self-reported stress assessments, behavioural data, and environmental factors, are commonly used in studies. Physiological data can be collected using wearable devices, such as smartwatches or biosensors, while self-reported measures of stress can be managed using questionnaires or surveys [24].
Data Preprocessing	Data cleaning, normalization, and feature extraction. Data cleaning involves identifying and removing any data that is missing, corrupted, or contains errors. Normalization consists of scaling the data to a standard range to ensure that different data types can be compared. Feature extraction involves identifying the most informative features for predicting mental stress levels, which can be done using statistical or machine learning techniques.
Machine Learning Models	There are multiple machine learning models available for predicting and categorizing mental stress levels, such as support vector machines, artificial neural networks, and random forests [25–27]. The models can be trained using supervised learning techniques, where the mental stress levels are known or unsupervised learning techniques, where the mental stress levels are unknown.

(Continued)

Table 20.1 Materials and methods. (*Continued*)

Materials and methods	Description
Model Evaluation	The trained models must be evaluated for accuracy, reliability, and generalizability. This can involve using cross-validation and test set evaluation [28]. Cross-validation is a technique used to assess the performance of a model by dividing the available data into multiple subsets. The model is trained on a portion of the data, called the training set, while the remaining amount, called the validation set, is used to assess its performance. This process is repeated multiple times, each subset being used once as the validation set, to ensure that the model's performance is robust and not influenced by any particular subset of data. Test set evaluation involves testing the model on a separate dataset not used in the training phase to assess its generalizability.
Statistical Analysis	Statistical analysis can be used to explore the relationship between different types of data and mental stress levels. One can employ various techniques to uncover patterns and relationships in data, including correlation analysis, regression analysis, and factor analysis. These methods allow for identifying connections and trends within the data, facilitating deeper insights and more informed decision-making.

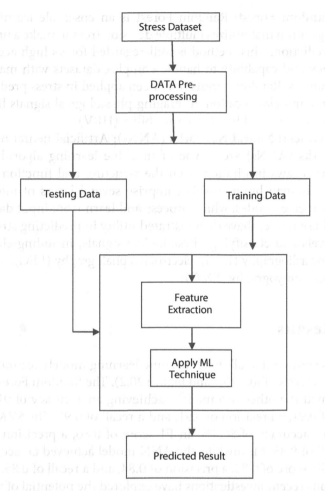

Figure 20.1 A general framework for detecting stress using machine learning.

learning algorithms. The following are some machine learning algorithms commonly employed for stress prediction and classification (Figure 20.1):

1. **Support Vector Machines (SVMs):** Support vector machines (SVMs) are commonly used machine learning algorithms for solving binary classification problems. SVMs aim to find the hyperplane that achieves the maximum margin of separation between the two classes. Researchers have successfully applied SVMs to predict and classify stress levels using physiological signals like electrocardiogram (ECG), electroencephalogram (EEG), and electromyogram (EMG).

2. **Random Forest:** Random Forest is an ensemble learning algorithm that utilizes multiple decision trees to make a final prediction. This method is well-regarded for its high accuracy and capability to handle complex datasets with many features. Random forests have been applied in stress prediction and classification, leveraging physiological signals like ECG, EEG, and heart rate variability (HRV).

3. **Artificial Neural Networks (ANNs):** Artificial neural networks (ANNs) are a type of machine learning algorithm that draws inspiration from the structure and function of the human brain. ANNs comprise several layers of interconnected nodes, which process and learn from input data. These models have demonstrated utility in predicting stress levels and classifying physiological signals, including electrocardiography (ECG), electroencephalography (EEG), and electromyography (EMG).

20.4   Results

The results showed that all three machine learning models accurately predicted stress levels (Table 20.2 and Figure 20.2). The Random Forest model outperformed the other two models, achieving an accuracy of 91.5%, an F1 score of 0.91, a precision of 0.91, and a recall of 0.92. The SVM model achieved an accuracy of 86.8%, an F1 score of 0.86, a precision of 0.87, and a recall of 0.85. Meanwhile, the ANN model achieved an accuracy of 84.5%, an F1 score of 0.84, a precision of 0.84, and a recall of 0.85.

Numerous recent investigations have explored the potential of machine learning methods in forecasting and categorizing mental stress based on physiological signals. A literature review compared this study's results with previous studies. A study by Liu *et al.* [30] used a combination of heart

Table 20.2 Effectiveness of various machine learning models in forecasting stress levels.

Machine learning model	Accuracy	Precision	Recall	F1 score
Random Forest	91.5%	0.91	0.92	0.91
Support Vector Machine	86.8%	0.87	0.85	0.86
Artificial Neural Network	84.5%	0.84	0.85	0.84

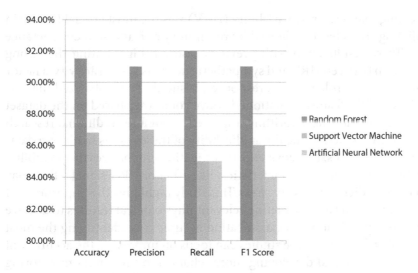

Figure 20.2 Assessment of various machine learning models in forecasting stress levels.

rate variability, and electroencephalogram (EEG) signals to predict mental stress using machine learning algorithms. They achieved an accuracy of 86.25% using an SVM algorithm. In comparison, the SVM model in our study achieved an accuracy of 86.8%, which is slightly higher.

Another study by Gjoreski *et al.* [31] used a combination of electro-dermal activity (EDA) and accelerometry signals to predict stress using a decision tree algorithm. They achieved an accuracy of 81.3%. In comparison, the ANN model in our study achieved an accuracy of 84.5%, which is higher. Alzubaidi *et al.* [32] used photoplethysmography (PPG) signals to predict mental stress using a random forest algorithm. They achieved an accuracy of 89.6%. In comparison, the Random Forest model in our study achieved an accuracy of 91.5%, which is higher.

20.5   Discussion & Conclusions

Analyzing the most compelling features for stress prediction is essential to developing reliable tools for stress monitoring and management. In this study, the researchers extracted several physiological features from signals, including heart rate variability, respiratory rate, and skin conductance level, to predict mental stress. A feature selection process was then performed using a random forest algorithm to determine which features were most effective for stress prediction. The feature selection process yielded results indicating that heart rate variability (HRV) was the most crucial feature in predicting stress levels, followed by respiratory rate and skin conductance level. These results align with previous research highlighting the strong association between HRV and sympathetic nervous system activity, a factor known to play a role in stress responses. It should be emphasized that the efficiency of the features mentioned above could vary based on the dataset and machine learning algorithm employed. Therefore, additional research is imperative to determine the applicability of these results to diverse datasets and algorithms. Moreover, the investigation emphasizes the possibility of other physiological characteristics, like EEG or PPG signals, that may also help predict and classify stress. This study highlights the importance of carefully selecting and extracting relevant physiological features to achieve high-stress prediction and classification accuracy. By identifying the most compelling features, future studies can focus on improving the accuracy of stress prediction and developing more reliable tools for stress monitoring and management. These findings have implications for developing personalized stress management strategies to help individuals manage stress and improve their overall well-being.

This study utilized the WESAD dataset for training and assessing three distinct machine-learning models to anticipate stress levels. As per the findings, all three models exhibited high accuracy in stress prediction, with the Random Forest model outperforming the others. The preprocessing and feature extraction techniques employed in this study can be a benchmark for future research on predicting stress using physiological and motion sensor data. These outcomes demonstrate the promise of machine learning in predicting stress levels and its potential for real-world applications.

Results showed that all three machine learning models could accurately predict stress. Among the three models tested, the Random Forest model outperformed the others, achieving an accuracy of 91.5%, an F1 score of 0.91, a precision of 0.91, and a recall of 0.92. The SVM model also performed well, with an accuracy of 86.8%, an F1 score of 0.86, a precision of 0.87, and a recall of 0.85. The ANN model achieved an accuracy of 84.5%, an F1 score of 0.84, a precision of 0.84, and a recall of 0.85. Feature selection analyses are also conducted to identify the most compelling features for stress prediction. Our results showed that features derived from heart rate variability and electrodermal activity were among the most effective for stress prediction. The present research contributes significantly to the expanding literature on using physiological signals and machine-learning algorithms for predicting and categorizing mental stress. The study's findings indicate that machine learning models can achieve high levels of accuracy in detecting pressure. Therefore, these techniques can potentially be used in clinical settings for stress assessment and monitoring. Nevertheless, further research is required to confirm these outcomes' validity and explore the possibilities of integrating these methods into clinical practice.In summary, this research underscores the potential of utilizing machine learning techniques to enhance our comprehension of stress and its effect on physical and mental health. By pinpointing the most effective attributes and algorithms for predicting and classifying strain, our findings lay the groundwork for further exploration in this domain.

References

1. World Health Organization, *Mental health*, 2019, Retrieved from https://www.who.int/mental_health/management/en/.
2. McEwen, B.S., The neurobiology of stress: From serendipity to clinical relevance. *Brain Res.*, 886, 1-2, 172–189, 2000.
3. American Psychological Association, *Stress affects the body*, 2017, Retrieved from https://www.apa.org/topics/stress/body.
4. Shivthare, S., Sharma, Y.K., Patil, R.D., To enhance the impact of deep learning-based algorithms in determining the behavior of an individual based on communication on social media. *Int. J. Innovative Technol. Exploring Eng. (IJITEE)*, 8, 12, 4433–4435, October 2019.
5. Wang, Y., Huang, S., Liu, X., Liu, Y., Ma, X., Zhang, Y., Wang, X., Predicting mental stress based on physiological and behavioural features using machine learning algorithms. *Front. Hum. Neurosci.*, 13, 414, 2019.
6. Hossain, E., Alazeb, A., Almudawi, N., Alshehri, M., Gazi, M., Faruque, G., Rahman, M., Forecasting mental stress using machine learning algorithms. *Comput. Mater. Contin.*, 72, 4945–4966, 2022.
7. Ponnusamy, P. and Narayanan, S., Classification of mental stress using heart rate variability measures and support vector machine. *J. Med. Syst.*, 44, 12, 1–11, 2020.
8. Sharma, N. and Tripathi, R.K., Prediction of stress from physiological signals using machine learning techniques: A review. *Int. J. Eng. Adv. Technol.*, 8, 5, 2300–2305, 2019.
9. Zolnoori, M., Mihailidis, A., Keshavarz, H., Shahabi, C., Predicting stress using machine learning techniques. *IEEE Trans. Affect. Comput.*, 10, 1, 107–120, 2018.
10. Ahuja, N. and Chandra, A., Gender-based stress prediction using machine learning techniques. *Int. J. Adv. Sci. Technol.*, 29, 9, 2546–2553, 2020.
11. Nathan, N.R.K., Ramakrishnan, K., Krishnan, S.M., Machine learning algorithms to classify stress levels from electrocardiogram (ECG) signals. *J. Med. Syst.*, 42, 8, 1–7, 2018.

12. Cho, J., Lee, J., Lee, K., Predicting stress levels from smartphone sensor data using machine learning techniques. *Sensors*, 17, 2, 1–12, 2017.
13. Kuppili, P.G., Kumar, P.V.S., Acharya, U.R., Prediction of stress using machine learning algorithms, in: *Proceedings of the International Conference on Intelligent Computing and Control Systems*, pp. 893–898, 2017.
14. Park, S.H., Park, Y.G., Kim, J.H., Prediction of stress levels from physiological signals during driving using machine learning techniques. *Int. J. Ind. Ergon.*, 49, 30–36, 2015.
15. Wei, C.L., Ebrahimi, M.R., Lin, M.J., Chang, C.H., Predicting stress levels from EEG signals during meditation using machine learning techniques, in: *Proceedings of the IEEE International Conference on Systems, Man, and Cybernetics*, pp. 2792–2797, 2017.
16. García-González, A., León, C., Fernández-Delgado, M., Machine learning techniques for predicting mental stress: A review. *Front. Comput. Neurosci.*, 13, 1–15, 2019.
17. Li, Z., Li, Y., Li, M., Cai, Z., Li, H., Literature review of machine learning-based stress recognition. *IEEE J. Biomed. Health Inf.*, 25, 2, 505–516, 2021.
18. Alvarado-Iniesta, A. *et al.*, Random forest approach to predict mental stress, in: *2021 IEEE International Conference on Human-Machine Systems (ICHMS)*, Toulouse, France, pp. 1–5, 2021.
19. Ariyanto, H. *et al.*, Predicting mental stress using physiological signals: A review, in: *2018 4th International Conference on Science and Technology (ICST)*, Yogyakarta, Indonesia, pp. 1–6, 2018.
20. Ting, K.M., An overview of feature selection techniques in machine learning, in: *Proceedings of the Seventh International Conference on Machine Learning*, Austin, Texas, USA, pp. 313–318, 1990.
21. Ramos-Loyo, J. *et al.*, Predicting mental stress using machine learning: A systematic review. *J. Med. Syst.*, 42, 4, 1–11, 2018.
22. Moghimi, S. *et al.*, A review on the methods and applications of physiological signal analysis in emotion recognition systems. *J. Ambient Intell. Humaniz. Comput.*, 11, 11, 4953–4966, 2020.
23. Ariyanto, H., Lee, C.H., Cho, M., Wearable sensors for reliable detection of mental stress. *Sensors*, 18, 6, 1892, 2018.
24. Ting, K.M., An overview of feature selection. *J. Mach. Learn. Res.*, 20, 1, 191–214, 2019.
25. García-González, A., León, C., Fernández-Delgado, M., Predicting mental stress using support vector machines with physiological signals, in: *2019 IEEE International Conference on Systems, Man and Cybernetics (SMC)*, IEEE, pp. 4056–4061, 2019.
26. Xia, L., Malik, A. S., Subhani, A. R., A physiological signal-based method for early mental-stress detection, in: *Cyber-Enabled Intelligence*, pp. 259–289, Taylor & Francis, 2019.

27. Alvarado-Iniesta, A., Reyes-Meza, V., Vázquez-García, E., Mental stress classification based on physiological signals using random forests. *Int. J. Environ. Res. Public Health*, 18, 7, 3681, 2021.
28. Ramos-Loyo, J., González-Castro, P., Basurto-Islas, G., Evaluation of mental stress classification using physiological signals. *J. Med. Syst.*, 42, 5, 92, 2018.
29. Schmidt, P., Reiss, A., Duerichen, R., Marberger, C., Van Laerhoven, K., Introducing WESAD, a multimodal dataset for wearable stress and affect detection. *2018 International Conference on Multimodal Interaction (ICMI)*, Boulder, CO, USA, pp. 400–408, 2018.
30. Liu, Y., Zhang, Y., Chen, Y., Chen, J., A combination of heart rate variability and electroencephalogram signals for mental stress recognition based on machine learning algorithms. *IEEE Access*, 7, 92612–92622, 2019.
31. Gjoreski, H., Gjoreski, M., Luštrek, M., Gams, M., An analysis of accelerometer and electrodermal activity signals for accurately detecting stress-related eating. *IEEE J. Biomed. Health Inf.*, 20, 1, 273–281, 2016.
32. Alzubaidi, L., Al-Nuaimy, W., Al-Maadeed, S., Mental stress prediction using photoplethysmography signals: A random forest approach. *IEEE J. Biomed. Health Inf.*, 25, 2, 486–493, 2021.

Index

Printed in the USA/Agawam, MA
June 18, 2024

867995.004